Alain Rouveret
Nonfinite Inquiries

Studies in Generative Grammar

Editors
Norbert Corver
Harry van der Hulst

Founding editors
Jan Koster
Henk van Riemsdijk

Volume 138

Alain Rouveret
Nonfinite Inquiries

Materials for a Comparative Study of Nonfinite
Predicative Domains

DE GRUYTER
MOUTON

ISBN 978-3-11-161956-9
e-ISBN (PDF) 978-3-11-076928-9
e-ISBN (EPUB) 978-3-11-076939-5
ISSN 0167-4331

Library of Congress Control Number: 2022946832

Bibliographic information published by the Deutsche Nationalbibliothek
The Deutsche Nationalbibliothek lists this publication in the Deutsche Nationalbibliografie;
detailed bibliographic data are available on the Internet at http://dnb.dnb.de.

© 2024 Walter de Gruyter GmbH, Berlin/Boston
This volume is text- and page-identical with the hardback published in 2023.
Typesetting: Integra Software Services Pvt. Ltd.

www.degruyter.com

Acknowledgments

Two scientific events are at the origin of the project that resulted in this book. The first one is a talk that Edwin Williams delivered on February 2013 at the Linguistics Department of the University Paris-7 Denis Diderot, where he was a visiting professor. It was entitled *The size of small clauses* and focused on such questions as how small small clauses can be, what is the size of infinitives, which clausal types are large enough to include a T head. The goal of Williams's inquiry was to try to unlock the systematicity of nonfinite domains. The second event was a talk on gerunds and verb-nouns I presented at the 17th China International Conference on Contemporary Linguistics, Beijing Institute of Technology, October 26–28, 2018, or rather the comments that followed, made to me by Pr Jianhua Hu and Pr Thomas Hun-tak Lee, who observed that much more had to be said about how nouns differ from verbs, particularly in the languages that have no person-number inflection and no overt tense marking at their disposal and yet have an expressive range as wide as that of heavily inflected ones. I was not in a position to contribute anything significant on Chinese, of course, but I could reflect on the many faces defectiveness could take in languages that were relatively familiar to me. This is how the *Nonfinite Inquiries* project began.

 I was fortunate. When I first mentioned the project to him, Henk van Riemsdijk not only reacted favorably, he also enjoined me to immediately get in touch with Norbert Corver, the new editor of the *Studies in Generative Grammar* series. Norbert provided encouragement and enthusiasm. When presented with a sketch of the book, Marcel den Dikken suggested new directions of research, manifesting as always an infectious love for linguistic puzzles.

 Most of the constructions examined in this book have given rise to a considerable literature. I am most indebted to the linguists (grammarians in the tradition, typologists or formal syntacticians), who first discovered their complexity and diversity. It has seemed just fair to dedicate substantial space to the detailed presentation of the proposals put forth and the results achieved by previous research. This book crucially relies on them. Another aspect of the present inquiry is that it is a comparative project dealing with several languages, none of which is my native language. Its success thus crucially depends on the linguistic judgments of the native speakers of English, Welsh, European Portuguese that I consulted. I am most indebted to Gwen Awbery and Emyr Davies for much needed help with the Welsh data, to Alexandra Fiéis, Ana Maria Madeira and Carla Soares-Jesel for discussion of the European Portuguese data. The mails exchanged with Gwen, Emyr, Alexandra, Ana and Carla were so numerous and substantial that they could advantageously be gathered into an autonomous volume. Anna Roussou supplied the Modern Greek examples. David Willis presented observations on the

Middle Welsh examples, which spared me several ignominious mistakes. All my informants were professional linguists, which, I am aware, is both a good and a bad thing. On the positive side, this means that all the colleagues that are mentioned here not only provided enlightened grammaticality judgments on their own language, but also offered enlightening, constructive and stimulating comments.

I am particularly indebted to Ion Giurgea, who agreed to read the pre-final version of the manuscript and suggested essential changes that substantially modified some of its conclusions, to Lea Nash whose generous help was decisive in improving chapter VII dealing with ergative alignment in Middle Welsh, to Benjamin Spector for precious advice concerning the ontology of abstract objects. I also want to express my gratitude to Bernard Bortolussi, Camille Denizot, Jaume Mateu, Daniel Petit and Georges-Jean Pinault, who generously shared their knowledge and expertise of Latin syntax with me.

I have discussed the nonfinite question with many colleagues and friends over the years, in particular Manuela Ambar, Nora Boneh, Huy Linh Dao, Joseph Emonds, Robert Freidin, Xiaoshi Hu, Richard Kayne, Jean Lowenstamm, Marc-Antoine Mahieu, Ora Matushansky, Jean-Claude Milner, Claude Muller, Patrick Sauzet, Christine Tellier, Chen Zhao.

I wish to dedicate this volume to the memory of Maurice Gross, Nicolas Ruwet and Jean-Roger Vergnaud, outstanding researchers, exceptional teachers, reliable colleagues and dear friends, who guided my first steps in the nonfinite labyrinth.

Contents

Acknowledgments —— V

Foreword —— XV

I Questions about nonfiniteness

1 Finiteness, tense, person agreement —— 3
1.1 The morphological and semantic bases of finiteness —— 3
1.2 The anchoring property of finiteness —— 6
1.3 The syntactic representation of finiteness —— 7

2 How nonfinite domains differ from finite ones —— 11
2.1 Defectiveness —— 13
2.2 Dependency —— 14
2.3 Size —— 15

3 Crossing the verb/noun border —— 18
3.1 Nonfiniteness vs. nouniness —— 18
3.2 Category mixing —— 19

4 A program —— 21

II Key concepts and emerging issues in recent syntactic theorizing

5 Categories and their labels —— 27

6 Categories and their features: Inheritance and the C-T connection —— 32

7 The licensing of overt and controlled subjects —— 39
7.1 The minimalist view —— 39
7.2 Landau's rule —— 40
7.3 The exhaustive control/partial control divide —— 43
7.4 Free alternation between PRO and overt subjects —— 44
7.5 A quick look at the Modern Greek case —— 45

7.6	Transposing Landau's generalization into Chomsky's probe-goal-Agree framework —— 49
7.7	Defectiveness and non-convergence —— 52

8 The semantics of nonfinite tense —— 55
- 8.1 Stowell (1982) —— 55
- 8.2 Wurmbrand (2001, 2014) —— 57
- 8.2.1 On the tense of infinitives —— 57
- 8.2.2 Explaining the simple present effect —— 59
- 8.2.3 Factive/emotive complements are tensed —— 61
- 8.3 Landau (2000, 2004, 2013, 2015) —— 64

III The morphosyntax of English gerund forms

9 The syntax/morphology interface —— 71
- 9.1 Lexicalism —— 71
- 9.2 Distributed Morphology —— 72
- 9.3 Bridging the gap between Distributed Morphology and Lexicalism —— 76

10 Transcategorial items, mixed projections —— 79

11 A preliminary classification of gerund phrases —— 81

12 Lexical approaches to trancategoriality —— 83
- 12.1 The neutralization approach —— 83
- 12.2 The underspecification approach —— 85

13 Syntactic accounts of transcategoriality —— 87
- 13.1 A DM analysis of gerund forms —— 87
- 13.2 Some shortcomings of the DM account —— 89
- 13.3 Category mixing and category switches —— 91
- 13.4 Some observations on switches —— 92
- 13.5 A generalized v analysis? —— 97

14 Conclusion —— 100

IV The syntax of English gerund clauses

15	**Some semantic properties of gerund domains —— 105**	
15.1	The tense of gerund clauses —— 105	
15.2	The aspectual value of the *-ing* suffix —— 106	
16	**How gerund constructions differ from one another —— 112**	
16.1	How verbal gerunds differ from nominal ones —— 112	
16.2	PRO-*ing* constructions —— 114	
16.3	Some differences between Acc-*ing* and Poss-*ing* constructions —— 116	
16.4	Two shared properties —— 120	
16.4.1	The syntax of gerund heads —— 120	
16.4.2	The subject of verbal gerunds —— 121	
17	**A labeling analysis of Acc-*ing* constructions —— 123**	
17.1	Categorial architecture and feature structure —— 123	
17.2	The effect of labeling —— 125	
17.3	The respective scopes of labeling and category switching —— 127	
18	**A category-switching analysis of Poss-*ing* constructions —— 129**	
19	**A note on nominal gerund constructions —— 133**	
20	**PRO-*ing* gerund constructions and the calculus of control —— 135**	
20.1	Controlled gerund clauses in prepositional phrases —— 135	
20.2	Is *-ing* an agreement marker? —— 137	
21	**Summary —— 141**	

V The morphosyntax of verbo-nominal heads in contemporary Welsh

22	**The two uses of the verb-noun —— 147**	
22.1	VNPs used predicatively —— 147	
22.2	VNPs used as arguments —— 150	
23	**The internal structure of VNP projections —— 154**	
23.1	Is the verb-noun a verb or a noun? —— 154	

23.2	A syntactic approach to word formation —— 159
23.3	Irish verbo-nominal projections —— 159
23.4	The internal structure of Welsh VNPs and clauses —— 163
23.5	Predicative VNPs can occupy nominal positions —— 164

24 Aspectual properties of Welsh verb-nouns —— 167

25 Conclusion —— 169

VI The syntax of Welsh verbo-nominal clauses

26 *i*-initial verbo-nominal clauses —— 175
26.1	*i* as a nonfinite complementizer —— 176
26.2	*i* as a case licenser —— 178
26.3	*i* as a nonfiniteness marker —— 180
26.4	Interim summary —— 184
26.5	The syntactic licensing of verbo-nominal clauses and of their subjects —— 185
26.6	Nonfinite interrogatives and relatives —— 189
26.7	The case of mandatory predicates —— 191
26.8	Verbo-nominal heads do not raise to T —— 194

27 *Bod*-initial constructions —— 196
27.1	Analysis of *bod*-clauses —— 196
27.2	Parallels between propositional types —— 200
27.3	Differences between propositional types —— 205

28 Labeling Welsh VN-clauses —— 210

29 The tense of VN-clauses —— 213

30 Conclusion —— 218

VII Verbo-nominal root clauses in Middle Welsh

31 Some remarkable data —— 223

32 A short excursus on unergative VNs —— 227

33	**Against the nominal analysis** —— **229**
33.1	Aspectual periphrastic constructions —— **229**
33.2	The "historic infinitive" —— **232**

34   The ergativity of verbo-nominal root and embedded clauses —— **234**

35	**Making the ergative analysis explicit** —— **238**
35.1	Is a unitary analysis of ergative structures possible? —— **238**
35.2	Deriving ergative alignment in VN-initial structures —— **239**

36   Coexistence of ergative-absolutive and nominative-accusative patterns —— **244**

37   The interpretation of tense —— **249**

38   Conclusion —— **251**

39   Appendix: Proposals for the analysis of ergative structures —— **252**

VIII The syntax of inflected infinitives in European Portuguese

40   Introduction —— **259**

41   Three asymmetries —— **265**

42   The non-existence of an auxiliary/main verb asymmetry —— **269**

43   The case licensing of IIC subjects —— **283**

44   The eventive/stative divide —— **286**

45	**The factive/nonfactive asymmetry and the categorial identity of IICs** —— **294**
45.1	A fundamental semantic divide —— **294**
45.2	Complementizers —— **295**
45.3	The categorial status of inflected infinitive clauses —— **296**

46	Labeling IICs —— 301
46.1	Labeling factive complements —— 301
46.2	Labeling epistemic/declarative complements —— 305

47	Inflected/uninflected infinitive clauses with a null subject —— 307

48	Conclusion —— 313

49	Appendix: Verb classes in European Portuguese —— 314

IX Extraposition phenomena

50	The extraposition of embedded finite clauses —— 323
50.1	The Case Resistance Principle —— 324
50.2	The nominal nature of propositional domains —— 326
50.3	The thematic properties of propositional arguments —— 329

51	Why Welsh VN-clauses obligatorily extrapose, why Welsh VN-phrases cannot —— 331
51.1	Extraposition of verbo-nominal *i*- and *bod*-clauses with an overt subject —— 331
51.2	A note on *synnu* —— 335
51.3	The non-extraposition of verbo-nominal phrases —— 338
51.3.1	Adjectival constructions —— 338
51.3.2	Subject control structures —— 341

52	A principled approach to extraposition —— 343

53	Why gerund clauses don't extrapose —— 346

54	Why Portuguese inflected infinitive structures sometimes extrapose, sometimes don't —— 351

55	Conclusion —— 356

X The Latin *ab urbe condita* construction

56   Domain of study —— 363

57   Basic syntactic and semantic properties of the DPC —— 368

58   The analysis of passive past participles: A few landmarks —— 374

59   DPCs as mixed projections —— 383

60   Agreement and case in DPCs —— 392
60.1   The problem —— 392
60.2   Formalizing agreement and case assignment in DPCs —— 395
60.3   A particular case —— 398

61   The origin of linguistic variation —— 401

62   Conclusion —— 404

XI Facts and events, attitudinal objects and states of affairs

63   Do gerund clauses name facts? —— 411

64   Verbo-nominal clauses —— 417

65   On attitudinal objects —— 421

66   Inflected infinitive constructions —— 424

67   Taking stock —— 426

XII Conclusion: The many faces of defectiveness

68   Semantics —— 433

69   Morphosyntax —— 435

70	Syntax —— 437
70.1	Classification of NFDs —— 437
70.2	The licensing of overt subjects —— 438
70.3	The movement of verbo-nominal heads —— 439
70.4	Labeling —— 440
70.5	Size —— 441

71	On defectiveness —— 442

References —— 445

Index —— 463

Foreword

Taking the path opened in the 60s and the 70s by Chomsky (1965), Rosenbaum (1967), Gross (1968), Kajita (1968), Kayne (1969, 1975), Kiparsky & Kiparsky (1970), Emonds (1970, 1976), Bresnan (1970, 1972), Wasow & Roeper (1972), Postal (1974), Horn (1975) and Chomsky & Lasnik (1977), followed by Chomsky (1981), Rouveret & Vergnaud (1980), Stowell (1981, 1982), Rizzi (1982), Burzio (1986), Rochette (1988), Kayne (1991), Pesetsky (1992), Rooryck (1992), Chomsky & Lasnik (1993) during the Principles and Parameters era, and further developed in a minimalist perspective by Chomsky (1995a, 2000a), Bošković (1996, 1997), Landau (2000, 2004, 2013, 2015), Mensching (2000), Wurmbrand (2001, 2014), Miller (2002), Cornilescu (2003), Pesetsky & Torrego (2004), Davies & Dubinsky (2004), Pires (2006), Tellier (2018) and many others, this book is intended as a contribution to the syntax of nonfinite domains.

The vast majority of the references that precede refer to works dealing with infinitival syntax, which constitutes a major chapter in the study of nonfinite complementation.[1] With the exception of the introductory chapter, where they are used to lay the theoretical foundations of this study, this book contains no systematic account of the syntax of standard infinitival clauses.[2] Infinitives belong to the class of forms that traditional grammars of Latin and Ancient Greek used to refer to as the "nominal forms of the verb", a class that also includes Latin and Romance past and present participles, Latin and Romanian supines, English gerunds and participles, Turkish inflected gerunds, Celtic verb-nouns, Arabic masdars.

What is intended here by "nonfinite domain" (henceforth NFD) should be made clear from the outset. This notion primarily refers to the syntactic structures lexically headed by a participle, a gerund, a verb-noun, or an infinitive, whose verbal/clausal nature cannot be questioned, and which are the *locus* of a predication relation between a nonfinite verbal predicate and an overt or a null subject. Some nonfinite structures functioning as adjuncts or restrictive modifiers – circumstantial small clauses, absolute participles, depictive constituents – no doubt correspond to this characterization, but they will only occasionally be alluded

---

[1] These references almost exclusively concern English and Romance languages. The list of the works dealing with complementation in other languages or other language families is too long to be reproduced here.

[2] But it includes a study of inflected infinitive constructions in European Portuguese, which appear to jointly display characteristics of both finite and nonfinite complement clauses. The question is not whether they are clausal – they are -, but whether they stand on the same side as standard infinitival constructions or should be characterized as concealed finite ones.

to in this study, the core target of the inquiry being constituted by the nonfinite clausal structures functioning as verbal or prepositional arguments. The label NFD also covers nominalized complex expressions that can be verbal to a varying degree (Latin dominant participle constructions) and are sometimes closely related to a verbal/propositional construction (English Poss-*ing* vs. Acc-*ing* constructions, Portuguese *o*-inflected infinitival clauses vs. bare ones). Although they fulfill the description to some extent, derived nominals like the nominalization *destruction* are left out.

The aim of this book is to propose an in depth investigation of the phrasal architecture of a restricted collection of NFDs – English gerund clauses, Celtic verbo-nominal sentential complements, Middle Welsh verbo-nominal root sentences, European Portuguese inflected infinitive constructions, as well as Latin dominant participle and gerundive constructions –, to define criteria on the basis of which their functional organization can be determined and to characterize their respective semantic profiles. With respect to each NFD, the main challenge that has to be taken up is to identify its categorial architecture, as well as the feature matrices associated with the functional heads it contains, and to propose a differentiated derivation and representation for it.

The terms used by the grammatical tradition to refer to nonfinite forms in the languages of the world and to their properties directly reflect their morphological, syntactic and semantic diversity. The infinitive is used to express the "meaning of the verb in the abstract", as Trask (1993) puts it. But one can find infinitives that are marked for tense, for aspect (Latin), for person (Portuguese). Participles are usually characterized as the nonfinite forms that denote a property linked to the participation of an actor in the process referred to by the verbal predicate. They can be viewed as the equivalents of attributive or predicative adjectival or adverbial phrases. But they also behave as genuine verbal forms functioning as argument-selecting predicates in dependent contexts, conveying an aspectual value, making voice distinctions, being modified by adverbs. This is precisely the case in the Latin dominant participle construction. Both gerunds in English and verb-nouns in Welsh should be conceived of as verbal nouns, which, in their predicative use, retain their ability to take complements, select arguments, be modified by adverbs. It will appear however that they differ in crucial respects. For example, English gerunds are natural vehicles for the imperfective value, Welsh verb-nouns do not convey any aspectual value. Although we are faced with superficially quite disparate phenomena, the various nonfinite domains and nonfinite forms under investigation will be looked at side by side from a unified perspective and the same set of questions will be raised about each.

I am aware that the particular nonfinite sampler selected here is comprised of a highly limited collection of languages and constructions, all of them belonging to the Indo-European family. Although they instantiate quite diverse choices and behaviors, it is clear that they illustrate only some aspects of the nonfinite phenomenology. It is to be hoped that they are nevertheless sufficiently representative of the possibilities found in the natural languages of the world.

Most of the constructions studied here have given rise to a considerable literature and the research in this book inevitably relies on previous work. But its goal is essentially comparative and typological. It is not to provide entirely novel and original accounts for each of the constructions examined, but, more modestly, to discover the properties they share and the extent to which they differ. Each of them sheds an interesting light on a particular facet of nonfiniteness. English gerund clauses raise the question of the nature of transcategoriality and the origin of mixed projections; Welsh nonfinite clauses exemplify a situation where the T head doesn't participate in the case licensing of subjects: they make accessible the effects of the absence of C-to-T transmission and illustrate the role of visibility in the distribution of clauses; the "historic infinitive" construction in Middle Welsh illustrates a situation where a structure traditionally analyzed as displaying a nominal syntax should in fact be viewed as a case of ergative alignment; inflected infinitives in European Portuguese show that labeling plays a crucial role in non overtly tensed domains in the fulfillment of the subcategorization requirements of matrix predicates; the Latin *ab urbe condita* construction illustrates a case where a predication relation involving a past or present participle displays the external distribution of a nominal structure. But in and of itself, none of these constructions allows us to unlock the systematicity of nonfinite domains. To have the full picture, it is necessary to assemble the different fragments together, to try to fit them into a consistent whole.

This study is couched within a resolutely minimalist approach. Minimalism in the 90s and in the following decades has opened new perspectives on the proper treatment of familiar phenomena, clarifying the modular organization of grammar, eliminating redundant principles and costly devices and making way to tighter accounts. The ultimate goal of this study is to determine whether the theoretical assumptions, derivational procedures and representational devices that are standardly used to account for infinitival syntax are also appropriate to deal with the clausal or nominal domains headed by other nonfinite categories. Recent theoretical advances will systematically be confronted with the phenomena studied here. Do they make a better job of the nonfinite problem than previous theories of syntax? I hope to show that they do and that a restricted set of minimalist ideas can be technically worked out across a wide range of data. To this extent, the book, which exploits quite recent aspects of syntactic theorizing, such as the Labeling Algorithm and feature inheritance, can be viewed as providing a laboratory for testing these new theoretical concepts.

I Questions about nonfiniteness

1 Finiteness, tense, person agreement

1.1 The morphological and semantic bases of finiteness

In order to reach a better understanding of the way nonfinite domains work, it is first necessary to get a clear idea of what finiteness is. The answer to this question cannot be simple, in part because it differs according to whether one adopts a morphological, a syntactic or a semantic perspective. The notion of finiteness appears not to be unitary and should probably be deconstructed. It could even turn out to be unnecessary, a result that would imply that the notion of nonfiniteness should also be dispensed with.

Jerzy Kuryłowicz's (1964) book, *The Inflectional Categories of Indo-European*, is devoted to the comparative study of the many grammatical dimensions that had a morphological expression in Indo-European. But finiteness is not included in the list. Finiteness has no place either in Roman Jakobson's (1957) classification of verbal categories, which primarily deals with the Russian verb and is exclusively based on morphological correlations and speech pragmatics. This absence reflects the fact that finiteness has no exponent of its own, but is dependent on other categories for its expression. The ones fulfilling this role are generally taken to be person/ number agreement and nominative case. Cowper (2016) writes that "the essence of finiteness is the ability to assign nominative case to a subject and to agree in person and number with that subject". To the extent that the assignment of nominative case to subjects generally goes along with the presence of tense, tense is also generally included in the list of the ingredients that are constitutive of finiteness. This rough preliminary morphological characterization immediately meets with serious difficulties, as recent typological studies have emphasized (see the contributions collected in Nikolaeva 2007a and Nikolaeva 2010). Deciding that some specific features are responsible for finiteness immediately excludes the languages in which these features have no overt expression. In Japanese, verbs inflect for tense, but not for agreement. In Chinese, no temporal or person-number inflection occurs on verbal heads. But it would be wrong to conclude that the finite/nonfinite distinction is not operative in these languages. According to some analyses of Chinese, finiteness, but not nonfiniteness, creates barriers to syntactic processes. The distinction between the finite and nonfinite clause types is further manifested by the distribution of null subjects and other properties.[1] Inflected

---

[1] Tang (1990) proposes eight criteria to distinguish finite clauses from nonfinite ones in Chinese. On finiteness in Chinese, see also Hu, Jianhua, Pan Haihua, and Xu Liejong (2001), Lin (2011, 2015).

infinitive constructions in Portuguese illustrate a still different case. The relevant forms are overtly specified for agreement – they agree with the subject, which is marked for the nominative case -, but not for tense. The fact that the nominative case is still available when inflectional agreement is dissociated from tense seems to indicate that it is agreement, rather than tense, that is responsible for the licensing of nominative and for the finiteness of the corresponding clause.[2]

The fact that the expression of clausal finiteness is generally parasitic on the spell-out of other grammatical features and that the list of the features that determine it varies across languages has led Givón (1990: 853) and other functionalist linguists to the conclusion that the finiteness/nonfiniteness distinction is not dichotomic in nature and that finiteness should be viewed as a scalar phenomenon, which cannot be handled by a single, discrete binary feature. This view is not shared by all those who adopt a functionalist perspective, however. Bisang (2007) claims that finiteness can indeed be described as a discrete binary phenomenon, once the grammatical and cognitive dimensions that languages choose to express in order to mark the asymmetry between independent and dependent clauses are carefully considered. According to him, finiteness is linked to the categories that "overtly mark structural independence at the highest level of sentencehood". It is uncontroversial that in the languages that establish a sharp distinction between finite and nonfinite domains, the verb forms used in the former "typically carry the maximum in morphological marking for such categories as tense and agreement permitted in [the] language" (see Trask 1993: 103–104, quoted by Nikolaeva 2007b).

An alternative approach relies on the claim that, since the morphological criterion is insufficient and subject to variation, the empirical basis for claiming that the finite/nonfinite distinction exists in a language L necessarily involves other, plausibly semantic and syntactic factors. The fact that the subject being assigned nominative is instrumental in the identification of the corresponding clause as finite indicates that syntax, not just morphology, is involved. A defining characteristic of finite clauses is precisely that their subject is licensed clause-internally

---

[2] Early work on European Portuguese inflected infinitives (see Rouveret 1980) suggests that, taken together, person-number agreement on the verbal head and nominative case on the subject suffice to identify the relevant clauses as finite, without the spelling out of tense being necessary. The study of Turkish inflected gerund constructions, which do not exhibit full verbal morphology and take genitive subjects, but display agreement, leads George & Kornfilt (1981) to the conclusion that agreement, not tense, is the hallmark of finite domains (see also Kornfilt's subsequent work). Modern Hungarian is also well-known for having both inflected infinitives in some nonfinite constructions and nominative infinitival subjects in others.

and establishes no relation with an external case assigner. The latter dimension is plausibly linked to the general status of finite clauses as opaque closed domains, that is, as domains that cannot be penetrated from the outside and that allow extraction only through the edge.

If one adopts a semantic perspective, finiteness can be defined as the ability for a subset of verbal forms to license independent predications, that is, to serve as the verbal elements in independent sentences. Positive declarative root clauses are taken to be the prototypical finite domains. But other constructions, whose finite status is controversial or quite uncertain, fulfill the independence criterion. Romance imperative forms, for example, which exhibit an admittedly reduced inflectional paradigm, can stand on their own in independent sentences.[3] The same conclusion holds for the optative conjugation in Ancient Greek and for the subjunctive one in Latin and Greek: They display full inflectional paradigms, whose forms can lexically head domains that can stand by themselves. An alternative option would consist in identifying finiteness with the semantic property possessed by the domains that qualify as propositions making an assertion that can be true or false, that is, are endowed with a truth-value. If this view is adopted, not all the constructions fulfilling the morphological criterion and containing a form able to stand as the main predicate in root clauses should be considered as finite. Imperative forms do not make an assertion and correspond to non-declarative speech acts. The optative and the subjunctive forms in Greek and Latin simple clauses denote an order, an exhortation or a wish, that is, an *irrealis* modality or intention. But interrogative clauses, which don't bear a truth-value, are plausible candidates for inclusion in the finiteness class. Conversely, infinitives, which morphologically qualify as nonfinite, have assertive force when they function as substitutes for finite tensed forms in independent sentences, where they convey a past interpretation in narrative discourse.[4] Finally, whether embedded finite or nonfinite clausal domains bear a truth-value or not depends on their denoting propositions or events, cf. ch. XI. The conclusion is that the notion of truth-value is not a reliable criterion for finiteness.

Whichever stand is taken on the interaction between finiteness and mood, there is no doubt that a proper characterization of finiteness should integrate a reference to various semantic dimensions. Landau's (2004) Finiteness Rule for Obligatory Control (Finiteness Rule for OC) can be interpreted as stating that

---

[3] The question of whether imperatives should be analyzed as [+ finite] or [– finite] is addressed in Platzack & Rosengren (1998).
[4] The subject of the "historical infinitive" in Latin is in the nominative.

both temporal reference and nominal reference should participate in the semantic characterization of finiteness. In Landau's view, as Adger (2007) summarizes it, the effect of the subject licensing relation in finite clauses is precisely to tie together the possibility of an independent nominal reference and the possibility of an independent temporal reference. Bianchi's (2003) aim is also to characterize the meaning of finiteness. She emphasizes the correlation between two defining characteristics of finite clauses, the ability of finite forms to license referentially autonomous subjects, that is lexical DPs, and their being assigned an absolute tense interpretation directly anchored in the speech time. Aiming at reducing these properties to a common source, she proposes an original conception of finiteness, based on the notion of "anchoring", a concept one inevitably comes across when one tries to understand the syntactic properties by which finite clauses distinguish themselves from nonfinite domains.

1.2 The anchoring property of finiteness

Enç (1987: 642) formulates an Anchoring Principle, according to which

> In main declarative clauses . . . events must be anchored to the utterance or to some other salient reference point.

This requirement is often cast in temporal terms. In most languages and constructions, it is the tense of each independent proposition that is anchored to the utterance context. Pursuing this line of research, Bianchi (2003) proposes that "the syntactic property of finiteness encodes the logophoric anchoring of the clause". The notion of Logophoric Centre is defined as follows:

> Every clause is anchored to a Logophoric Centre: a speech or mental event, with its own participants and temporal coordinates, which constitutes the centre of deixis (Bianchi 2003, proposal 3).

She argues that finiteness has a meaning, which has to do with the way tense and the Logophoric Centre of the clause, understood as including the relation between the speaker, the subject and temporal coordinates, are identified. In finite root clauses, the Logophoric Centre is determined autonomously: Absolute tense and person agreement are directly anchored to the utterance context. At the same time, the sensitivity of nominative case to the finiteness of the clause containing the marked subject is not coincidental. The licensing of nominative case is tightly linked to the person features that constitute the Logophoric Centre. The person features are themselves licensed in a local selectional relation with the speech event, which constitutes the centre of deixis with respect to which they are interpreted.[5] In other words, nominative case is directly related to the anchoring property of finite clauses, which is a manifestation of person agreement.

The question that immediately arises is how anchoring is achieved in embedded nonfinite clauses. Bianchi boldly confronts this question and argues that control is mediated by an internal Logophoric Centre, syntactically represented in the complementizer area (more precisely in the Finite head, see 1.3) and usually resorting to the temporal and logophoric centres of a higher clause. Obligatory control structures and non-obligatory control ones propose two different ways to solve the difficulty. In non-obligatory control structures (and also, in partial control ones), anchoring is achieved anaphorically, via the mediation of a semantically/pragmatically licensed internal Logophoric Centre, which corresponds to a contextually defined mental event or state, involving at least one human/animate participant that grammatically functions as a controller. In exhaustive control ones, the Fin head of the infinitival complement clause takes the matrix clause Event as its antecedent, the complement clause being anchored to it. The extension of the construct "Logophoric Centre" to nonfinite domains is clearly not a trivial task. The ingredients involved in its definition seem to vary in function of the clause type: Whereas the speech event and the temporal structure play a crucial role in finite clauses, the relevant notions in non-obligatory control domains are those of participants and person structure.

1.3 The syntactic representation of finiteness

In the non-functionalist formal approach adopted here, the fact that a language L provides no morphological expression for some features in the phonological forms of sentences (PF) doesn't mean that these features are absent from their logical representations (LF). The fact that Russian, Finnish, Japanese, Chinese don't have a definite article at their disposal doesn't mean that definiteness is not operative in their grammar. The lack of copula in the present tense in Russian and Arabic doesn't imply that these languages are unable to build predicative structures with a present time interpretation. Finiteness could be just one of the categories that some languages choose to express, while others simply have no expression for it. This situation is reminiscent of Jakobson's (1959) insightful remark in his article on Boas.

---

[5] Bianchi refers to Jakobson's (1957) characterization of *person*.

> person characterizes the participants of the narrated event with reference to the participants of the speech event.

> the true difference between languages is not in what may or may not be expressed, but in what must or must not be conveyed by the speakers.

Once again, what makes finiteness a difficult notion to grasp is that in the vast majority of the cases covered by typological research, finiteness has no representation of its own, its expression being parasitic on other dimensions. It can thus be viewed as a global property of clauses, relying on a disparate set of grammatical (semantic, syntactic, morphological) properties, a kind of epiphenomenon, as Kornfilt (2007: 305) proposes.

Formal grammatical approaches make available elegant solutions to some of the questions about finiteness raised by typological and functional research. Of course, it remains to be checked whether these solutions have a real explanatory power. A major concern of the Principles and Parameters framework was the nature and origin of syntactic representations, conceived of as arising from the integration of lexical projections into larger structures headed by functional categories. While lexical heads are responsible for making accessible the descriptive content of verbal, nominal and adjectival entities, as well as the argument structure they select, functional heads take care of the items endowed with a non-lexical, purely grammatical meaning. Mood, tense, aspect, as well as number, person and definiteness are functional entities in this sense.

Kayne (1994) explicitly argues that finite clauses are full CPs and that finiteness is not encoded on the Tense head, but on the Complementizer head. Rizzi (1997), in his cartographic account of the clausal left periphery, assumes that the finiteness specification is indeed not pinned in the inflectional domain, but on an independent category in the left-periphery of clauses, labeled Finiteness and occupying a low position in the complementizer system. This implies that the content of the periphery necessarily participates in making a proposition finite. Since Finiteness (or Finite or Fin) is a head, it necessarily determines a projection, namely FinP. Since Fin encodes a global property of clauses, it necessarily occupies a high position in the cartography of sentences. The functional categorial organization of propositional domains Rizzi (1997) arrives at is the following:

(1) Force > Topic > Focus > Topic > Finiteness > Tense > v > V ...

In this model of clausal architecture, Finiteness is dominated by Force (abstracting away from Topic and Focus), the category where the features related to the illocutionary force of the proposition (which can be an assertion, a question, an order, a wish...) reside. Force is the *locus* of the relation between the proposition and the utterance context. It is less easy to understand what the semantic content of Fin is, which is the lowest head of the complementizer system, interfacing with the inflectional system. Rizzi is not fully explicit on this point. He only states that Fin has a grammatical meaning, which is represented by the binary opposition [+ finite]/[− finite] ...

Cartographic approaches take the functional architecture in (1) as recording distributional regularities recurring across natural languages. Should we limit ourselves to registering the empirical generalizations that underlie (1) or can a conceptual motivation be provided for it? Categorial hierarchies can at least partly be conceptually motivated, because functional items have a grammatical meaning that assigns them a particular rank in a semantic hierarchy. Abstracting away from the left periphery, Ramchand & Svenonius (2014: 161–165) show that the categorial architecture standardly assigned to finite domains (T > Asp > v > V) simply reduplicates the semantic hierarchy between propositions, situations and events.[6] If one considers the left periphery, the fact that the Topic head occupies a position hierarchically higher than Focus corresponds to the expected situation. Similarly, it is not surprising that Force is located higher than Finite. From a semantic point of view, the relation between D and Number in nominal expressions can be thought of as being analogous to the relation between Fin and T. The tense-agreement system at the T-level specifies the temporal and pronominal coordinates of the predication relation, but the proposition gets anchored to the utterance context only when the content of Fin and that of Force are taken into account. Similarly, Number in noun phrases only specifies that a plurality (or non-plurality) of occurrences is involved. The content of D provides the whole expression with a reference value.

(1) is used by Bianchi (2003) to couch her discussion of finiteness. In her view, the Logophoric Centre of the clause, which includes elements such as speech time, speech location, speaker, address, resides in Fin. The licensing relation of person features in the syntax takes the form of a selectional relation between the Fin head that encodes the Logophoric Centre and the Infl head that encodes person agreement. Let us provisionally assume that Fin in finite clauses encodes the relation between the logophoric elements and the grammatical dimensions of the event (event time, event location, agent, patient) and that Force in turn encodes the relation between the illocutionary operator binding a propositional variable, the context of utterance and the Logophoric Centre. The presence of a Force head specified [+ assertion] above Fin makes the corresponding clause temporally independent and referentially autonomous.

---

6 In the semantic ontology they use, (i) *events* are atemporal; θ-roles are relations between individuals and events; (ii) *situations* presuppose the existence of an eventuality; they have a Time parameter; they have a World parameter; (iii) *finite propositions* presuppose a situation that is existentially closed; they are anchored to the utterance context, having force in the discourse.

In most versions of cartography, functional heads are endowed with features which flatly recapitulate the definition of the category itself (the Topic head bears a [+ topic] feature, the Focus head a [+ focus] feature . . .). In Chomsky's (2000a) probe-goal-Agree approach to syntactic dependencies, functional heads bear features that can be interpretable or uninterpretable and, when uninterpretable, must first be valued, then deleted. This is the case of the [number] and [person] features on the category T, which in Romance languages hosts the verbal forms that are specified for these features. Checking is achieved via the establishment of an Agree relation with an expression also bearing the relevant features. The entity targeted by the Agree process in this case is the subject noun phrase, which is by definition endowed with interpretable [number] and [person] features and is the closest nominal expression to the T head (since it resides in the specifier of vP). What about the feature [+/− finite] associated with Fin? It is itself interpretable and hence doesn't need to be checked. The question is why it is manifested the way it is. We have concluded that finiteness is generally dependent for its expression on the spell-out of other features, namely [tense] and [person]. [tense] is visible on the tensed verbal forms residing in T (or in the verb phrase), not on the category Fin itself. A sharpening of our understanding of the relation between these two categories is in order. Chomsky's inheritance theory, discussed in section 6, is in a most favorable position to derive this property, the idea being that all the uninterpretable features involved in the C-T complex originate in a single cluster in C (that is, Fin) and that a subset of them, the uninterpretable [φ] features, are transferred to T, which is already the *locus* of the interpretable [tense] feature. If this idea is on the right track, the claim that C/Fin is the original locus of finiteness can be maintained in the face of the data. The [finite] feature uncontroversially resides in C/Fin, but, when transmission occurs, the two affixes that manifest finiteness, [tense] and [agreement], are both morphologically spelled out on the immediately lower category, namely T.

2 How nonfinite domains differ from finite ones

The preceding observations explain the way finite tensed clauses work, but say nothing about nonfinite ones.

Some of the elements that have been listed in the preceding section are only present when the [finite] feature is positively specified. It is negatively specified in standard nonfinite clauses. If one reasons in Bianchi's terms, the Logophoric Centre in these domains is necessarily of a different nature from the one in finite clauses. The property that seems to crucially distinguish nonfinite from finite clauses is precisely the absence in their temporal structure of a speech point/ utterance time to which the reported event and its participants could be independently related, as argued in sct. 1.2.[7]

Adopting a syntactic/morphological point of view, I will take the combination of syntactic defectiveness and morphological deficiency as a defining hallmark of nonfinite constructions and nonfinite heads. The primary goal of this work is precisely to explore the "syntax of defective domains" in a minimalist perspective.[8] This basically amounts to following in the footsteps of Chomsky's (2000a) probe-goal-Agree approach to syntactic dependencies, which is based on the idea that infinitival domains are φ-defective and to extend this insight to other NFDs. But, as observed by Adger (2007), "although there is just one way to be finite (which is to be specified as [+ finite] . . .), there is more than one way to be nonfinite". Edwin Williams (personal communication) compares nonfinite domains to the particles in the physics of the 50s or 60s: "There is a 'zoo' of them, with what seem to be randomly assorted properties, and no one has found the key that unlocks their systematicity".

There are indeed many ways in which NFDs can descriptively differ from one another. The syntactic, morphological, and semantic dimensions possibly relevant to the study of nonfiniteness constitute a quite heterogeneous set. It should

---

[7] On the opposition between the external and internal Logophoric Centre, see sct. 1.2.
[8] Tracking the "minimalist syntax of defective domains" is exactly the program (and the title) of Acrisio Pires's remarkable book (cf. Pires 2006). I basically pursue the same goal here, but my account is based on different explanatory principles and resorts to different technical devices. In Pires's view, the range of properties shared by English gerunds and Portuguese inflected infinitives, which both present some sort of defectiveness, can be explained by the same mechanisms, in particular by Hornstein's (1999) movement theory of control. This theory plays no role here. Acquisition data are not discussed either. But this book has a broader empirical coverage since, besides English and European Portuguese, Latin, Welsh and Middle Welsh data are also taken into account.

be determined whether these dimensions are themselves direct reflexes of defectiveness or constitute autonomous areas of variation.

A first key potentially opening the way to a systematic account of NFDs is provided by Williams's (2013) claim that the relevant differences between nonfinite domains and finite ones and among nonfinite domains themselves could reduce to size, that is, to the complexity of their respective functional architectures.

Closely related to size is the question of the categorial identity of nonfinite domains: Which functional category heads them? What is their label? The properties of the extraposition process, which are seldom capitalized on, may help to find an answer: Some projections are forced to extrapose, others are prevented from doing so, and this variation is closely related to their categorial identity, in a way that will be made explicit.

Another way to tackle the nonfiniteness question is to characterize the various NFDs in function of their tenseness, extending Stowell's (1982) initial insight and Wurmbrand's (2001, 2014) and Landau's (2004, 2013) fine-grained classifications of infinitives. Although the relevant forms are not morphologically marked for tense, the embedded domains they lexically head are assigned different tense construals, depending on the identity of the affix they bear, on the class and selectional requirements of the matrix predicate (propositional attitude, speech act, factive, emotive . . .), on the lexical type of the embedded one (stative, eventive).[9] Tense construal phenomena have an intrinsic semantic interest, but they will mainly be used here as evidence that a T head is projected in the corresponding syntactic structures. Deciding whether a projection of T is present or absent in the internal structure of the various nonfinite constructions is of a crucial importance in their analysis and, we will see, a point of variation between them.

In other words, morpho-syntactic (defectiveness/deficiency), syntactic (size, categorial identity) and semantic (tenseness) aspects of nonfiniteness should be explored in order to discover which properties are shared by all nonfinite domains and which ones are subject to variation, which ones are defining characteristics and which ones are accidental features. Once the values taken by these properties have been established, it will be possible to identify the categorial architecture of each construction, as well as the feature matrices associated with the functional heads it contains, and to propose a differentiated derivation and representation for it. An important variation can be detected among NFDs as to the identity and

---

9 The eventive/stative asymmetry also manifests itself in languages that are deprived of inflectional verbal morphology. For example, stative predicates in Creole languages are construed as denoting a state of affairs contemporary with the utterance time, eventive predicates systematically refer to a past event, see Déchaine (1993).

number of the verbal and/or nominal projections they incorporate, but it will appear that they can also project similar functional architectures and differ as to the feature matrices associated with the functional heads they include. The intuition that underlies the research strategy adopted here is that the set of properties associated with a specific NFD doesn't constitute a cluster that should be tackled separately, but a combination of characteristics that should be studied in relation to the other nonfinite domains and to finite ones.[10]

2.1 Defectiveness

It must be acknowledged that the leading ideas on which the analyses of infinitival domains are built have changed a lot in the last 50 years. In the 70s, syntactic research focused on the distribution of complement clauses, on their categorial identity and on the rules that affect them. Contrary to the early transformational hypothesis that entailed that *that*-clauses, *for-to*-clauses and gerund clauses were not distinguishable at deep structure, the phrase-structure approach developed by Bresnan (1972) took into consideration the fact that complementizers have a meaning and that verbs are subcategorized for the type of complement they take. During the Principles and Parameters period, the major concern was the distribution of subjects in the various types of infinitive constructions and both Case Theory and Binding Theory were resorted to to account for it. Overt referential subjects, when present, needed case (*John wants very much for Mary to leave*; *Paul expected Lucy to win*); the null subjects associated with infinitives didn't require case, but had to fulfill specific government and binding requirements: The subject of control structures, PRO, had to be ungoverned (*Max intended* [PRO] *to leave*); the subject of raising structures, NP-trace, had to be properly governed and locally bound (*Paul seems* [t] *to speak fluent Chinese*), cf. Chomsky (1981).[11]

---

[10] Note that we are used to think of NFDs as dependent domains. But the finiteness/nonfiniteness question also arises in the systems in which root clauses display no temporal or person-number inflection, as is the case in isolating languages (cf. fn. 1). One cannot a priori exclude the possibility that a better understanding of these languages could help to evaluate some of the proposals argued for in this book, either directly (if NFDs and isolating structures appear to share a common core of properties) or indirectly (if they turn out to be radically different). This angle won't be pursued here.

[11] At a later stage, it was argued that PRO itself should be marked for a special non-lexical case, namely null case, which is such that the only DP that can bear it is PRO and that only nonfinite T can assign it, cf. Chomsky & Lasnik (1993), Bošković (1996). One of the advantages of the claim that PRO must be case-marked just like any other DP is that it dispenses with the assumption, made by the theory of Principles and Parameters, that PRO is both pronominal and anaphoric.

The perspective changed again in the 90s with the advent of the Minimalist Program, when it was realized that there exist many more classes of infinitive-taking verbs than the previous framework allowed. An important trend of research exploits Chomsky's (2000a) idea that infinitival clauses should be thought of as defective domains headed by a morphologically deficient tense. The full significance of this assumption appears clearly when it is combined with the probe-goal-Agree approach to syntactic dependencies developed in *Minimalist Inquiries*. Nominal subjects, like other nominal expressions, must get rid of their uninterpretable case feature. In finite clauses, this is achieved without the argument subject being forced to move, via Agree between the external argument in SpecvP and finite T, which simultaneously gets rid of its uninterpretable φ-features. The movement of the argument subject, when it occurs, can only be traced back to an independent requirement, the Extended Projection Principle (EPP), now modeled as an uninterpretable feature on T. An alternative way to interpret subject raising in finite clauses is to claim that it reflects the requirement that all derived projections, clauses included, should be assigned a label.[12] No problem arises in null subject finite sentences, where the T head is strong enough to provide a label for the clause it heads, whatever the position of the subject. But in the languages where T is weak, an alternative strategy must be resorted to. Feature sharing between T and the raised subject provides the solution.

Can the syntax of subjects in nonfinite domains be dealt with along similar lines? One expects nonfinite T, if present at all, to be too weak to perform the labeling of its clause. It must be determined whether the cases of subject raising observed in nonfinite domains instantiate the same strategy as the one at work in finite clauses.

2.2 Dependency

The defectiveness of nonfinite domains and the deficiency of some of their components play a crucial role in the establishment of dependency relations, since they force the elements involved to look for interpretable/uninterpretable features within the domain they belong to or to establish relations with the outside

---

Landau (2013) shows that the claim that PRO bears case is supported by ample crosslinguistic evidence, but that the relevant case cannot be null case. The account proposed here makes no claim concerning the case status of PRO.
12 On labeling, cf. sct. 5.

environment.[13] Dependency is a rather vague term that combines a notion of hierarchy – dependency relations are asymmetric, one of the terms functions as a complement to the other – and a notion of syntactic integration – as an effect of Merge, the dependent phrase becomes an integral part of the constituent headed by the selecting head. The notion of dependency has a wider scope than that of subordination, which is exclusively relevant to sentential complementation and modification, or that of government (in its traditional sense), which also concerns non-sentential complementation, but is exclusively structural.

More should be said about dependency, however. Nonfinite domains are generally syntactically and semantically dependent, but nonfinite forms don't exclusively occur in dependent contexts – this is the case of root infinitives – and finite forms occur in embedded contexts, without displaying reduced marking in terms of person-number agreement and tense-aspect-mood on the verb or reduced case marking on the subject. The dependency between propositional complements and the matrix predicates that select them must be marked in some way or other. To achieve this result, finite clauses resort to complementizers and, in some cases, to specialized moods (the subjunctive is found with factive and volitional predicates in French, it has a larger distribution in Italian). Nonfinite ones do not object to the use of complementizers, but they can also dispense with them by making the selectional dependency parasitic on the existence of other dependencies, for example the lack of a referentially independent subject and the necessity to interpret the silent one (usually PRO) or the impossibility to case license the overt subject clause-internally and the necessity to find an external licenser for it. The relatively impoverished endowments of nonfinite domains, as compared with those of finite clauses, are a proof that several strategies exist in the realm of clausal complementation to syntactically represent the relevant dependencies.

2.3 Size

A general characteristic of the generative approaches to nonfiniteness is that they essentially resort to the same phrase-structural schema to deal with *infinitive* clauses and with *finite* ones. The source of the difference between the two lies in the feature endowment of the functional categories involved, T and C in particular, and in the strength/weakness of these features, rather than in the identity of the categories themselves. It is worth asking whether the other NFDs

---

[13] The case of tense defectiveness is complex since, as will be shown in section 8, morphological tense deficiency doesn't systematically correspond to the lack of semantic tense.

(gerund clauses, participial phrases...) involve different clausal architectures or basically resort to the same clausal patterns. It is one of the aims of this study to establish this point.

It soon appears that the full battery of functional verbal heads is not necessarily present in all NFDs. If one attempts to extend the cartographic schema in (1) to nonfinite structures, several possibilities should be considered: (i) Fin is present in nonfinite domains, but is negatively specified for the feature [finite]; or (ii) some nonfinite domains lack the category Fin entirely, but include an instance of T; or (iii) non-clausal vP-domains exist, which include no instance of T. This would leave us with the following options:[14]

(2) a. (V) [$_{FinP}$ Fin [$_{TP}$ DP$_s$ T [$_{AspP}$ Asp [$_{vP}$ v VP]]]]
    b. (V) [$_{TP}$ DP$_s$ T [$_{AspP}$ Asp [$_{vP}$ v VP]]]
    c. (X) [$_{AspP}$ Asp [$_{vP}$ v VP]]

Williams (2013) argues that the first two options are instantiated by the structures which he labels "small clauses" and which, in his view, are the *loci* of a predication relation between an unsaturated verbal or nominal predicate and an external argument that saturates it. These include absolute constructions, Acc-*ing* gerund constructions, perception verb complements... He claims that only a structure of a certain size (say TP) licenses saturation by an external argument (which generally stands in SpecTP). No PRO and no saturation are involved in the third structure, (2c), which underlies the -*ing* phrases functioning as restrictive modifiers.[15] This case is illustrated in (3a), where the phrase headed by *hiding* is unsaturated as modifiers must be. On the contrary, *hiding* in (3b) has a PRO subject and the resulting combination functions as a saturated predicate.

(3) a. *The man hiding his hands came into the room backwards.*
    b. *John, hiding his hands, came into the room backwards.*
         [Williams 2013]

---

[14] In (2a), (2b) and (2c), (V) stands for the matrix predicate. An additional functional head, namely Aspect, has provisionally been inserted between T and v. One should not conclude that Aspect is systematically projected in nonfinite domains.

[15] Representation (2c) presupposes that obligatory control complements should be analyzed as unsaturated predicates, as Williams (1980) assumes. The works in the tradition of Lexical Functional Grammar refer to them as open complements. Chomsky (1981) and the vast majority of scholars after him characterize them as propositions. This is the position I will adopt in the following chapters. See Landau (2004: 812) for discussion.

In (3a), the *-ing* form heads the smallest possible projection it can head, namely vP or AspP, cf. (2c). In (3b), V-*ing* is the lexical head of a constituent embedded in a TP domain, which is the smallest phrase in which saturation by an external argument can be achieved.

If the three cases schematized in (2) are indeed attested, it could be proposed that the full clausal structure represented in (1) can be truncated at different levels. The complements to ECM verbs like *expect* or *believe* and to raising verbs like *seem* are truncated at the T-level and, as a consequence, the licensing of the subject entirely depends on the external environment.[16] Structure (2b) illustrates this situation. In (2c), the clause is truncated at the Asp/v-level. This case corresponds to the situation where a nonfinite verbo-nominal category heads a phrase that functions as an attributive restrictive modifier. This phenomenon will only be briefly alluded to in this study, which focuses on the predicative uses of these heads and confronts them with their argumental use.

Cases of cross-linguistic variation confirm that NFDs come in different sizes. It has long been known that the infinitive phrases occurring in *tough*-movement constructions in French have a reduced size as compared with their English counterparts: They cannot involve a long-distance relation between the null embedded object and the "matrix" subject (cf. 4a/4b).[17]

(4) a. *This book would be difficult to convince your sister to read* [e].
　　b. * *Ce livre serait difficile à convaincre ta soeur de lire* [e].

We are now in a position to propose a preliminary characterization of nonfinite domains.
(i)　NFDs are morphologically deficient and syntactically defective with respect to finite ones.[18]
(ii)　NFDs are syntactically and semantically dependent.
(iii)　NFDs can structurally come in different sizes.

---

16 This is consonant with Chomsky's (2008) claim, at the basis of the inheritance idea, that T, when it is not selected by C/Fin, doesn't inherit φ-features that would turn it into an active head (cf. sct. 6). C/Fin is not projected in ECM and Raising nonfinite clauses. If the uninterpretable φ-features of T originate in C/Fin, both the donor Fin and the receiver T must be present for T to be active.
17 Williams (2013) also discusses this case. The French examples are from Authier & Reed (2009).
18 Among the constructions considered in this study, European Portuguese inflected infinitive constructions are tense-defective, but display person inflection, cf. ch. VIII.

3 Crossing the verb/noun border

3.1 Nonfiniteness vs. nouniness

The notion of finiteness is usually considered to be exclusively relevant to clausal domains. But it would be artificial to dissociate the study of the clausal domains lexically headed by verbo-nominal forms from the nominal structures in which the same forms occur. Gerund phrases in English provide a particularly clear example of this situation.

(5) a. *John reading* War and Peace *surprised me.*
    b. *John's reading* War and Peace *is unlikely.*
    c. *John's reading of* War and Peace *in public was a huge success.*

In the Acc-*ing* construction (5a), the gerund form has a verbal status and the domain it heads has the internal structure of a clause and the external distribution of a nominal expression. In the Poss-*ing* construction (5b), the lexical head also behaves as a verb, but the expression has the external distribution and, in part, the internal make-up of a noun phrase. In the nominal gerund construction (5c), both the internal structure and the external distribution of the gerund phrase are nominal. The gerund is nominal in (5c), verbal in (5a) and (5b).

The proposal has been made by Ross (1972) that the standard lexical categories in English appear to be arranged according to a quasi-continuous hierarchy, which in his view supports a non-discrete conception of grammatical categories and of the grammar itself. He proposes (6):

(6) verb > present participle > perfect participle > passive participle > adjective > preposition > adjectival noun (like *fun*) > noun

In a later paper, Ross (1973) establishes the existence of another hierarchy, the "nouniness squish", whose outcome is a classification of syntactic entities in function of their nouniness:

(7) *that*-clauses > *for...to*-clauses > embedded questions > Acc-*ing* constructions > Poss-*ing* constructions > action nominals > derived nominals > nouns

In Ross's view, the expressions on the top of the list in (7) are less nominal than the terms at the bottom. This conclusion is based on the observation that some syntactic phenomena (which at the time were dealt with in transformational terms) exclusively affect the lower members of the list, others the higher members, but that no phenomenon exists that is such that it affects, say, *for . . . to*-clauses and derived nominals, but not Acc-*ing* constructions that intervene between the two in the hierarchy. Relying on Ross's (1972) insight and dealing with gerunds, Alexiadou (2013) claims that "the distinction between nouns and verbs doesn't represent a dichotomy". She refers to a "gradience in verbal traits" and tries to discover how this gradience can be explained. In my view, this state of affairs, although quite suggestive, should not be taken as supporting a non-discrete conception of categories and constructions. I will stick to the traditional view that takes categories to be discrete entities and try to show how the properties exhibited by each verbo-nominal construction can be made to follow from the interaction between the featural make-up of the affix they contain and other dimensions, in particular the lexical classes to which the embedded predicate and the matrix verb belong.

3.2 Category mixing

The final items in Ross's (1973) nouniness squish are action nominals, then derived nominals, then nouns. There is no doubt that the corresponding constituents are nominal expressions, with an internal nominal structure.[19]

The case of intermediate elements such as English gerunds is less straightforward. An aspect of gerundive syntax is that some gerund clauses appear to have a mixed categorial status. This is the case of Poss-*ing* constructions (cf. 5c), which simultaneously display syntactic and morphological traits that define verbs and traits that define nouns and should thus be viewed as "mixed" projections.[20] Although they differ from the verbal/clausal constructions involving the same heads, they raise the same type of questions, which are detailed in sct. 4 below.

---

19 The structures that are exclusively nominal (noun phrases, derived nominals) are not taken into consideration in this work. For in depth studies, see Grimshaw (1990), Alexiadou (2001) and Borer (2005).
20 The expression "mixed category"/"mixed projection" has been introduced by van Riemsdijk (1978) to deal with prepositional syntax in Dutch. It is the label used by Rouveret (1987, 1994, 2020), Bresnan (1997), Harley & Noyer (1998), Alexiadou (2001), Nikitina (2008), Panagiotidis (2015) and others to refer to gerund constructions and to structures in other languages displaying similar properties. Grimshaw (1990) and Borsley & Kornfilt (2000) refer to them under the label "mixed extended projections". In *Remarks*, Chomsky (1970) also uses the term "mixed", but it assigns it a different meaning. In his view, confronted with gerundive nominals (*John's refusing the offer*) and derived nominals (*John's refusal of the offer*), structures like *John's refusing of the offer* should be viewed as mixed forms.

A rarely made observation is that mixing could be seen as a characteristic of non-finite domains which could be linked to their defectiveness (but in no way should be taken to support a non-discrete view of grammar). One of the aims of this book is to try to determine which approaches to the definition of lexical categories and to the labeling of derived projections are in the most favorable position to capture this possible correlation.

4 A program

In what follows, the class of NFDs will be taken to include both the verbal/clausal and the nominal structures headed by a verbo-nominal head. At a descriptive pre-theoretical level, it must be determined for each NFD whether:
(i) the lexical head of the domain can coexist with adverbs/adjectives;
(ii) the head can/cannot be preceded by the definite article or by other determiners;
(iii) the head can/cannot have an overt/null subject of its own;
(iv) when the head governs an object, the relation between the two is direct/mediated by a preposition; when it is direct, the case assigned to the nominal complement is the verbal case (accusative)/the case typically available in nominal domains (genitive).[21]
(v) the NFD must/cannot occupy argument positions.

These criterial properties are in part intended to distinguish between verbal and nominal projections.

In more general terms, it must be decided how the basic syntactic and morphological characteristics of NFDs listed in (i)–(v) should be formally represented, which principles and mechanisms are involved in their derivation. The discussion will be organized around five major questions:[22]
(i) What is the origin of verbo-nominal nonfinite forms? Are they built in the lexicon or derived in the syntax? More generally, which assumptions about the nature of word-building processes are in the best position to account for their properties?
(ii) Which principles determine the distribution of NFDs? How are they assigned a categorial label?
(iii) Is a T head present in the internal structure of nonfinite constructions?
(iv) What is the syntax of features within the functional architecture of the various NFDs?

---

[21] This question is worth asking because the two options are sometimes instantiated within the same construction. See the discussion of the alternation between the SOV and SVO orders in Irish nonfinite clauses, section. 23.3.
[22] Recall that the case of the nonfinite phrases functioning as restrictive modifiers or adjuncts is left out in this study.

(v) How are nonfinite subjects licensed? If they move, which principle triggers their movement?

(vi) Nonfinite verbal/verbo-nominal heads sometimes raise, sometimes do not. Which grammatical dimension is responsible for this difference?

Providing a principled answer to (i) presupposes that we have formed a clear conception of the properties of the lexicon/syntax and the syntax/morphology interfaces. (ii) will receive a principled answer only if we have a labeling theory at our disposal, able to determine how heads and projections are assigned a categorial label. Concerning (iii), syntactic properties, such as the distribution of sentential negation and of temporal adverbials can provide diagnostics for the presence or absence of the category T in the internal structure of NFDs; a reference to the temporal interpretation of these domains cannot be dispensed with either. (iv) presupposes that the features on functional heads indeed have a syntax and are allowed to agree with the features on other heads or be copied on them. This imposes the definition of both a feature-sharing mechanism and a feature-transmission device. Question (v) stands at the core of any theory of nonfiniteness. Overt subjects, when present in NFDs, generally raise to the clause-initial position, even in the languages that do not display a subject-initial order in finite clauses.[23] Is this movement triggered by the necessity to case license the subject, or to satisfy the EPP requirement, or to provide a label for the whole nonfinite domain? Is the deficiency of nonfinite verbal forms in some way or other responsible for subject raising? (vi), a rarely asked question, can only receive an answer if an adequate theory of head movement is available.

Providing (i)–(vi) with principled-based answers should help us to approach the most fundamental questions raised by nonfiniteness: Is the cartography of NFDs identical to that of finite clauses? Or does it differ from the latter by the value assigned to the features on functional heads? Or is it a truncated version of the latter? Or a totally specific one? More generally, does the analysis of NFDs impose the definition of specialized formal devices and specific principles or can their properties be derived from the same set of principles and devices as the ones at work in finite domains?

---

23 As is the case in the verbo-nominal clauses of Celtic verb-initial languages (the Irish nonfinite constructions where the subject takes the form of a prepositional phrase introduced by *do* are an exception to this generalization).

II **Key concepts and emerging issues in recent syntactic theorizing**

Syntactic research has been developing since the end of the 50s by focusing on some crucial areas of grammar and on their interaction, defining new theoretical constructs, novel principles and formal devices, fueled by continuous empirical discoveries. Chomsky (2013) lists the following as the "core properties of concern": compositionality, order, projection and displacement. With the advent of the Minimalist Program, the necessity to simplify computational procedures and the search for a greater explanatory adequacy led to a reassignment of the above properties to different principles and to distinct grammatical components. Whereas compositionality, order and projection were initially taken care of by phrase structure principles and displacement by the transformational component, the consensus today is that compositionality and displacement should be assigned to "the operation Merge, applying in its simplest form", that order should be interpreted as "a reflex of sensorimotor externalization" and labeling as a special case of minimal search in the syntax. A novel approach to syntactic dependencies, the probe-goal-Agree approach, was developed, which relies on a sophisticated theory of features and of the various processes that can affect them (valuation, transmissibility, inactivation) (cf. Chomsky 2000, 2001).

Developing in parallel to the minimalist enterprise, cartographic research has given rise to precise proposals concerning the fine internal structure of syntactic domains, that of clauses at their core and at their periphery and that of nominal expressions (cf. Rizzi 1997, Cinque & Rizzi 2008).

Finally, although they played a less prominent role at certain periods in the history of the field than at others, the concern for construal phenomena and the interface with interpretation were never absent. Dealing with obligatory control, Landau (2004, 2013) has shown that in order to achieve a proper classification of clausal domains, it was necessary and sufficient to refer both to the interpretive properties of tense (irrespective of whether it is overt or null) and to the presence or absence of agreement inflection on C or on T. The latter proposal stems from a better understanding of the properties of null tense. Indeed, much progress has been done concerning the knowledge of the interpretive properties of tense across domains (cf. Wurmbrand 2001, 2014, Landau 2004).

The aim of this chapter is to present and briefly discuss these proposals, which provide key insights into the Faculty of Language. Most of them have been put forth independently of the nonfinite constructions. There is no doubt that they also should play a prominent role in the analysis of the nonfinite phenomena considered here and in the implementation of the research agenda outlined in the preceding chapter.

At the same time, with the exception of the probe-goal-Agree approach, the Labeling Algorithm and the Theory of Inheritance, which are part of the minimalist trend and are obviously tightly interconnected, they have different origins and distinct scopes. Simply putting them together in their current form will clearly not give rise to a coherent theory. For them to be integrated into a consistent whole, several adjustments must be carried out. Some preliminary observations on the way this integration can be achieved will be made as the presentation proceeds.

5 Categories and their labels

The determination of the categorial identity of linguistic units is one of the most complex problems syntactic theory must face. It has two facets and raises two types of questions. First, how do words and lexical items get a categorial label? Section 9 will provide indications about the various ways this question can be answered. Second, how is the identity of the complex syntactic objects resulting from Merge determined? This is the topic of this section.

The idea that the construction of categorial identity is a purely syntactic affair is present in several forms in contemporary theorizing: It is directly involved in labeling, a processus that has become a necessary ingredient of derivations in recent years, interacting with the internal word order and external distribution of phrases. In Chomsky's (2008, 2013a, 2015) approach, the principles of construction of expressions and projection mechanisms are kept apart. The projections resulting from structure building (that is, External Merge) and those created by movement (that is, Internal Merge) need to be labeled and labeling involves a specific procedure. The deep reason why projections must be assigned a label is that the information concerning headedness and endocentricity plays a crucial role in the syntactic computations they are involved in, as well as at LF and at the C-I interface, the levels at which interpretive procedures check whether the subcategorization and selectional requirements of the heads involved in a structure are fulfilled and whether predication relations are well-formed. The technical motivation for adding a Labeling Algorithm to the computational system is that the free structure-building operation Merge, when it combines two objects, just creates a binary set and says nothing about the label of the resulting complex object (the concept of *specifier* is not present anymore in a Merge-based conception of grammar). Chomsky proposes an algorithm based on the operation Label, which, like Agree, performs a minimal search in order to detect the most accessible element in a domain. In configurations like {X, YP}, where X is a head and YP is not, no problem arises: X gives its label to the whole structure.[1] But if we are dealing with a symmetric structure {XP, YP}, minimal search identifies two heads, X and Y, and the procedure fails. Symmetric structures in which a constituent immediately contains two sister maximal projections XP and YP can nevertheless be provided with a label, if certain conditions are met. They are specified in (1).[2]

---

[1] What is intended by "exocentric" is simply that the label of the object [XP YP] is neither X nor Y.
[2] The necessity to define precise constraints on the selection of the candidates for labelling appears clearly when one considers the labeling properties of some *wh*-constructions, which are not systematically assigned the label of the host head, but can also inherit the one of the moved

(1) **Labeling Algorithm**
If X and Y are identical in one respect and, in particular, share some feature, this feature is selected as the label of SO; in this case, the label is the "pair of agreeing elements" (Chomsky 2015).

The situation referred to by (1) arises in simple and embedded finite clauses. Recall that in this approach to phrase structure building, the applications of Internal Merge (phrasal movement) don't target the specifier of the attracting category,[3] but systematically create a set-merge symmetric exocentric structure.[4] This is the case in (2).

(2) [C [$_\alpha$ [$_{DP}$ John] [$_{TP}$ T [$_\beta$ [$_{DP}$ ~~John~~] [$_{vP}$ killed the mocking bird]]]]]

Recall that the applications of Merge don't target specifiers, but systematically create set-merge symmetric exocentric structures. This is the case in (2). The vP and the adjoined subject form a symmetric structure β. Chomsky claims that the symmetry is neutralized by the further raising of the subject, which makes the lower occurrence of *John* invisible and the label β equal to vP/v. (1) is relevant to the determination of the label α. According to (1), the label of a simple finite clause is the union of the two matching sets of φ-features borne by the raised noun phrase and the head T of the TP it adjoins to. α in (2) is <φ, φ>, since both *John* and T are endowed with φ-features and since these features match. In Chomsky's view, T in English is too weak to serve as a labeling head. But the relevant configuration can be assigned a label if subject raising occurs, in which case (1) applies. The Extended Projection Effect observed in (2) should be viewed as in indirect effect of the labeling requirement. The claim is not that the labeling

---

element (cf. Chomsky 2008). These structures can be interpreted as free relatives or as interrogative clauses, depending on the lexical context, cf. *I read what you wrote* vs. *I wonder what you wrote*. The free relative interpretation of the sequence obtains when it is the moved *wh*-head that projects and provides the label for the whole expression.

3 The treatment of the relation between category-defining heads and roots with their complement (see the non-lexicalist approaches discussed in section 9) should also be made explicit. Chomsky (2013, 2015) assumes that roots cannot serve as labels. The selected root inherits the uninterpretable features of the category-defining head (v or n) and merges with it. Since the two heads share features, no symmetry problem arises.

4 Although the traditional notion of specifier has been abandoned, it can informally be used, to refer to the YP that is sister-of-XP in the exocentric structures resulting from Merge, as Chomsky (2020) does. The structures in which the subject ends up being a sister of TP, as an effect of Internal Merge, will occasionally be referred to as structures in which the subject has raised to the "specifier" of TP.

requirement is the driving force behind subject raising. It cannot be, because the subject-raising process involved is a free untriggered operation, which, contrary to Agree, is not launched by the necessity to value and delete an uninterpretable feature. The Labeling Algorithm can indeed be viewed as subsuming the effects of the EPP principle, which generally concerns expressions that have been independently licensed, in particular case licensed. But by itself, it plays no role in subject licensing, it is limited to providing the complex object resulting from Internal Merge with a label. The scopes of the two processes, subject licensing and clausal labeling, do not overlap.

It is also well-known that clausal structures exist that are undoubtedly appropriately labeled, but do not resort to (1). Null subject Romance languages are a case in point. These languages allow constructions in which EPP effects are not observed and the subject argument is allowed to remain in its original position. This is so because finite T, which is endowed with rich agreement, is strong enough to label the clause it heads as TP. Italian differs from French in this respect.[5]

(3) a. *I ragazzi giocano. insieme.*
    the children play.3PL together.

   b. *Giocano i ragazzi insieme.*
    play.3PL the children together

   c. *Giocano insieme.*
    play.3PL together

(4) a. *Les enfants jouent ensemble.*
    the children play.3PL together

   b. **Jouent les enfants ensemble.*
    play.3PL the children together

   c. **Jouent ensemble.*
    play.3PL together

In null subject Romance languages, the EPP seems to be suspended in finite clauses: The subject argument can remain in the postverbal position (cf. (3b)),

---

5 In this book, I use capitalized regular font (e.g., Aspect or Asp. Tense or T) for syntactic nodes/categories, lower case font (e.g., past, perfect) to indicate the semantic features merged in the syntactic structures and small caps (e.g., PAST, PERFECT) to gloss the morpho-syntactic realization of the semantic features in the examples.

is not forced to raise, but is of course allowed to (cf. (3a)). The contrasts between (3b) and (4b), (3c) and (4c) follow from the fact that T in Italian is strong enough to provide the clause with a label, whereas it is too weak in French to do so, which leaves subject raising and feature sharing as the only available labeling procedure.[6,7]

By the same logic, one expects defective/deficient nonfinite T heads not to have the same labeling force as complete finite ones and not to be strong enough to provide a categorial label for the projections that dominate them. How is the labeling of these structures achieved? Is it necessary to resort to a procedure specific to nonfinite domains? Or is (1) sufficient to achieve the desired result? It will be shown that the second option is correct.[8]

The interaction of the labeling procedure with other grammatical requirements should be made explicit at this point. Since only one label can be assigned to a given configuration under Chomsky's (2013a, 2015) account (contrary to what Chomsky 2008 assumed), labeling via feature sharing necessarily interferes with the satisfaction of subcategorization and selectional requirements. But, if it does, one would expect insuperable difficulties to arise in many syntactic configurations, as has been pointed out to me by Marcel den Dikken.[9] The labeling of finite {DP$_{subj}$, TP} structures is precisely such a case. C in (2) selects a verbal complement, not a nominal one, but α is labeled <φ, φ> by the shared features of T and the DP subject. This situation, Den Dikken takes as a clue that labeling

---

[6] What has just been said implies that two labels are potentially available for (root) finite clauses: TP (in the null or postverbal subject constructions in Romance languages, cf. 3b, 3c) or <φ, φ> (in English and French and in subject-initial structures in null subject Romance languages, cf. 3a).

[7] Gallego (2017) proposes an alternative account of the EPP effect. He argues that (5) doesn't instantiate a subcategorization relation between C and T, but a movement relation: C is just the head of a movement chain also including T, T should be rewritten C. A copy resulting from movement is not strong enough to label. In fact, strength is not at stake: The copy is invisible for labeling and for all the other computational processes. See also Pesetsky & Torrego's (2001) proposal that *that* actually corresponds to the way T is spelled out when moved to C/Fin. The authors also take the complementizer *for* to originate in T.

[8] A priori, the labeling of (finite and nonfinite) propositional domains in languages such as Chinese, that have no inflectional morphology at their disposal and allow both overt and null subject structures, should raise no specific difficulty since, in Chomsky's system, the labeling procedure proceeds along the same lines whether the relevant φ-features are overt or not. The same observation holds for Scandinavian languages whose finite verbal forms display no overt agreement morphology.

[9] ECM configurations like *Mary expects Paul to win* are one of these. See Chomsky (2020) on the best way to solve the problem raised by these confifgurations. In his view, the external argument doesn't stop in SpecTP, but raises higher and ends up adjoined to matrix vP.

via feature sharing *does not* interfere with subcategorization requirements and that it must be completed by a feature percolation mechanism, ensuring that T and the projection that dominates it share a T or [+ V] label. It seems that in (7a), it is the label resulting from percolation that takes care of C's subcategorization requirement, not the one resulting from feature sharing. Den Dikken's objection is real and well-grounded and it must absolutely be kept in mind as we proceed. But I will argue that the general claim that labeling via feature sharing interferes with the satisfaction of subcategorization requirements can be maintained once the very restricted conditions under which this device can be resorted to are made explicit.

6 Categories and their features: Inheritance and the C-T connection

Finiteness and nonfiniteness can only be properly characterized if a better understanding of the connection between C and T is achieved.[10] Chomsky's (2008) notion of inheritance could provide an elegant and explanatory mechanism to represent this connection. In this section, I will present the Inheritance Theory and check whether it can handle some of the cases that raise a potential difficulty against the conception of the finiteness/nonfiniteness divide sketched in chapter I. It should be kept in mind that the inheritance claim, whose initial theoretical motivation is internal to the Theory of Phases, cannot be dissociated from the probe-goal-Agree approach to syntactic dependencies that governs the syntax of formal features. In some sense, it is just an ingredient of this approach. The ensuing discussion will of necessity be a bit technical.

The claim made by the Inheritance Theory is that the uninterpretable features that are active in a derivational domain – in Chomsky's approach, these domains define "phases" – originate on the functional head of this domain and that a subset of them is transmitted to the immediately lower head, after the phase head has been merged. The Agree relations involving the relevant features can only be established after transmission has taken place. One of the goals of the inheritance proposal is precisely to deal with the relation between C and T. T is inserted into derivations with an interpretable [tense] feature, but no uninterpretable φ-features. The latter originate on C which transmits them to T, making it active, that is, equipped to function as a probe. As a consequence, the corresponding person-number affix, when it is spelled out, is realized on the inheriting head T, not on the source head C. This is the situation in English declarative clauses. The pre-Agree structure resulting from the transfer of features is something like (5).[11]

(5)   C   T DP_s
      ~~u- φ~~   u- φ   i- φ
      ~~u-case~~   u-case   u-case
                 i-tense

---

10 In the discussion to follow, I use the traditional symbol C ("complementizer"), as Chomsky does, to refer to the category Fin of cartographic schemas.
11 The letter i prefixed to a feature label indicates that we are dealing with the interpretable version of this feature, the letter u that the uninterpretable version of the relevant feature is at stake.

If C kept its φ-features in (5), it would have to probe over T to agree with the subject, violating locality. As Ouali (2008) observes, a possible way out is to lower the relevant features onto T, which makes the probe head closer to the goal. Transmission in this case is forced by the Principle of Minimal Search.

But the case of English subject questions shows that the transmission to the internal head doesn't systematically take place, revealing that the C-T relation can take several forms. According to Ouali (2008), three cases should be distinguished. In some languages and constructions, the phasal head C transmits its uninterpretable φ-features to the phase-internal head T, making C inactive and T active; in others, the relevant features stay on C and the head T, exclusively endowed with an interpretable [tense] feature, remains inactive; in others, the uninterpretable φ-features are shared by the phase head and the internal head, which are thus both active. Ouali refers to the first case as Donate, to the second one as Keep, to the third one as Share.[12] As was just shown, English root declarative clauses illustrate a situation where Donate is operative (cf. (5)). But Keep is involved in root interrogatives like *Who drinks coffee?*, where the interrogative element is the subject. If Donate was involved, T would φ- agree with the *wh*-subject, valuing its own φ-feature and deleting the case feature on the *wh*-subject. But, after transmission has occurred, C would only bear an interpretable *wh*-feature and would thus be inactive. As a result, the corresponding uninterpretable feature on the *wh*-word would remain unvalued. In this case, Keep is the only option that gives rise to a converging derivation.

Languages provide other examples of situations where Keep, rather than Donate, is resorted to. Verb-initial languages are a case in point. Dealing with Berber, Ouali proposes to account for the anti-agreement effect in inheritance terms. The hallmark of the structures displaying anti-agreement is that the form of finite verbs don't vary according to the singular/plural status of the subject. What is found instead is an impoverished form, usually homophonous to the third person singular. In Berber, this effect is observed in subject interrogative clauses, subject clefts and subject relative clauses, but not in finite declarative affirmative root clauses, in which number agreement between the finite verb and the subject is systematically observed. Ouali's conclusion is that in Berber, Keep is involved in subject-extraction structures, Donate in the simple structures where no subject extraction occurs.

Welsh differs from Berber in that anti-agreement is observed not only in the structures displaying the local extraction of the subject (cf. 6a), but also in simple finite declarative root clauses (cf. 7a).[13]

---

[12] In other words, the operation Donate is parametrized. Some languages and some constructions have it, others don't.
[13] In (6a) and (6b), *a* is the relative particle used in gap constructions.

(6) a. y   dynion   a ddarllenodd   y   llyfr
       The men   a read.PRET.3SG the book
       'the men who read the book'

   b. *y   dynion   a ddarllenasant y   llyfr
       the men   a read.PRET.3PL the book

(7) a. Canodd   y   merched.
       sing. PRT.3SG   the girls
       'The girls sang.'

   b. *Canasant   y   merched
       sing.PRT.3PL   the girls

Let us look at simple declarative clauses first, which in Welsh display the anti-agreement effect (cf. 7). The form of the solution depends on the assumptions that are made about the scope of verb movement in the language. The early accounts of Welsh clausal syntax took the finite verb to stand in T. But many scholars today propose that Celtic finite clauses essentially have the same syntax as finite root clauses in Germanic (modulo the nature of the element preceding the finite verb, which in Welsh can be nothing or a simple sentential particle): Celtic finite verbal forms stand in C.[14] These two analyses are schematized in (8).

(8) a. **verb-in-T analysis**
       [$_{CP}$ C [$_{TP}$ v-T   [$_{vP}$ DP$_s$ v ...]]]
             u-φ   i-tense   i-φ
             u-case   u-case

   b. **verb-in-C analysis**
       [$_{CP}$ v-T-C   [$_\beta$ [DP$_s$] [$_{TP}$ v-T   [$_{vP}$ DP$_s$ v ...]]]]
             u-φ   i-tense   i-φ
             u-case   u-case

Suppose that Donate is not involved in these constructions and that C systematically withholds its uninterpretable case and φ-features from T. The case feature

---

[14] In the cartographic approach to the left periphery, finite verbs would stand in Fin in both root and embedded clauses; sentential particles would either occupy the Fin position, where they would coexist with the finite verb (this seems to be the case of the declarative complementizer *y*) or occupy a higher functional head. Some particles, such as the negative ones *ni(d)* and *na(d)*, have access to several positions. See Rouveret (2017) for an overview.

on both C and the subject and the uninterpretable φ-features on C must be deleted/valued via Agree. If the verb-in-T analysis (8a) is adopted, C will have to probe the subject in SpecvP across T to get rid of the former and value the latter. If the finite verb in T displayed full agreement, the corresponding φ-matrix would count as a goal closer to the C probe than the nominal subject and would block the establishment of an Agree relation between the uninterpretable features on C and the features of the subject. Anti-agreement can thus be viewed as a strategy aiming at voiding the potential locality violation induced by the intervening T and its content.

A similar conclusion can be drawn within the verb-in-C analysis, schematized in (8b). An advantage of this analysis is that v-T has raised and doesn't intervene between the C probe and the subject goal. But if the verb in C bears a rich inflection and if this inflection is assigned a status equivalent to that of an incorporated pronoun, it should block the establishment of an Agree relation between the uninterpretable φ-features of C and the DP subject. The φ-features on C would be valued, but the uninterpretable case feature on the subject would not be eliminated. Only if the agreement on the verb is poor, that is, φ-incomplete can the necessary Agree relation be established between C and the subject. No minimality problem arises because v-T has raised to C. This is the analysis that will be adopted in this book.

An additional observation should be made at this point, concerning the derivation schematized in (8b). The argumental subject raises to the edge of the TP domain, a claim supported by the distribution of medial negation and adverbs (cf. ch. VI). If the C head witholds the uninterpretable features it is initially endowed with and if long-distance Agree is not an option (or, at least, not the preferred one), subject raising, which positions the subject in the immediate locality of C, is not an untriggered movement allowing the resolution of a labeling problem (cf. sct. 5), but a movement imposed by the necessity to check the Case feature of the subject and to value C's φ-features. The motivations behind subject raising in verb-initial and in subject-initial (cf. sct. 5) languages differ.

Let us now consider *wh*-structures. They can be represented as in (9), if one adopts the verb-in-C analysis.

(9) [$_{CP}$ DP$_s$ [$_C$ a] [$_{TP}$ v-T [$_{vP}$ D̶P̶$_s$ v̶ ...]]]
$\quad\quad\quad$ u-φ $\quad\quad\quad$ i-tense $\quad$ i-φ
$\quad\quad\quad$ i-wh $\quad\quad\quad\quad\quad\quad\quad$ u-wh
$\quad\quad\quad$ u-case $\quad\quad\quad\quad\quad\quad$ u-case

The English and Berber facts already show that Donate is not a possible choice when subject extraction is involved. If Donate was involved, that is, if C didn't retain its uninterpretable φ-features and became inactive, it would not be able to value the [wh] feature on the subject and the derivation would crash. If Keep is selected, C remains active and T, with its interpretable [tense] feature, inactive. Which derivational path is followed? Ouali's account, which can be extended to the Welsh case, takes the well-formedness of the structures displaying the anti-agreement effect as a sure indication that C in the relevant structures is able to probe the *wh*-word and agree with it. When the verbal form doesn't bear a rich inflection that would block the establishment of the Agree relation, the goal closest to C is the relativized *wh*P in the lower subject position.[15] It bears interpretable φ-features, an unvalued case feature and an uninterpretable *wh*-feature. As a result of Agree with φ-complete C, [wh] and [case] on the subject are valued, [φ] on C also is. T doesn't participate in these checking relations.[16]

The merit of this account, based on Ouali's (2008) proposal, is that it succeeds in establishing a link between the anti-agreement effect and a specific choice concerning the transmission of φ-features: Anti-agreement on the finite verb goes together with the selection of Keep, full agreement is compatible with Donate, as the discussion of Berber declarative clauses has shown. The analysis of Welsh verbo-nominal clauses in chapter VI relies on the claim that no φ-feature transmission from C to T takes place in the sentential domains of this language.

Another piece of the puzzle resulting from the featural relations between C and T comes from Irish and specifically concerns [tense]. A tense connection exists between C and T in this language, as shown by interesting data first discussed by Cottell (1995).[17] But there are strong reasons to doubt that a transmission of a [tense] feature from C to T is involved in the corresponding structures.

In Irish, finite complementizers display tense distinctions, as (10) shows.[18]

---

[15] This *wh*P ends up in the SpecCP position.
[16] In both Berber and Welsh, full agreement reappears when the subject is long-distance extracted. Ouali argues that the third option, namely Share, is involved in the relevant structures. Of course, it remains to be explained why anti-agreement is not observed in English matrix questions. For a suggestion, see Ouali (2008, sct. 5).
[17] For a different analysis of the closely related Scottish Gaelic data, see Adger (2007).
[18] McCloskey (1996) has provided examples which, when interpreted in the light of the cartographic approach, uncontroversially show that finite complementizers in Irish stand in Fin, rather than in Force as in Romance languages (see Rizzi 1997). Roberts (2005) resorts to this characteristic to account for the close relation between C and T in Irish. The verb-initial property and the anti-agreement effect are also observed in this language, which suggests that Irish Fin retains its uninterpretable features.

(10) a. *Deir   sé go dtógfaidh   sé   an peann.*
       say.PRES.3.SG he go take.FUT.3SG 3SG the pen
       'He says that he will take the pen.'

   b. *Deir   sé gur   thóg   sé   ann peann.*
       say.PRES.3SG he go.PAST take.PAST.3SG 3SG the pen
       'He says that he took the pen.'

The complementizer *go* has an unmarked present form (*go*) and a form marked for past (*gur*), cf. (10a) vs. (10b). A similar alternation is found with other complementizers, such as relative particles and negative complementizers. From these data, Cottell concludes that a [tense] feature is present on C. But the situation illustrated by (10) is complex. Tense is represented on both finite verbal forms and on complementizers, but its representation on the latter is impoverished with respect to its representation on the former: It reduces to the past/non-past distinction on complementizers, whereas finite verbal paradigms also include future forms. There are several reasons why the phenomenon under consideration should not be tackled in inheritance terms. Why would [future] be the only feature not represented on the source head, but represented on the heir category? Moreover, [tense], which clearly is interpretable on T, is uninterpretable on C. Transmission certainly cannot turn an uninterpretable feature into an interpretable one. When it occurs, the uninterpretable status of the transmitted features is not affected. If some kind of transmission was involved in the relevant structures, it should be performed upward. The only way out is to assume that Irish C, which doesn't transmit its uninterpretable φ-features, is also endowed with an uninterpretable [tense] feature, which enters into an Agree relation with the interpretable [tense] feature on T. The impoverished tense mark on the complementizer is the morphological reflex of the Agree relation between the uninterpretable [tense] on C and the interpretable one on T.[19] What about [finite]? Someone arguing that [finite] resides on C in all the structures under discussion and coexists with uninterpretable φ-features and possibly uninterpretable [tense] would be on the safe side. Since it is interpretable, this feature has no reason to lower onto T.

---

19 For Agree to occur, the matrices on T and on C must count as non distinct, a condition that is satisfied only if the presence of [tense] on the two heads, not its specific value, is taken into account or if [present] is a cover feature for both [present] and [future], that can take either value when on T, but is exclusively realized as present when on C.

The overall conclusion of this section is as follows. The reason why the tense and agreement features that manifest finiteness are not spelled out on the C head that bears [finite] in English and Romance is that C's φ-features have been derivationally transferred from the cluster on C to which, together with [finite], they initially belong, to T, where they coexist with T's interpretable [tense]. Celtic verb-initial languages appear to make a different derivational choice. First, there is no transmission of uninterpretable φ-features from C to T. The verb-initial property and the anti-agreement effect can be explained along these lines. Second, tense in Irish is also represented at the C- level, where it is uninterpretable (its interpretable counterpart is on T). This property could be linked to the fact that Irish belongs to the family of languages that select the Keep option. An alternative possibility is that tense has a featural representation on C in the finite clauses of all languages, but that the corresponding feature is spelled out only in a restricted subset of them.

7 The licensing of overt and controlled subjects

7.1 The minimalist view

Both before and after the advent of Case Theory in Vergnaud (1977) and Chomsky (1981), linguists have struggled silently, often painfully, to discover the conditions governing the distribution and the overtness of referential noun phrases, of subjects in particular. Case Theory, the PRO theorem and the EPP principle, which were essential ingredients of the Principles and Parameters framework at the end of the 70s, no doubt mark a huge step forward in this respect. The studies couched within this framework argue that nominative case licensing is possible when either one of two structural relations is borne out: a specifier-head agreement relation or a government relation with an inflected verbal category bearing a tense-agreement suffix.

The minimalist approach to syntactic dependencies makes available a novel theory of subject licensing that is in a position to derive this double option. Government and the specifier-head relation don't define syntactically relevant configurations anymore and the licensing of the subject is taken care of by an Agree relation established at the T-level (or at the C-level) between the person, number *and case* features of the T (or C) head, eventually hosting the inflected verb, and those of the subject it c-commands.[20] Uninterpretable case features play an ancillary role in the overall system, which is reduced to the identification of the nominal expressions that bear them as appropriate goals for the valuation operation. When the relevant features are on T, as is the case in subject-initial languages, case checking occurs early in the derivation, when the subject still resides in the vP. If the subject raises from its original position – and it undoubtedly does in a lot of finite constructions -, its movement is not triggered by the necessity to establish an additional probe-goal relation between the elements involved. As observed in section 5, Internal Merge, which is henceforth totally dissociated from case checking, applies freely in this case. It is an untriggered movement, whose effect is to produce a labelable representation that fulfills the Labeling Requirement.

---

[20] See Chomsky (2000a, 2001, 2004, 2008). [case] is uninterpretable on both the inflected verbal form (or the T head) and the argument subject, [person] and [number] are uninterpretable on the verbal form (or on T) only. For the Agree operation to be possible, *minimal* c-command is not required; it is sufficient that the subject occupy a position c-commanded by T or by the inflected verbal form bearing the finite affix.

The basic operations that are involved in the derivation of finite and nonfinite clauses in the minimalist approach have now been identified. These are:
(i)   External Merge
(ii) Transmission
(iii) Valuation (Agree)
(iv) Internal Merge
(v)   Labeling

There are in fact several ways to combine them. Müller (2008) observes that an indeterminacy may arise in the application of the two elementary operations Merge and Agree, which both obey Pesetsky's (1989) Earliness Requirement, and he claims that the way each language solves this indeterminacy determines the type of argument alignment it displays, ergative-absolutive or nominative-accusative (cf. sct. 35.1). In a recent paper, Chomsky (2020) claims that Merge (both Internal Merge and External Merge) applies freely everywhere, with the resulting deviant expressions and interpretations being filtered out. This proposal is intended to solve a major problem raised by the assumption that probe-goal relations are triggered. In the relevant structures, the transmission of the uninterpretable features from C to T, a CP-level process, takes place before the Agree operation between T's inherited features and those of the subject, a T'-level operation: a counter-cyclic derivational scenario that should absolutely be avoided if a minimalist perspective is adopted. I will ignore this problem and Chomsky's elegant solution to it, but I will retain the idea that, besides probe-goal relations that are triggered by definition, instances of Internal Merge exist, which are not triggered at all. This is indeed the case of the Internal Merge operation that results in the <φ, φ> labeling of finite clauses in English (cf. sct. 5).

7.2 Landau's rule

Since the early 2000s, Idan Landau has been developing a new perspective on control phenomena and the licensing of subjects (cf. Landau 2000, 2004, 2013, 2015). In his view, two distinct grammatical properties are relevant to the determination of the availability/unavailability of overt/controlled subjects in finite and nonfinite complementation: *semantic* tense and *morphological* agreement. Concerning tense, the dimension that motivates the assignment of a + or − value to the [T] feature of an embedded clause is the possibility of a temporal mismatch between the matrix and the embedded event.²¹ In this system, [– T] on Infl encodes the absence of semantic tense in the clause; [+ T], which may or may not be associated with overt tense morphology, occurs in *semantically* tensed clauses, that is, indicative clauses and a large subset of infinitive clauses, but not exhaustive control ones, nor Hebrew and Balkan subjunctives. Whereas the criterion for [+ T] is purely semantic, an inflectional head Infl is positively specified for [Agreement] (henceforth [Agr]) only if the verbal form is overtly inflected for φ-features. In other words, [Agr] must be visible to be active. Landau proposes the following generalization, which he dubs the Finiteness Rule for OC (cf. Landau 2013: 90):²²

(11) In a fully specified complement clause (in which the Infl head carries slots for both [T] and [Agr]):
 a. If Infl carries both semantic tense and agreement ([+T, +Agr]), NC (no control) obtains.
 b. Elsewhere, Obligatory Control (OC) obtains.

(11) distinguishes non-control (NC) environments from obligatory control (OC) ones on the basis of the presence of semantic tense and of overt person and number inflection. Clause (11b) is intended to cover the basic cases of obligatory control in English, as well as the structures that instantiate what Landau refers to as "finite control", a well-known phenomenon illustrated by the subjunctive clauses in Hebrew, Modern Greek and other Balkan languages, which are overtly inflected propositional domains but define environments for obligatory control. Given (11), OC is available in [–T, –Agr] complements (cf. 12), in [+T, –Agr] complements (cf. 13), and in [–T, +Agr] complements (cf. 14, 15).²³

(12) *Mary remembered/forgot* [PRO/*Bill *to lock the door*]

(13) *Mary hated/planned* [PRO/*Bill *to lock the door*]

---

21 For example, the infinitive is [– T] in (i); it is [+ T] in (ii) (cf. Landau 2013: 66).

(i) *Last. night, Tom condescended to help us today.
(ii) Last night, Tom planned to help us today

Various classifications of verbal predicates in function of the tense properties of their complements have been proposed in the literature. They are discussed in sct. 8.
22 (11) reproduces Landau's notation.
23 Landau (2004) adopts Iatridou's (1993) idea that control *na*-clauses in Modern Greek lack tense and characterizes the subjunctive complements in (14), (15) as [–T, +Agr]. In other words, the absence of overt tense marking in a clausal domain doesn't show that it is [– T], overt mood marking in a clausal domain doesn't show that it is [+ T].

(14) Rina bikša me-Gil [še-[e] yivdok šuv et ha-toca'ot]
Rina asked from-Gil that would.check.3SG again ACC the-results
'Rina asked Gil to double-check the results.' [Hebrew]

(15) O Yannis kseri [e] na kolimbai
the Yannis.NOM knows PRT swim.3SG
'Yannis knows how to swim'. [Greek]

(11) predicts that semantically tensed and untensed complements will not differ in control as long as they are both uninflected (compare 12 and 13) and that inflected and uninflected clauses will behave the same as long as they are both untensed (compare 12 and 14–15). When the two features [T] and [Agr] are specified, that is, when semantic tense and agreement inflexion coexist on the inflectional head of the complement, control is blocked, a case instantiated by finite indicative clauses.[24]

In the most recent versions of his theory, Landau claims that the computational system must take into account the distribution of [T] and [Agr] on both T and C. These formal features can also be manifested on the C head. In Landau's view, the full range of complement types in natural languages can be classified on the basis of the specifications assigned to the [T] and [Agr] features on the two clausal functional heads Infl and C.

The claim that two autonomous and differently characterized features are jointly relevant to the determination of both finiteness and control is indeed a major insight that cannot be ignored. It should be clear by now that what Landau proposes is not just a theory of control, but a theory of the alternation between controlled subjects and overt case marked subjects in both finite and infinitival clauses, which considerably spreads its empirical coverage.[25] A further aspect of

---

[24] Technically, an explicit correlation must be established between the T and Agr values of Infl and the occurrence/non-occurrence of PRO. To achieve this result, Landau (2004) resorts to a referentiality feature R, which is negatively specified on PRO and positively specified on lexical DPs and pro. In tensed clauses, where all specifications on T are positive, a [+ R] feature is introduced, which can only be checked by a referential DP. In the complement structure associated with, say, the verb *prefer*, a verb allowing partial control and, in this case, selecting a complement with dependent tense (*Mary would prefer* PRO *to meet at 5*), T is negatively specified for [agreement] and, as a consequence, PRO must be selected as a subject, because it is the only element that can check a [−R] feature.

[25] Landau (2013: 90) insists that (11) only applies in "potentially OC contexts", that is, non defective complement clauses, which includes standard infinitives, subjunctive, indicative clauses, but excludes ECM and raising structures, small clauses and possibly gerunds. The fact that a restriction of this type must be integrated into the system is slightly worrying.

Landau's approach that must be emphasized is that it makes the licensing of overt and silent subjects independent of the [+ finite]/[– finite] status of the clause: [γ finite] is dissociated from [α T]/[β Agr].

7.3 The exhaustive control/partial control divide

The Finiteness Rule for OC (11) also addresses the interpretation of PRO in obligatory control structures. Landau (2000, 2004, 2013) proposes that exhaustive control and partial control should both be viewed as instances of OC, whose signature they share, but that the corresponding constructions involve different feature structures and distinct derivations. The proposal is that exhaustive control infinitives are untensed and that only tensed infinitives can display partial control.[26]

Let us look at the infinitives hosting exhaustive control first. They are characterized as [–T] domains. Landau proposes that Agree operates to match the features of the antecedent DP or those of an external functional head (F) with the φ-features of PRO, which are unvalued when PRO is inserted. The relevant representation at Transfer is given in (16):

(16) [... [$_{FP}$ F [$_{VP}$ DP [$_{V'}$ V [$_{CP}$ C [$_{TP}$ PRO [$_{T'}$ T [$_{VP}$ t$_{PRO}$ ...]]]]]]]]

This analysis has been criticized by Hornstein (2003: 38–42), who observes that the reason why F can see PRO in (16) remains a mystery, since a phasal CP boundary and a full DP intervene between the two (both the PIC and minimality should block the relation). This objection is partially unfounded however because, since it was formulated, constructions have been discovered in various languages that show that Agree can take place across phasal boundaries.[27] This is exactly what happens in (16).

---

26 Partial control arises when the reference of the controlled subject PRO properly includes the reference of the controller. Landau (2013) provides the following examples.

(i) *We thought that*
    a. *the chair$_i$ preferred* [PRO$_j$ *to gather at 6*].
    b. *Bill$_i$ regretted* [PRO$_j$ *meeting without a concrete agenda*].
    c. *Mary$_i$ wondered* [*whether* PRO$_j$ *to apply together for the grant*].

Control is optional in the following environments: absence of c-command, non-locality of the relation. Arbitrary control falls into this category.

27 The relevant data come from long-distance agreement in Icelandic, a phenomenon in which a finite T head licenses nominative case on an embedded object contained in a lower phase, see Chomsky (2008 : 143) for discussion.

According to Landau, the major difference between exhaustive control complements and those that allow partial control is that the former are semantically untensed, whereas the latter are semantically tensed.[28] Assuming that a semantically active tense is indeed present in partial control complements, the following derivation can be proposed: The embedded T moves to C; the resulting intervening unit prevents Agree from taking place between PRO and an external antecedent or a higher functional head, which is matrix T when subject control is at stake. The relevant structure at Spell-Out is given in (17).

(17) [... [$_{FP}$ F [$_{VP}$ DP [$_{V'}$ V [$_{CP}$ T+C [$_{TP}$ PRO [$_{T'}$ t$_T$ [$_{VP}$ t$_{PRO}$ ...]]]]]]]]

The absence of a movement of this type in structure (16) is precisely what allows PRO to have direct access to F/DP in the matrix clause. Again, Hornstein (2003: 37–42) rightly observes that the technical workings of the blocking effect of T+C in (17) are far from clear.

7.4 Free alternation between PRO and overt subjects

An additional distinction that turns out to be relevant to the proper characterization of the finiteness/nonfiniteness divide is the one between the predicate complement constructions that exclusively define obligatory control structures and those that display a free alternation between overt subjects and PRO. In a subset of natural languages, DP and PRO are not in complementary distribution and can occupy the same syntactic position in some constructions. Two situations must carefully be distinguished in this respect. In some languages, the NC cases display and spell out a syntactic feature that is absent from the OC constructions.

---

28 This analysis is supported by the following contrasts:

(i)   * *Yesterday, John managed to solve the problem tomorrow.*
(ii) *Yesterday, John hoped to solve the problem tomorrow.*

manage is an exhaustive control predicate, *hope* allows the partial control reading of its complement. For additional arguments that verbs compatible with the partial control interpretation of their complement like *hope* in English should be analyzed as tensed domains, contrary to exhaustive control verbs like *try*, see Landau (2000, 2004). See also fn. 21.

As will be shown at length in chapter VI, this is the case in Welsh *i*-initial constructions, where *i* occurs in presence of an overt subject, but is generally absent in controlled structures. It is clear that the non-complementarity problem doesn't arise when the competing constructions manifest a syntactic or a morphological difference. But in other systems, no feature distinguishes the NC structures from the OC structures. As has been observed by McCloskey (1984), Chung & McCloskey (1987) and Bondaruk (2006), Irish falls under this characterization. Burukina (2019, 2020) argues that Russian provides a "true case of DP/PRO alternation in the same embedded environment, restricted by the availability of case outside of the non-finite clause". It just happens that several of the nonfinite constructions examined in this book display a free alternation of the second type. The English verbal gerund constructions, complements to predicates like *regret*, for example, admit strictly parallel variants with an overt and with a null subject, cf. ch. IV, sct. 20.

This situation raises a potential difficulty against Landau's general approach. It is unexpected if the environments in which overt subjects are licensed form a natural class and if all the other ones correspond to the elsewhere case, as (11) implies. Landau convincingly argues that the frontier between control structures and the other configurations should be displaced, in order for Hebrew and Greek subjunctive clauses to fall within the realm of control, but his system basically retains the standard idea that the positions that are accessible to control cannot host an overt DP (or a pro). He is keenly aware of the existence of situations of non-complementarity and refers to the English, Irish, Welsh and also Portuguese cases, which are analyzed in this book. But he argues that, for the most part, they are linked to the variation in the agreement or tense properties of the clauses involved. Checking whether the attested alternations are real or involve different or differently specified functional structures is one of the most difficult challenges this work has to face. To illustrate the difficulty, it may be useful to briefly look at the Modern Greek case.

7.5 A quick look at the Modern Greek case

A salient property of Modern Greek is the absence of infinitives and the use of finite forms in the contexts where Romance languages resort to infinitives (cf. example 15). The relevant structures are usually characterized as subjunctive clauses, although, strictly speaking, Modern Greek has no morphological subjunctive at its disposal. What makes the relevant constructions subjunctive is the presence of the particle *na*, which immediately precedes the inflected verb.

Na-clauses can correspond either to OC structures or to non-OC structures with a null or an overt subject.[29]

Modern Greek has at its disposal a set of obligatory control verbs, that select finite subjunctive *na*-clauses as their complements. These clauses display all the standard properties of OC, as examples (18) show.

(18) a. *I Maria   prospathi   na elegsi   tin oreksi   tis.*
       the Maria   try.3SG   na control.3SG   the appetite her
       'Maria tries to control her appetite.'

   b. *Ta pedhja   arxisan   na trexun.*
      the children began.3PL   na run. 3PL
      'The children began to run.'

   c. *O   Kostas matheni   na odhiji.*
      the Kostas learn.3SG   na drive.3SG
      'Kostas learns how to drive.'

   d. *O Yannis   kseri   na kolimbai.*   (cf. 15)
      the Yannis   know.3sg   na swim.3sg
      'Yannis knows how to swim.'

The situation is different with other verbal predicates whose complements can, but need not define control contexts. A disjoint reference reading of the null embedded subject is possible in (19a) and (19b). A "together" reading, that is, a split control interpretation, is available in (20b).

(19) a. *O Yannis   elpizi   na pari   tin ipothrofia.*
       the Yannis   hope.3SG   na get.3SG   the scholarship
       'Yannis hopes to get the scholarship.'
       'Yannis hopes that (he/she) will get the scholarship.'

   b. *O Kostas   theli   na odhiji.*
      the Kostas   want.3SG   na drive.3SG
      'Kostas wants (him) to drive.'

---

[29] The functioning of control and the nature of the controlled subject of *na*-complements – is it pro, PRO or a trace of movement ? – are much discussed topics in the linguistic literature on Modern Greek, see Terzi (1997), Landau (2004, 2013), Pires (2006), Spyropoulos (2007), Roussou (2009) for discussion.

(20) a. I Maria parakalese ton Yannni na djavasi.
        the Maria ask.PRET.3SG the Yiannis na read.3SG
        'Maria asked Yannis to read.'

   b. I Maria parakalese ton Yanni na djavasun mazi.
        the Maria ask.PRET.3SG the Yanni na read.3PL together
        'Maria asked Yanni to read/study together'

In these constructions, the embedded verb is sometimes coupled with a lexical subject referentially disjoint from the matrix subject (the overt subject obligatorily follows the verb which forms a complex with *na*, cf. 21 a-c). An overt subject can even be present in the embedded domain when the matrix verb is an OC predicate, provided that it can be interpreted as coreferential with the matrix subject. In (21d), the subject is a reflexive expression.

(21) a. I Maria prospathise na diavasoun ta pedia.
        the Maria try.PRET.3SG na read.3PL the children
        'Maria tried to make the children read.'

   b. Thelo na fiji o Kostas.
        want.1SG na leave.3SG the Kostas
        'I want Kostas to leave.'

   c. Ipa ton Kosta na fiji o yios tou.
        tell.PRET.1SG the Kosta na leave.3sg the son his
        'I told Kosta that his son had left.'

   d. O Janis arxise na kapnii o idhjos.
        the Janis started.3SG na smoke.3SG the same
        'Janis started smoking.'

Landau (2004), partially following previous proposals, refers to the obligatory control constructions of the type of (18) as C(=control)-subjunctives and to the ones in (19), (20) and (21a, b, c) as F(= free)-subjunctives. It is a lexical property of individual predicates to select a control subjunctive or a free subjunctive or another complement type. He analyzes the C-constructions as involving a PRO subject and a clausal complement with an *anaphoric* [− T] tense identified with that of the matrix clause and the F-constructions as involving a complement with a *dependent* [+ T] tense. Since the overt agreement inflection on the verb is present in both complement types, the variation between the two constructions can only concern the status of [T]. If one assumes that what crucially distinguishes the two complement types is their tense specification, the cases that instantiate free control (cf. 19–21) involve a [+T, +Agr] head, the cases illustrating obligatory control involve a [–T, +Agr] head.[30]

Terzi (1997) and Pires (2006), who argue against a tense-based account, show that the link between control options and the tenseness status is more tenuous than was initially thought. For example, *hope* (cf. 19a) and *want* (cf. 19b), which are known to select complements with different tense properties – tense mismatches between the embedded predicate and the matrix verb are observed when the matrix verb is *hope*, not when it is *want* – turn out to display identical control properties. But the major difficulty raised by the Modern Greek control data is not the existence of two well-identified predicate classes, one selecting C-subjunctive complements and the other selecting F-subjunctive complements, but the fact that a subset of predicates that allow disjoint reference also function as well-behaved control predicates (compare 18a and 21a). How should this mixed status be represented? A first possibility is to claim that the predicates under consideration exclusively select a [+T, +Agr] complement and that the subject, when it is null, should uniformly be analyzed as a kind of pro. The OC interpretation would be strongly favored or even forced by the lexical/syntactic context and also obviously the absence of an overt subject. The pro-analysis of free control is not implausible in a language in which "finite control" involves subjunctive forms (it is more problematic in the languages where controlled subjects don't coexist with any inflexion). This is basically the analysis developed by Spyropoulos (2007), who proposes to view the free control subjunctive complement clauses as cases of "augmented coreference", since they do not obey the defining conditions of partial and split control. It is clear however that the adoption of the pro-analysis would deprive Landau's system of one of its major motivations, namely incorporating the finite control phenomenon with an integrated theory of control. The second option, which is the one favored by Landau, consists in assuming that PRO is indeed present whenever a control interpretation is involved, whether an obligatory or a free control predicate is at stake. The characterization of PRO in Landau's system is precisely that it can freely cooccur with a [–T, –Agr] inflection (corresponding to exhaustive control structures), with a [+T, –Agr] inflection (corresponding to partial and other control structures) and with a [–T, +Agr] inflection (corresponding to finite control structures). The gist of the Finiteness Rule for OC is precisely that the control interpretation can have several possible sources. But the free alternation phenomenon documented in 7.4 shows that some predicates can select either a [+T, +Agr] or a [+/–T, –Agr] complement, freely shifting the value of [Agr] from + to – or the reverse with no concomitant morphological

---

[30] See Roussou (2009) for extensive discussion and criticism.

change. And the Greek case shows that some predicates can take a [+T, +Agr] or a [−T, +Agr] complement, freely shifting the value of [T]. This aspect of Landau's analysis could turn out to be a negative one.

7.6 Transposing Landau's generalization into Chomsky's probe-goal-Agree framework

Let us ask whether rule (11), henceforth taken to express a correct generalization, and Chomsky's probe-goal-Agree approach to syntactic dependencies can be integrated into a consistent whole. This result will be achieved only if the claim that agreement inflection must be overt in order to be syntactically active can be derived on principled grounds.

Landau's account is based on a system of features that is quite different from the current minimalist one, since it ignores the notion of valuation and refers to that of interpretability only implicitly (via semantic tense). Let us make explicit the exact meaning of the positive and negative specifications associated with the two features [T] and [Agr] present on the T and C/Fin heads, which, in Landau's view, constitute the basic ingredients of finiteness. The positive specification of [T] encodes the presence of a semantically interpretable tense in the clause, whose exact value has yet to be determined. [+T] can be referentially autonomous (when the head of a root clause) or dependent (when embedded). The negative specification notes the absence of tense or its anaphoric status. Being morphologically realized or silent has no impact on the functioning of [T]. On the contrary, [Agr] is positively specified only when it is overt; the negative specification refers to "abstract agreement", as Landau (2013) puts it, or simply to the absence of agreement.

How should the asymmetry between tense and agreement be reinterpreted within Chomsky's minimalist perspective? At a preliminary stage, it can be taken to reflect the fact that the presence of tense in a domain doesn't crucially depend on its being morphologically manifested and that, on the contrary, uninterpretable φ-features can reasonably be said to have a value only when an overt content can directly or indirectly be associated with them.

Let us look at the [tense] feature in embedded finite clauses first. It doesn't require to be valued since it is interpretable. Binding suffices to establish the necessary interpretive link between the embedded tense and the matrix one, Agree is not involved. But we know that there are situations where an embedded clause contains more than one instance of [tense] and where the claim that an uninterpretable [tense] feature is present on C/Fin is well-supported, as the Irish data discussed by Cottell (1995) indicate (cf. sct. 6). When it is the case, the relation between the embedded tense and the matrix one is mediated by the [tense] feature on C/Fin, which is valued via a phase-internal Agree relation with the interpretable occurrence of [tense] on T.

The case of φ-features is more delicate. In Chomsky's system, plays no role in the probe-goal procedure. But a plausible assumption about φ-feature matrices is that their value must be recoverable. This is the case only if one of the following conditions is fulfilled: (i) φ-features are spelled out as an affix, or (ii) they are linked to an affix, or (iii) they are bound by an overt nominal expression.[31] Technically, the uninterpretable φ-features on the T or C heads must satisfy an additional condition to be properly valued, namely enter into an Agree relation with a DP subject. This Agree operation is not sensitive to the overtness of the elements it targets. But the two preceding conditions, namely feature sharing and content recoverability, can naturally be collapsed into a single one. The result is as follows: Uninterpretable φ-features present on functional heads must be spelled out as an affix (or linked to an affix-bearing head) for valuation via Agree to be successful.[32] A final property of Agree relations is that φ-valuation obeys strict locality conditions, notably Relativized Minimality and the Phase Impenetrability Condition. In Chomsky's (2000a) terms, "phases are exactly the domains in which uninterpretable features are valued" (the relevant phase is the one that minimally contains the probe). For the derivation to converge, a finite CP phase must contain a verbal form bearing an affix which can be viewed as the spell-out of inflectional features that match the uninterpretable ones on T (or on C) and enter into an Agree relation with the interpretable ones on a nominal subject.[33]

The empirical soundness of rule (11) can be questioned however. In English, an agreement affix is present only at the 3rd person singular of the present tense of verbal paradigms; in Mainland Scandinavian, agreement has completely disappeared. This situation can easily be handled in Chomsky's system, where the φ-features involved in the valuation procedure and those that serve as labels in

---

[31] Case (i) corresponds to the situation where a fully inflected verbal form occupies the T position, case (ii) to the situation where the inflected verb doesn't raise to the φ-bearing T, case (iii) to raising structures where the embedded T is chain-linked to the matrix subject (it is also linked to matrix T, a relation which makes it similar to case ii).
[32] Note that in the lexicalist approach, the inflectional affix has already been spelled out in finite tensed clauses when Agree takes place This claim is a departure from the DM architecture in which Late Lexical Insertion takes place on the PF branch, in the Morphological Component.

Although at no point does Landau raise the question of the derivation of morphologically complex verbal forms, his proposal is clearly compatible with a lexicalist approach to word formation of the type adopted in the Minimalist Program.
[33] In Welsh, the relevant affix is attached to a prepositional complementizer or to the verb-noun *bod* hosted by C/Fin (cf. ch. VI).

the feature sharing process don't have to be overt. Clauses in these languages obviously fulfill both the checking requirement and the labelling requirement. The solution is less straigntforward in an approach relying on Landau's Finiteness Rule for OC, which insists on morphologically overt agreement being a necessary condition for NC subjects to be available.

It remains that Landau's Finiteness Rule for OC proposes a solid characterization of exhaustive control. Can this phenomenon be given a plausible representation within the minimalist approach adopted here? It must be decided whether a T head is syntactically present in the internal structure of the corresponding domains and, if it is, which is its feature endowment. I adopt the assumption that in the complements selected by exhaustive control predicates, T is anaphoric and specified for an unvalued [tense] feature, that gets a value from matrix tense from which it is semantically non distinct (cf. sct. 7.3).[34] Anaphoric T doesn't bear any (inherited) φ-features either. PRO, being itself deprived of interpretable φ-features when it is inserted into derivations, would not be in a position to value uninterpretable features on T. Overt subjects are not possible choices in the corresponding SpecTP position because, embedded T being deprived of φ-features, they would be unable to get rid of their own case feature. The only possibility is for PRO to enter into an Agree relation with a functional head and an antecedent in the matrix clause. Binding doesn't suffice in this case. The characteristic of this relation is that the two elements it associates do not belong to the same phase. If correct, this analysis confirms that inter-phasal Agree relations should be allowed, contrary to what Chomsky's (2000a) initial characterization implies. Summarizing: If one adopts a minimalist perspective, the major difference between NC structures and exhaustive OC ones is that in the former, the overt inflectional features that, along with the subject, participate in the valuation of T's- or C's φ-features are internal to the minimal CP/FinP phase that also includes the subject, and that, in the latter, the determination of PRO's φ-features relies on an inter-phasal Agree relation.

This analysis, in spite of its seductiveness, leaves an important question unanswered. From a minimalist point of view, it would be important to form a clear idea of the way the controlled clause is labeled. Several solutions present themselves, but they are all essentially speculative.

Another question that still awaits an answer is how exactly partial control structures distinguish themselves from exhaustive control ones. Transposing Landau's account within the probe-goal-Agree framework, I assume that C/Fin in

---

34 The idea that tenses in natural languages, like pronouns, can have indexical, anaphoric and bound variable uses has been put forth by Partee (1973) in a famous paper.

the relevant constructions bears an uninterpretable [tense] feature that is valued via Agree with the interpretable [tense] on T and that the existence of this relation blocks the establishment of a direct relation between embedded T and matrix T. The existence of this phase-internal relation is compatible with the embedded tense (that is, the C/Fin-T chain) having a dependent status, not an anaphoric one. No Agree relation with matrix T should be invoked, binding suffices to provide it with an interpretation. The null subject is itself interpretively dependent on the subject of the matrix clause, but only partially because we are dealing with partial control. In this respect, the functioning of partial control resembles that of NC structures displaying a coreference relation between an embedded pronoun and one or several entities in the matrix clause. No Agree relation can be established between PRO and its antecedent (or with the φ-features of matrix T). This explains why the range of interpretations accessible to the null entity that stands as the partially controlled subject is larger than the ones available to PRO in exhaustive control constructions. But partial control resembles obligatory control in that the value of the φ-features of the null subject is only known during the next phase. In English infinitival clauses, the relevant entity cannot strictly be identified with pro, since φ-features are not locally accessible. A possibility is to adopt Landau's claim that we are dealing with PRO in both the exhaustive and partial control cases. This claim forces on us two conclusions: first, exhaustive control relations systematically involve inter-phasal relations; second, PRO occupies a case position in non-exhaustive control structures. Only the first one will unreservedly be adopted here.

7.7 Defectiveness and non-convergence

Reinterpreted in this way, Landau's proposal can be viewed as opening the way to a novel characterization of defectiveness. In order to make further progress towards this goal, one should make explicit the link that exists between feature defectiveness and non-convergence and between feature completeness and convergence. It should be recalled that a phase that still contains a single unvalued uninterpretable feature when it is completed doesn't converge and that the derivation can go on only if the relevant feature stands at the edge.

Finite complement clauses raise no specific difficulty: An interpretable [tense] feature is present in the embedded domain and φ-features are spelled out on one of the inflectional heads (T or C/Fin). The clause thus forms a featurally complete syntactic entity. It also corresponds to a converging phase if it is assumed that binding suffices to establish the necessary relation between the embedded dependent tense and the matrix one and that Agree is not involved. The relevant interpretation is of the pronominal type (the tense dependency can give rise to different readings, depending on the matrix predicate). It would be implausible to consider indicative complement clauses, which by definition have a non-deficient dependent tense, as non-convergent. The resulting objects should thus be characterized as closed featurally complete convergent domains. To make the analysis tighter, I assume that in embedded finite clauses, an uninterpretable [tense] feature is systematically present on C/Fin and that an agreement relation is established between the interpretable and uninterpretable occurrences of [tense] on T and C/Fin respectively. The presence of uninterpretable [tense] on C/Fin qualifies it as an active head; the transmission of φ-features to T also makes the latter active. The two heads of the C-T pair participate in an Agree relation.

If we now consider nonfinite domains, two situations arise depending on the status of embedded T. T is anaphoric when no interpretable [tense] is associated with it. It must have a direct access to matrix T, which provides it with features and with an interpretation. The embedded subject itself can only be PRO, which is assigned φ-features via an inter-phasal Agree relation. The result is exhaustive control. In exhaustively controlled domains, defectiveness and non-convergence clearly work tandem.

What about control constructions which are not exhaustive control structures, partial control ones in particular? I assume that in this case, an interpretable [tense] feature is associated with embedded T and that the relevant tense is a dependent tense. Embedded finite complement clauses show that, although the embedded finite tense is ultimately dependent on the matrix one for its interpretation, it doesn't suffice to mark the embedded domain as non-convergent. I will assume that in these nonfinite structures as in embedded finite ones, whenever an interpretable [tense] is present on T, an uninterpretable [tense] is associated with C/Fin, which is valued by its interpretable counterpart. The question that arises is whether the relevant domains are convergent, as NC structures are, or non-convergent, as exhaustive control domains are. The answer exclusively depends on the status that is assigned to the null entity, call it PRO, that functions as the controlled subject. I have suggested that PRO in the relevant structures displays pronominal properties that are partly similar to those of coreferent embedded overt subject pronouns: It is inserted in the derivation with φ-features that have an unspecified value, a value that is fixed only when the derivation reaches the matrix clause, where the features share the value of the φ-features of one or several entities. Once again, the relevant relation is reminiscent of standard coreference. No Agree is involved between PRO and its antecedents. If this view is adopted, the relevant controlled domains are convergent, but not, strictly speaking, featurally complete ones.

The constructions that Landau refers to as "finite control structures" illustrate still a different case. They are featurally incomplete, defective domains, where φ-features are spelled out on T or on C/Fin, but no [tense] is present (or an anaphoric tense is). They cannot function as closed entities and are dependent on the matrix clause for licensing and interpretation.[35]

There are other situations where convergence and completeness do not coincide. Chomsky (2000a, example 19) observes that the embedded finite clause in (22) defines an inflectionally complete syntactic object, that is, a NC configuration, but it doesn't converge.

(22) Which article is there some hope [that John will read t_{wh}]

Parallel extraction cases, involving nonfinite domains, can easily be found. In spite of this uncertainty, I propose to replace (11) by (23):

(23) In a C/Fin complement clause,
   a. NC obtains if
      (i) the clause is featurally complete (either T or C/Fin or both are specified for [tense] and [φ] features);
      (ii) the clause is convergent (both uninterpretable [tense] and uninterpretable [φ]'s are valued within the C/Fin phase).
   b. OC (exhaustive control) obtains elsewhere.

(23 a i) and (23 a ii) state that, in the general case, agreement [φ] features must be morphologically overt on T or on C in the FinP phases containing an overt subject. (23 a ii) plays a crucial role in distinguishing NC structures from OC ones: OC structures involve an interphasal Agree relation, contrary to NC ones. All in all, formulation (23) captures the gist of Landau's generalization and is conceptually more satisfying. It also inherits some of its difficulties.[36]

---

[35] Calling them "finite control structures" is, in my view, an unfortunate terminological choice. The relevant structures should better be viewed as nonfinite domains, all the more so that, in the approach under discussion, only the pair [tense]/[φ] plays a role in the licensing of subjects, [finite] being irrelevant.

[36] For example, the difficulties mentioned in 7.5 are not solved by the account sketched in 7.6 and 7.7.

8 The semantics of nonfinite tense

Pursuing the preliminary exploration of the functional makeup of nonfinite domains and keeping in mind Adger's observation that it is relatively easy to form a clear idea of what finite clauses are, but that the proper analysis of nonfinite domains remains quite uncertain, one should look for additional evidence that the T category is projected in at least a subset of nonfinite morphologically untensed clauses. This move is important because both the probe-goal-Agree approach to syntactic dependencies and Landau's Finiteness Rule for OC rely on the existence of silent semantically interpretable and syntactically active T heads in these domains. The relevant evidence comes from the conclusions of the research on the grammar of tense, produced during the last decades in the traditions of formal syntax and formal semantics. Tenseness/tenselessness could turn out to be a grammatical dimension, partly independent from, but as significant as the finiteness/nonfiniteness divide and much easier to handle.

8.1 Stowell (1982)

A remarkable characteristic that these approaches to tense try to make sense of is that the absence of overt tense morphology in infinitival clauses should not systematically be taken as an indication of the lack of semantic tense, as first emphasized by Stowell (1982). According to him, future *irrealis* infinitival constructions like those in (24), in which the embedding predicate (*promise, decide, remember, ...*) requires that the tense of the infinitive complement be understood as "unrealized" with respect to the tense of the matrix event, should be analyzed as being tensed. Bresnan (1972) had already observed that infinitive tense is essentially *irrealis*. It just happens that English has no nonfinite inflectional affixes at its disposal to manifest it.

(24) a. *Albert promised to leave tomorrow.*
b. *Max decided to read this novel next week.*
c. *John remembered to bring the wine at the party.*

Stowell's idea that infinitival constructions should be semantically classified according to whether they are tensed or tenseless immediately raises two closely related questions: (i) which *semantic* properties should be taken as criterial for dividing infinitival constructions into tensed and untensed ones? (ii) which *syntactic* properties are related to the presence or absence of the category T in infinitival domains? Concerning (ii), Stowell observes that the future *irrealis* tense in

English is specifically found in control structures and, conversely, that it is plausible to characterize raising structures as untensed. If an embedded CP boundary was present in examples (25), it would prevent the trace in subject position to be licensed (the latter wouldn't be "properly governed"). Anticipating a proposal developed by Enç (1990), Stowell speculates that SpecCP is the natural *locus* of Tense operators and that the clauses that lack a CP projection cannot be tensed domains, since they make no host position available for these operators.

(25) a. *John appears to like poker.*
 b. *The president is believed to be corrupted.*

Concerning (i), later studies have identified several interpretive properties as potentially relevant. But all authors insist on the significance of the "simple present effect", that is, the impossibility in English for a verbal form in the present tense to be assigned an episodic punctual interpretation when an eventive predicate is involved. It is well-known that English root clauses containing a bare main verb in the present tense do not allow this type of interpretation (cf. 26a). These clauses are well-formed only if they allow a habitual or generic reading (cf. 26b). To express an eventive interpretation, the progressive form must be used (cf. 26c).

(26) a. * *Lady sings the blues right now.*
 b. *Lady sings the blues every night at Carnegie Hall.*
 c. *Lady is singing the blues right now.*

Importantly for us, Stowell (1982, 1995) and also Pesetsky (1992), Bošković (1996, 1997), Wurmbrand (2001, 2014) argue that the "simple present effect" also manifests itself in infinitival domains, which appear to distribute into different classes with respect to this property. For example, the clausal complement to *want* doesn't display it (cf. 27), but the complement to *prove, suspect, believe* does (cf. 28), an asymmetry which should be traced back to the tense statuses of the relevant complements.

(27) a. *John wants to read War and Peace.*
 b. *John wants Mary to read War and Peace.*

(28) a. *This proves him to (*cheat + be cheating) the exam right now.*
 b. *Paul suspects him to (*steal + be stealing) the jewels right now.*
 c. *Lady is believed to (*sing + be singing) the blues right now.*

8.2 Wurmbrand (2001, 2014)

8.2.1 On the tense of infinitives

Wurmbrand (2001, 2014) proposes a fine-grained classification of English infinitival constructions, based on an in-depth study of the distribution of episodic readings with eventive verbal predicates, the basic assumption being that the status of tense in each complementation type reflects a requirement imposed by the selecting predicate. Her observations lead to the identification of four distinct types:

(a) future *irrealis* infinitives, complements to predicates like *decide, plan* ... , do not block the episodic interpretation of embedded verbal predicates (cf. 29);[37]
(b) propositional attitude predicates do not allow a bare eventive infinitive in their complement to be assigned an episodic interpretation (cf. 30a); as expected, the use of the progressive or perfect form of the eventive (cf. 30b, 30c) or its replacement by a stative (cf. 30d) gives rise to a syntactically well-formed and semantically interpretable result; the present form of eventive predicates is also welcome in this context, provided that the embedded clause is assigned a habitual/generic interpretation (cf. 30e).
(c) the simultaneous infinitives found in *try-* and *manage-*constructions do not display the present tense effect (cf. 31);
(d) the complement of raising verbs like *seem* and *begin* does not allow the episodic interpretation of bare eventive predicates in present tense sentences (cf. 32a, 32b, 32c).

(29)   *Leo decided to bring the toys tomorrow.*
                              episodic interpretation

(30) a.   * *Leo believes Julia to bring the toys right now.*
                              *episodic interpretation

   b.   *Leo believes Julia to be bringing the toys right now.*
                              episodic interpretation

   c.   *Leo believes Julia to have solved the problem already.*
                              episodic interpretation

---

[37] The term *irrealis* used here refers to the fact that "the infinitival complement to these verbs is interpreted as unrealized at the time of the matrix clause" and that "its truth at the time of utterance is left unspecified", cf. Pesetsky (1992).

    d.   *Leo believes Julia to like modern painting.*
                                stative interpretation

    e.   *Paul believes the earth to turn around the sun.*
                                habitual interpretation

(31)   *Yesterday, John tried/managed to sing.*
                                episodic interpretation

(32) a.   * *Leo seems to sing in the shower right now.*
                              *episodic interpretation

    b.   *Leo seems to be singing in the shower right now.*
                                episodic interpretation

    c.   *Leo seemed to sing in the shower yesterday.*
                                episodic interpretation

Wurmbrand interprets these distributions as follows.

(a) the reason why the episodic interpretation is not blocked in future *irrealis* infinitives is that they do not include any tense (*pace* Stowell), but a future modal element that she refers to as *woll*, which, combined with finite present tense, produces *will* and contributes the temporal orientation of future infinitives (cf. 29);

(b) propositional attitude infinitives semantically impose the Now of the propositional attitude holder as the reference time of the infinitive; they are specified for tense, which happens to be zero, and display the present tense effect (cf. 30);

(c) the infinitive clauses selected by *try* or *manage* semantically form a single temporal domain with the matrix one; their reference time *is* the reference time of the matrix predicate (cf. 31); it is plausible to analyze the complement of these domains as tenseless; the lack of the present tense effect thus corresponds to the expected situation.

(d) the fact that *seem*-constructions display the present tense effect indicates that we are dealing with nonfinite tensed domains (cf. 32a vs. 32b, 32c).

The tense/tenseless distinction thus appears to play a crucial role in the distribution of eventive (i.e. non stative, non generic, non habitual) VP predicates, and in the availability of the episodic interpretation.

Stowell (1982) assumed that the infinitive tense in English is future *irrealis* and that it is specifically found in control structures. One of Wurmbrand's discoveries is that the tensed/untensed distinction cuts across the control/raising/ECM divide. (29) is a control structure and doesn't object to the embedded verb being an eventive predicate. But the present tense effect is observed in (33a), where *claim* also selects a control structure.[38]

(33) a. * Leo claims to sing in the shower right now.
     b. Leo claims to be singing in the shower right now.

8.2.2 Explaining the simple present effect

It is interesting at this point to ask what kind of explanation can be proposed for the present tense effect. Several ones have been offered in the literature. Enç (1990), Pesetsky (1992), Bošković (1997) suggest that eventive predicates contain an event variable that can only be bound by a modal or temporal operator other than PRES (it can be PAST or FUTURE or GEN).[39] Wumbrand's (2014) account is quite different and capitalizes on the interaction between tense and aspect in clausal domains. She adopts Pancheva & von Stechow's (2004) definition of perfective and imperfective aspect:

> perfective aspect requires that the event interval be included in the reference time interval, whereas imperfective aspect requires the reference time interval be included in the event time interval.

In past and future sentences, episodic interpretations are available, because the event time interval is included in the reference time interval, as required.

---

38 The behavior of *expect* confirms Wurmbrand's general conclusion. It can have the syntax of a control predicate and that of a raising predicate. The present tense is possible in both cases.

(i) *John expects to win.*
(ii) *The wall is expected to fall.*

Williams (2013) suggests that the futurity intrinsic to *expect* could be responsible for this double possibility. The complement of *expect* can plausibly be analyzed as future *irrealis*.

39 Enç's idea that eventive predicates include a temporal position that needs to be bound but stative predicates do not is not without problems. Pesetsky (1992) observes that the past tense morpheme cooccurs freely with stative predicates, although there is no place to bind in this case. Enç points out that in the past constructions where eventive predicates receive an habitual/generic interpretation (cf. i), we don't know whether the PAST tense operator binds the temporal position or whether the quantifier does.

(i) *Mary usually sang the Marseillaise at political meetings.*

(34) a. *John sang in the shower yesterday.*
b. *John will sing in the shower.*

But a characteristic of the present tense in English is precisely that it is exclusively compatible with imperfective aspect.[40] The perfective aspectual interpretation underlying the episodic construal of eventive predicates requires that the event time interval be included in the reference time interval. This condition, Wurmbrand claims, cannot be met by the infinitive in the complements to propositional attitude predicates, because these predicates impose the restriction that the attitude holder's Now (rather than the matrix event or reference time) functions as the reference time for the embedded aspect (the time that the aspect uses to position the embedded event time relative to). The attitude holder's Now, like the utterance time, is a "near-instantaneous interval that cannot include the event time". In other words, present tense statements inevitably give rise to an interpretation in which the reference time (the "speaker's Now", that is, the utterance time) is included in the event time (the time of singing). This is the reason why (30a) is excluded. The only possible aspectual interpretation is the imperfective one and English obligatorily resorts to the progressive form in this case (cf. 30b). In generic/habitual statements such as (30e), on the other hand, "the event intervals are included in the reference interval", which dispenses with the necessity to resort to the progressive construction.[41] Finally, concerning stative constructions (cf. 30d), Wurmbrand assumes that "(im)perfective aspect is not projected; hence, the verb combines with tense directly, and the aspect distinction is irrelevant".

The idea that the distribution of eventive predicates is sensitive to aspect also explains the availability of the episodic interpretation in the other classes of infinitival constructions. Those where the infinitive is interpreted as future *irrealis* are modal constructions, which, by definition, have little to say about tense. Episodic interpretations are predicted to be possible. Conversely, the perfective interpretation is excluded and the simple present effect manifest in the infini-

---

[40] This property is specific to a subset of languages. English displays it, French and German do not. It just happens that the two other languages examined in this book, Welsh and European Portuguese, stand on the same side as English in this respect. This makes it possible to resort to the simple present effect to decide whether a T head is projected in a domain or not.

[41] If the interpretive behavior of episodic predicates perfectly fits Wurmbrand's characterization, things are different when the generic/habitual interpretation is at stake. As observed by Ion Giurgea, the earth's turning around the sun cannot easily be conceived of as being included in the attitude holder's Now (cf. 30e). Generics and habituals are usually considered as forming stative predications. Giurgea suggests that they are imperfective by default. But, of course, it could also be said that these embedded structures allow the Now interpretation because they are true at a point.

tive clauses complements to predicates like *believe*: Since the matrix predicate imposes its reference time as the reference time of the embedded infinitive, the effect pops up when the matrix predicate is in the present tense.

Although Wurmbrand (2014) is very cautious not to draw hasty syntactic conclusions from these semantic phenomena, her contribution points towards the conclusion that nonfinite domains come in different sizes and instantiate different labels, each reflecting the selectional requirement of the selecting predicate. In future *irrealis* constructions, we are not dealing with tensed domains, but with constituents headed by *woll*: T is absent, but a Modal head is projected, giving rise to a ModP projection. In simultaneous infinitive structures, no T is present, no C is either. In her view, they should be analyzed as "truncated structures", that is, as vPs or AspPs, not as TPs or CPs. In raising infinitive clauses, T is present, C is not.

8.2.3 Factive/emotive complements are tensed

One should ask whether other infinitival classes can be added to this list without making the whole system inconsistent. One predicate class, which Wurmbrand (2014) explicitly decides to leave aside, considerably complicates the picture: Factive/emotive predicates like *regret, like, hate, resent*. Is there a place for factives/emotives in her system? (There is none in Stowell's 1982 one). I will first introduce the basic properties of the factive class, relying on Pesetsky's (1992) discussion. I will then try to interpret the results attained from the vantage point of Wurmbrand's classification.

A major difference between the infinitival complements to factive/emotive predicates and the complements to verbs of the *believe*-class is that the subject position of the former doesn't seem to be accessible to an external governor: It can host a PRO-element, but not a NP-trace.

(35) a. *Billy likes to sing the blues.*
b. * *Billy is liked to sing the blues.*

(36) a. * *John believes to be a leading linguist.*
b. *Billy is believed to sing the blues.*

These observations suggest that factive/emotive complements define opaque domains, contrary to the propositions complements to *believe* that do not. This picture is oversimplified, however, since factive/emotive predicates are indeed allowed to enter into ECM-like constructions in which the embedded subject position hosts a full NP. This option however is available only under restricted conditions, as Pesetsky (1992) has discovered.[42]

(37) a. *John hated his students to smoke in class yesterday.
     b. *John hates his students to smoke in class right now.
     c. John loved to smoke in class yesterday.
     d. John would hate his students to smoke in class.

The ill-formedness of examples (37a) and (37b), which are understood as describing a single episodic event, indicates that eventive predicates cannot receive an episodic interpretation in this context, a phenomenon that very much looks like the simple present effect. But the episodic interpretation of the eventive predicate is accessible in (37c), which closely resembles a control structure, suggesting that an alternative construction of the matrix predicate is involved. Finally, (37d), which contains a matrix involving a modal and an *irrealis* complement, is also semantically well-formed. The fact that the present tense effect is not observed in this case is a clear indication that the interpretive status of the complement is not exclusively determined by the lexical class of the matrix predicate, but also depends on the modal environment. This is in sharp contrast with what is observed with other predicate classes and could be related to the fact that the trigger of an emotional state can be a specific anterior event or an event that has not occurred yet.

The status of (37a), (37b), (37d) is not affected if *for* is inserted before *his students*. But, as Pesetsky observes, the sentence greatly improves if the context makes the generic/habitual interpretation of the complement possible, as shown by the contrast between (38a) and (38b); *for* can also be used in constructions where the complement clause refers to an unrealized state of affairs (cf. 38c).

(38) a. *John hated (very much) for his students to smoke in class yesterday.
     b. John always hates (very much) for his students to smoke in class.
     c. John would hate (very much) for his students to smoke in class.

Accounting for the presence/absence of *for* across English infinitival structures is precisely Pesetsky's (1992) and Pesetsky & Torrego's (2004) major concern. They observe that complement infinitives with PRO may be *realis* or *irrealis*/generic, depending on the selecting matrix predicate, but that infinitives in subject position are generally confined to *irrealis*/generic semantics.

---

[42] All examples are from Pesetsky (1992).

(39) a. *Mary hated* [PRO *to learn the election results*].
 b. *Mary hates* [PRO *to lose games*].

(40) a. [PRO *to learn the election results*] *would shock me.*
 b. ?? [PRO *to learn the election results*] *shocked me.*

They also note that *for* cannot be dispensed with when subject infinitives with an overt subject are involved (cf. 41), whereas it is optional in complement clauses (cf. 37d).

(41) [*(For) Sue to leave*] *would be desirable.*

A correlation can thus be established between the *irrealis* semantics of some infinitive clauses and the non-omissibility of the complementizer *for* in the relevant structures. Pushing this idea further, they propose that *for* (or its null variant) is just nonfinite T moved to C – this movement takes place when *irrealis* semantics is involved – and that the absence of *for* in a structure can reflect a derivation in which T has not moved at all and the nominal subject has raised to SpecCP – this happens when a realis interpretation is at stake. This account indeed presupposes that complement and subject factive clauses are tensed.

As the discussion of Wurmbrand's classification has shown, it is sometimes a tricky matter to decide whether an infinitive domain should be classified as tensed or untensed. The decision concerning the tenseness of factive complements is no exception.[43] Let us take for granted that the present tense effect provides robust evidence in favor of infinitival tense. (37a), (38b) and (38d) show that eventive predicates are excluded in factive complements when the intended interpretation of the embedded clause is realis and that of the embedded predicate episodic, but acceptable when the sentence has an *irrealis* interpretation and when the infinitive clause refers to a generic/habitual situation or to a state. This contrast unambiguously indicates that the relevant embedded structures display the simple present effect and suffices to show that they are tensed domains. Factive nonfinite complements do not differ in this respect from propositional attitude complements. The long-known differences between *like* and *believe* (cf. 35)/36) thus cannot be exclusively traced back to the tenseness status of the nonfinite domains under discussion.

---

[43] Pesetsky (1992) classifies factive complements as [– tense], despite the evidence that has just been presented; Landau (2000) classifies them as [+ tense].

8.3 Landau (2000, 2004, 2013, 2015)

Wurmbrand (2001, 2014) takes the distribution of the episodic interpretation, a property directly associated with tense, as the key dimension for distributing infinitival constructions into different classes. Landau's (2004) classification of verbal predicates capitalizes on a different dimension, namely the possibility of temporal mismatches between the matrix and the embedded event. We know that his aim is to propose a classification that can serve as a basis to derive the difference between various types of control, first the distinction between obligatory and optional control, second the distinction between various subclasses within each of these two types.

As already mentioned, Landau (2004, 2013) substitutes a two-entries partition based on the distinction between [+ T] and [− T] complements, for the four semantic types of infinitives identified by Wurmbrand (2001, 2014). The complements to factive (*like, hate, regret, surprise*), propositional (*believe, imagine, say, assert, deny*), desiderative (*prefer, hope, agree decide, intend*) and interrogatives (*wonder, ask, know*) predicates are [+ T]; the complements to aspectual (*begin*), modal (*may, should, need*), implicatives (*manage, dare, remember, forget, avoid*) predicates, as well as evaluative adjectives (*crazy, rude, silly, difficult*) are [− T].

Wurmbrand's and Landau's classifications differ as to the analysis of future *irrealis* complements, which are taken by Landau to select a tensed complement, as if a zero T head was projected above the Modal. They also assign different analyses to the complements of implicative verbs like *remember* and *forget* and more generaly to the complements of so-called restructuring verbs. In Landau's view, exhaustive control constructions are full clauses with a PRO subject and a [− T] head. Wurmbrand (2001) defends a different position. She takes the fact that the relevant predicates often behave as restructuring verbs to point towards the absence of a T head. If such a head was present, restructuring would be impossible.

As Wurmbrand (2014: 405) rightly observes, the reference to control and the reference to episodic interpretation sometimes yield contadictory results. She notes that "*claim*-infinitives would need to be tensed for the purpose of control, but tenseless for the purpose of episodic interpretation". The relevant examples are the following:

(42) a. *Leo claimed to be rich.*
      b. *Leo claimed to eat dinner (*yesterday/*tomorrow).*
      c. *Leo claimed to be eating dinner right then.*

The bare infinitival VP in (ii) cannot receive an episodic interpretation. She concludes that, at least for her purposes, the distribution of the episodic interpretation has a greater indicative value than control properties, which should be accounted for in different terms. One could add that well-formed examples of factive/emotive constructions instantiating temporal mismatches between the matrix event and the embedded event are difficult to find and that the data do not really provide the expected support in favor of the claim that the relevant complements are tensed.[44] But the two classifications also match up to a large extent and converge on the conclusion that a T head is projected in a large subset of infinitival domains.

In conclusion, the line of research followed by Stowell, Wurmbrand, Landau consists in showing how the verbal predicates of a language L are distributed into lexical classes on the basis of the semantic tense properties shared by their complements and in identifying the syntactic correlates associated with these properties. To the extent that tense construal phenomena, in particular the simple present effect or the possibility of temporal mismatches between matrix and embedded clauses, provide robust evidence in favor of the presence or absence of a T head in nonfinite domains, they will figure among the properties resorted to to "unlock the systematicity of nonfinite domains", together with the eventive/stative and factive/nonfactive divides and along with the syntax of verbo-nominal forms, the syntactic licensing of subjects and extraposition processes. It could be objected that the projection of a T head in the syntactic structure of nonfinite domains is not absolutely necessary to account for their tense construal and can be dispensed with once an appropriate semantic calculus is defined. But it will appear that the structures where formal semantics detect the presence of tense coincide with those where formal syntax is led to posit a T head.[45]

Of course, it must be kept in mind that tense construal phenomena are just one aspect of the semantics of nonfinite complementation. Other semantic dimensions should be explored for a full characterization of the properties of NFDs to be reached.

---

[44] (i) is marginal (*resent* selects a gerund complement, not an infinitive one). The infinitive variants with *love* and *hate* are fully ungrammatical.

(i) ?? Today, the government members very much resent a mass mailing being done yesterday, before the President's speech.

[45] Evidence in favor of this claim is provided by control phenomena in European Portuguese inflected infinitive clauses, cf. ch. VIII.

III The morphosyntax of English gerund forms

A sharp distinction should be established at the outset between the functional and lexical architecture underlying morphologically complete nonfinite lexical *forms* (English gerunds, Celtic verb- nouns, inflected infinitives, Latin passive perfect participles, . . .) and the internal structure of the nonfinite verbal/clausal or nominal *domains* lexically headed by these forms (Acc-*ing*/Poss-*ing* gerund structures, verbo-nominal clauses, inflected infinitive clauses, dominant participle constructions, . . .). When the focus is on nonfinite *forms*, the questions that arise are that of their derivational origin (under the assumption that inflectional morphology makes a systematic use of the computational operation Merge), how they are assigned a categorial identity, how transcategoriality obtains, how mixed projections arise. These questions directly bear upon the definition of lexical categories. When the emphasis is on the syntax of nonfinite *domains*, the problem is to determine how the construction of a predication relation between a nominal expression functioning as a subject and a projection qualifying as a predicate is achieved in these domains, how this initial predication structure is embedded in a larger one, which strategy is used to syntactically license the embedded subject.

The investigation launched in this book resolutely focuses on the second issue, but the origin of verbo-nominal forms should also be discussed. As a matter of fact, there is no way to keep apart the syntax of words and the syntax of phrases and clauses, that is, the properties of the affixes the various verbo-nominal forms incorporate and the structures these forms enter into . . . All the verbal forms considered in this study (English gerunds, Celtic verb-nouns, Portuguese inflected infinitives, Latin participles) happen to be morphologically complex units, whose derivation necessarily involves a word-formation process. With respect to gerunds, it should be asked what is the status of the -*ing* affix, what kind of object it is combined with (is it a stem or a root?) and more generally to what extent gerund forms can be accounted for in syntactic terms. To provide appropriate answers to these questions, it is first necessary to briefly reconsider the current assumptions concerning the origin of words and the location of morphology in the grammatical architecture. If one uses a derivational framework, it must be decided in which grammatical component morphology is located, at which level of derivation lexical items are built.

9 The syntax/morphology interface

The question of whether morphology precedes syntax or follows syntax or whether syntax is interspersed with morphological episodes divides contemporary morphological theories into two classes: Lexicalist theories assume that the formation, derivation and inflection of words are performed in the lexicon, that is, before syntax; syntactic approaches claim that word formation takes place in the syntax and/or after syntax.

9.1 Lexicalism

In *Remarks on Nominalization*, Chomsky (1970) opposes the early generative view that nominalizations are derived in the syntax by transformation from sentences and claims that the grammar must incorporate a word-formation component, the lexicon, that transmits fully derived and, possibly, fully inflected units to the computational system. In this type of lexicon, lexical entries include several types of information concerning the lexemes: their syntactic category, their subcategorization frame, their argument structure, the properties and featural content of the derivational and inflectional affixes they contain and, of course, the sound-meaning pairs they correspond to. The interaction of the syntax with the lexicon was constrained by the claim that syntax couldn't refer to units smaller than words, an assumption known as the Lexical Integrity Hypothesis. Thirty years later, the probe-goal-Agree approach to syntactic dependencies developed in *Minimalist Inquiries* (cf. Chomsky 2000a) and after revives the lexicalist approach to word-formation: Inflected words are created in the lexicon and inserted fully formed into syntactic derivations; the checking by valuation procedure is here to help them and the functional items they are related to to get rid of their uninterpretable features.

Remarks didn't claim that word formation is exclusively lexical. There was no doubt at the time that syntactic operations and principles could also be involved in the process. Chomsky (1970) both assumed that nominalizations are built in the lexicon and that the *-ing* gerund forms, which are entirely regular and display all the properties of the verbs embedded within them, are derived in the syntax. The assumption that some word formation takes place in the syntax, which was explicit in *Lectures on Government and Binding*, was fully developed in Baker's

(1985, 1988) work.[1] Baker's Mirror Principle states that the order of affixes in a complex word faithfully reflects the hierarchy of functional projections, because the latter directly determines the order in which the affixes residing in the corresponding functional heads are successively attached to the root.[2] It thus embodies the claim that the internal structure of words mirrors the syntactic architecture of clauses.[3] At first sight, only the syntactic approach to word formation is in a position to capture this generalization. It makes interesting predictions concerning both the internal make up of complex words and their distribution. For example, if a complex verbal form includes two affixes (say, a tense affix and a person-number affix), the movement of the verbal root/stem will not stop until it reaches the highest inflectional head, hosting the most external matrix to be spelled out as an affix. Concerning the syntactic position of verbal heads, it predicts that infinitival forms should not raise as high as finite ones, because they generally have to pick up a tense/mood affix (Romance *-r-*), but no person-number affix. It is easy however to find cases where the syntax of verbal heads doesn't reflect their morphological richness/poverty. In null subject Romance languages, infinitives raise as high in the structure as finite forms; in the Swedish dialect spoken in Kronoby (Finland), finite verbs, which in no way can be considered as richly inflected, raise in embedded clauses.

9.2 Distributed Morphology

In the last decades, an important body of research has emerged in which all words and lexemes, not just the complex units resulting from an incorporation process as in Baker (1988), are defined on a syntactic basis. The Distributed Morphology approach initiated by Halle & Marantz (1993) and further developed by Marantz (1997, 1999, 2001, 2007), Harley & Noyer (1999), Embick (2004), Embick

---

1 Some earlier studies had argued that both options, the lexical one and the syntactic one, were in fact necessary to account for the full range of possibilities and that a divide had to be established between words derived in the lexicon and words derived in the syntax. An example is Wasow's (1977) analysis of verbal and adjectival participles in English: The former are built in the syntax, the latter originate in the lexicon.
2 At least in concatenative languages and provided that all functional heads are linearized in the same direction.
3 Embick & Halle (2008) rightly observe that this generalization has a different status in the syntactic and in the lexicalist approaches to word formation. In the former, it directly follows from the way the grammar is organized: The non-attested morphological forms are excluded by independently motivated syntactic constraints. In the latter, the relevant generalization has to be stipulated.

& Noyer (2001, 2007) aims at reintegrating word formation into the syntax, thus reducing the mass of information listed in the lexical entries and deriving some of the relevant properties from another component of the grammar. The result is a highly impoverished lexicon reduced to the listing of sound-meaning pairs. This theory promotes the "single engine hypothesis", according to which all computation, whether of words or of larger units such as phrases and sentences, is syntactic and performed by the computational system. The grammatical architecture includes no lexical space anymore, where complex objects could be built. The syntax manipulates two kinds of elements: (i) abstract morphemes, exclusively consisting of matrices of non-phonetic features, such as [definite], [past], [imperfective], [plural], and (ii) roots that make up the lexical vocabulary. Lexical roots and stems successively raise to the functional nodes that host feature matrices and merge with them, via a process akin to head movement.[4] Morphological structure *is* syntactic structure and what is usually referred to as "morphology" reduces to a sequence of operations that apply at PF to interpret this structure. The function of this process, taking place late, on the PF branch and called Vocabulary Insertion, is to assign phonological content to abstract morphemes.[5]

A defining feature of the Distributed Morphology approach (henceforth DM) is that roots are category-neutral when inserted into derivations and that the construction of the categorial identity of lexical items is a purely syntactic affair. It results from the association in the syntax of a root with a category-defining head, v or n, that minimally c-commands it.[6] (1) and (2) are two basic assumptions of this approach.

(1) L-heads (lexical heads, namely verbs and nouns) are broken up into a categorially neutral root X and a F-head (a functional head v, n) that defines its categorial membership.

---

[4] But Distributed Morphology also resorts to rules such as lowering and local dislocation, which are implementations of Affix Hopping and can be viewed as specific forms of morphological merger (see Embick & Noyer 2001).

[5] For example, it is at this stage that it is decided which exponent the [plural] feature in English receives in various contexts (it can be Ø, *-en* or [-z]). The reason why it is necessary to "distribute" morphology into different components is that it is difficult to account for suppletion and syncretism phenomena in a natural way in a theory that assumes that features are supplied by morphemes with an already specified phonological form. A strong argument in favor of late insertion comes from the observation that some properties of lexical heads are only accessible in the syntax, not in the output of morphology, but mismatches are known to exist between the full specification of lexical heads in syntax and their underspecification in morphology.

[6] This conception is in sharp contrast with the view of lexical classes developed by Baker (2003), who claims that nouns and verbs are already distinguished at the root level, nouns being inherently referential and verbs being inherently predicational.

(2) v and n can host F-words or F-affixes or just F-features.[7]

(1) and (2) state that all lexical categories are syntactically complex and result from a *construction* process, operating on specific syntactic structures. The minimal elements entering word formation are not words or stems, but roots. Categorial membership depends on the identity of the category-defining head present in the immediate environment of the root. A verb corresponds to the combination of a category-neutral root with v, a noun to the combination of a category-neutral root with n. In transitive and unergative structures, v introduces the external argument in its specifier (in informal terminology), bears an accusative case feature when the root is transitive, activates the θ-grid of the root, is the locus of the *agentive* and *eventive* interpretations, coexists with adverbs, cf. (3a). n allows the derivation of a nominal item; the complex n-root head corresponds to ordinary and derived nouns, coexists with adjectives and is deprived of any argument selection (the only θ-role that is available within a nominal expression headed by the word *house* is configurational: it is the Possessor role endorsed by the dependent genitive). It is natural to assume that in (3b), at least under the resultative/stative interpretation of the nominalization, we are dealing with a fully nominal construction, created directly from a root and including no v.[8]

(3) a. v : *The witness describes the accident* transitive verbal form
T [$_{vP}$ [the witness] [$_v$ [$_{RootP}$ √DESCRIBE the accident]]]

b. n : *the description of the accident* result nominalization
[$_{DP}$ D [$_{nP}$ n [$_{RootP}$ √DESCRIBE the accident]]][9]

In other words, corresponding to the traditional N and V, there are no terminal nodes anymore, but a more complex structure which is a combination of a cate-

---

[7] In a strict DM approach, v and n can only host features because the spell-out of abstract morphemes occurs late.
[8] I leave aside the question of whether the representation of complex event nominals should also include a v head. They probably should, because they display a number of verbal properties that are not found in simple event nominals (they can include *by*-phrases for example). The decision of course depends on whether they are taken to have an argument structure which, like that of verbs, must be mapped onto a syntactic structure. For opposite views, see Grimshaw (1990) and Reuland (2011), as well as Alexiadou's (2010a, 2010b) state-of-the-art article on nominalizations and the contributions in Alexiadou & Borer (2021a). In Grimshaw's (1990) view, only referential nominals allow plural; argument-supporting event nominals do not, which tallies well with the claim that they have a verbal internal structure, possibly including an Aspect projection. Yet, argument-supporting nominals display a nominal external distribution, a situation that suggests that some kind of category mixing is involved.
[9] Note that in (3a) and in (3b), complements are properties of the root.

gory-neutral root with a functional head belonging to a restricted set of category-defining heads. As has been often observed, there is no way, in this approach, in which *description* can be characterized as deverbal, that is, as being related to *describe*: The two items just happen to share the same root.[10]

It should be asked on which basis the lexicalist approach and the syntactic one could be differentiated. One dimension of the word-formation process, namely head movement, could provide an answer, because it has a distinct status in the former and in the latter. The movement of verbal heads in Minimalism cannot be traced back to a syntactic word-formation process – morphologically complex words are already formed when inserted into derivations -, nor to feature sharing between T and the verb – if sharing is also relevant to the relations between heads, it involves Agree, not Move. This leaves open the possibility that the verbal head doesn't move at all. Raising may be forced for other reasons, for example in order to provide a substantive/lexical support for the interpretable feature of some functional head, say, the [tense] feature of T. In the DM approach, the syntactic incorporation of the root to the local category-defining head hosting the feature matrix of the relevant affix is an integral part of the derivation of lexical categories. But, once formed, words can continue to move and the operation involved is also head movement (for example, finite verbs in verb-second and verb-initial languages no doubt leave the vP). Arad (2003) insightfully observes that the DM approach must assume that the heads n and v that merge with a root form a closed domain with it and determine its interpretation and its pronunciation and that any further operation takes as input not the root itself, but the derived word. Words derived from words have access only to the words they are derived from, not to the initial root. She concludes that word-formation from roots and word-formation from words should be carefully distinguished and formulates locality constraints on the interpretation of roots that imply that only the lowest instance of v or n has access to the root, the higher ones only deal with words. If this distinction has detectable effects in the syntax, they cannot be captured in the lexicalist approach where fully formed words are available from the start. In other words, head movement is a necessary feature of both the syntactic approach and the lexicalist approach to word formation, but it has a different status in each. The conceptually distinct analyses this difference gives rise to are potentially empirically distinguishable. This prediction will be tested in chapter IV, when the derivation of gerund clauses is dealt with.

There are other areas where the lexicalist approach and the syntactic one lead to quite different accounts of some phenomena. Syncretism is one of them.

---

[10] Alexiadou & Borer (2021b) also make this observation.

It is well-known that bare verb stems in English function as indicative present forms (except at the 3rd person singular), as imperative forms, as infinitive forms and as subjunctive ones (cf. *open*) and that the *ed*-affixed forms correspond both to indicative past forms and to perfect passive adjectival participles (cf. *opened*). The kind of account that can be put forward to deal with that type of phenomenon depends on the conception of the syntax-morphology interface one adopts. In a lexicalist approach, the syntax, as shown by Kayne (2010), should be viewed as disambiguating morphological forms. On the contrary, Manzini & Roussou (2019) observe that in a DM approach, where lexical exponents are inserted late, syncretism should be taken to "result from the underspecification of the lexicon or the application of impoverishment rules to fully specified syntactic forms".

9.3 Bridging the gap between Distributed Morphology and Lexicalism

The DM theory relies on three basic assumptions, which are in part independent from one another. The first one has lareadly been discussed: Lexical categories result from a-categorial roots being categorized in the syntax by the functional structure dominating them. The second one is that lexical insertion is distributed over different syntactic levels. The third one is that roots are inserted early, inflectional affixes are assigned a morphological shape late in the derivation. For each of these claims, it is possible to propose a version weaker than the one adopted by the supporters of the DM approach.

Some languages appear to allow the insertion of any root in any environment to produce a verb or a noun. Panagiotidis (2015) refers to Lillooet Salish as being a language of this type. Semitic languages are also reputed to be plausible candidates for a treatment along these lines. But the availability of category-neutral roots should not necessarily be viewed as a universal of language. It could also be a language-specific property. It is easier, in the languages of the Indo-European family, to describe derivational morphology using categorially specified bases, simply because the vast majority of them do not occur with more than one category.

Concerning the nature and the locus of lexical insertion, it is true that late lexical insertion is in a good position to deal with non-concatenative morphology, with various cases of allomorphy . . . But, in many cases, lexical derivations can appropiately be accounted for in a pre-syntactic component. Chomsky (2001) in *Derivation by phase* insists that with respect to LI (Lexical Insertion), the simplest choice should win in all situations.

For roots and highly predictable inflectional elements (say, English progressive), the distinction between single-LI and several independent contributions to LI (as in DM systems postulating universal late insertion ULI) seems to have little empirical content, but they might, for example, when an idiosyncratic feature F of a root has syntactic effects.

In other words, it is not easy to think of situations where the DM approach to word-formation makes empirical predictions that are different from those of the minimalist checking procedure, except in some very specific cases.

At first sight, a huge conceptual gap exists between the syntactic approach to word-formation and the lexical one. But it is less important than it could appear at first. The Minimalist Program seems to adopt a resolutely lexicalist stand. But Williams (1996) shows that appearances are deceptive in this respect. Affixation is done in the lexicon and words are inserted fully formed in syntactic derivations, but affixes are still associated with syntactic positions, although indirectly. Each affix is coupled with a matrix of features, which enter into an agreement relation with the uninterpretable features of a functional head, in order to check, value and delete them.[11] This means that, exactly as in non-lexicalist approaches, the spine of functional projections recapitulates the internal structure of verbs. According to Williams, the dividing line should be established between the theories in which the only component involved in word formation is the lexicon and those in which movement or checking operations are necessary to combine or license the different parts of a word within narrow syntax, in other words, those in which "compositionality involves syntactic elements". If this view is adopted, Chomsky's probe-goal-Agree approach relies on a conception of the syntax-morphology interface which is not strictly lexicalist and is even anti-lexicalist in some respects.

Another feature that bridges the gap between DM and the Minimalist Program is that Chomsky's theory integrates at least one category that can be thought of as a category-defining head, namely v, although it was initially characterized as a light verb. There is no doubt that n should be added to the list. The label of the Root-x configurations resulting from the raising of the root should also be clarified. Recall that, in Chomsky's (2013, 2015) view, roots cannot serve as labels, voiding ambiguity. Rather, a root selected by some x inherits x's uninterpretable features when it raises to x and gets a label.

---

11 Still another possibility would be to claim that affixes and roots are introduced as separate entities into derivations, as the syntactic approach claims, and are separately attracted by the functional heads the features of which they value or lexicalize, as the lexicalist approach proposes. See Rouveret (2018a) for preliminary discussion.

The analyses developed in this book make a massive use of category-defining heads. They are couched within a conception of the syntax-morphology interface in which "compositionality involves syntactic elements". But they are essentially neutral with respect to the various options concerning the early or late lexical insertion of inflectional (and derivational) affixes.

10 Transcategorial items, mixed projections

Some languages have at their disposal a particular class of lexical objects, usually referred to as *transcategorial items*, which cannot be univocally identified as belonging to one of the three major lexical classes (V, N, Adj), but manifest different categorial signatures depending on the context, with interpretive effects correlated with the change of categorial identity. Languages differ as to the extension of the phenomenon. Concerning Mandarin Chinese, Lee (2018) observes that "the same form (*hao*) can appear as an adjective, an intensifier adverb, a verb complement or a noun" and that "the same form of the verb can be used as the main verb, a complement verb, or a subject". Another salient characteristic of Mandarin Chinese is that some words are ambiguous between a lexical and a functional status, a property that stems from the fact that functional elements often have a word status, which goes hand in hand with Chinese displaying a much impoverished affixal morphology. The fluidity of the boundaries between word classes in Chinese and their apparently exclusively contextual definition has led some linguists, most notably Gao Mingkai, to claim that, as far as the lexicon is concerned, Chinese can do without syntactic category labels.[12] The distinction between nouns and verbs has also been called into question in the languages of the Mayan and of the Austronesian families, although it turns out to be maintained in one form or another.[13] Indo-European languages, which have rich declension and/or conjugation systems at their disposal and tend to define rigid categorial classes via morphological marking, usually include a relatively restricted set of transcategorial items.

One of the basic claims of this chapter is that, in order to reach a better understanding of *transcategoriality*, it is necessary to contrast it with another phenomenon, *category mixing*, predominantly found in inflected languages and which cannot easily be detected in isolating languages. Let us call "mixed category" a projection with a dual nature, exhibiting features that are characteristic of more than one category.

The existence of both transcategoriality and category mixing obviously raises crucial questions concerning the characterization of lexical categories. The two phenomena seem to militate against the traditional rigid classification of parts of speech into nouns and verbs (and adjectives). The rest of this chapter is devoted to identifying and hopefully solving some of the difficulties they raise through

---

12 This proposal must be distinguished from Shen Jiaxuan's position, who claims that Chinese verbs should be seen as a subclass of nouns. See Lee (2018) for an extensive criticism.
13 See Lois & Vapnarsky (2006) on Mayan, Sabbagh (2009) on Tagalog, Coon (2014) on Mayan and Tagalog.

the study of a particular case, English gerund constructions. The basic opposition between verbal (Acc-*ing* and Poss-*ing*) and nominal gerund constructions is briefly presented in section 11. Two lexicalist approaches to gerund-formation are discussed in section 12. A Distributed Morphology account of gerund forms is developed in section 13, which proposes first a characterization of transcategoriality based on the existence of category-defining heads, then a characterization of category-mixing relying on category-changing (or category-switching) heads. The limits and shortcomings of these two proposals are also discussed. The results achieved in the chapter are summarized in the conclusion (section 14).

11 A preliminary classification of gerund phrases

Although it has been extended to cover various phenomena, the label "mixed category" in the literature on English has primarily been reserved to refer to a rather restricted set of constructions, most notably those containing an -*ing* gerund form, which are usually taken as paradigmatic.[14] The following examples are borrowed from Malouf (2000).

(4) a. *Everyone was impressed by Pat's artful folding of the napkins.*
          [Nominal gerund]
   b. *Everyone was impressed by Pat artfully folding the napkins.*
          [Accusative-*ing*]
   c. *Everyone was impressed by Pat's artfully folding the napkins.*
          [Possessive-*ing*]

(4a) is a nominal gerund construction: The lexical head of the construction, i.e. *folding*, has a clearly nominal syntax (adjectival modification, prepositional complementation); the phrase as a whole occupies a site accessible to nominal expressions. (4b) illustrates the Acc-*ing* construction: *folding* manifests the internal syntax of a verb (argument selection, direct complementation, adverbial modification) and functions as the lexical head of a verbal/propositional domain; but the expression as a whole has the external distribution of a noun phrase. (4c) exemplifies the Poss-*ing* construction: It combines a verbal (accusative) marking of the object with a nominal (possessive) marking of the subject; the -*ing* form heads a verbal predicate (adverbial modification, direct complementation); but the structure above the verb phrase is that of a noun phrase (the subject is realized as a "saxon" genitive); and the construction has the external distribution of

---

14 The syntax and semantics of English gerunds has given rise to a considerable literature, see, among others, Chomsky (1970), Emonds (1970), Wasow & Roeper (1972), Horn (1975), Williams (1975), Reuland (1983), Abney (1987), Johnson (1988), Milsark (1988), Portner (1991a, 1991b, 1994), Asher (1993), Zucchi (1993), Kratzer (1996), Harley & Noyer (1998), Marantz (1999), Malouf (2000), Cornilescu (2003), Moulton (2004), Pires (2006), Emonds (2007), Alexiadou (2013, 2021), Panagiotidis (2015). This section draws heavily on Cornilescu's luminous state of the art chapter *Gerund clauses* in her 2003 book *Complementation in English. A minimalist approach*, as well as on Pires's (2006) analysis of Acc-*ing* constructions, and Panagiotidis's (2015) discussion of Poss-*ing* constructions.

a nominal expression. (4b) and (4c) are often grouped under the label "verbal gerunds".

If looked at in this light, the syntax of English gerunds clearly illustrates both transcategoriality and category mixing. Some constructions with a gerund as their core exclusively display internal and external nominal characteristics: this is the case of nominal gerunds. Others occupy positions usually hosting nominal expressions, but display strictly verbal/clausal internal properties: this is the case of the Acc-*ing* constructions. The coexistence in English of verbal and nominal gerunds supports the conclusion that gerunds are transcategorial items or, equivalently, that the -*ing* suffix is a bivalent morpheme (if one takes it for granted that the suffix is responsible for the categorial identity of the lexeme). At the same time, a third construction exists, namely the Poss-*ing* construction, whose external distribution is exclusively nominal, but whose internal structure jointly displays characteristics typically associated with verbs and others typically associated with nouns.

The two types of mixing instantiated by verbal gerund constructions should be carefully distinguished. In Poss-*ing* gerund constructions, mixing affects the internal structure of the mixed projection: The categorial features of the phrase appear to change at some point in the projection line, with the lower part verbal and the higher part nominal. I will refer to this case as "mixing in the narrow sense" or "strong mixing". Acc-*ing* gerund constructions instantiate a different case, which will be referred to as "mixing in the broad sense" or "weak mixing": They have a verbal/clausal internal structure and, at the same time, are allowed to occupy positions that are reserved for nominal expressions. There is thus a mismatch between the internal structure of the phrase and its external distribution. Although the two cases are usually confused, I will show that the two types of mixing constitute distinct phenomena and should be assigned separate analyses.

12 Lexical approaches to trancategoriality

The various approaches to transcategoriality and category mixing fall into two major families: the lexical ones, that take gerunds and other verbo-nominal categories to be lexical items of a special type, specified as such in the lexicon, but whose specific categorial membership in each sentence is context-sensitive; the syntactic ones, that take gerund words to be formed in the syntax and resort to category-defining heads to derive transcategorial items and to specialized category-switching heads to derive mixed categories, via a process akin to nominalization.

12.1 The neutralization approach

When one attempts to establish which combinations of nominal and verbal properties are possible within a single projection, three options should be contemplated: the projection can be a bivalent category, a hybrid category or a mixed category (cf. Rouveret 1987, 1994, 2020).

(i) If a head X displays all the properties of a standard nominal head in nominal structures and all the properties of a standard verbal head in verbal structures, X should be thought of as a *bivalent* category or, equivalently, as a *transcategorial* item.

(ii) If a head X defines a specific entity in the inventory of lexical categories, showing a unitary behavior in the two types of constructions, which distinguishes it both from standard nominal heads [+N, –V] and from standard verbal heads [–N, +V], X should viewed as a *hybrid* category. If one adopts a system founded on the binary features [αN], [βV]), such a category should be specified [+N, +V].

(iii) The projection XP of a category X is *mixed* if XP has the external distribution of a noun phrase, but X internally manifests some of the properties of verbal heads, or if XP has the external distribution of a verb phrase, but X internally manifests some properties of nominal heads.

The potential existence of *hybrid* categories, that is, of categories specified in the lexicon as [+N, +V], immediately raises a question that is fundamental to the theory of lexical categories. Suppose that gerunds in English are authentic *hybrid* categories. Can a single syntactic element be simultaneously nominal and verbal? Baker (undated) raises the question and concludes that such a possibility should be discarded, because it goes against a principle he has been arguing for, the Reference-Predication Constraint, stating that "no syntactic node can have both a specifier and a referential index". The property that distinguishes verbs from nouns in Baker's (2003) theory is that verbs are coupled with a specifier, nouns with a referential index. The problem with gerunds and gerund phrases is precisely that they seem to have both.[15]

The hybrid analysis also meets with problems having to do with lexical insertion and with labeling. It raises serious difficulties against the approaches that, like the Principles and Parameters framework, distinguish between terms and positions and for which the list of possible labels for positions necessarily coincides with the list of the categorial signatures available to items. The point is that no [+N, +V] position exists in phrase-structure trees and that [+N, +V] terms can be inserted neither in [+N, −V] nor in [−N, +V] positions.

A possible way out compatible with the strictures imposed by X-bar theory, consists in claiming that a categorial neutralization process affects the corresponding syntactic positions (see Rouveret 1987, 1994 for an analysis along these lines). Phrase-structure trees in the relevant languages would exclusively make available [+ N] and [+ V] positions, both appropriate hosts for [+ N, +V] terms. English doesn't provide any clue in favor of this scenario. But Celtic does to some extent. It is known that in Welsh, some prepositions inflect for person and number and that prepositional inflection is quite similar to the verbal one,[16] suggesting that the neutralization hypothesis – the categorial neutralization of phrase-structure positions to either [−N] (i.e [+ V]) or [+N] – could be on the right track.

Another promising way to look at the problem is to assume that neutralization doesn't affect syntactic positions, but the lexical items themselves. In order to account for the case marking properties of German adjectives, van Riemsdijk (1983) claims that the distinction between V and A can be neutralized to [+V] in some languages. Dealing with Arabic participles, Aoun (1981) proposes that [+N, +V] items can switch to either one of the core categories, namely [+N, −V] or [−N, +V]. In his view, a change of this type is at the origin of the difference between standard Arabic participles, which are hybrid items, and Lebanese Arabic ones, which are exclusively verbal, and could underlie the corresponding diachronic process. But the neutralization proposal is not in a position to provide a principled explanation for the existence of the Poss-*ing* construction besides the Acc-*ing* and the nominal ones.

---

15 To solve the difficulty, Baker (undated) revives the time-honored analysis of gerunds as fusions of a true verb with an affix with nominal features, which he takes to be inserted into Infl. This proposal is reminiscent of Jackendoff's (1977) deverbalizing rule scheme that was intended to restrict the category changes that are not immediately compatible with the core assumptions of X-bar theory, but nevertheless appear to be possible within phrases.
16 But they inflect for gender at the third person singular, which is not the case of finite verbs.

At a general level, it should be observed that the problem raised by the feature mismatch between the inserted item and the host position doesn't arise in the bare phrase structure approach to constituent structure, in which phrase structure doesn't exist independently of the lexical items that participate in it. The existence of hybrid categories, if it was confirmed, could even be taken as an argument against pre-built categorially-labeled phrase-structure trees: A feature system exclusively based on [αN] and [βV] is not in the best position to adequately characterize the categories that have been coined "hybrid categories" and the difficulty to represent gerunds in this system could simply reflect a deficiency of standard X-bar theory.

Given these observations concerning the notion of hybridity and the insuperable difficulties that are encountered when one tries to assign it a formal status, it comes as a relief to discover that hybrid categories, as they are defined here, probably don't exist, contrary to bivalent and mixed ones. In the course of this study, I have not met any clear case of hybridity. This means that the *Nominalization* categorial feature system can provisionally be maintained. But the other two types, the bivalent one and the mixed one, are indeed attested and it must be determined which set of assumptions is in the best position to represent their basic properties.

12.2 The underspecification approach

A possible approach to bivalent and mixed categories consists in tracing back their duality to the categorial *underspecification* of verbo-nominal heads. This is the way Blevins (2005) proposes to deal with English gerunds and Welsh verb-nouns. He refers to van Riemsdijk's (1983) treatment of German adjectives and Malouf's (2000) analysis of gerunds as possible theoretical antecedents of the perspective he adopts. He particularly insists on the tight connection that should be established between his proposal and Chomsky's (1970: 190) position, summarized in the following passage.

> We can enter *refuse* in the lexicon as an item with certain fixed selectional and strict subcategorization features, which is free with respect to the categorial features [noun] and [verb]. Fairly idiosyncratic morphological rules will determine the phonological form of *refuse*, *destroy*, etc, when these items appear in the noun position . . .

> Let us propose, then, as a tentative hypothesis that a great many items appear in the lexicon with fixed selectional and strict subcategorization features, but with a choice as to the features associated with the lexical categories noun, verb, adjective. The lexical entry may specify that semantic features are in part dependent on the choice of one or another of these categorial features.

The gist of this passage is that categorial identity is not necessarily determined early, an idea that clearly anticipates the debates on the relation of the lexicon to the syntax in the 80s and the 90s. In this conception of the lexicon as underspecified, related lexemes share an entry associated with meaning and subcategorization, but not with categorial membership. In an approach in which a distinction is drawn between lexical and syntactic operations, there is no doubt that gerunds should remain within the jurisdiction of the syntax, whereas derived nominals should be taken care of by an enriched lexicon. The fact that gerunds show clear signs of mixing and function either as verbs or as nouns or as verbs embedded in noun phrases is a further clue to the syntactic origin of gerunds. To achieve the appropriate distinctions among the various gerund uses and assign to gerund heads and projections a specific categorial label, reference must be made to the structural and categorial environment. Resolution is necessarily contextual and, in Blevin's (2005) view and to some extent in Chomsky's (1970) one, can be performed on the basis of category-specific X-bar expansions, such as V' → V or NP N' → N PP: *signing the treaty* will be interpreted as a verbal projection in (5a), as a verbal projection embedded in a noun phrase in (5b), as a nominal projection in (5c).

(5) a. *They are relunctantly signing the treaty.*
    b. *their reluctantly signing the treaty.*
    c. *the reluctant signing of the treaty.*

The suffix *-ing* is thus underspecified for its context of insertion and endorses different characteristics depending on the verbal or nominal environment in which it occurs.

Both the neutralization approach and the underspecification approach rely on the local context to resolve categorial ambiguity and are natural candidates to account for the existence of transcategorial items. But if they succeed in providing a precise characterization of transcategorial items, they shed no light on the existence and nature of mixed projections and do not explain which nominal and which verbal properties are retained, nor how these properties are distributed in the internal structure of mixed categories. A second weakness of lexicalist approaches is that they resort to theoretical assumptions and constructs that date back from the early 70s and don't take into consideration the role of functional heads in the syntax of natural languages, nor the interplay between functional and lexical items which, in contemporary syntactic thinking, largely contributes to the form and interpretation of linguistic expressions. This undoubtedly constitutes a limitation of these approaches.

13 Syntactic accounts of transcategoriality

13.1 A DM analysis of gerund forms

In the conception defended by Distributed Morphology, word formation is reintegrated into the syntax and lexical heads are assigned a categorial identity exclusively on a syntactic basis. But this conception differs from Chomsky's (1970) one in that the traditional categories, N, V, . . ., are not analyzed as terminals, but result from the combination in the syntax of a category-neutral root and a designated category-defining functional head, n or v. The basic assumptions of this approach are given in (6)–(7), reproduced from (1)–(2).

(6) L-heads (lexical heads, namely verbs and nouns) are broken up into a categorially neutral root X and a F-head (a functional head v, n), which defines its categorial membership.

(7) n and v can host F-words or F-affixes or just F-features.[17]

Let us tentatively adopt (6) and (7) and consider the derivation of -*ing* forms, focusing on Acc-*ing* gerunds first. The null hypothesis is that their internal functional structure differs from that of nominal gerunds: A v head that both introduces the external argument and case marks the internal one is projected in verbal gerunds; no such head is present in nominal ones, which include a n head that is responsible for their nominal characteristics.[18] We end up with the following tentative representations (where all lexical items occupy their first Merge position).

(8) a. *John describing the accident*   Acc-*ing*
    b. (C) [$_{TP}$ T [$_{AspP}$ Asp [$_{vP}$ John [$_{v'}$ [$_v$ -*ing*] [$_{RootP}$ √DESCRIBE the accident]]]]]

(9) a. *the killing of the mocking bird*   nominal gerund
    b. [$_{DP}$ [$_D$ the] [$_{NbP}$ Nb [$_{nP}$ [$_n$ -*ing*] [$_{RootP}$ √KILL of the mocking bird]]]]

The Acc-*ing* construction in (8b) incorporates an Aspect head. The nominal gerund one in (9b) does not; it includes a Number head instead, a decision that is

---

17 In strict DM terms, only a matrix of F-features can be associated with the v and n heads, since the lexical insertion of functional morphemes occurs late in derivations, on the PF branch of the grammar.
18 But see sct. 13.5.

supported by the observation that this construction doesn't allow perfective auxiliaries to be present, but can occasionally be pluralized, as example (10a) from Wasow and Roeper (1972) shows (verbal gerunds are never pluralized, cf. 10b).

(10) a. *Sightings of UFO's make Mary nervous.*
b. *Sighting(*s) UFO's makes Mary nervous.*

The well-formedness of (10a) can be taken as a strong indication that a Number head is present in the domain, as (9b) presupposes or, alternatively, that the n head projected above RootP is endowed with a [number] feature, making the projection of the Number head superfluous. It has been proposed that Number and Aspect generally exclude each other in a given extended projection, cf. Rouveret (1994). If a strict distributional complementarity exists between Number and Aspect, the absence of Aspect in nominal gerund structures corresponds to the expected situation.

Representations (8b) and (9b) tentatively identify the verbalizing and nominalizing heads with the affix *-ing* that shows up upon the root. It is taken to spell out the relevant category-defining head, that is v in the Acc-*ing* construction and n in the nominal gerund construction. But under the DM approach, all lexical categories, not just gerunds, are constructed in the syntax. What then is the defining characteristic of transcategorial items? A tentative answer is that these items are x-Root combinations, where the category-defining head x is underspecified: The range of x is {v, n}; the selection of a value for x is performed contextually. As already emphasized, the functional environment actually suffices to define categorial membership. In the case of nominal gerunds (cf. 1a), the constituent is a nominal headed by a D head;[19] the complement of D can only be a nominal projection nP; x is n and the gerund is n-Root. No positive evidence supports the claim that a D head is present in Acc-*ing* constructions. The subject of an Acc-*ing* construction cannot be replaced by the definite article. The resulting ungrammaticality strongly militates against the nominal analysis:

(11) a. *I disapproved of John killing the mocking bird.*
b. **I disapproved of the killing the mocking bird.*

---

[19] I leave it an open question whether 's is realized in D or is a simple genitive marker. The representations of Poss-*ing* constructions and of nominal gerunds proposed below presuppose that 's is D.

13.2 Some shortcomings of the DM account

Both the syntactic approach to lexical categories and the account of transcategoriality it makes available can be criticized on various grounds.

The syntactic approach presupposes that there is nothing like "primitive nouns" or "primitive verbs" and that there is no direction of derivation. The surface morphological differences between verbs, nouns and adjectives reduce to the syntactic structures in which roots appear, in conjunction with agreement processes defined to operate on these structures. The full responsability for determining the categorial status of a lexical item is endorsed by the functional heads in the local environment of the root. These consists of abstract morphosyntactic features and are labeled v or n (or a). Vinokurova (2005), however, shows that a distinction indeed exists between nouns and verbs at a basic level. More needs to be said about the category-defining heads themselves in order to capture the traditional characterization of verbs as representing intrinsically relational concepts and of nouns as representing intrinsically non-relational concepts (and of adjectives as being intrinsically 1-place concepts).[20] According to Reuland (2011), these dimensions play a decisive role in the formulation of the instructions determining the way the relevant items are inserted into syntactic representations. These reservations do not specifically concern the DM account of gerund constructions. But the following observations do.

The claim that the lexical entries of -*ing* forms are underspecified and that their resolution is contextual indeed provides a satisfactory answer to the question of which specific property underlies their dual behavior and their transcategorial status. As mentioned above, the contextual sensitivity of underspecified categories can be expressed by saying that the relevant items are x-Root combinations, where x ranges over {v, n} and the selection of a value for x is performed contextually. But this assumption says nothing about the property that makes some syntactic objects eligible for functioning as transcategorial items (or as lexical heads in mixed projections). The solution is not straightforward at all in an approach which, like Marantz's one, postulates categorially neutral roots at the origin of *all* lexical categories, not just of verbo-nominal ones.

Moreover, if the value of x is exclusively determined on the basis of the context, the result achieved via categorizing heads could as well result from taking into account the subcategorization frames of the heads that are found in the local environment (as Blevins 2005 does; cf. 5). For example, if an a-catego-

---

[20] This presentation makes things simpler than they are. Relational nouns and relational adjectives exist, which select more than one argument.

rial root is found in the complement position to the category T, the root and the projection it heads are generally verbal. Similarly, if some root is the head of the complement of a D or Nb category, it is definitely nominal. Observations of this type provide strong support for alternatives to DM such as Borer's Exo-Skeletal framework. I reproduce a passage from Borer (2014).

> Within Distributed Morphology . . .., a root must merge with a categorizer before merging with any functional node (in the conventional sense). But why should that be? Why can a root merge directly with v but never with T or D? Are these conditions on the distribution of roots? Are these conditions on the distribution of functors? If these are conditions on roots, e.g., the need for roots to instantaneously merge with a category label, what does such a requirement follow from? If, on the other hand, these are conditions on functors, e.g., T selects v, D selects n and so on, and then n or v merge with the root, don't such conditions amount, effectively, to a surrogate categorization of the root by T or D, rendering the presence of an additional n or v categorizer superfluous? [Borer 2014: 120].

There is no doubt that any selecting category, not just v or n, can potentially be taken to function as a categorizing head. But if it turns out to be the case, it is necessary to draw up the list of the categories that indeed function in this way.

It is clear that what has been described in subsections 12.1 and 12.2 is more a research agenda that remains to be completed than a full-fledged theory of the lexicon-syntax and syntax-morphology interfaces. Besides the ones that have just been listed, many questions haven't received precise answers yet. For example, we don't know how the properties standardly associated with "words" emerge from the combination of roots and functional features, how the resulting units get an argument structure and even a meaning.

In conclusion, DM's generalized a-categorial approach to lexical categories turns out to be quite efficient when phenomena like transcategoriality are considered. But this approach certainly doesn't find strong empirical support in all categorial and morphological systems and it seems difficult to unreservedly adopt it. Similarly, inserting an affix in the lexicon or later in many cases makes no empirical difference. Distributed lexical insertion, the late insertion of functional items included, are inevitable choices only in a very restricted set of morphological situations. In what follows, I will remain agnostic on this question, but, contrary to the DM stance, I will make the claim that the feature matrices corresponding to affixes are spelled out either in a pre-syntactic component or in the overt syntax, *but not after syntax*.[21]

---

[21] This claim is necessary to capture Landau's generalization concerning overt inflection, cf. sct. 7.2 and 8.3.

13.3 Category mixing and category switches

How do these assumptions fare in the analysis of category mixing?[22] In order to solve the projection problem raised by category mixing across languages, scholars generally adopt the view that the nominal properties of mixed categories are contributed by a nominal functional head merged above a verbal projection, which functions as a category switch. In Bresnan's (1997: 4) terms, "a mixed projection can be partitioned into two categorially uniform subtrees, such that one is embedded as a constituent of the other". In the Poss-*ing* construction, the structure displays nominal properties above the verbal projection, which is the locus of verbal properties. The approaches that take it for granted that lexical categories are primitives entities and reject (6)–(7), admit the existence of category-switching heads or of specialized functional heads having the same effect, cf. Reuland (1983), Rouveret (1994), Bresnan (1997), Borsley & Kornfilt (2000), Malouf (2000). For these researchers, neither the existence of transcategoriality nor that of category mixing constitute arguments in favor of a-categorial lexical entries. Others take up the opposite stand and adopt the assumptions that underlie the syntactic approach to the definition of lexical categories promoted by DM, cf. Marantz (1997, 1999, 2001), Alexiadou, Iordachioaia & Soare (2010), Panagiotidis & Grohmann (2011), Carnie (2011), Panagiotidis (2015), Rouveret (2020). Their account of category mixing relies on something like (12).

(12) Besides being category-defining heads, n and v also are category-switching heads, that can respectively be merged above a vP and an nP projection.

Recall that in Poss-*ing* constructions, a verbal substructure is embedded inside a nominal one. Arguments supporting the claim that a verbal substructure is present come from the examples which manifest properties standardly associated with verb phrases: adverbial modification, direct case marking of the object, cf. (4b) and (4c). The contrast between (13a) and (13b) can be taken to confirm that v is absent in nominal gerunds, but present along with n in the Poss-*ing* construction.

(13) a. *Lucy's frequent/*frequently reading of War and Peace.*
 b. *John's *continual/continually playing the sonata.*

---

[22] The basic ingredients of the DM account of category mixing developed here, as well as of the one of transcategoriality in the preceding subsections, are borrowed from Marantz (1999, 2001).

The nominalizer, if present in (13b), is attached rather high and could be inserted immediately below the "subject" position, as adverbial distributions suggest. We end up with the analysis of (14a) schematized in (14b): vP is topped by a nominalizer; the nominal properties of the construction are contributed by the nominal functional projection above vP.[23]

(14) a. n > v : *John's describing the accident.*   Poss-*ing*
        [DP [DP John] [DP [D 's] [nP [n -*ing*] [vP v [RootP √DESCRIBE the accident]]]]]

In this account, a category-switching head n is present above the category-defining head v.[24] Contrary to what happens in derived nominal constructions (at least in a large subset of them), where n directly attaches to the root (cf. 3b), the category-switching head n in Poss-*ing* gerunds attaches on top of the vP projection. This analysis directly captures Panagiotidis & Grohmann's (2011) observation that nominal and verbal properties do not intersperse. It is also compatible with Arad's (2003) claim that word-formation from roots and word-formation from words should be distinguished. In Poss-*ing* constructions, there is no evidence that the switch has access to the initial root: it only sees the verbal word.

13.4 Some observations on switches

Several questions should be raised at this point. First, it must be asked whether, in the generalized syntactic approach, category-defining and category-switching heads should be considered as instantiating a single categorial type. Marantz (1997, 1999) gives a positive answer to this question and proposes (12). Panagiotidis (2015) rejects (12) and assigns to category-switching heads a specific status, endowing them with both an uninterpretable feature, representing complement selection, and an interpretable one, registering the categorial status and the semantic import of the higher part. For example, the nominal switch Ger that he postulates in Poss-*ing* constructions contains both a subcategorization [uV] feature, checked by the lexical verbal root that it c-commands, and an interpret-

---

[23] In (14), all the lexical elements are represented in their first Merge position. The question of the origin of the subject argument is left open for the moment.
[24] In the treatments that reject (6) and (7), that is, in which words are formed and categorially specified in the lexicon, the domains under consideration include a category-switching (nominalizing) head, but no category-defining head.

able categorial [N] one. Panagiotidis (2015: 145) states: "Switches are no ordinary categorizers (no ordinary nominalizers in the case of Poss-*ing* gerunds)".[25] Even if one sticks to some version of (12), there is an inescapable difference between category-defining and category-switching heads, already emphasized by Arad's (2003) contribution. By definition, the former are associated with a-categorial roots, the latter are coupled with already categorized word units. As a matter of fact, the DM approach cannot do without a principle having the effect of Arad's locality constraints on the interpretation of roots, ensuring that only the lowest instances of v or n (that function as category-defining heads) have access to the root and that the higher ones (that function as switches) exclusively deal with words.[26]

Second, it should be established at which hierarchical level category switches can be inserted, that is, where exactly in the structure the change from a verbal status to a nominal one takes place. To properly answer this question, it is necessary to discover and state the restrictions on the size of the verbal and nominal subtrees whose union constitutes a mixed projection (in the narrow sense). Is a unified characterization of the size of the nominalizers' complements possible? Panagiotidis & Grohmann (2011) propose that it can only be the size of a prolific domain, in Grohmann's (2003) sense, Panagiotidis (2015) that it should be the size of a phase. But deciding whether the complement of a switch is a phase is a delicate matter. To provide a principled solution to this problem, it is first necessary to characterize the status of the -*ing* affix in gerund constructions more accurately. Some scholars have observed that, contrary to what (14b) presupposes, -*ing* cannot itself be the nominalizing affix, but should rather be analyzed as an aspect marker, homophonous to the imperfective suffix that derives the present participle morpheme (cf. Ackema & Neeleman 2004: 175–181, Panagiotidis 2015: 143). If an autonomous Aspect head is indeed present, at which point in the structural architecture is it merged? Let us assume that it stands above vP in (14b). But if the overtly realized affix is not the one that is responsible for categorial change, a second silent affix, functioning as a nominalizer must be present somewhere, merged with the AspP phrase, not with vP. (15) should be substituted for (14b).

(15) [$_{DP}$ [John] [$_D$'s] [$_{nP}$ n [$_{AspP}$ [$_{Asp}$ -*ing*] [$_{vP}$ [v [$_{RootP}$ √DESCRIBE the accident]]]]]]

---

25 If Panagiotidis is right, mixed projections are not special in any way with respect to their phrase-structure status, since they strictly conform to the Endocentricity Condition: a most welcome result.

26 Note that a syntactic framework can do without category-defining heads, but it cannot dispense with a device that has the same effect as category-switching heads, which points toward their being different.

Now, AspP is not a phase. On the other hand, if Asp was merged below v, between V and v, it would disrupt the relation between v and the root it identifies as verbal, a situation that shouldn't arise in the category-defining approach.

But there is reason to doubt that -*ing* is an exponent of external/grammatical aspect. It will be shown in chapter IV that V-*ing* forms and verbal gerund constructions do not function as vehicles for any specific aspectual value. The aspectual interpretation of gerund clauses entirely depends on the inner aspectual profile of the lexical head and on the class of the matrix predicate. Moreover, if -*ing* was taken to be an exponent of aspect in verbal gerund constructions, it would be extremely difficult to provide it with a status in nominal gerund constructions. It certainly cannot be conceived of as an exponent of number.

Let us drop the assumption that the -*ing* affix is an exponent of aspect, while maintaining the claim that it is not the manifestation of a categorizer either. What is its status? Lowenstamm (2014) has recently provided arguments to the effect that derivational affixes such as -*ness* or -*ity*, which are usually analyzed as categorizing (nominalizing) categories, should better be viewed as roots. He further suggests that the insertion of a categorizing head can be an adjunction to a complex root, rather than to a simple one. An immediate effect of the root analysis of derivational affixes is to make it possible to postpone the adjunction of the categorizing head. If one extends this logic to the case under consideration, it can be proposed that the representations associated with nominal gerunds and verbal (Acc-*ing* and Poss-*ing*) gerunds are as follows (all lexical items are represented in their first Merge position):[27]

(16) a. *the killing of the mocking bird* nominal gerund
     b. [$_{DP}$ [$_D$ the] [$_{NbP}$ Nb [$_{nP}$ n [$_{RootP}$ [Ving] [√KILL of the mocking bird]]]]]

(17) a. *John describing the accident* Acc-*ing*
     b. (C) [$_{TP}$ [T] [$_\alpha$ John [$_{vP}$ v [$_{RootP}$ [Ving] [√DESCRIBE the accident]]]]]

(18) a. *John's describing the accident* Poss-*ing*
     b. [$_{DP}$ [John] [$_D$'s] [$_{nP}$ n [$_{TP}$ T [$_{vP}$ [v [$_{RootP}$ [-*ing*] [√DESCRIBE the accident]]]]]]]

---

[27] The specifics of these representations, in particular the presence of T in (17) and (18) will be fully justified in the next chapter.

T, which is projected in Acc-*ing* constructions, is taken to be also present in Poss-*ing* ones. If analysis (18b) is on the right track, the complement of the category switch is not a phase, since it is a TP domain.

The decision to analyze -*ing* as a derivational (not inflectional) affix and to assign derivational affixes a radical status has a further consequence: It implies that one cannot adopt Abney's (1987) and Moulton's (2004) proposal that gerund constructions differ from one another only by the attachment height of the -*ing* suffix, which can be merged with different segments of a verb's extended projection. According to Abney, what distinguishes the various types of gerunds is simply the size of the verbal constituent they contain. And the higher the affix attaches, the more verbal properties the resulting structure displays. In nominal gerund constructions -*ing* attaches to V itself, in Poss-*ing* to vP, in Acc-*ing* to the whole TP. In the approach adopted here, -*ing* originates in the complex root governed by the categorizing head in all verbal and nominal gerund constructions.[28]

Still another consequence of the root analysis of affixes is that gerund forms cannot be used to choose between the syntactic approach and the lexical approach to word-formation, a possibility alluded to in section 9. The relevant forms are morphologically complete at the v-level in the two analyses, which do not distinguish themselves by the way they deal with fully formed words.

We already know that not all combinations of nominal and verbal properties are legitimate. An additional question is whether all mixed projections are externally nominal. Panagiotidis's (2015) answer is positive. In effect, we haven't met with any situation where a mixed projection is externally verbal, although some Welsh verbo-nominal constructions could at first give the impression that they are (see chapter VI). If empirically supported, this restriction has to be stipulated. It doesn't follow from any independently motivated assumption of the category-switching approach.

Let us now carefully consider a last aspect of the generalized category-defining/category-switching approach to the definition of syntactic categories and projections, which is potentially problematic. The syntactic account adequately captures the observation that Poss-*ing* gerunds have a more verbal/clausal nature than nominal gerunds and derived nominals, but are more nominal than Acc-*ing* gerunds. In traditional analyses, the nominalization process is characterized as a category-shifting operation, turning an essentially verbal item into the lexical head of a domain displaying the properties of a nominal expression or, in seman-

---

28 In this respect, the behavior of the *ing*-affix contrasts with that of the nominalizing head. Representation (18b) presupposes that the nominalization process can affect various pieces of structures, including whole TPs. For a recent account of nominalization along these lines, see Alexiadou (2021).

tic terms, allowing the formation of referential terms from predicative expressions. Nominal gerunds and Poss-*ing* constructions clearly fall under this general characterization.[29] Whenever a category-shifting process is involved, one should ask which lexical, morphological, syntactic, semantic properties of the input are preserved (usually, only a subpart of them is), which ones are altered. Adopting the traditional perspective, it is natural to attribute the relevant changes to the nominalization process itself and to the category or marker responsible for it. But, once again, the question of the status of nominalized constructions arises in quite different terms in an approach that takes *all* lexical categories to be derived in the syntax and to involve a categorizer. In an approach of this type, nominal gerunds don't instantiate a category shift, strictly speaking, because what is nominalized is an unspecified root, not a category. On the contrary, Poss-*ing* constructions uncontroversially instantiate such a shift. The major question nevertheless remains: Which properties of finite verbal forms or infinitives are absent from gerund forms? In an approach relying on (6)–(7) and (12), the only possible answer is that the apparent loss of some properties or the gain of new ones should be traced back to the properties of category-defining heads or to the combinations of category-defining and category-switching heads, together with the specific characteristics of inflectional affixes, registered by the feature matrices associated with them, or by the functional heads that host them. In this respect, Chomsky's (2000) probe-goal-Agree approach to syntactic dependencies can advantageously be combined with the DM theory based on category-defining/switching heads: When inserted into derivations, the v and n heads bear the collection of features that are responsible for the licensing and movements internal to the vP and nP projections. The latter, which are also the domains where the arguments of lexical heads originate, qualify as phases, that is, as computational, interpretive and spell-out units. When it functions as a category-switching head, n modifies the range of properties of the vP projection it governs. It should have no access to v and should not affect the accusative case feature it is endowed with. But it deprives the specifier of vP of its thematic status. This is only possible if a verbal gerund word has already been formed and has raised to a position where it is accessible to n. This position in (18) can plausibly be identified with T.

---

[29] Lees (1960) referred to nominal gerunds as "action nominalizations" because, unlike verbal gerunds, they don't allow stative verbs as a derivational base.

13.5 A generalized v analysis?

The proposals developed in the preceding sections take it for granted that the distinction between verbal and nominal gerunds, as it is standardly stated, adequately describes the distribution of verbal and nominal properties in gerund constructions. This distinction, promoted by Chomsky (1970), Wasow & Roeper (1972), Kratzer (1996), Harley & Noyer (1998), Fu, Roeper & Borer (2001), Pires (2006) and many others, in fact, amounts to classifying gerunds in function of the way they mark their object. The so-called verbal gerunds are the ones that directly case mark their object and, in this respect, Acc-*ing* and Poss-*ing*, to which one should adjoin PRO-*ing* constructions (cf. (19)), are just subclasses of verbal gerunds.

(19) a. *Pat enjoys* [PRO *artfully folding the napkins*].
   b. [PRO *artfully folding the napkins*] *is a challenge for everyone.*

But Moulton (2004) insightfully observes that an alternative grouping of the data is possible, once one takes into account the ability of gerunds to cooccur with an external argument in some environments, not in others. Whereas the contrast between (20a) and (20b) could be taken to be "a classic case of Burzio's generalization", (20c) and (20d) show that the absence of accusative case assignment does not necessarily correlate with the absence of an external argument.

(20) a. *Michael running the marathon*
   b. *the running of the marathon (by Michael)*
   c. *Michael's running the marathon*
   d. *Michael's running of the marathon regularly*

If external arguments are taken to be systematically introduced by a light v head, a head of this type must be projected in a larger range of structures than initially thought.[30] Even gerund constructions like (20d), because they contain an external argument position, should incorporate a defective light v head, whose effect is not to value accusative case, contrary to the v head present in (20a) and (20c), which is not defective.[31] Moulton's overall conclusion is that the truly relevant divide is between the gerunds that contain a position for an external argument

---

[30] This conclusion extends to event nominals, which are known to allow *by*-phrases, corresponding to the projection of an external argument.
[31] If they are taken to originate exclusively in SpecvP, external arguments must be allowed to move to a pre-gerund site, either SpecDP or a position sister-to-DP.

and those that do not, irrespective of whether they assign accusative case to their object or not. In his view, only a subset of nominal gerunds, dubbed "relational NGs", should be viewed as true nominalizations, that is, as domains deprived of a v head, contrary to "syntactic NGs". This "generalized v" proposal has the merit to account for a set of data in which a manner adverb unexpectedly cooccurs with a nominal gerund.

(21) *The shutting of the gates regularly at ten o' clock had rendered our residence very irksome to me.* [Mary Shelley]

(22) *From the daily reading of the Bible aloud to his mother, ...*

(21) and (22) are quoted by Jespersen (1940) from literary sources. Other examples show that the distribution of properties between the verbal and the nominal types has not always been as clear-cut as it is today. Jespersen provides examples where the subject of a verbal gerund is replaced by the definite article or another determiner and its object assigned accusative case:

(23) *in the delaying death* [Shakespeare, *Measure for measure*, IV, 2.]

(24) *this continual working-up afresh the old materials into slightly different forms* [Spencer]

(25) *He may press me to the immediate signing the deed.*

Examples (23)–(25) are strictly ungrammatical in contemporary English and differ from (21)–(22), which are almost fully acceptable. This situation is not specific to gerund constructions: It is reminiscent of Fu, Roeper & Borer's (2001) conclusions about derived nominals, which sometimes show evidence for a syntactically active verbal substructure (through adverbial modification again and *do so*-anaphora).

Can the existence of these additional data be reconciled with the DM approach sketched in the preceding sections? At this point, I can only present some preliminary observations that anticipate the full account that will be given in the next chapter. Moulton is right to claim that the absence of accusative case assignment doesn't always correlate with the absence of an external argument. This suffices to show that Burzio's generalization doesn't hold in the domains under consideration. But it is equally true that, in contemporary English, the availability of accusative case systematically goes along with the presence of an external argument (cf. 26a) and that, in the absence of accusative case, the external argument, when there is one, can only be built as the specifier of a DP (cf. 26b).

(26) a. * *the running the marathon*
   b. *Paul's running of the marathon* / * *Paul running of the marathon*

I won't adopt Moulton's assumption that external arguments systematically originate in SpecvP and that SpecDP is both a first merge and a movement site. Instead, I will assume that, when D is absent, as is the case in Acc-*ing* constructions, the subject has raised from within vP, but that when D is projected, as it is in Poss-*ing* constructions, SpecDP is the first Merge position of the external argument realized in __'s. Nothing prevents the occurrence of a v head in the structures headed by D. But nothing forces them to occur either: D can indeed head a domain not including a vP substructure! When v coexists with D, it never introduces an external argument and licenses accusative case only optionally. When it does, a Poss-*ing* structure is produced, cf. (20c). When it doesn't, a case illustrated by (20d), it is identical to unaccusative v: It doesn't select an external argument and doesn't make accusative case available, but it does allow adverbial modification.

14 Conclusion

The syntactic approach to the formation of gerund forms is unquestionably more successful than the lexical analyses considered previously, but it leaves several questions unanswered and, at least in the format assigned to it in the DM framework, remains conceptually unsatisfactory on several points. I will nevertheless tentatively adopt its basic assumptions in what follows, in particular (27i) and (27ii).

(27) (i) in a system that incorporates a restricted set of designated category-defining heads, transcategoriality can elegantly be dealt with (the categorizer associated with the root can take different values); but the transcategoriality phenomenon doesn't suffice to show that a-categorial roots are necessary.
 (ii) category-switching heads have a status distinct from that of category-defining heads (they function at the word/phrase level, not at the root level); they are natural candidates to account for category mixing.

Concerning specifically gerund forms, two preliminary conclusions can be drawn.

(28) (i) *-ing* is neither an exponent of aspect, nor the morphological spell-out of a categorizer or of a switch, but a derivational morpheme with radical status;
 (ii) when v coexists with D or n, it is defective: It doesn't introduce an external argument; it licenses accusative case only optionally.

IV The syntax of English gerund clauses

The preceding chapter has provided gerund *forms* with a morphosyntactic status. A framework that combines the Distributed Morphology approach to the definition of lexical categories with the assumptions of the probe-goal-Agree theory of syntactic dependencies was introduced, which accounts for the existence of transcategorial items and mixed projections. This chapter focuses on the various problems raised by the derivation and representation of gerund *constructions*. It is shown that, whereas positing a category-switching head, in fact a nominalizing head n, in their internal structure is the best formal choice to account for the strongly mixed properties of Poss-*ing* constructions, the weakly mixed properties of Acc-*ing* constructions are appropriately captured and their existence explained if one takes into account the way they are labeled.

Before embarking on the syntactic study of these constructions, it will be useful to get a better understanding of their semantic properties.

15 Some semantic properties of gerund domains

In this section, the tense properties of gerund clauses and their aspectual profile are briefly considered. They provide strong support for the claim that the internal structure of these constructions includes a defective Tense head and no outer Aspect head.

15.1 The tense of gerund clauses

According to Stowell (1982: 561–563), infinitives have tense, gerunds have no tense, or more accurately "no internally determined tense". He states that "the understood tense of the gerund is completely malleable to the semantics of the governing verb", contrary to what happens in infinitival constructions, where the embedded tense has a certain freedom with respect to the matrix one and, in the examples he discusses, has a clear future *irrealis* orientation. Interpretive differences can indeed be detected between the infinitives and gerund clauses complements to predicates that can select either construction. Stowell (1982) gives examples (1 a, b), Bolinger (1978) examples (1 c, d), Cornilescu (2003) examples (1 e, f).

(1) a. *Jenny remembered* [PRO *to bring the wine*].
 b. *Jenny remembered* [PRO *bringing the wine*].
 c. *Try* [PRO *to move it with your hand*]; *you'll see how hard it is.*
 d. *Try* [PRO *moving it with your hand*] *and see if that doesn't get it in the right position.*
 e. *I regret* [PRO *to say that you are a liar*].
 f. *I regret* [PRO *saying that you are a liar*].

The infinitive form is strongly preferred with verbs whose complement is understood as unrealized at the time of the matrix event, that is, when a future *irrealis* interpretation is involved. In (1a), Jenny has not yet brought the wine at the time of remembering; the gerund clause in (1b) refers to an act that has already taken place and is assigned a past tense interpretation with respect to the matrix tense. Commenting on the complementation of *try*, Bolinger (1978) observes that (1c) refers to an act that is not necessarily even possible, whereas (1d) "envisages an action about the accomplishment of which no doubt is raised." With other predicates, the tense of the gerund clause can refer either to an event anterior to the state of affairs described by the main clause or to an event contemporary with the matrix tense. This is the case in (1f), where the tense of the embedded clause complement to *regret* is ambiguous between present and past. These observations point to the conclusion that at least some gerund clauses are tensed and that their temporal interpretation largely depends on the semantic requirements of the matrix predicate. Direct evidence in favor of the presence of tense in the gerund clause is provided by constructions where the tense of the gerund clause and the tense of the matrix one are fixed by adverbial expressions.

(2) a. *Jenny remembers now having brought the wine yesterday.*
    b. *Jenny remembers their having brought the wine on Christmas Eve.*

I will henceforth assume that a syntactic T head is projected in verbal gerund constructions and, more generally, in the nonfinite structures where tense construal is a source of variation.[1]

However, the considerations that support the conclusion that some infinitival structures are untensed also hold in the case of gerund constructions. Pires (2006: 29) provides the following examples:

(3) a. * *Bill tried today* [PRO *talking to his boss tomorrow*].
    b. * *Philip avoided last night* [PRO *driving in the freeway this morning*].
    c. *Sue favored (yesterday)* [PRO/*Anna moving to Chicago today*].

He traces back the ungrammaticality of (3a) and (3b) to the absence in the embedded domain of a tense specification independent of that of the matrix clause. On the contrary, a tense specification is present in the embedded domain in (3c), a difference which appears to be correlated with the free alternation between null and overt subjects.

15.2 The aspectual value of the *-ing* suffix

Beside tense, another potentially relevant dimension is aspect. It has long been observed in the literature that nominalizations have specific aspectual properties

---

[1] Temporal mismatches occur in many guises in natural languages and are not specific to embedded nonfinite clauses. Ion Giurgea observes that disjoint temporal reference may also be detected in genuine nominal and adjectival espressions, as in *I remember their marriage last year, last year's presents, these formerly so fashionable clothes* . . . Of course, one doesn't want to conclude that a T head is projected in the phrases under consideration. For interesting observations on this phenomenon, see Kaneko (2002).

and both lexical and syntactic approaches have been proposed to account for their aspectual sensitivity (for an overview and references, see Alexiadou 2010b). English gerunds also manifest aspectual sensitivity, but it turns out that the -*ing* suffix exhibits almost identical properties in all its uses.[2]

Before we move forward to the characterization of the aspectual value of -*ing*, let us briefly reconsider the distinction between inner and outer aspect. The former is also referred to as Aktionsart or situation aspect, the latter as grammatical or viewpoint aspect. The latter is associated with notions like perfectivity/imperfectivity, the former with several distinct ontological dimensions concerning the internal temporal structure of the event that is referred to (Vendler's 1967 classification distinguishes between states, activities, accomplishments, achievements, to which Smith 1997 adds semelfactives). The consensus today is that the features relevant to viewpoint aspect reside in an Aspect head projected above vP, whereas situation aspect and the features that relate to the semantic class of the verbal predicate are a property of verbal heads or of verbal phrases themselves.[3] The two aspectual dimensions interfere with the distribution of V-*ing* phrases.

Among the environments where the suffix -*ing* is found in English, three cases should be distinguished: (i) the V-*ing* form appearing in the progressive construction is generally thought of as a present participle form; (ii) among the -*ing* forms that occur in non-progressive environments, verbal gerunds should be distinguished from nominal gerunds; (iii) within the class of verbal gerund structures, Acc-*ing* constructions should be distinguished from Poss-*ing* ones. It must be determined whether the V-*ing* form gives rise to different interpretations in these various uses. Let us briefly examine each of them in turn, first presenting the facts, then proposing an analysis.

It has long been known that not any verbal root can occur in the *be*+V-*ing* construction, which usually displays an imperfective interpretation independently of the inner aspect of the verb. Stative predicates however are not welcome, as (4a) shows (cf. Borer 2005, Alexiadou, Iordachioaia & Soare 2010). Imperfectivity means ongoingness at some reference time and is generally incompatible

---

[2] The idea that -*ing* has the same status in all its uses has been advanced by Milsark, who doesn't specifically apply it to aspectual value, but to syntactic categorization. According to him, this status leads one to expect that all categorial options exist: nominal, verbal, adjectival (*an interesting book*) and prepositional (*concerning your paper*). Only verbal and nominal gerunds are considered here.

[3] The reason why it is appropriate to refer to the whole verb phrase in this case is that situation aspect is a property of event descriptions and that any phrase that describes an event can have a situation aspect feature. This is the case of verbal expressions like *eat for 10 minutes, eat the cake in 10 minutes, run for 10 minutes*.

with adverbial expressions measuring the event. This is what is observed in (4b) and (4c).

(4) a. *John is knowing the answer.*
 b. *The ship was sinking for two hours.*
 c. *Yesterday, at 7, the president was speaking for two hours.*

There is no doubt that V-*ing* forms in the progressive construction function as [– perfective], [+ progressive] verbal entities. But it is not necessary to assume that they are *inherently* imperfective. The negative value of the [perfective] feature in the progressive construction could be transmitted to the gerund word (or to v) by the verb *be* itself.[4]

Let us now consider the aspectual properties of verbal gerunds and nominal gerunds. In their quantitative corpus-based analysis of the aspectual features of gerunds in present-day English, Heyvaert, Maekelberghe & Buyle's (2019) don't detect much difference between the aspectual behaviors of the two classes of constructions.

> the claim that gerunds designate unbounded activities or activities that are in progress cannot be upheld, because a significant number of both nominal and verbal gerunds denote non-durative (achievements, semelfactives) or telic (accomplishments) ones, and because most gerunds lack explicit markers of "completeness" or "ongoingness". [Heyvaert, Maekelberghe & Buyle 2019: 32]

They conclude that the suffix -*ing* has no aspectual meaning in English gerunds. As the preceding quotation shows, this conclusion encompasses both situation and viewpoint aspect. With respect to situation aspect, it means that -*ing* can potentially be affixed to any verbal stem, whatever its lexical/aspectual class, although admittedly very rarely to stative predicates in Romance and Germanic languages. With respect to viewpoint aspect, it means that -*ing* doesn't function as an imperfectivizing suffix in the relevant structures.

Considering specifically nominal gerunds, Borer (2005) has discovered that the "nominalizer -*ing*" is sensitive to the Aktionsart of the predicates involved. It is legitimate with activity or accomplishment predicates (cf. 5a), excluded with achievement predicates (cf. 5b); only a nominalization is possible in this case (cf. 5c); but the context may force the interpretation of an achievement predi-

---

4 Alternatively, if an Aspect head is assumed to be projected above vP in the relevant structures (an option that is dismissed in the following sections), V-*ing* forms could systematically raise to Asp to check or "lexicalize" their [aspect] feature; the negative value of [perfective] could be made to depend on the positive value of [progressive] in the feature matrix of Aspect.

cate as an accomplishment or an activity, as is the case in (5d) and (5e). Nominal gerunds occur very naturally with activities.[5]

(5) a. *the sinking of the ships*
    b. * *the arriving of the train*
    c. *the arrival of the train*
    d. *I was amazed at the way . . . the British newspapers combined to blame the shooting of peaceful demonstrators in the Ciskei . . .*
    e. *Third World countries are especially worried about the dumping of nuclear waste.*

But, as emphasized by Heyvaert, Maekelberghe & Buyle (2019), it would be wrong to say that "nominal gerunds zoom on activities represented as ongoing rather than completed". The only reasonable conclusion is that nominal gerund phrases inherit their inner aspect from the verb.[6] In Borer's view, nominal gerunds do not project an outer Aspect head either, since they appear to be neutral with respect to viewpoint aspect.

Verbal gerunds display similar aspectual properties. *-ing* in (6)–(8) manifests no preference for the event type of the root it attaches to. And it imposes no imperfective interpretation on the corresponding gerund phrase.[7]

(6) a. *The train arriving on time surprised us.*
    b. *The ships getting lost in the Northwest passage was a huge shock.*

(7) a. *Marcel's reading books until late in the night worries his mother.*
    b. *Mary's blinking is annoying.*
    c. *John's arriving at 5 pm is unlikely.*

(8)   *Leaving at seven, they reached the city at about one.*

Once again, verbal gerunds can refer to unbounded activities or activities in progress, but can also denote non-durative situations or telic ones, achievements or accomplishments. In (8), we find the temporal succession typical of perfective

---

[5] Examples (5a), (5b), and (5c) are discussed by Borer (2005), (5d) and (5e) come from Heyvaert, Maekelberghe & Buyle's (2019).
[6] But explaining how the inner aspect sensitivity of the affix in nominal gerunds comes about is a delicate enterprise, see Borer's (2005) and Alexiadou's (2010b) proposals.
[7] (7a), (7b), (7c) are given by Alexiadou (2010a) and Alexiadou, Iordachioaia & Soare (2010); (8) is provided by Ion Giurgea.

aspect. *-ing* can contribute a process reading or a result reading. No imperfective interpretation is imposed on telic (cf. 6a, 7c, 8) or atelic (cf. 7a, 7b) predicates which, as examples (9) show, can coexist with time measuring expressions (these expressions are excluded from the progressive construction, cf. 4 b, c).

(9) a. *John's rehearsing the opera for three days annoyed everybody.*
   b. *The ship sinking in 30 minutes surprised everyone.*
   c. *Teaching from 6 to 8 is not a good idea.*

Two analytic options present themselves: Either an Aspect head is present in non-progressive verbal gerund constructions, but it is not aspectually restricted, or no Aspect head is projected in these domains. It is the second option that is retained in the following sections: The representations that will be proposed for Acc-*ing* and for Poss-*ing* incorporate no Asp head.[8]

It must be acknowledged that some aspectual differences can be detected between verbal and nominal gerunds, as Borer's (2005) observations already establish. Heyvaert, Maekelberghe and Buyle (2019: 32) observe that "nominal gerunds tend to denote activities more often and are more likely to occur in contexts which are explicitly marked for temporal bounding or for ongoingness; verbal gerunds . . . represent significantly more often achievements or semelfactives and occur more often than nominal gerunds in neutral or unmarked contexts in terms of temporal bounding".[9] I am not in a position to propose a well-founded explanation for this subtle difference.

But these generalizations in no way jeopardize the claim that the *-ing* suffix is aspectually neutral in all the environments where X-*ing* forms occur. Recall that this conclusion also holds for the progressive construction if the verb *be* is taken to be the source of the imperfective interpretation. This means that Acc-*ing* and

---

[8] This decision conforms to Alexiadou, Iordăchioaia & Schäfer's (2011: 32–33) claim that, when there is no aspectual operator, there is no AspP projection either. The inner aspect information given by an atelic root is sufficient to give the construction its aspectual value.

[9] Among the many examples they provide, we find (i) and (ii) in which an activity or an achievement predicate is embedded in a nominal gerund and (iii) (iv) and (v) in which a state, an accomplishment or an iterative predicate heads a verbal gerund.

(i)   . . . *not connected with the running of the mine.* [activity]
(ii) . . . *within one week of the signing of the agreement.* [achievement]
(iii) . . . *holding a position . . . which is subject . . . to popular election.* [state]
(iv) . . . *the right . . . of converting a dramatic into a non-dramatic work.* [accomplishment]
(v)   . . . *by referring to a similar decision of Marcus Aurelius* [semelfactive]

Poss-*ing* constructions are not aspectually restricted and usually get an aspectual value from the predicate the -*ing* suffix attaches to.[10]

In an approach making use of a category-switching head to derive Poss-*ing* constructions, it is tempting to argue that it is the n head that is responsible not only for the categorial switch, but also for the aspectual profile of the gerund (distinct from that of finite tensed verbs). If I am right, no category switch is involved in the derivation of Acc-*ing* constructions (cf. sct. 17). Since an aspectual calculus also takes place in the structures where there is no n and no switch, n cannot be assumed to initiate the aspectual computation in Poss-*ing* constructions.

Let me summarize the results arrived at in this section.
(i) The understood tense of verbal gerund clauses is basically malleable to the semantics of the governing verb. It can refer to an event overlapping with the state of affairs described by the main clause, to a past event or to an event unrealized with respect to the tense of the matrix predicate.
(ii) V-*ing* forms are not inherently imperfective. The suffix -*ing* conveys no specific aspectual meaning. Neither nominal nor verbal gerund phrases project an outer Aspect head.

The picture that emerges is that the temporal and aspectual interpretations of verbal gerund clauses are not determined by inherent tense or aspect values attached to the -*ing* suffix, but by the *Aktionsart* of the embedded verbal root and by the tense of the matrix predicate, as well as by the lexical class it belongs to.

---

10 In the analyses that postulate an outer Aspect head in verbal gerund structures, this head is not aspectually restricted, but gets a value from situation aspect; a complex semantic calculus is required to perform the transmission of the inner aspect value to the outer Aspect head, cf. Borer (2005).

16 How gerund constructions differ from one another

16.1 How verbal gerunds differ from nominal ones

Examples (10)–(16) further illustrate the distribution of verbal gerund constructions. (10a)/(10b) are expected to be well-formed if both nominal expressions and (a subset of) clausal domains define appropriate prepositional objects.[11] Gerund phrases can also occupy a position standardly assumed to be a site where accusative case is assigned, namely the subject position of small clauses (cf. 10c, 10d).

(10) a. *I disapproved of John's killing the mocking bird.*
b. *I disapproved of John killing the mocking bird.*
c. *I consider his selling the house a big mistake.* [Cornilescu 2003]
d. *I consider him selling the house a big mistake.*

Whereas Poss-*ing* constructions are clearly welcome in positions where nominal expressions are legitimate – this is the case in (11b) and (11d) -, there is some disagreement among native speakers as to whether Acc-*ing* structures are allowed to occur in the subject position of tensed clauses. Bresnan (1982) states that "it is generally true that an Acc-*ing* construction cannot function as a subject, even in nonfinite clauses" and she gives examples (11a) and (11c) as unacceptable; she doesn't make explicit the status of (11b) and (11d); (11e) is adapted from Marantz (1978), who marks it as ungrammatical (contrary to (11f)). But Freidin (personal communication) gives (11g) as a bit awkward, but not frankly deviant, and (11h) as perfectly grammatical; Pires (2006) provides (11i) and (11j); Cornilescu (2003)

---

11 Gerund clauses can function as objects of prepositions, *that*-clauses and *for*-clauses cannot, which indicates that they are not welcome in all NP/DP positions. The following examples are ungrammatical:
(i) * *Aristotle based his theory on that Plato never contradicts Socrates.*
(ii) * *Maybel was relieved by that John killed the mocking bird.*

This suggests that they should probably not be assigned a nominal analysis (if they are not noun phrases, no explanation has to be given for the fact that they don't occur in NP/DP positions). The nominal analysis of complement clauses is discussed and rejected in ch. IX. Any account of gerund clauses has to deal with the fact that, on the contrary, they can appear in almost any noun phrase position. The labeling analysis developed in section 17 fulfills this requirement.

observes that both Acc-*ing* (cf. (11k)) and Poss-*ing* (cf. (11l)) are possible in the sites that are uncontroversial non-topic subject positions.

(11) a. Fred losing again is worried about by all his friends.
      b. Fred's losing again is worried about by all his friends.
      c. I'd like for Fred losing again not to bother you.
      d. I'd like for Fred's losing again not to bother you.
      e. * John killing the geese destroyed the liver business.
      f. John's killing the geese destroyed the liver business.
      g. John killing the geese destroyed our faith in him.[12]
      h. The grand jury indicting those bankers for fraud will shock Wall Street.
      i. John reading the book was much preferred.
      j. Sue showing up at the game surprised everybody.
      k. Would John performing the aria please you?
      l. Did John's performing the aria please you?[13]

Four additional characteristics shared by the two constructions are their non-extraposability ((12)), their compatibility with clausal negation ((13)) and with sentential adverbs ((14)) and the possible occurrence of perfect auxiliaries ((15)).

(12) a. * It's unlikely Bill's making a fortune.   [Cornilescu]
      b. * It's unlikely Bill making a fortune.

(13) a. We protested against his not receiving the grant.
      b. We protested against him not receiving the grant.

(14) a. John's probably being a spy was hard news for the director of the Agency to take.
      b. John probably being a spy was hard news for the director of the Agency to take.

---

12 Examples (11g), (11h) and (11j) also marginally admit an analysis and an interpretation in which the gerund is built as a clausal adjunct (this would be the only choice if commas were inserted at the beginning and at the end of the gerund phrase). But the adjunct construal of the gerund is not available in examples (11i) and (11k).

13 Here are some additional (attested) examples, coming from various sources.

(i) a. John doing that makes zero sense.
     b. Him doing that makes you feel cheated.
     c. Him throwing it over his shoulder completely destroyed all that.

(15) a. *His having criticized the book came as a huge surprise.*
b. *Him having criticized the book came as a huge surprise.*

The compatibility with clausal negation and with sentential adverbs is a clue that T is projected, cf. (13) and (14). Examples like (15) indicate that verbal gerund complexes can include an additional head, which is the first Merge site of auxiliaries and can be an Aspect head or an additional verbal head. Cornilescu (2003) notes that given the general tendency of English auxiliaries to end up in T, the presence of *have* in (15a) and (15b) in fact provides additional support for the claim that T is present in verbal gerunds.

It is easy to check that nominal gerund phrases, which can only occupy argument positions, cannot function as predicates in absolute constructions (cf. 16a), cannot include a sentential negation (cf. 16b), cannot display aspectual distinctions (cf. 16c, 16d) and are not allowed to extrapose (cf. 16e).

(16) a. * *The chess champion's making of a decisive move, the other player resigned.*
b. * *We protested against her not folding of the napkins.*
c. * *We protested against her having folded of the napkins.*
d. * *His having criticized of the book was unexpected.*
e. * *It's unlikely Bill's winning of the race.*

They cannot define control domains either, a property to which we turn in the next subsection.

16.2 PRO-*ing* constructions

In the contexts that allow Acc-*ing* and Poss-*ing*, gerunds can also be subjectless. If a subject position is indeed projected in the relevant structures, the most plausible candidate to occupy it is PRO. A third construction should thus be defined, namely PRO-*ing*.[14]

(17) *I avoided* [PRO *meeting him*]

PRO-*ing* is found in object positions (cf. 18a, 18b) and subject positions (cf. 18c-18e).

---

14 This label is used by Abney (1987).

(18) a. *I abhor singing.*
 b. *I abhor singing operas.*
 c. *Reforming the French educational system turned out to be an impossible task.*
 d. *Listening to Bob's obsessional criticism of the TGG bored Andy to death.*
 e. *Interviewing Richard Nixon gave Norman Mailer a headache.*

These verbal PRO-*ing* constructions should be distinguished from nominal gerund ones, which display a different syntax, as the comparison between (19a) and (19b)/(19c) and between (19d) and (19e) demonstrates.[15]

(19) a. *I detest loud singing.*
 b. *I detest singing loudly.*
 c. *I enjoy singing the blues.*
 d. *The killing of his dog upset John.*
 e. *Killing his dog upset John.*

Wasow & Roeper (1972) conclude that control occurs in verbal gerund constructions, which they call "activity gerunds", not in nominal ones. If the former are analyzable as clauses with a PRO subject, the latter are subjectless domains. Some verbal gerund structures clearly display obligatory control (cf. 19b, 19c), but it is easy to find cases illustrating the phenomenon usually referred to as optional control. The null subject of the gerund may be assigned an arbitrary generic interpretation (cf. 20a, 20b) or an unspecified one (cf. 20c); control may be long-distance with the controller not being included in the immediately higher clause (cf. 20d); partial/split control, which Landau classifies as a particular case of obligatory control, is also available (cf. 20e).

(20) a. *The law forbids shooting deers.*
 b. *I disapprove of shouting loudly.*
 c. *Building a bridge was undertaken.*
 d. *Harold knew that forgetting his umbrella would make it rain.*
 e. *I argued with John about leaving the country.*

The null hypothesis is that the PRO subject of gerunds is interpreted along the same lines as the PRO subject of infinitives.

---

[15] The pairs (19a), (19b) and (19d), (19e) are from Wasow & Roeper (1972). (20a), (20b), (20c) are from Wasow & Roeper (1972), (20d) and (20e) from Cornilescu (2003).

Examples (3) show that subjectless gerunds do not constitute an homogeneous class. The complements to aspectual verbs, like *start, finish, continue*, and verbs like *try* and *avoid* (cf. 3a, 3b) are characterized by Pires (2006) as "TP-defective gerunds", because they do not display a tense (and aspect) specification independent from that of the matrix clause. This is not the case of the null-subject gerund clauses found with other predicates, *favor* for example (cf. 3c). In Landau's classification, the gerund complement of exhaustive control predicates like *try* and *avoid* would be specified as [– T], the complement of *favor* as [+ T].

Now that four gerund types have been identified, it remains to be decided whether each constitutes an independent syntactic entity or whether some pairs can be collapsed into a single type. Pires (2006) argues that the PRO-*ing* construction should be viewed as the subjectless counterpart of the Acc-*ing* construction – the two function as complements to the same predicates – and that both should be conceived of as clausal domains: They are "far more sentential" in their internal structure and external shape than the other two. Conversely, Poss-*ing* constructions and nominal gerund constructions resemble each other as far as the surface realization of the external argument is concerned. It must be decided whether these parallelisms are real and whether they each reflect identical mappings of external arguments onto syntactic structures.[16]

16.3 Some differences between Acc-*ing* and Poss-*ing* constructions

Some differences can be detected between Acc-*ing* and Poss-*ing* constructions. The contrast between (21a) and (21b) confirms the clausal status of the former and the nominal status of the latter. Extraction out of propositional domains is generally possible, whereas extraction out of definite noun phrases produces ungrammaticality.

(21) a.   *the city which we remember him describing* [__]
      b. * *the city which we remember his describing* [__]

Other operations that clearly cannot apply to Poss-*ing* constructions are *there*-insertion and expletive insertion, as shown by the ungrammaticality of examples (22a) and (22b), given by Yoon (1996) and left for future research by Borsley &

---

[16] For a very clear exposition of the problem, see Moulton (2004).

Kornfilt (2000). These elements freely occur in Acc-*ing* constructions, as the minimal pair (23a)/(23b) provided by Pires (2006) illustrates.

(22) a. *there's being a spy in the closet.*
 b. *its being obvious that Bill is a spy.*

(23) a. *You may count on there being a lot of trouble tonight.*
 b. **You may count on there's being a lot of trouble tonight.*

Another syntactic difference distinguishing the two constructions is mentioned by Horn (1975) and concerns agreement in coordinate structures.

(24) a. *John coming so often and Mary leaving so often bothers / *bother Mum.*
 b. *John's coming and Mary's leaving *bothers / bother Mum.*

Once again, Poss-*ing* constructions in subject positions behave as full DPs, triggering agreement, whereas coordinated Acc-*ing* structures exclude it, which, at least in this respect, makes them similar to tensed clauses.

Acc-*ing* structures can, Poss-*ing* structures cannot function as absolute constructions, which confirms the clausal status of the former and the non-clausal status of the latter.[17]

(25) a. *John obviously being a spy, Bill tried to avoid him.*
 b. **John's obviously being a spy, Bill tried to avoid him.*

An additional asymmetry between Poss-*ing* and Acc-*ing* gerunds is that whereas Poss-*ing* are not allowed to extrapose, (cf. 16e), Acc-*ing* can, but under very strict conditions: The gerund domain must be separated from what precedes by a pause, cf. (26a)/(26b).[18]

(26) a. **It surprised me Mary's leaving town.*
 b. *It surprised me # Mary leaving town.*

---

[17] The V-*ing* form involved in absolute constructions is often analyzed as a verbal participle, rather than as a gerund.
[18] Tensed complements do not require a pause when extraposed.

Similarly, Poss-*ing* gerunds cannot host result clauses, as discovered by Williams (1975).¹⁹ A quick survey reveals that Acc-*ing* gerunds can (cf. 27a, 27b, 27c, 27d).

(27) a. * *Mary's leaving so much money to John that he became snobbish is a pity.*
 b. *Mary leaving so much money to John that he became snobbish is a pity.*
 c. * *John's leaving town so quickly that no one knew he was gone was unexpected.*
 d. *John leaving town so quickly that no one knew he was gone was unexpected*

Sentence adverbs like *probably* are ungrammatical in Poss-*ing* gerund phrases, awkward but not ungrammatical, with Acc-*ing* (cf 28a, 28b).

(28) a. * *John's probably giving the book to Mary bothers me.*
 b. ? *John probably giving the book to Mary bothers me.*

The distribution of *probably* and that of result clauses can be viewed as scope-sensitive phenomena. Williams (1975) also discusses an interpretive characteristic of Poss-*ing* having to do with the scope of *because*:

(29) a. *John's not killing his wife because he loved her...* [unambiguous]
 b. *John not killing his wife because he loved her...* [ambiguous]

Sentence (29a), which contains a Poss-*ing* construction including a *because*-clause, is unambiguous: The *because*-clause is necessarily interpreted as being in the scope of negation. The parallel sentence with Acc-*ing* (29b) is ambiguous: The *because*-clause can also be interpreted as being outside the scope of negation, which indicates that it can occupy a position outside the c-command domain of negation. Finite clauses with *because* display a similar ambiguity.

Cornilescu (2003) also discusses interpretive differences between the two constructions related to the scope of quantifiers.

(30) a. *John doesn't approve of everyone taking a day off.*
 b. *John doesn't approve of everyone's taking a day off.*

---

19 Examples in (27a), (27c), (28a), (29a) are to be found in Williams's (1975) celebrated paper on small clauses, which only takes Poss-*ing* gerunds into consideration. Williams's initial goal was to show that the relevant phrases are not NPs dominating CPs, but clauses with no C and no T, "shallow clauses". The Acc-*ing* examples (27b), (27d), (28b), (29b) reproduce the judgments Edwin Williams gave me when I submitted them to him.

(30a) is unambiguous: *everyone* can only take narrow scope with respect to negation. (30b) has two readings, in function of the relative scopes of the quantifier and the negation.

Can these phenomena be integrated into a consistent whole? The interpretive contrast between (30a) and (30b) is as expected if the calculus of quantifier scope is taken to be a clause-bound process. The fact that the quantifier is allowed to take wide scope (i.e to scope over negation) in the Poss-*ing* construction and cannot do so in the Acc-*ing* construction is easily explained if the former is analyzed as a nominal expression and the latter as a clausal domain. It is more delicate to account for the scope phenomena discussed by Williams. Some semantic relations appear to require wide scope (interpretation of *probably*, of *because*, of result clauses). The interpretive contrasts observed between Acc-*ing* (where these relations are possible) and Poss-*ing* (where these relations are blocked) do not necessarily show that the former have a greater size than the latter.[20] But they indicate that the space available to the semantic calculus is larger in Acc-*ing* than in Poss-*ing*: In Acc-*ing*, it encompasses the whole structure, which is a clausal domain, in Poss-*ing*, it coincides with the internal vP and doesn't extend further (because the category-switching n is the head of a different non-clausal projection, possibly the head of a distinct phase).

With respect to the divide between Acc-*ing* and Poss-*ing*, all analytic options have been contemplated and argued for by linguists. Abney (1987) observes that Poss-*ing* constructions are less sentential than Acc-*ing* ones, but strongly differ from nominal gerund phrases. Extending to Acc-*ing* Emonds's (1970) and Chomsky's (1970) analyses of Poss-*ing*, Portner (1994), Asher (1993), Cornilescu (2003) claim that the two constructions are DP projections embedding a TP. On the contrary, Williams (1975), as just mentioned, argues that Poss-*ing* gerund phrases never are NPs, but projections of V, Miller (2002) that they should be viewed as TP domains in all their uses. Finally, Reuland (1983), Johnson (1988) and Pires

---

[20] To account for these distributions (and for the cases where Poss-*ing* and Acc-*ing* behave alike), Williams (1975) distinguishes several levels of structure within the clause, which each contain elements and phrases that are more and more distant from the verb: Subcategorized direct objects form class I, *for*-datives belong to class II, the grammatical subject position defines class III, the complementizer system is included in class IV. Transformations can be categorized as to whether they strictly apply within a given domain and not within a higher one. Passive and nominative case assignment occur when domain III is reached. Subject auxiliary inversion, result clause extraposition exclusively take place in domain IV. We know today that clauses don't have the type of fishbone structure he presupposes (see also Williams 1974) and that binary and uniform downward branching phrase structures should be preferred (the adjuncts he locates high in the tree in fact occupy a low position, result clauses are a case in point). The fact remains that some of his findings on gerunds still await a solution within current syntactic theorizing.

(2006) describe Acc-*ing* as IPs/TPs, Poss-*ing* as NPs (in fact DPs). My contention is that the differences between Acc-*ing* and Poss-*ing* listed in this section provide sufficient evidence against a unified account and motivate the assignment of distinct categorial analyses to them. As already argued in chapter III, Acc-*ing* should be identified as CPs/FinP domains, Poss-*ing* as DP projections.

16.4 Two shared properties

The two types of verbal gerund constructions with an overt subject share a couple of syntactic properties that have not been mentioned up to now and can help to fix the limits of variation: Auxiliary gerund forms clearly raise out of vP; the subject argument occupies the phrase-initial position, which is the highest one in the gerund domain.

16.4.1 The syntax of gerund heads

Up to now, I have left it a moot point whether the gerund forms in Acc-*ing* and Poss-*ing* constructions move to some higher head: Do they reach T or do they remain within vP?

In Poss-*ing* constructions, manner adverbs can freely follow the gerund+object complex or immediately precede it, but they cannot occur in between the gerund and its object.[21]

(31) a. *Their launching the ship promptly* ...
 b. *He proposed our immediately drinking a bottle together.* [Fielding]
 c. *That it is the same movement is clearly shown by their often at the same time taking a bit in their mouth.* [Darwin]
 d. *His throat ... cut ... without his ever knowing it ...*

Interestingly, *all* and *both* systematically precede the gerund form of lexical verbs, but follow *being*, as the contrast between the two following Jane Austen's examples shows.

---

[21] Most of the examples in this section come from literary sources and are drawn from Jespersen (1940).

(32) a. *the assurance of their being all settled in London for the winter* ...
 b. *the confusion that might arise from our both addressing the same lady assurances of their both being alive* ...

This contrast suggests that *being* raises higher than the *-ing* forms of lexical verbs (*addressing* in 32b) and strongly recalls what is observed in English finite tensed clauses. We conclude that *being* raises as high as T and that non-auxiliary V-*ing* forms stay in v.

Acc-*ing* and PRO-*ing* constructions basically follow the same distributional pattern in this respect and point to the same conclusion. (33d) confirms that *having* has the same syntax as *being*.

(33) a. *John cleverly selling the house when prices were high amazed all of us.*
 b. *Peter probably arriving late worried his wife.*
 c. *She liked to think of Trafford very rapidly and easily coming forward.*
 d. *Without Paul having ever offered to help them* ...

(34) a. *Demosthenes with often breathing up the hill amended his stammering.*
 b. *Always eating cabbage when I had dinner was no fun.*
 c. *Being all settled in London for the winter is a nice perspective.*

In conclusion, adverbial distributions in English verbal gerund constructions reveal that gerund heads display the same syntactic properties as the finite verbal forms in this language.

16.4.2 The subject of verbal gerunds

A sometimes overlooked characteristic of Acc-*ing* verbal gerund structures is that they constitute appropriate domains for DP-raising.[22] The fact that in these constructions, sentential adverbs, which are projected high in the structure, intervene between the raised subject and the gerund form (cf. 33a, 33b) indicates that the subject itself moves to an even higher position. In a bare phrase structure approach, the relevant adverb is pair-merged with TP and the subject is merged with the object resulting from the first operation. Adopting Chomsky's (2013a,

---

22 Following Chomsky's (1970) lead, the question of the subject of gerunds was a much discussed topic at the beginning of the 70s, see Wasow & Roeper (1972) and Thompson (1973). For more recent contributions interested in the syntactic mapping of the external argument in gerund structures, see Kratzer (1996), Moulton (2004) and Pires (2006).

2015) claim that Internal Merge systematically gives rise to an exocentric structure, the raising of the subject from its original position inside vP produces configurations where it successively occupies the positions adjoined to the higher functional projections TP and CP, as representations (35b), (35c) and (35d) assume.

(35) a. *John describing the accident*   Acc-*ing*
      b. [$_{CP}$ C [$_{TP}$ [T] [$_a$ John [$_{vP}$ v [$_{RootP}$ [ing] [√DESCRIBE the accident]]]]]]
      c. [$_{CP}$ C [[$_{DP}$ John] [$_{TP}$ [T] [John [$_{vP}$ v [$_{RootP}$ [ing] [√DESCRIBE the accident]]]]]]
      d. [[$_{DP}$ John] [$_{CP}$ C [[$_{DP}$ John] [$_{TP}$ [T] [John [$_{vP}$ v [$_{RootP}$ [ing] [√DESCRIBE the accident]]]]]]]

I will argue in section 18 that a different scenario is involved in the derivation of Poss-*ing* constructions: There is no internal movement of the subject argument in this case, which is spelled out in its first merge position (SpecDP) and case licensed there, as shown in (36b).

(36) a. *John's describing the accident*   Poss-*ing*
      b. [$_{DP}$ [$_{DP}$ John] [$_{DP}$ [$_D$'s] [$_{nP}$ n [$_{TP}$ T [$_{vP}$ v [$_{RootP}$ [ing] [√DESCRIBE the accident]]]]]]]

Tightly linked to the selection of different derivational paths is the choice of distinct strategies to determine the categorial identity of each domain: A labeling account is appropriate for Acc-*ing* constructions, a category-switching one for Poss-*ing* ones.

17 A labeling analysis of Acc-*ing* constructions

The aim of this section is to flesh out Pires's (2006) insight that Acc-*ing* structures with an overt subject include a null T head that "carries a special feature that is instrumental in the assignment of case to the subject". Gerund T, which is neither overt nor finite, is exceptional in this respect and it must be asked how it comes to enjoy this privilege in the first place. The consensus has long been that it displays this property because it is accessible to a case licensing external head, which checks the case of the whole gerund expression it governs, allowing T itself to function as a case assigner for the subject. The governing head can be P or V or matrix T (before the gerund clause adjoins to TP). Several accounts indeed rely on the claim that the case licensing of the subject in these constructions indirectly depends on the presence of an external governor, which we know is there because gerund clauses generally occupy positions where case is available. In Reuland's (1983) analysis, the element -*ing* is a nominal agreement marker that must be assigned case to itself function as a case assigner (see also Johnson 1988, Cornilescu 2003). An alternative approach assumes that the licensing of the subject doesn't depend on the presence of an external head, but strictly relies on resources available within the gerund expression. Adopting Schütze's (1997) proposal that accusative is the morphological default case in English, Miller (2002) argues that the case of the subject in Acc-*ing* constructions is a default. In this section, I defend the view that the licensing of Acc-*ing* subjects is performed exclusively within the boundaries of the gerund expression and that their raising directly contributes to the labeling of the latter.

17.1 Categorial architecture and feature structure

Evidence was provided that supports the presence in Acc-*ing* gerund constructions of a v head (direct assignment of accusative case to the internal argument; possibility of an overt external argument plausibly originating in the "specifier" of vP) and of a T head (compatibility with negation, semantic tenseness). To account for the well-formedness of perfect auxiliaries in these constructions (cf. 15b), it can be assumed that auxiliaries originate in an external v head projected immediately above vP.[23] This proposal, which dispenses with the projection of an Aspect head, takes care of the tight relation existing between T and aspectual auxiliaries. It was

---

[23] Emonds (1970) proposes to analyze auxiliaries as verbs selecting verb phrases. The extra vP projection is such that it is a sister to T and its v head selects a vP projection.

also assumed that C is projected in Acc-*ing* constructions, cf. (35 b, c, d). We end up with the functional architecture (37). Representation (38), where all lexical and functional elements occupy their first Merge position, includes the feature information that is lacking in (35b).

(37) C > T > (v) > v > √ing – √X

(38) C   [$_{TP}$ T   [$_α$ John [$_{vP}$ v [$_{RootP}$ [√ing – √DESCRIBE the accident]]]]]
      u-φ   u-φ   i-φ
      u-case   u-case   u-case

As has been argued in 16.4, the positioning of gerund forms with respect to adverbs in these constructions can be made sense of if one assumes that T has properties comparable to those of finite T. Lexical verbs are not allowed to raise to T, auxiliaries must raise to T. The same conclusion is arrived at if one considers the way the subject is case licensed. If one follows Pires's (2006) claim, the availability of Acc-*ing* constructions, as well as that of absolute constructions, is a sure indication that null T in the relevant structures is endowed with a case feature and uninterpretable φ-features, plausibly inherited from C, that have the same checking strength as the corresponding features in finite tensed clauses.

But if the minimalist checking-by-valuation procedure works in gerund clauses along the same lines as in finite clauses, one can immediately dismiss Case Theory as a possible trigger of DP-raising in Acc-*ing* structures. In (38), T is endowed with uninterpretable φ-features that must be valued and erased; it also bears a case feature that must be checked. This is achieved via the establishment of an Agree relation between T's uninterpretable features acting as a probe and the features of the nominal expression in SpecvP acting as a goal. The case licensing of the subject is achieved internally to T' and the identity of the case assigned doesn't depend on the presence of an external governor.[24] The inherited case feature, which, like its counterpart on the vP-internal subject, is uninterpretable on T, is checked together with T's φ-features. Once its case feature has been checked and deleted, the nominal expression is not active anymore and cannot enter into a relation with another checking head. In particular, no relation can be established between the raised subject occupying the edge of the gerund clause and the external environment. In a theory of grammar in which case checking

---

[24] "Government" is here taken as a purely descriptive term with no theoretical content and refers to the structural relation existing between a head that minimally c-commands a phrase (which, in the general case, it is subcategorized for) and this phrase. It also covers the relation between the head and the specifier of the phrase that it minimally c-commands.

reduces to an Agree relation and that has the EPP at its disposal, whichever form is given to it, the obligatory raising of the subject in finite clauses can only be traced back to an EPP-type principle, not to Case Theory. Verbal gerund constructions also display an EPP-like effect. The problem is to discover the best way to derive this effect. A crucial question to which EPP cannot provide an answer is how come Acc-*ing* constructions, if they are analyzed as in (38), that is, as CP domains with an overt subject, and derived as in (35), are allowed to occupy nominal positions. These questions receive a unified answer once the way gerund clauses are labeled is taken into consideration.

17.2 The effect of labeling

An explanation of the raising property seems to be attainable if one reasons in labeling terms. Chomsky proposes the Labeling Algorithm in (39) in order to guarantee that symmetric structures are assigned a label:[25]

(39) **Labeling Algorithm**
If X and Y are identical in one respect and, in particular, share some feature, this feature is selected as the label of SO; in this case, the label is the "pair of agreeing elements" (Chomsky 2015).

Simple finite clauses in English are among the configurations to which (39) is directly relevant, if one adopts the conception of phrase-structure building developed in Chomsky (2013a, 2015), where the applications of Internal Merge (phrasal movement) systematically create set-merge exocentric structures. Recourse to (39) is unavoidable in the clausal domains headed by a category that is not strong enough to provide the projection that dominates it with a categorial label. The clausal domains headed by a defective or categorially unspecified head fall into this category and V-*ing* forms and their projections fit the description. If one grants the claim that the labels resulting from (39) contribute to the satisfaction of the subcategorization requirements of selecting heads, the DP-raising process taking place in Acc-*ing* constructions should be viewed as a free untriggered operation, whose result is to produce a labelable structure. The resulting label is <φ, φ>. This noun-like label explains why these essentially verbal structures are welcome in nominal positions (recall they are legitimate in the direct object position of transitive verbal predicates, in the complement position of some prepositions, in the

---

25 (39) has been introduced and discussed in (4), ch. II.

subject position of clauses). But it would be foolhardy to claim that a projection labeled <φ, φ> is undistinguishable from a NP/DP projection, in other words that the labels <φ, φ> and NP/DP are strictly equivalent. It would also be meaningless: There is no way in which a nominal expression like *the description of the accident* can be thought of as being <φ, φ>. Keeping on the safe side, one can assume that the label <φ, φ> suffices to mark the domain that bears it as a content appropriate to occupy nominal positions; it certainly doesn't identify it as a NP/DP projection. In the analysis proposed here, Acc-*ing* constructions are not NP/DP projections, but CP/FinP projections labeled <φ, φ>.

Let us go through the derivation of the expression *John describing the accident*. (35d), reproduced here as (40), represents the final stage.

(40)   [$_γ$ [$_{DP}$ John] [$_{CP}$ C [$_β$ [$_{DP}$ ~~John~~] [$_{TP}$ T [$_α$ ~~John~~ [$_{vP}$ [$_v$ describing]
        [$_{RootP}$ [Ving] [~~√DESCRIBE~~ the accident]]]]]]]]

The DP subject first externally merges with the vP projection. It is case licensed in its first Merge position via the establishment of an Agree relation with the uninterpretable features on T. But the domain α, which contains it, is an exocentric structure if one assumes that External Merge also gives rise to such configurations. It is not labelable. Internally merging the DP subject with the TP projection again creates an exocentric structure. But this time, we are dealing with a configuration in which DP and T share φ-features, which suffices to label the {DP, TP} configuration as <φ, φ>. This is the stage represented in (35c). What happens at the CP-level? A possibility is that the procedure at work at the TP-level is repeated at the CP-level. To the extent that C transmits features to T, it is natural to analyze it as being included in T's extended projection and to assume that the relevant φ-features on C survive until the completion of the CP phase.[26] DP adjoins to CP and shares φ-features with C, ensuring the labeling of the resulting complex object. The resulting label is again <φ, φ>. This label, being nominal in nature, allows Acc-*ing* constructions, which are essentially verbal expressions, to occupy positions reserved for nominal expressions.

Under which conditions is labeling via feature-sharing available ? The T head must be endowed with φ-features, which is the case (recall that the null T present in gerund clauses has the same checking potential as finite T, as far as their respective subjects are concerned). For this scenario to go through, it is

---

[26] Another possibility would consist in claiming that the Share option (cf. Ouali 2008) is involved in the relevant structures: C keeps a copy of the uninterpretable φ-features it transmits to T, with the result that the two heads are active.

necessary to assume that the uninterpretable φ's on T remain accessible after valuation. As already mentioned, the recourse to labeling via feature-sharing is the only option when the head of the projection that is adjoined to is not in a position to insure the proper labeling of the corresponding projection. In gerund clauses, the T head is weak because -*ing* is not itself specified for any specific φ-feature value.[27] I leave it an open question whether this strategy remains available when the relevant head is strong or whether the label of the whole constituent is necessarily that of the head (cf. sct. 5).

In this approach based on the labeling requirement, the nominal distribution of Acc-*ing* gerund constructions is traced back to a property they independently display: the raising of the nominal subject. The EPP effect observed in these constructions is captured without invoking the presence of an [EPP] feature on the internal T. Before it can be concluded that the labeling strategy has a real advantage over alternative options, the conditions that govern it must be made explicit and its scope properly defined.

17.3 The respective scopes of labeling and category switching

In the framework of assumptions in which my analyses of nonfinite domains are couched, the Labeling Algorithm (39) coexists with the claim that the grammar has at its disposal a set of dedicated category-defining heads including v and n. n can also function as a category-switching head, that is, be inserted above a vP projection or above an extended verbal projection and nominalize it.[28] The latter assumption gives rise to structures like (41):

(41) [$_{nP}$ n [...[$_{vP}$ DP [v ...]]]]

On the other hand, the effect of the Labeling Algorithm LA is to identify the label α in (42) as <φ, φ>.

---

[27] When one deals with Acc-*ing* constructions, the φ-features that the verbal head and T make available are those of -*ing*, an affix that is not specified for any value and can thus agree with any nominal or pronominal expression, whatever its person and number specifications. One must conclude that the Agree relation that assigns a value to these φ's is sensitive to their not being distinct from those of the DP goal, not to their being identical to them, as is the case in standard agreement relations. The same observation holds for the <φ, φ> pair involved in labeling : The two φ's are required to be non-distinct. The status of the -*ing* affix is reconsidered in subsection 20.2. in relation to control structures.
[28] See sct. 9 and 10.

(42) [$_\alpha$ [DP]$_\varphi$ [X$_\varphi$ [~~DP~~$_\varphi$ [v ...]]]]

The grammar thus makes available two ways in which an initially verbal projection can be turned into a domain having the external distribution of a nominal expression, LA and category switching. The coexistence of two mechanisms which apparently produce similar results potentially raises a serious difficulty. It appears however that the conditions under which each device can be used strongly differ and that the resulting structures in fact display quite distinct properties.

The resort to the category-switching device is appropriate when the structure dealt with has a clearly deverbal status and combines verbal properties (at the bottom of the tree) and nominal ones (at the top). It will be argued that Poss-*ing* constructions incorporate a nominalizer and that the '*s* subject doesn't originate in the vP substructure, but is first merged in its spell-out position. In this particular case, there is no movement from the vP substructure to the nP/DP superstructure.

The conditions that must be met for labeling via movement and φ-sharing to be available are quite different (and turn out to be irrelevant when a strongly mixed projection is involved):

(i) DP movement is not triggered by case or agreement considerations. In simple finite clauses and in Acc-*ing* constructions, the moved DP has already been case licensed when it moves and is not an active goal anymore;

(ii) DP movement is not an Agree (probe-goal) operation, but a *free untriggered process*, whose effect is to make labeling via feature sharing possible;

(iii) the φ-sharing condition is fulfilled only if the initial DP and the head of the sister projection XP are endowed with φ-features (this relation identifies the two entities involved as standing in a predication relation); in order to make the theory tighter, it could be assumed that X can only be T (and maybe C, see the discussion of 40).

(iv) no change of categorial identity is involved – the verbal/clausal status of the sister constituent is preserved from bottom to top.

In conclusion, no overlap exists between the structures where category switches are needed and those where the Labeling Algorithm can be used.

18 A category-switching analysis of Poss-*ing* constructions

It has been argued in section 17 that Acc-*ing* constructions exclusively resort to the Labeling Algorithm and entirely dispense with the insertion of a switch above the vP projection. I now intend to show that Poss-*ing* constructions make use of a nominalizer.

I will take the functional architecture in (43) as a working hypothesis. The representation it generates is schematized in (44) (all elements are represented in their first Merge position).

(43) D > n > T > (v) > v > √*ing* – √X
      v is defective

(44) [$_\alpha$ [$_{DP}$ John] [$_{DP}$ [$_D$'s] [$_{nP}$ n [$_{TP}$ T [$_{vP}$ v [$_{RootP}$ √*ing* √kill the mocking bird]]]]]][29]

A priori, we don't know whether the DP subject originates within the vP, as in Acc-*ing* constructions, or is first merged in its spell-out position __ 's, as is the case in standard nominal constructions resorting to the Saxon genitive (and also plausibly in nominal gerund constructions). (44) presupposes that the second option is correct. The movement option encounters several difficulties and should be discarded. First, it assumes that DP-movement can and, in this case, must take place within a structure that, in some of its aspects, looks very much like a nominal phrase. This goes against Williams's (1982) observation that DP-movement is much restricted inside complex nominals, a restriction which he traced back to their not being domains for subject-predicate relations. The same observation holds for Poss-*ing* constructions.

(45) a. * *John's appearance* [~~John~~ *to leave*]
      b. * *John's appearing* [~~John~~ *to leave*]

---

[29] Representation (44) assumes that D is projected in the relevant structure. An alternative analysis would be to claim that D doesn't systematically head nominal expressions, which can also be "bare" nPs. If this assumption was the one adopted for the analysis of Poss-*ing*, the ungrammaticality of the definite article in these structures (cf. 11b, ch. III) would follow straightforwardly. The raising of the argument subject and its merger with TP would suffice to identify the label of the nominal expression with <φ, φ>. This proposal should be discarded however because D is the *locus* of the [definiteness] feature and Poss-*ing* constructions systematically have a definite interpretation, not an indefinite one.

As shown by examples (25), repeated here as (46a) and (46b), Poss-*ing* constructions don't accept expletive subjects either.

(46) a. * there's being a spy in the closet
　　　b. * its being obvious that Bill is a spy

The reason why (46a) and (46b) are ungrammatical is twofold. First, if one assumes that *there* and *it* are spelled out in their first Merge position and that they are endowed with uninterpretable features that need to be disposed of, no head in the Poss-*ing* structure is equipped to value them. In (46a), T has not inherited φ-features from a higher C and, if such features were available, they would be used to license the postverbal argument *a spy*. Second, there is no position in (46b) the expletive *it* could have raised from and it couldn't be inserted in a θ-position anyway. Grimshaw (1990: 82–83) adduces examples (47a) and (47c) as evidence that the SpecDP position (the position adjoined to DP in my analysis) in Poss-*ing* gerunds is not a target for A-movement and correlates this restriction with its θ-status. The comparison between (47a) and (47b) and between (47c) and (47d) confirms that Poss-*ing* gerunds lack a passive form.[30]

(47) a. * the tree's felling the trees
　　　b. John's felling the trees
　　　c. * the city's destroying the city
　　　d. the enemy's destroying the city

It must be concluded that Poss-*ing* and Acc-*ing* constructions do not follow the same derivational paths and that the strategies used to license the subject are different. The introduction of the external argument is necessarily done differently in the two constructions, since the __'s position is a θ-position. It cannot be claimed either that the internal structure of Poss-*ing* and that of Acc-*ing* are parallel (up to the higher DP or CP projection), with the vPs in the two constructions having identical properties, and, at the same time, assume that [$_D$'s] is responsible for the case licensing of the subject. If the subject had been previously case licensed (via Agree with T), it couldn't get an additional case at the

---

30 But the fact that (i) has a reading where *John* is interpreted rather low in the nominal tree could support the movement analysis of __'s nominals, as Ion Giurgea observes.

(i) I will leave the question open.
　　John's former house
　　meaning "the house that belonged to John, but doesn't anymore."

D-level. Similarly, if the external argument is θ-licensed within the vP, it cannot move to the __'s position, taken to be an unrestricted θ-position in constructions such as *John's house, Mary's willingness to help* ... [31]

But if the subject is first merged at the edge of DP, the v head itself must be assumed to be defective: It doesn't host an external argument in its specifier, even when the root is transitive or unergative. The only feature the T head is endowed with is in fact an interpretable [tense] feature. If the T head was endowed with the same features as in the Acc-*ing* construction, the presence of φ-features on T and the absence of a subject argument in SpecvP would be difficult to reconcile. What does the θ-defectiveness of v – the fact that its specifier doesn't host an external argument – result from? The φ-defectiveness of T could play a role and should itself be traced back to D not transmitting φ-features to T, contrary to C. But the category-switching head n inserted immediately above TP in (44) could also hold the key to the problem under discussion. What are the effects of the insertion of n on the various relations internal to TP? Concerning direct objects, the licensing properties of v are not affected, which indicates that the features that the phase head v transmits to the root it c-commands are preserved. But no external argument is inserted into the specifier of vP, which ceases to function as a θ-position. My proposal is that n is responsible for v not introducing any external argument. Since n in this case functions as a category-switching head, not a category-defining head, it can only access full words, not roots. And the elements that can be affected should probably stand in the immediate locality of n. I will nevertheless assume that n in (43)/(44) has access to v and to vP over T, deleting v's external argument slot. In other words, the gerund form behaves in all cases as if it had raised to T, which it does only when it is an auxiliary.

In this connection, it must be determined which dimension triggers the raising of auxiliary gerunds in Poss-*ing* constructions. Since no feature valuing is involved in this case, the movement of auxiliaries to T (cf. 15a) evidenced by adverbial distributions (cf. 32a, 32b), would not result from the necessity to make the interpretable [tense] feature on T visible (it needn't be made visible in the constructions that do not contain an auxiliary), but from the auxiliaries being inherently tensed, which non-auxiliary lexical heads are not.

In support of this analysis of Poss-*ing* constructions, it should be noted that the motivation underlying the subject-raising process in Acc-*ing* nominals is absent in these constructions. The presence of D suffices to label the expression as nominal, without the movement of the subject being necessary. More gener-

---

31 If no movement of the subject is involved in gerund domains like *John's killing the mocking bird*, the grammar must include a specific "θ-checking device" making sure that the role borne by the __'s DP matches one of the roles made available by the lexical root. This proposal also holds for derived nominal constructions, see Rouveret 1987, 1994.

ally, Poss-*ing* constructions display the mismatches that are typical of mixed projections and the movement analysis would not capture this mixed status.

Summarizing: In Poss-*ing* constructions,

(i) v makes accusative case available, when the gerund is a transitive predicate;
(ii) v is θ-defective: it doesn't host an external argument in its specifier (that is, doesn't stand in a sister relation with an external argument);
(iii) no C head is projected above TP; T exclusively bears an interpretable [tense] feature and is thus syntactically inactive;
(iv) a category-switching head n is projected above TP, turning the resulting structure into a nominal expression;
(v) a D head is projected above n;
(vi) the position where the expression functioning as the external argument is spelled out is its first Merge position; it either occupies the specifier of DP or is adjoined to DP (if it is assumed that not only movement, but also first Merge gives rise to exocentric structures);
(vii) the case licensing of the subject is achieved at the D-level, internally to DP.

19 A note on nominal gerund constructions

In the light of the preceding analyses, it is easy to understand how nominal gerund constructions are similar to Poss-*ing* ones and at the same time how they differ from them. The derivation of nominal gerund constructions also involves the insertion of a category-defining head n above the Root. It is usually assumed that the presence of n goes along with the availability of nominal features such as case, gender, number, possession, and determiners, and with the absence of verbal features such as tense, aspect, mood and a drastic reduction or a complete neutralization of valency. The complementation options in these domains are very limited, as examples (48) discussed by Hoekstra (2004: 269) establish. For example, nominal gerunds don't accept small clause or ECM complements.

(48) a. * *the letting of children sleep*
b. * *the hearing of John climb the fence*
c. * *the finding of the students incompetent*
d. * *the electing of Bill president*

As is the case in Poss-*ing* constructions, the external argument, when there is one, is first merged in its Spell-out position SpecDP.

(49) *John's running of the marathon regularly*

A first difference between the two types is that nominal gerunds do not project a T head: Neither auxiliaries, nor the negation can occur in these domains. They presumably don't project an Aspect head either, since their aspect is neutral with respect to viewpoint aspect, as Borer (2005) has discovered.[32] And if an additional head is projected above TP, it certainly is not C, but D. There is every reason to believe that the lexical head in these domains displays strictly nominal properties. The overall phrase qualifies as a DP projection, as Poss-*ing* constructions do.

(50) $D > Nb > n > \sqrt{ing} - \sqrt{X}$

The second difference concerns the presence and the status of v. The fact that one finds well-formed examples such as (49), in which a manner or frequency adverb coexists with a nominal gerund indicates that a verbal substructure is present in at least some nominal gerund phrases, as Moulton (2004) has argued, cf. sct. 13.5.

---

32 See sct. 15.2.

But when a v head is present below n in a nominal gerund, it is strongly defective. It is like Poss-*ing* v in that it does not introduce any external argument but, contrary to it, it is not endowed with an [accusative] case feature either and doesn't license an internal argument. Its unaccusativity forces the insertion of the case marker *of* in front of the object.

20 PRO-*ing* gerund constructions and the calculus of control

20.1 Controlled gerund clauses in prepositional phrases

It is time to look more closely at PRO-*ing* gerund constructions and to check whether they can be given a natural analysis within the framework of assumptions resorted to in the preceding sections. Johnson (1991) observes that progress towards a better understanding of these constructions can be achieved if one considers the behavior of gerund structures embedded under a preposition. An interesting asymmetry can be detected among prepositions in their behavior with respect to gerund phrases. Some freely take a complement structure with an overt or a null subject, others only accept the PRO-*ing* construction.

(51) a. *Mary was bothered about him/her son/PRO stealing apples.*
 b. *Liz left before *him/*his son/PRO telling a story.*

Johnson suggests that the prepositions that do not accept an Acc-*ing* complement select a CP. In an expression headed by *before*, a temporal operator must be present, which can only reside in the specifier of some CP. The subject position SpecTP in the resulting structure is ungoverned from the outside and can only contain the element PRO. In the well-formed preposition+overt subject+V-*ing* configurations, the subject seems to be syntactically case licensed by the governing preposition. The fact that, with prepositions belonging to the *about*-class, PRO and overt subjects appear not to be in complementary distribution seems to indicate that C can be present or absent in these structures. Just like some prepositional structures, a subset of verbal predicate constructions does not give rise to a complementarity effect. Some emotive/factive verbs can be followed either by an Acc-*ing* construction or by a PRO-*ing* construction (cf. 52a), others disallow gerund structures with an overt subject (cf. 52b), cf. sct. 7.4.

(52) a. *I regret Mary leaving / her leaving / PRO leaving.*
 b. *I hate*
  * *my students smoking in class*
  ? *their smoking in class*
  PRO *being left alone.*

Should Johnson's government account of prepositional syntax – either a C is present or there is no C – be transposed to verbal structures? The claim would be that *hate* excludes overt subjects because it exclusively selects a CP complement, whereas *regret* is more flexible. Or should the difference between *regret* and *hate* be considered as an exclusively lexical, not structural, property?

Johnson (1991) formulates his analysis within the Principles and Parameters framework, which states that PRO must be ungoverned. In contemporary syntactic theory, the PRO-theorem has no theoretical status anymore. But it could still express a valid generalization. If it did, the very existence of PRO-*ing* constructions would confirm that C is projected above TP in at least a subset of gerund structures. But it was argued in section 17 that C is projected in *all* Acc-*ing* constructions and that their subject is never licensed by an external head. Johnson's account cannot be incorporated into the present analysis.

Examples (3), repeated here as (53), point towards a quite different direction. A correlation seems to exist between the non-complementary distribution of overt and null subjects displayed by some gerund clauses and the possibility of temporal mismatches between the embedded and the matrix clauses in these constructions. This fact has been interpreted by Landau (2000, 2004) and Pires (2006) as a clue that some gerund clauses are tensed (cf. 53a, 53b), whereas others are tenseless (cf. 53c, 53d).[33]

(53) a. *Sue favored (yesterday)* [PRO/*Anna moving to Chicago today*].
b. *Sue insisted (yesterday) on* [PRO/*Anna moving to Chicago today*].
c. * *Bill tried today* [PRO/*Jane talking to his boss tomorrow*].
d. * *Philip avoided last night* [PRO/*Paul driving in the freeway this morning*].

Let us assume that the functional architectures of Acc-*ing* and of PRO-*ing* both include a T head and that what distinguishes them is the presence of an interpretable [tense] on T (or, in Landau's terms, of a positively specified [T] feature) in the verbal gerund clauses that allow both overt and null subjects, and the absence of an interpretable [tense] on T (or the presence of a negatively specified [T]) in the gerund complements that exclusively qualify as control structures. T can be thought of as "dependent" in the first case, as "anaphoric" in the second one. The claim here cannot be that the structures of the second type include no T head. That such a head is indeed projected in these domains is confirmed by the occurrence of sentential negation and of auxiliaries.

---

33 Of course, we know that the clausal complements to *try* and *avoid* cannot contain an overt subject. What is important is that the constructions that illustrate the impossibility of temporal mismatches between the embedded and the matrix clauses remain ungrammatical when PRO is substituted for the overt subject, cf. (53c) and (53d).

(54) a. *Langston Hughes tried not to talk about jazz at the party.*
 b. *I confess not being convinced by her argument.*
 c. *I remember having heard Samson François in my youth.*

20.2 Is -*ing* an agreement marker?

Pursuing this approach, one would expect Acc-*ing* and PRO-*ing* gerund constructions to fit into Landau's Finiteness Rule for OC (cf. 11, ch. II) in a straightforward way. But, as acknowledged by Landau (2013) himself, the syntax of these constructions appears to fall outside the generalization expressed by his rule. He specifies that the claim underlying his Finiteness Rule only holds for domains that qualify as non-deficient clauses and *potentially* define control structures. In his view, this class includes finite and infinitive clauses, but excludes raising structures, ECM constructions, small clauses *and possibly gerunds*. Recall that at the core of his system is the idea that the association of semantic tense and overt agreement on T and/or on C makes the corresponding domain a non-control (NC) structure and that the lack of either semantic tense or of explicit agreement suffices to turn it into an obligatory control (OC) one. His decision to exclude gerunds from the scope of the rule seems to be well-supported, as shown by a careful examination of the three relevant cases:

(i) Acc-*ing* constructions with an overt subject;
(ii) PRO-*ing*/Acc-*ing* constructions (that is, constructions where PRO freely alternates with overt DPs);
(iii) PRO-*ing* constructions (that is, OC constructions where PRO is the only possible choice).

Constructions (i) instantiate a situation where an embedded predicational domain contains an overt referential subject. The well-formedness of Acc-*ing* constructions is unexpected if agreement markers are assumed to obligatorily display variation in person and number, which is not the case of the -*ing* affix, which doesn't manifest the morphological covariation typical of agreement. Let us provisionally assume, however, that the suffix -*ing*, although invariable, nevertheless qualifies as an overt agreement marker in Landau's sense. But then, it is the fact that the same gerund V-*ing* form also occurs in control structures (see ii and iii) that should be a matter of concern. The affix -*ing* must count as positively specified for agreement in constructions (i), as negatively specified in constructions (ii) when the subject is null, because the [tense] specification is positive, as irrelevant in constructions (iii), which are deficient anyway because they lack tense. The difficulty is not that the same predicates can select tensed and untensed complement clauses, but that the variation should concern the status of both [tense] and [agreement]: *-ing*, which is overtly present in all structures, must be analyzed as an active agreement marker in some constructions, as inactive or irrelevant in others. As mentioned in 7.4, in some of the languages where overt subjects and obligatorily controlled ones freely alternate in embedded clauses, the corresponding structures are often morphologically or syntactically distinguished. But in gerund clauses, the difference is not manifested in any way.

The difficulty can be circumvented in several ways, none of them fully compatible with Landau's general approach. Recall that overt agreement has an observable effect only when it coexists with semantic tense. As already mentioned, there is absolutely no objection to analyzing it as a full-fledged agreement marker when it doesn't coexist with tense, as is the case in (iii). If the null subject is taken to be a pro-like element in constructions (ii), not standard PRO as in constructions (iii), *-ing* can be analyzed as an agreement marker in all contexts. In (ii), the interpretation of the null element as a controlled pronominal would be imposed by the syntactic context and lexical environment. But the pro-analysis is not available in Landau's approach. It implies that the identity of the controlled element varies and that control relations cannot be taken to uniformly target PRO, contrary to Landau's wish. A similar difficulty has been mentioned in the discussion of the Modern Greek data (cf. sct. 7.5).

The pro vs. PRO-analysis can easily be reformulated within the probe-goal-Agree approach integrating the Labeling Algorithm and the inheritance mechanism. In this approach, interpretability matters; φ-features can be active without being overtly manifested; valuation always involves two terms, a probe and a goal. Uninterpretable φ-features are, along with [tense], a property of T, not an independent dimension. It is quite natural to assume that T inherits φ-features from C only if it is itself endowed with interpretable [tense] or, equivalently, that φ-features on T are syntactically active only when they coexist with interpretable [tense]. Exhaustive control complements illustrate a different case : The anaphoric T head, which bears an unvalued [tense], lacks φ-features. The hallmark of the *ing*-suffix is precisely that it is compatible with two possible feature endowments of T and can coexist both with dependent/interpretable [tense] and anaphoric/unvalued [tense].

In order to make the analysis tighter, a sharpening of the characterization of the *-ing* affix is necessary. In some contexts, *-ing* behaves as if it spelled out a full matrix of φ-features. This is the case in constructions (i), where its features are sufficient to case-license the embedded subject and, in Landau's terms, to make the corresponding gerund clause a featurally complete domain. But it undoubtedly has a φ-deficient status in OC gerund constructions, where it doesn't block the establishment of a control relation between embedded PRO and an antecedent (and a functional head) in the matrix. How can these two characterizations be reconciled? A natural assumption is that -*ing* indeed functions as a *substitute* for agreement and qualifies the gerund form as a φ-endowed entity – whence its case-licenser role in gerund clauses with an overt subject -, but cannot transmit number and person features to an entity that is deprived of such features, namely PRO, because the -*ing* affix itself doesn't specify the value of these features. This scenario explains why OC is available in constructions headed by V-*ing* : Because the value of its φ-features is unspecified, -*ing* doesn't block the establishment of an Agree relation between embedded PRO and a functional or a nominal antecedent in the matrix. It is also compatible with the claim that the internal raising of their subject makes Acc-*ing* gerund clauses appropriate contents to occupy positions belonging to an A-chain, in particular the grammatical subject position of the sentence (cf. ch. IV). Importantly, this process is not sensitive to the complete/defective status of the clause it affects. As already observed, the only condition for the derivation to converge is that the two agreeing elements, the verbal form and the raised subject, share *non-distinct* φ-features. -*ing* transmits to T's φ-features its unspecified value, which counts as non-distinct from that of the raised subject.

No mention has been made of the structures instantiating non-complementary distribution (case ii). Two analytic options can be considered. These structures can be subsumed under the type of account that was proposed for Acc-*ing* constructions, assuming that we are dealing with pro-like null subjects that raise to the edge of gerund projections, exactly as overt referential subjects do in Acc-*ing* structures. Or one can rely on the idea that -*ing* is unable to transmit person and number features to the relevant null entity in subject position. The control mechanism involved would then be identical to the one at work in structures (iii). I personally favor the first option because, as shown in several parts of this book, partial control appears to observe restrictions similar to the ones obeyed by other cases of control and different from the ones that govern exhaustive control. The second option is more in line with Landau's general approach.

An important consequence of the characterization of the -*ing* affix and of the analysis of gerund clauses that has just been sketched is that Acc-*ing* constructions are converging, but not strictly speaking featurally complete domains: -*ing* is only a *substitute* for agreement, in which the values of the relevant features are not specified. Extraposition phenomena will be shown in chapter IX to support this analysis.

Can this analysis handle Johnson's prepositional paradigm (51)? It can, but the analysis that is arrived at is the reverse of the one he defends. In (51b), no interpretable [tense] is present on T, no uninterpretable counterpart resides on C/Fin. The only available strategy is the elsewhere OC one. On the contrary, in (51a), [tense] in its interpretable and uninterpretable versions is present on T and on

C/Fin respectively, uninterpretable φ-features are transmitted by C/Fin to T. The procedure at work when a null (necessarily pro-like) subject is involved is the same as the one used in Acc-*ing* constructions. The clausal complement is labeled <φ, φ>. The contrast between *regret* and *hate* in (52) can presumably be accounted for along similar lines.

21 Summary

The study of gerund clauses reveals that a set of complex expressions with a verbal head display a nominal external distribution. The main proposal of this chapter is that this behavior can a priori be traced back to one of two grammatical processes and result either from the insertion of a "nominalizer" in the structure (or from another category-switching device), as is usually assumed, or from the normal functioning of labeling. It was argued that Poss-*ing* constructions, which are strongly mixed projections, illustrate the first case and that Acc-ing constructions, which are weakly mixed projections, illustrate the second one. The latter do not incorporate any nominalizing head; it is a syntactic process, subject raising, that allows an essentially verbal/propositional domain to be assigned a $<\varphi, \varphi>$ label and to take the external distribution of a nominal.[34] In the former, the syntactic inertness of T and the defectivity of v conspire to make the resort to a nominalizer both necessary and possible.

The functional structures arrived at for each gerund type are as follows.

> Acc-*ing* constructions, cf. (37)
>> C > T > (v) > v > √*ing* – √X
>>> with T's uninterpretable features inherited from C and v not defective;
>
> Poss-*ing* constructions, cf. (43)
>> D > n > T > (v) > v > √*ing* – √X
>>> with T syntactically inactive and v θ-defective (v doesn't introduce an external argument);
>
> Nominal gerund constructions, cf. (49)
>> D > (Nb) > n > v > √*ing* – √X
>>> with T syntactically inactive and v θ-defective (v doesn't introduce an external argument) and unaccusative (v doesn't case license an internal argument).

---

34 As a final observation, note that the transcategoriality of the gerund morpheme or of V-*ing* forms can also be taken care of in labeling terms. The fact that the labeling of x-X heads (the assignment of a value to x) is performed derivationally and is context-dependent correctly predicts that the same projection can be assigned a verbal or a nominal label. This analysis naturally captures the link between the categorial underspecification of gerund heads and the labeling properties of the corresponding projections.

It is time to take stock and check whether the preceding analysis is in a position to account for the differential properties of the three constructions. Acc-*ing* constructions have been characterized as CP/FinP domains with a syntactically silent but active T, Poss-*ing* constructions as DP projections incorporating an inactive T.[35] The extraction asymmetries illustrated in (21) directly follow, as well as the possibility/impossibility of *there*-insertion and *it*-insertion in the two structures (cf. 22, 23), the agreement facts illustrated in (24), the variable tolerance to extraposition (cf. 26), the availability of scopal relations requiring an extended clausal domain in Acc-*ing* constructions and the exclusion of such relations in Poss-*ing* constructions (cf. 27–30). The specific/presuppositional status of Poss-*ing* structures, as opposed to the basically non-presuppositional status of Acc--*ing* structures, which will be further discussed in chapter XI, is also fully compatible with the DP vs. CP/FinP analysis. As for nominal gerund constructions, they should be characterized as DP projections including no T, in which the external argument is first merged in SpecDP, in a way parallel to what happens in Poss-*ing*. But it must be acknowledged that some nominal gerunds appear to incorporate a (strongly defective) v head, a fact which is potentially problematic for the analysis developed here.

---

[35] Recall that, although inactive, T is the landing site of gerund auxiliaries, a property which reflects the tenseness of auxiliaries as opposed to the tenselessness of lexical stems. The anaphoric/unvalued T in OC constructions also 'attracts' gerund auxiliaries.

V The morphosyntax of verbo-nominal heads in contemporary Welsh

This chapter and the two following ones report the results of a research devoted to Welsh verbo-nominal constructions. My initial goal was to show that the assumptions and devices that were introduced to tackle the transcategoriality and categorial mixing of English gerunds could be extended to account for the Celtic data. Verbo-nominal phrases (henceforth VNPs) in contemporary Welsh have two kinds of uses, a dominant verbal one and a peripheral nominal one, and transparently illustrate the transcategoriality of verb-nouns or of the verbo-nominal suffix. But contrary to what could appear at first, the evidence supporting a mixed projection analysis of a subset of VNP projections is shaky. The structures that seem to give rise to a category-mixing effect and are plausible candidates for an analysis along these lines can also be accounted for in different terms. And it is often difficult to determine whether this effect is best thought of as resulting from the projection of a category-switching head or from another factor.[1]

In this chapter, I first draw up a list of the syntactic contexts where verb-nouns are found; I then broach the question of the derivation of verb-noun heads.

---

[1] In this respect, Welsh differs from Irish which seems to provide clear examples of category mixing.

22 The two uses of the verb-noun

All Celtic languages have a verb-noun at their disposal, that is, a differentiated form of verbal paradigms that is not inflected for tense, aspect, voice, person and number and is used in a heterogeneous set of constructions, in syntactic situations where the other Indo-European languages resort to infinitives, participles, gerunds, or to inflected verbal forms.[2]

The Welsh "verb-noun" (*berfenw*, henceforth VN) is a morphologically complex form. Several morphological classes can be distinguished, depending on the presence and the form of the suffix. We can have a bare verbal stem (cf. *dilyn* 'follow'; *dechrau* 'begin'; *gostwng* 'lower'), or a suffixed formation (*briw-o* 'hurt', *lliw-io* 'dye', *crynu* 'tremble' *oer-i* 'grow cold'), or a derivation with vocalic mutation when the root is nominal (cf. *gweithio* 'work', root *gaith*; *goleuo* 'light up', root *golau*; *rhoddi* 'give', root *rhodd*).

Verb-nouns are morphologically complex entities, much like the infinitival forms of the Romance languages which incorporate a nonfinite inflection *-r-*. But their syntax sharply differs from that of Romance infinitives and English *to* constructions and requires a different account.[3] Two types of uses should be distinguished, depending on whether the verbo-nominal constituent should be identified as a predicative phrase or as an argumental expression.

22.1 VNPs used predicatively

(i) Serial constructions
In "serial" constructions, the verbal predicate of the first member of a sequence of coordinated clauses is finite, the predicates of the following clauses take the form of verb-nouns. All the members of the coordination structure semantically share the same subject and the same temporal interpretation, which are those of the finite verbal form of the first member.

---

[2] The topic of verb-nouns, which is omnipresent in the traditional linguistic literature on Celtic, is also tackled in various contributions completed within the tradition of formal syntax, see the articles mentioned in the discussion, as well as the following book-length works aiming at covering the syntax of Welsh: Awbery (1976), Jones & Thomas (1977), Sadler (1988), Rouveret (1994), Willis (1998), Roberts (2005), Borsley, Tallerman & Willis (2007).
[3] Adger (2007: 46) provides a list of diagnostic properties characteristic of infinitival forms and concludes that Celtic VN-clauses should not be viewed as infinitives.

(1) Aeth   y ffermwr at y   drws   a   churo   arno
     go.PAST.3SG   the farmer to the door and knock.VN   on.3M.SG
     ac aros   am dipyn heb   gael   ateb.
     and wait.VN   a little without get.VN answer
     'The farmer went to the door, knocked at it and waited a little without getting an answer.'

(ii) Nonfinite clauses[4]

The subject of a nonfinite clause precedes the verbo-nominal projection and is governed by the preposition-like element *i*.[5]

(2) a. *Dywedodd   Emyr i Siôn fynd   i Gaerdydd.*
        say.PAST.3SG   Emyr to Siôn go.VN   to Cardiff
        'Emyr said that Siôn went to Cardiff.'

   b.   *Bwriadai   'r athro   i   'r plant   ddarllen*
        intend.IMPF.3SG   the teacher to the children read.VN
        llyfr   arall.
        book   other
        'The teacher intended to have the children read another book.'

(iii) V+VNP sequences (VNPs complements to auxiliaries, modals, control and raising predicates)

---

4 The predicate in adjunct clauses often takes a verbo-nominal form. This is the case of purpose clauses introduced by the preposition *i* (cf. i). When preceded by the prepositions *dan* or *gan*, the verb-noun is equivalent to an English present participle functioning as a secondary predicate (cf. ii and iii).

(i)   *Daethant   yma i 'n   gweld.*
      come.PAST.3PL   here *i* us   see.VN
      'They came here to see us.'

(ii) *Daeth   y   ferch   i mewn dan ganu.*
      come.PAST.3SG   the girl   inside *dan* sing.VN
      'The girl came in singing.'

(iii) *Euthum   i 'r dref   gan feddwl   gweld fy nghyfaill.*
      go.PAST.1SG to the town *gan* think.VN see.VN my friend
      'I went to town, thinking to see my friend.'

5 The complement clauses dependent on verbal or prepositional predicates can also be realized as *bod*-initial structures, where *bod* is the verb-noun form of the verb "be". *i*-initial and *bod*-initial constructions are extensively studied in chapter VI.

(3) *Mi   wneith   Mair   ganu   heno.*
    PRT do.PRES.3SG Mair sing.VN tonight
    'Mair will sing tonight.'

(4) a. *Fe.   ddylai   Gwyn   ei   ddisgrifio.*
       PRT should.3SG Gwyn   CL.3M.SG describe.VN
       'Gwyn should describe it.'

   b. *Ni   allwn   ddweud   yr un gair.*
       NEG can.IMPF.1SG say.VN   the one word
       'I could not say one word.'

   c. *Ni   allai   eu   rhwystro.*
       NEG can.IMPF.3SG CL.3PL stop.VN
       'She could not stop them.'

(5) *Ceisiodd   pawb   ganu   'r anthem.*
    try.PAST.3SG everyone sing.VN the anthem
    'Everyone tried to sing the anthem.'

The nominal expression that immediately follows the finite main verb or auxiliary or modal and is the grammatical subject of the clause is also interpreted as the subject of the verbo-nominal projection.

(iv) Asp+VNP in small clauses

In aspectual small clauses, such as (6), the Aspect head selects a verbo-nominal projection and is preceded by the subject of predication.[6] The same holds for periphrastic aspectual constructions (cf. 7) and absolute constructions (cf. 8).

(6) *Clywais   i   ef   yn   canu   *(yn)   hyfrid.*
    hear.PAST.1SG 1SG 3M.SG PROG sing.VN PRED pleasant
    'I heard him sing pleasantly.'
    [Borsley 1993]

(7) a. *Mae   'r dyn wedi   lladd   yr offeiriad.*
       be.PRES.3SG the man PERF kill.VN the priest
       'The man has just killed the priest.'

---

6 (6) would be ungrammatical in the absence of *yn* before *hyfrid*. In Welsh, manner adverbs are formed by combining the corresponding adjectives with the predicative particle *yn*.

b. *Roedd   Megan yn   canu   yn   hyfryd.*
   be.IMPF.3SG Megan PROG sing.VN   PRED pleasant
   'Megan was singing pleasantly.'

c. *Yr   oedd   Ifan wedi cysgu   yn   hwyr*
   PRT   be.IMPF.3SG   Ifan PERF sleep.VN PRED late
   y   bore   hwnnw.
   the   morning   that
   'Ifan had slept late that morning.'

(8) *Aeth   i 'r ystafell   a   'r dynion*
    go.PAST.3SG   to the room   and   the men
    yn   bwyta.
    PROG   eat.VN
    'He went into the room, while the men were eating.'

22.2 VNPs used as arguments

(v) VNP as the second element in a noun + complement construction.

(9) a. *amser hau*
       time   sow.VN
       'the time of sowing'

    b. *gwialen bysgota*
       rod   fish.VN
       'fishing rod'

(vi) VN modified by an adjective[7]

(10)   *rhedeg   cyflym*
       run.VN   fast
       'the fact of running fast'

---

[7] In Welsh, attributive adjectives immediately follow the noun; predicative adjectives and nouns are systematically preceded by the predicative particle *yn* triggering soft mutation (lenition).

(vii) VNP in subject position

(11)   *Mae   canu   da   yn   werth ei   wrando.*
       be.PRES.3SG sing.VN good PRED worth CL.3MSG listen.VN
       'It is worth to listen to a well-played song.'

(viii) VNP preceded by the definite article

(12)   *Deffrowyd   ef   gan y   gweiddi.*
       wake.up.PAST 3M.SG by the shout.VN
       'He was woken up by the shouts.'

(ix) VNP preceded by a possessive article

(13) a. *Y   mae   ei   chanu   yn   gwella.*
        PRT be.PRES.3SG CL3M.SG sing.VN PRED better
        'His way of singing is getting better.'

   b. *Nid wyf   yn   deall   ei   siarad.*
      NEG be.PRES.1SG PROG understand.VN CL.3M.SG speak.VN
      'I don't understand his way of speaking.'

   c. *Clywais   i   ei   ganu   (*yn) hyfrid.*
      hear.PAST.1SG 1SG CL.3M.SG sing.VN PRED pleasant
      'I heard his pleasant song.' [Borsley 1993]

The clearest cases of argumental VNPs are those where the VN is preceded by the definite article, cf. (12). The interpretation of prefixed and infixed pronouns draws a sharp distinction between the predicative and the argumental uses. With VNPs used as arguments, the pronominal article is systematically interpreted as a possessive, cf. (13a), (13b), (13c); with VNPs used as predicates, the prefixed or infixed pronoun can only be understood as the pronominalized form of the direct argument (and can occur only with transitive VNs), cf. *ei* in (4a), *eu* in (4c), *ei* in (11).

This asymmetry in turn reflects the different ways in which the argument structure of the original root is mapped syntactically in the argumental and the predicative uses. In the argumental use, a DP in construction with the VN can only be a genitive/possessive complement.[8] In the predicative use, all the inter-

---

[8] The resulting reading is exclusively stative/resultative. Derived nominals, which also exist in Welsh, behave differently since they allow both an eventive and a stative/resultative interpretation.

nal arguments selected by a transitive verbal root can potentially be present, but a DP directly constructed with the VN is systematically interpreted as the direct argument of the root. The contrast between the following examples discussed by Borsley (1993) can be explained on this basis.

(14) a. *Cafodd   canu   Emrys ei   glywed   gan bawb.*
　　　　get.PAST.3SG sing.VN Emrys CL.3M.SG listen-to.VN by all
　　　　'Emyr's song was listened to by all.'

　　 b. * *Cafodd   canu   'r   anthem ei   geisio gan bawb.*
　　　　get.PAST.3SG sing.VN the anthem CL.3M.SG try.VN by everyone
　　　　'Singing the anthem was tried by everyone.'

We know that VNPs in the argumental use exclusively occupy nominal positions, the subject position included. The well-formedness of (14a) confirms the nominal status of the VNP projection in the argumental use. *canu Emrys* in (14a) can only be nominal because *Emrys* cannot be interpreted as the semantic object of *canu*, only as a genitive. On the contrary, VNPs in the predicative use occupy positions from which standard nominal expressions are generally excluded, cf. (1)–(5). (14b) necessarily illustrates the predicative use because the complement DP can only be interpreted as the direct argument of *canu*. It confirms that VNPs in this use are not legitimate in the positions where nominal expressions are welcome, suggesting that they are analyzed as vPs or clauses rather than DPs.

A further characteristic of the predicative use should be emphasized: The order VN-DP$_s$ (-DP$_o$) is strictly excluded in contemporary Welsh, whatever the lexical class of the root.[9] The absence of independent VN-initial clauses is presumably linked to the lack of tense/agreement morphology on verb-nouns, which makes it impossible for them to value the case feature on the nominal subject, and to provide the interpretable feature of the null Tense head with a lexical support. VN-initial dependent clauses are also excluded when VN is a lexical verb.[10]

(15) a. * *Dywedodd   ddod   y   dyn.*   (unaccusative)
　　　　say.PAST.3SG come.VN the man,
　　　　　　meaning 'He said that the man had come.'

---

9 But this order was attested in Middle Welsh in "historic infinitive" constructions, see chapter VII.
10 *Bod*-initial clauses, studied in chapter VI, are an exception to this generalization.

b. *Credaf   barhau 'r oedfa ychydig amser. (unaccusative)
   believe.PRES.1SG last.VN the concert little time
       meaning 'I believe that the concert didn't last long.'

c. *Credaf   ddawnsio 'r plant   neithiwr.   (unergative)
   believe.PRES.1SG dance.VN the children last night
       meaning 'I believe that the children danced last night.'

Finally, the examples given in this subsection confirm that VNPs can be modified by an adjective in the argumental use (cf. 10, 13c), by an adverb in the predicative use (cf. 6, 7b, 7c).[11]

---

[11] An adjective can also occur before the verb-noun and form what the Welsh grammars identify as a compound verb. (i) has the same meaning as (ii). (iii) is a literary example quoted by Thorne (1993: 327).

(i)   Mae   'r dyn yn   cyflym gerdded.
      be.PRES.3SG the man PROG fast walk.VN

(ii) Mae   'r dyn yn   cerdded yn gyflym
      be.PRES.3SG the man PROG walk.VN PRED fast
      'The man is walking fast.'

(iii) Yr oedd   yn   prysur gerdded y   llwybr hwnnw.
      Prt be.IMPF.3SG   PROG fast   walk.VN the path   that
      'She/he was rapidly going along the path.'

23 The internal structure of VNP projections

23.1 Is the verb-noun a verb or a noun?

Traditional accounts argue that the morpho-syntactic properties of Welsh verb-nouns identify them as nouns, both diachronically and synchronically, cf. Anwyl (1899), Morris-Jones (1913, 1931), Lewis (1928), Richards (1938, 1950–1951), S. Williams (1980). In his *Welsh Grammar for Schools*, Anwyl (1899: 164) writes:

> The verb-noun in Welsh, inasmuch as it is the *name* of an action, is treated in many respects like a noun; but, as it is the name of an *action*, some of its constructions resemble those of the verb . . .

> Modern Welsh, doubtless influenced in the course of centuries by the practice of translating from other languages, tends to be conscious rather of the verbal aspect of the verb-noun as the name of an *action*, than of its nominal aspect as the *name* of an action.

Morris-Jones's (1913: 317) characterization is as follows:

> The verbal noun is not strictly an infinitive; it governs the genitive, not the accusative case. It may be used, like an abstract noun, with the article or an adjective, as the subject or object of a verb or the object of a preposition; but it is sufficiently distinct from an ordinary abstract noun by reason of certain constructions in which it cannot be replaced by the latter.

Empirical support for the claim that verbo-nominal projections preserve a nominal internal syntax, even when they function as nonfinite verb phrases, is provided by the following often repeated observations:

(i) a sequence [VN DP] can be analyzed as a possessive construction of the "construct-state" type [N DP], cf. (16a)/(16b);[12]

(ii) there is no mutation on the initial consonant of the dependent term (cf. 16b); this behavior is parallel to that of the genitive complement in the possessive construction (cf. 16a); it contrasts with that of the direct argument of inflected verbs in the VSO order, which is affected by lenition (cf. 16c);

(iii) like N, VN can support a prefixed clitic, cf. (17b), (17c) vs. (17a);

---

[12] The hallmark of construct-state constructions in Semitic languages is the absence of any preposition-like element mediating the relation between the head noun and its complement – the possessive relation is marked by the construction itself -, by the absence of a definite determiner when the expression as a whole is interpreted as definite and, in Hebrew, by the use of a special form of the possessed noun. Celtic languages instantiate a variant of the construct-state construction, in which there is no adjacency requirement between the head noun and its dependent. See Rouveret (1994) among many others.

(iv) properties (i)–(iii) are observed in both the predicative and the argumental uses;
(v) in Welsh, because case inflection was lost, there is no morphological distinction between the genitive complement of the noun (and of the verb-noun) and the accusative complement of the finite verb; but in literary Irish, a language that has kept a system of morphological cases, the object of VN in VN-DP sequences is marked for the genitive case in the nominal uses, but also in clearly predicative uses, for example in progressive periphrases containing the particle *ag*, cf. (18). As in Welsh, the VN has the same internal syntax in the predicative uses and in the argumental uses, that is a nominal syntax.

(16) a. *plant cymydog* / children neighbor / 'the children of a neighbor'
   [rad. cymydog]
   b. *Mae Megan wedi gweld cymydog* 'Megan has seen a neighbor.'
   c. *Gwelodd Megan gymydog ddoe* 'Megan saw a neighbor yesterday.'

(17) a. *ei dŷ (ef)* / his house him / 'the house that belongs to him'
   b. *Mae   rhywun   yn   ei   weld.*
      be.PRES.3SG someone PROG CL.3.M.SG see
      'There is someone that sees him.'
   c. *Clywais   i   ei   ganu (*yn) hyfrid.*
      hear.PAST.1SG 1SG CL.3.M.SG sing PRED pleasant
      'I heard his pleasant singing.'

(18) *Nuair a bhí   siad ag   ceannach an tí,* ...
    when C be.PAST 3.PL PROG buy   the house-GEN
    'When they were buying the house ... ' [Irish]

Some contemporary treatments have adopted (or adapted) the nominal analysis, see Awbery (1976), P. Willis (1988), Fife (1990), Rouveret (1994), among others. Awbery (1976: 20) states the challenge facing the supporters of the nominal analysis very clearly.

> It is ... necessary to reconcile the need to analyze the uninflected verb as a verb and the need to analyze the unit formed by the uninflected verb and the direct object as a noun phrase.

A second family of accounts, which includes Jones & Thomas (1977), Borsley (1993, 1997), Borsley & Kornfilt (2000) treats verb-nouns as nonfinite forms of the verb.[13]

Both analyses have their own merits. The nominal one straightforwardly accounts for the morphosyntactic aspects of verbo-nominal constructions. And it doesn't preclude characterizing VNPs as predicative domains. In the absence of a determiner, nominal projections are nothing more and nothing less than predicative domains. In a framework that distinguishes between lexical and functional categories, this is indeed what NPs are. They only acquire a referential status when coupled with a determiner, a definite article for example. But when a VNP projection complements an aspectual head or occurs in a serial verb construction, its verbal status must be guaranteed some way or other. A rudimentary solution would consist in claiming that the immediate categorial environment suffices to derive the required distinction – the VN is verbal when it finds itself in the locality of a T head, of an Aspect head or of a modal verb, nominal when it is preceded by a determiner[14] or a pronominal article.[15]

The nominal analysis is generally dismissed in contemporary approaches, see in particular Borsley (1993, 1997). The verbal analysis, which is favored today, has more plausibility, since predicative uses are overwhelmingly dominant in the modern language, as is the case of the infinitive in Romance, and since verb-nouns in the relevant structures behave exactly as if they were ordinary nonfinite verbal forms. But it leaves us without an explanation for the convergence between verbo-nominal constructions in the predicative use and nominal constructions (the nominal use of VN included), on which the traditional nominal analysis is founded.

The verbal analysis could be unreservedly adopted, if it could be shown that the similarities exemplified in (16)–(18) are spurious and do not necessarily indicate that verbo-nominal domains are internally structured as nominal expressions are. This is the conclusion arrived at by Borsley (1993, 1997) with respect to Welsh and by Carnie (2011) in his study of Irish verb-nouns, who successfully establish that the convergences discovered by traditional grammar can be accounted for

---

[13] See also Rouveret (2017, 2020).
[14] It must be kept in mind however that some determiners in Welsh have no morphological exponent. This is the case of the singular and plural forms of the indefinite article.
[15] A variant of this account is developed in Rouveret (1987, 1994). In these references, I took Welsh VNs to be verbs, but verbs embedded in a DP (more precisely embedded in a Nominalization Phrase NomP, itself embedded in a DP), and claimed that VNs move to the head Nom to pick up their morphology. D was postulated to host proclitics, which usually stand in a D head. Borsley (1997) rightly points out that the assumption that D is present in the relevant structures has unfortunate consequences.

differently and hence cannot be invoked to support the nominal analysis. Let us focus on the Welsh data, for the moment.

Possessives pronouns are a case in point. They correspond to full-fledged genitives in nominal constructions and in VNPs functioning as arguments, but have nothing specifically genitive in their predicative use, where they can simply be viewed as pronouns signaling the presence of a gap in the argument position following the VN.[16]

There is also a major interpretive difference between VN-DP$_0$ structures and standard construct-state constructions. In the latter, the definiteness of the whole nominal expression is determined by the definiteness of the dependent genitive. Nothing similar is observed in verbo-nominal structures.[17]

The deconstruction approach can be extended to the absence of mutation on the dependent genitive in DPs (cf. 16a) and on the complement in transitive VNPs (cf. 16b), contrasting with the mutation on the direct object in verb-initial clauses (cf. 16c), a situation which should not be taken to support a "generalized NP/DP" analysis. A purely structural explanation is possible, making no reference to categorial identity and relying on the traditional insight that two types of mutation should be distinguished, "lexical" mutation, triggered by specific lexical items, "structural" mutation which, by definition, is exclusively structure-dependent.

---

[16] It remains to be explained why possessive articles and argument clitics are basically homophonous, an unfrequently asked question. Note that the definite article and third person accusative pronominal clitics in French illustrate a similar situation. The elements of the two classes are clearly definite.

[17] An additional clue confirming the verbal status of verb-nouns is provided by colloquial Welsh, where no possessive pronoun occurs in the aspectual constructions (cf. i) or verbo-nominal clauses (cf. ii) containing a pronominal object, which makes them quite different from genitive constructions. What is invariably found in object position is an independent pronoun. The personal pronouns functioning as objects in verb-initial clauses are also realized as independent pronouns in colloquial speech, cf. (iii) (and in the literary language).

(i)   oedd   Siôn   wedi   gweld   e.
      be.IMPF.3SG   Siôn   PERF   see.VN   3M.SG
      'Siôn had seen him.'

(ii)   mi   alli   di   fenthyg   o.
      PRT   can/may.2SG   2SG   borrow   3M.SG
      'you can/may borrow it.'

(iii)   Fe   weles   i   e
      PRT   see.PAST.1SG   1SG   3M.SG
      'I saw him.'

The phenomenon is not a particular feature of a specific construction (the aspectual one), but a general property of verbo-nominal structures, as (ii) confirms. It obviously militates against the nominal analysis of verb-nouns in contemporary Welsh.

The object mutation in (16c) illustrates the second type: It is triggered by the non-adjacency of the object to the finite verb. There is no mutation in (16a) and (16b), where the head and its dependent are structurally adjacent.[18]

Finally, one cannot deny that the aspectual particles (cf. *yn*, *wedi* in 6, 7b and 7a, 7c) are at first sight homophonous to prepositions,[19] leaving open the possibility that Asp-VNP sequences be analyzed as P-NP sequences, as the traditional nominal analysis presupposes. But it is well-known that in contemporary Welsh, they trigger mutations that are distinct from the ones that are observed in prepositional contexts and should be viewed as instances of an autonomous functional category Aspect: Whereas prepositional *yn* 'in' triggers nasal mutation, cf. *ym Mangor* 'in Bangor', progressive *yn* is followed by the radical form. We are thus dealing with distinct grammatical morphemes, not with polyfunctional/transcategorial items.

If the morphosyntactic, syntactic and semantic evidences are taken to be inconclusive to settle the status of predicative verb-nouns in Welsh, we are left with two uses of verbo-nominal forms, a dominant use, which is verbal, and a peripheral nominal use. If this picture is correct, VNs in Modern Welsh don't illustrate the category-mixing phenomenon at all. They are transcategorial items and the analysis that was devised to account for the transcategoriality of verbal and nominal gerunds in English can be extended to the alternation between the argumental use and the predicative use of verb-nouns in Welsh. This is tentatively done in section 23.2. But the Irish constructions discussed in section 23.3 definitely indicate that mixed projections exist in at least one Celtic language. Additional Welsh data are discussed in sections 23.4 and 23.5, which show that the situation is more complex that could appear at first. A syntactic analysis intended to cover these data is proposed.

---

18 As already mentioned, attributive adjectives follow the noun they modify. When modifying the head noun in a possessive construction, they are interpolated between the noun and the possessive complement. And in this case, the latter display no mutation. Intervening adjectives don't count in the calculus of adjacency, as (i) confirms.

(i) merch   bert   tad   difrifol
     daughter pretty   father   strict
     'the pretty daughter of a strict father'

Conversely, the initial consonant of direct objects mutate in null subject constructions, which indicates that what matters is structural (non-)adjacency, not linear adjacency. Everything works as if the null subject was visible to the mutation process.

(ii) *Gwelodd gymydog ddoe*
      'He/she saw a neighbor yesterday.'

19 *newydd*, which occurs in periphrastic constructions marking recent past, is an exception to this claim.

23.2 A syntactic approach to word formation

Several affixes, a zero affix included, can be involved in the formation of verbo-nominal words. I suggest that, on a par with the gerund suffix *-ing*, the verbo-nominal suffixes should be analyzed as roots, following Lowenstamm's (2014) suggestion. Keeping in mind that in the contemporary language, Welsh verbal nouns are generally verbs, sometimes nouns, let us assume that in the predicative use, there is a v above the complex object formed by the combination of the affix root and the category-neutral root, without any additional category-switching head being present.

(19) Y [$_\alpha$ DP$_S$ [$_{vP}$ v-√X-aff [$_{RootP}$ [√aff] [√X DP$_o$]]]
where Y ranges over Asp, T, auxiliaries and modals

The VNPs used predicatively should be analyzed as vP projections selected by Asp (in periphrastic constructions, cf. 6, 7, 8), by T (in non-finite clauses and in serial constructions, cf. 1, 2) or by an auxiliary or a modal (cf. 3, 4, 5).

Examples (9)–(13), illustrating the argument use, raise no particular difficulty either. They provide absolutely no evidence for the presence of an internal verbal component and should be analyzed as nP projections in which the θ-grid of the root is deactivated, cf. (20).

(20) Y [$_{nP}$ ... [n-√X-aff [$_{RootP}$ [√aff] [√X DP]]]

For the sake of simplicity, (19) and (20) can be rewritten as (21) and (22).

(21) Y [$_\alpha$ ... [$_{vP}$ VN [$_{RootP}$ [√aff] [√X DP$_o$]]]

(22) Y [$_\alpha$ ... [$_{nP}$ VN [$_{RootP}$ [√aff] [√X DP]]]

23.3 Irish verbo-nominal projections

As (18) and (23a) illustrate, the object of VN in literary Irish is marked for the genitive case in the argumental *and* in the predicative use.[20] As observed by McCloskey (1983), Ó Siadhail (1989: 277), Carnie (2011), this marking is a conservative feature of nonfinite verbal syntax. What is usually found in spoken Irish in the progressive construction is the "common case" or "direct case", which is the form used in the nominative and accusative positions, cf. (23b).

---

[20] All the Irish examples in this section are discussed in Carnie's (2011) study.

(23) a. *Tá   mé   ag   ól   an leanna.*
       be.PRES 1.SG PROG drink.VN the beer.GEN
       'I am drinking beer.'

   b. *Tá   mé   ag   ól   an leann*
       be.PRES 1.SG PROG drink.VN the beer.COM

As reported by Carnie (2011), the complement in the possessive construction displays a partly similar, partly different behavior. In written Irish, both the dependent noun and its determiner are marked for the genitive case, cf. (24a). In spoken Irish, the dependent noun displays the common case, but its determiner is in the genitive, cf. (24b).

(24) a. *teach an   ghasúir*
       house the.GEN boy.GEN
       'the boy's house'

   b. *teach an   ghasúr*
       house the.GEN boy.COM
       'the boy's house'

From these and similar data, Borsley & Kornfilt (2000) conclude that neither in the possessive nor in the progressive construction does the nominal complement bear a "true genitive" case. The morphosyntactic features displayed by spoken Irish do not provide sufficiently robust evidence in favor of the nominal analysis of verbo-nominal constructions; they are at best neutral between this analysis and the one that takes VNP projections to be standard verbal projections and assigns to VNs in the predicative use the status of verbal heads.

The properties of some Irish VN-clauses, discussed by McCloskey (1980, 1984), Chung & McCloskey (1987), Guilfoyle (1990, 1997), Bobaljik & Carnie (1996), Borsley & Kornfilt (2000) and Carnie (2011), seem to point to a different conclusion and to support a mixed analysis of a subset of verbo-nominal projections in this language. In the Northern dialects (Ulster and Connemara), nonfinite transitive structures display an SOV order, in which the subject and the object arguments both precede the verb-noun and are marked for the "common case", cf. (26)–(27). The particle *a* is interpolated between the object and the verb-noun. In the Southern dialects (Munster), only one DP can precede the verb-noun. If there is no overt subject, the object marked for the common case appears preverbally, cf. (28). If there is a subject, it precedes the verb-noun and the object is relegated to the post-VN position and is marked for the genitive case, cf. (29). Again, the particle *a* immediately precedes the verb-noun, provided that an argument precedes it.

(25) *Ba   mhaith liom   an teach   a thógáil.* [all dialects]
    be.PAST.3.SG good   with.1.SG the house. COM *a* build.VN
    'I would like to build the house.'

(26) *Ba   mhaith liom   Seán   an teach   a thógáil.* [Ulster]
    be.PAST.3.SG good   with.1.SG Sean.COM the house.COM *a* build.VN
    'I would like Sean to build the house.'

(27) *Ba   mhaith liom   sibh an doras   a phéinteáil*
    be.PAST.3.SG good   with.1.SG 2.SG the door.COM *a* paint.VN
    'I would like you to paint the door.'

(28) *Ba   mhaith liom   an doras   a phéinteáil.* [Munster]
    be.PAST.3.SG good   with.1.SG the door.COM *a* paint.VN
    'I would like to paint the door.'

(29) *Ba   mhaith liom   Seán   a thógáil. an tí.*
    be.PAST.3.SG good   with.1.SG Sean.COM *a* build.VN the house.GEN
    'I would like Sean to build the house.'

Summarizing: Whenever a pre-VN position is available, the object of the verb-noun shifts around the verbo-nominal head and takes a common case form. The particle *a* systematically occurs in the corresponding structures and is presumably involved in the case licensing of the raised argument, although it is not necessarily a case licenser itself. We can think of this particle as a functional head, maybe Aspect as Carnie (2011) suggests, merged immediately above vP, endowed with φ-features that require to be valued and functioning as a probe. The major difference between the two dialects is that, in the Northern one, *a* is able to successively attract more than one argument[21] – the result is a structure in which both the subject and the object stand outside the domain of existential closure -[22], and that in Munster, *a* can only attract a single argument – the attracted term

---

21 On the possibility for a given head functioning as a probe to attract several items or expressions and on the reason why the one that is attracted later intervenes between the attracting head and the one that is attracted first, see Richards's (2001) treatment of multiple clitics and multiple *wh* structures. His assumptions can be extended to the Irish case.
22 Ramchand (1993) for Scottish Gaelic, Kratzer (2004) for German and Finnish, Carnie (2011) for Irish insist that object shift has a semantic import. In sentences with a shifted accusative (or neutral case) object, the nominal receives a bounded interpretation, whereas it doesn't when no shift occurs, cf. Ramchand (1993) and Carnie (2011: 1218).

is either the subject which is structurally closer, hence immediately accessible, or the object, when there is no overt subject. The remarkable feature of these constructions is that the object is marked for the genitive case when it is forced to remain in the low post-VN position – this is the case in the Munster dialect when an overt subject is present and precedes the verb -, and for the common case when it is allowed to raise and occupies the high pre-VN position.

The cooccurrence in the Munster dialect of the postverbal genitive with the preverbal common case is unexpected in Borsley & Kornfilt's (2000) analysis and raises a potential difficulty against it. Concerning the origin of this case, two assumptions can be made. The simplest one consists in the claim that the genitive is assigned/valued by a n head minimally c-commanding the root; when the nP phase has been completed, a category-switching head v is merged with the nP projection, as shown in (30).[23]

(30) T [DP$_s$ a [~~DP~~$_s$ v [n [Root DP$_o$]]]]

Under this analysis, the relevant structures instantiate a case of strong categorial mixing. The occurrence of the genitive case corresponds to the expected situation since the genitive is the only structural case available in nP domains. Another option consists in assuming that the genitive case functions as a default marking, as Carnie proposes.[24] No n is projected in this case. The genitive marking on the object reflects the fact that in the structures where a subject is present, the complement in the post-root position is the only argument within the vP to which a has no access, cf. (31).

(31) T [DP$_s$ a [~~DP~~$_s$ v [Root DP$_o$]]]

But in order to reconcile the genitive marking of the post-VN argument with the verbal analysis in (31), an additional assumption has to be made concerning the status of the nonfinite v or of the v-root complex in Irish. The necessity to resort to a default case in the post-root position is a sure indication that the v head doesn't transmit any [accusative]/[common] feature to the head it categorially identifies as V. This state of affairs can have two origins: Either v is an unaccusative head and doesn't make any [accusative]/[common] feature available; or

---

[23] The possibility to analyze these structures along these lines is considered, then rejected by Carnie (2011).
[24] In fact, Carnie develops a much more sophisticated version of this idea. Although it differs from Borsley & Kornfilt (2000) analysis, the default case approach also amounts to treating the genitive as a fake genitive.

v is endowed with an [accusative]/[common] feature, but doesn't transmit it to root/V. If the unaccusative hypothesis is adopted, the obligatory presence of *a* in the pre-VN position is a sure indication that the particle *a* is the head that makes [accusative]/[common] available. If the no-transmission hypothesis is correct, it is difficult to decide which of *a* or v is responsible for the case licensing of the object.

A salient feature of this analysis of Irish VN-clauses is that T is not involved at all in the licensing of nominal arguments. Adger (2007) defends a similar position in his study of parallel (but not identical) VN-structures in Scottish Gaelic. But his general conclusion is that VN-clauses lack T entirely and are just PredPs/VPs.[25] My position is that the constructions under consideration do not impose the conclusion that truncation can operate at the PredP-level. T is present, but inert, which correctly predicts that the syntactic processes that require the presence of an active TP or a CP domain cannot take place in the relevant structures.

23.4 The internal structure of Welsh VNPs and clauses

The Welsh structures in (32) differ from the Irish ones in two major respects: the direct argument never precedes the VN; the VN is not preceded by a particle.

(32) a. *Bwriadai   'r athro   i 'r plant   ddarllen llyfr arall.*
        intend.IMPF.3.SG the teacher *i* the children read.VN book other
        'The teacher intended to make the children read another book.'

    b. *Gwn   i Mair orffen   y gwaith*
        know.PRES.1.SG *i* Mair finish.VN the work
        'I know that Mair has finished the work.'

In contemporary Welsh, the casual evidence is lacking, so that it is difficult to decide whether the nonfinite clauses in (32) should be viewed as mixed projections with a n-related genitive complement or as structures with an abstract default genitive case or as constructions instantiating a nominative-accusative alignment. In other words, three analytic options can be contemplated: Either the internal argument is marked for a structural (within a nP shell) or a default (in the absence of n) genitive case in its original position, or it raises to the edge of vP (if

---

[25] Adger (2007) resorts to an Agr head projected above VNP to license the object and claims that verb phrases are headed by a Pred category (which should be viewed as a generalized version of Chomsky's v) dominating AgrP.

v doesn't transmit its features) and is marked accusative; in the latter option, the movement of the object would be followed by the subsequent raising of the VN head to a higher position. It will be shown in the next chapter that C and T are projected in VN-clauses, that the subject is licensed by the content of C, which can be the nonfinite complementizer *i* or the complementizer-like verb-noun *bod*. As for the object, there is unfortunately no way to decide how it is licensed, beyond the fact that licensing necessarily takes place within the extended verbal projection.[26]

23.5 Predicative VNPs can occupy nominal positions

The main topic of the preceding subsections was the functional architecture of Welsh verbo-nominal phrases. The central question was that of the identity of the category-defining head minimally c-commanding the Root and the potential presence of an additional switching category projected above the first functional projection. The goal of this inquiry was to determine whether the structures under consideration should be viewed as instantiating strong categorial mixing.

The discussion of the gerund Acc-*ing* construction in chapter IV has shown that some structures display a different kind of mixing, namely weak categorial mixing, induced by a mismatch between the internal structure of the domain and its external distribution. A priori, we don't know whether such a situation should be dealt with using the device of category-switching heads or whether a different syntactic process is involved. With respect to Acc-*ing* constructions, it was concluded that an analysis based on labeling should be preferred.

The Welsh examples (33a) and (33b) show that an adverb can occur in a VNP projection that has the external distribution of a nominal phrase.

(33) a. *Rhedeg yn   gyflym yw   priodwedd gyntaf milwr.*
       run.VN PRED fast   be.PRES.3.SG quality   first soldier
       'Running fast is the soldier's first quality.'

   b. *Mae   ymarfer   yn   gyson   yn   llesol.*
       be.PRES.3.SG train.VN PRED regular PRED beneficial
       'Training regularly is beneficial.'

---

[26] In chapter VII, it will be shown that Middle Welsh root VN-clauses solve the case problem raised by verbo-nominal transitive constructions in a different way: They resort to an ergative alignment strategy.

23.5 Predicative VNPs can occupy nominal positions

The challenge here is to explain how an apparently argumental VNP projection can contain an adverb. The presence of the adverb suggests that some v is part of the internal make-up of the VNP. At the same time, the expression occupies a site which usually hosts noun phrases. This combination of verbal and nominal properties could indicate that we are not dealing with a homogeneous domain, but with a mixed projection. The decision to characterize Welsh VNPs as instantiating strong or weak category mixing much depends on the analysis of examples of this type.

A first analytical option, represented in (34), consists in claiming that a category-switching head n is present above the vP constituent headed by the category-defining v.

(34) $[_{nP} \ldots n \, [_\alpha DP_s \, [_{vP} v\text{-}vX \, [\, \cancel{vX} \, DP_o \,]]]]$

If this analysis is correct, the verbo-nominal phrases in the relevant structures are nominals derived from verbs, "nominalized verb phrases". They are neither "verbalized nouns", nor nominals directly derived from categorially neutral roots. If one reasons in these terms, the apparently dual nature of VNPs in these constructions is traced back to the presence in their internal structure of an additional functional head, a switch in Panagiotidis's (2015) terminology, inserted at the cut-off point between two projections and determining a categorial change. It presupposes that, within the VNP projections in (33a) and (33b), there is an internal partition between two categorially homogeneous subparts, the lower one (verbal), the higher one (nominal). Alternatively, it could be argued that examples like (33) do not in and of themselves suffice to show that VNPs are mixed categories in the strong sense. The possibility that they display a homogeneous verbal internal structure that happens to have a nominal external distribution, much as Acc-*ing* constructions do, should not be dismissed. And the situation could be dealt with along the same lines as the ones followed in the case of Acc-*ing* constructions. The only condition for this analysis to go through would be to assume that the relevant structures contain a null pro-like subject that derivationally moves from the original external argument position internal to vP to a position adjoined to the projection XP minimally containing VNP. X can only be T. The raising of the null subject out of vP would have the effect of assigning the label <φ, φ> to the resulting syntactic object, which can thus display a nominal distribution. To explain that the labeling strategy can be used in this case, it must be assumed that the null subject and the T head itself are endowed with φ-features, so that a φ-feature-sharing relation between the raised subject and the TP projection can be established.[27]

In chapter VI, I show that the insertion of a category switch is not required in the relevant structures. It seems that, contrary to the situation found in Irish (cf. sct. 23.3), category switches can be dispensed with entirely in the account of contemporary Welsh verbo-nominal projections. Situations indeed exist where the resort to these heads is an option, but, contrary to what happens in Irish, the relevant facts can also be dealt otherwise. This conclusion meets up with the one that was reached in chapter IV with respect to Acc-*ing* constructions, which could be accounted for without resorting to the category-switching device.[28]

As a final remark, it should be noted that the claim that natural languages resort to structures like (35) would be highly implausible.

(35)   n > v > n > Root

(35) would arise if (i) the lowest projection within a complex phrase was analyzed as nominal, a result obtained via the insertion of the categorizing n head above Root (explaining genitive marking), if (ii) it underwent a first categorial change via the insertion of a v switch (which would account for the possibility of adverbs), and if (iii) this categorial change was followed by a second one performed by the insertion of a second n switch (intended to account for the nominal distribution of the expression). The situation schematized in (35) is not excluded by the assumptions made so far about category-defining and category-switching heads. A reasonable constraint on the use of switches could be that a given extended projection can only include one of them and cannot be the *locus* of two successive categorial changes, going in opposite directions.[29]

---

[27] Recall that in Landau's analysis, PRO bears no φ-features when it is inserted into derivation. If the labeling analysis is adopted in the case under consideration, the null subject must be assumed to be a φ-endowed, hence a pro-like entity.

[28] An unquestionable advantage of the category-switching approach over the labeling one is that it opens the way to a precise characterization of where, in a mixed projection, the properties of one category end and the properties of another category begin. But this result can also be obtained in the labeling approach: The verbal properties end up at the derivational stage where subject raising (the movement of the silent pro in examples (33)) takes place, producing a <φ, φ>-labeled configuration. This analysis certainly cannot be extended to examples like (12) and (13) where VNP is preceded by the definite article or a possessive article. For these constructions, we maintain the analysis schematized in (22): We are dealing with categorially homogeneous nominal projections.

[29] Panagiotidis (2015) draws a similar conclusion from different data. He claims that "flip-flopping" is in principle impossible.

24 Aspectual properties of Welsh verb-nouns

Constructions (6)–(8) indicate that, in a subset of contexts, VNs are coupled with an explicit aspectual head that allows the verbo-nominal projection to have fully verbal properties and defines its aspectual profile. In the relevant structures, the VN head is responsible for introducing the lexico-semantic part of the predicate, but the insertion of an Aspect head above VNP is necessary for a predication relation to be established. Dealing with the corresponding Scottish Gaelic constructions, Ramchand (1997) argues that VNs in the predicative use are endowed with an argument structure that specifies the number and the type of the selected arguments, but that it is the Asp head that introduces the event variable in the semantic representation; she suggests that it could also assign the θ-roles that represent the mapping to the event.

A well-known interpretive characteristic should be mentioned at this point. In Welsh, the *yn*+VNP periphrastic construction, usually translated as a progressive, is possible with stative predicates that exclude *-ing* in English. For example, it is compatible with stative verbs, like *adnabod, gwybod* 'to know'.

(36) a. Mae   'n   gwybod   yr   ateb.
        be.PRES.3SG PROG know.VN the answer
        'He/she knows the answer.'

   b. * She is knowing the answer.

As a matter of fact, this construction has not the meaning of a progressive, but acts like a simple imperfective/atelic present tense. The same situation holds in Scottish Gaelic. Ramchand (1997) concludes that verb-nouns (or verbal roots) in this language don't come lexically specified for an event type and are not classified as inherently introducing a bounded or an unbounded event.[30] The outer aspect marker (perfect/perfective *wedi*, imperfective *yn*) imposes its value to the predicate. And *yn*, if it is imperfective, is not progressive. As she observes, the fact that in Celtic periphrastic constructions, the information about outer aspect and the tense information making explicit the temporal anchoring of the process are associated with distinct words, not to affixes to which the lexical root derivationally adjoins, opens the way to a sharper characterization of the respective semantic contributions of the VN, Asp and T heads to the construction of predication

---

[30] Note that *knowing the answer* can also be a temporary state, manifested in a particular situation.

relations. This feature sharply distinguishes verbo-nominal constructions from gerund constructions, where the aspectual value of the -*ing* form is not explicitly marked.

This first difference is correlated with a second one, which resides in the status of the respective suffixes. One cannot exclude that gerund -*ing*, although being neutral with respect to aspectual distinctions and not conveying a specific aspectual value itself, indirectly signals that the corresponding form is aspectually interpretable. On the contrary, the verbo-nominal suffix cannot be an exponent of outer aspect, since the complements of aspectual particles are full-fledged verb-nouns, not verbal roots. An alternative possibility would be that, in the verbal use, the affix marks the verb-noun as being specified for inner aspect. But a dedicated head or suffixal root is not necessary anyway because the inner aspect value of a predicate can be computed on the basis of the verbal root and its arguments. The initial structure of a periphrastic aspectual construction can only be as follows, where Asp stands for the external aspect head:

(37) $[_{CP}\ C\ [_{TP}\ T\ [_{AspP}\ Asp\ [_{\alpha}\ DP_S\ [_{vP}\ v\ [_{RootP}\ \sqrt{aff}\ \sqrt{X}\ DP_o\ ]]]]]]$

This situation can be interpreted as a clue that the Welsh verbo-nominal affix is not itself specified for aspect and tense. When these dimensions are present, they must have independent words as their exponents.

25 Conclusion

Verb-nouns in contemporary Welsh occur either in a verbal/propositional structure (cf. (21)) *or* in a nominal structure (cf. (22)) and should thus be characterized as bivalent categories/transcategorial items. When the category-defining head v is selected, the resulting word has verbal properties; when n is selected, the resulting word has nominal properties. We have not met any indisputable cases of category mixing in the syntax of verbo-nominal constituents: The genitive case, if one assumes that it is abstractly assigned to the direct argument of VNs, should be viewed as a default case; the fact that verbo-nominal constituents in the predicative use are allowed to occur in nominal positions should be dealt with in labeling terms.

We are left with a minimal characterization of the Welsh verbo-nominal suffix. It doesn't convey any specific aspectual interpretation and is not specified for voice or tense. It has no properties (or it has exclusively negative ones), which means that the voice, aspect and tense specifications, when they are present in a verbo-nominal domain, must be borne by independent words.

VI **The syntax of Welsh verbo-nominal clauses**

Welsh epistemic and declarative predicates such as *credu* 'believe' and *dweud* 'say', as well as future *irrealis* predicates like *disgwyl* 'expect' and *bwriadu* 'intend', which take finite *y*-clauses as objects, can also govern nonfinite clauses.¹ These clauses come in two varieties, depending on whether the embedded predicate (i) designates a state of affairs contemporary with or anterior to the situation or the event denoted by the matrix predicate, or (ii) refers to a punctual event localized in the past or interpreted as unrealized at the time of the matrix clause. The first type is the *bod*-initial aspectual periphrasis [*bod* DP Asp VNP], where *bod* is the verb-noun form of the highly irregular verb 'be'.² The second type is the [*i* DP VNP] construction, that generally includes no aspectual specification and in which the lexical subject is preceded by the element *i*, homophonous to the preposition *i* 'to', 'for', the prototypical marker of destination. How are these two constructions derived? What are their respective functional architectures? Let us concentrate on *i*-initial constructions first.

---

1 Jones & Thomas (1977) provide the following list of verbs taking a verbo-nominal clause with an overt or covert subject as a complement: *addo* 'promise', *anghofio* 'forget', *arfer* 'get used to', *bwriadu* 'intend', *bygwth* 'threaten', *ceisio* 'try', *cofio* 'remember', *cytuno* 'agree', *darfod* 'finish', *dechrau* 'start', *dewis* 'choose', *digwydd* 'happen', *dioddef* 'suffer', *disgwyl* 'expect', *dymuno* 'will', *gobeitio* 'hope', *gorffen* 'finish', *gwrthod* 'refuse', *licio* 'like', *meddwl* 'think', *methu* 'fail', *mwynau* 'enjoy', *mynnu* 'wish', *ofni* 'fear', *penderfynu* 'decide', *smalio* 'pretend', *trio* 'try'.
2 The *bod*-initial construction is studied in section 27. The indicative present tense third person singular form of *bod* is *mae*, the indicative imperfect third person singular form is *oedd*.

26 *i*-initial verbo-nominal clauses

Here are some illustrative examples of *i*-initial clauses.

(1) a. *Dywedodd   Emyr i Siôn fynd   i Gaerdydd.*
        say.PAST.3SG Emyr *i* Siôn go.VN   to Cardiff
        'Emyr said that Sîon had gone to Cardiff.'

   b. *Gwn   i Mair orffen   cyn   i 'r   lleill   ddod.*
        know.PRES.1SG *i* Mair finish.VN before *i* the others come.VN
        'I know that Mair had finished before the others arrived.'

   c. *Yr   oedd   Mair yn   credu   iddo   ei   gweld.*
        PRT be.IMPF3SG Mair PROG believe.VN *i*.3M.SG CL.3F.SG see.VN
        'Mair believed that he had seen her.'

   d. *Bwriadai   'r athro   i'r   plant   ddarllen   llyfr arall.*
        intend.IMPF.3SG   the teacher *i* the children read.VN   book other
        'The teacher intended to make the children read another book.'

   e. *Disgwyliodd   Sîon iddi   ennill.*
        expect.PAST.3SG Sîon *i*.3F.SG win.VN
        'Sîon expected her to win.'

From a semantic perspective, two uses should be distinguished. The verbo-nominal predicates included in the complements to epistemic/declarative predicates in (1a), (1b), (1c) denote an event or a process that is anterior to the one referred to by the matrix predicate. On the contrary, the nonfinite complements to expectation or desiderative predicates such as *disgwyl* or *bwriadu* (cf. 1d, 1e) are interpreted as unrealized at the time set by the matrix clause, which fixes the reference time of the whole sentence. In both constructions, the verbo-nominal clause (henceforth VN-clause) conveys a temporal interpretation that is distinct from the one of the matrix clause. This gives some plausibility to the claim that a T head (or a Modal head) with no morphological realization is projected in the relevant domains.[3]

---

[3] On the tense of Welsh nonfinite domains, see section 29.

Note: This chapter is an updated and much revised English version of the chapter IV of my *Syntaxe du gallois*, published in 1994. The proposals made in this chapter are couched within a different framework, but I remain loyal to some of the ideas put forth in my former contribution.

The major challenge taken up in this section is to determine the status of the particle *i* preceding the overt subject in the relevant structures.

26.1 *i* as a nonfinite complementizer

When the subject is pronominal, it is morphologically represented by an inflectional mark affixed to *i* (cf. 1c, 1e). This property recalls the behavior of the inflected preposition *i*, which is also specified for the grammatical features of its pronominal complement (as all the so-called "inflected prepositions" are). Suppose that an incorporation-like process is involved in the derivation of these configurations. If it is the case, the host category must minimally c-command the original site of the incorporated category, a condition that is fulfilled if *i* stands in C/Fin and the pronoun has been merged in SpecTP. Coordination data, however, indicate that *i* doesn't find itself with respect to the subject in the same structural relation as a preposition with respect to its complement. Harlow (1983) discusses the following examples:

(2) a. *Disgwyliai   Emrys i Siôn ganu   ac   i Mair ddawnsio.*
       expect.IMPF.3SG Emrys *i* Siôn sing.VN and   *i* Mair dance.VN
       'Emrys expected that Siôn would sing and that Mair would dance.'

   b. ?? *Disgwyliai   Emrys i Siôn ganu   a   Mair ddawnsio.*
         expect.IMPF.3SG Emrys *i* Siôn sing.VN and Mair dance.VN

   c. * *Disgwyliai   Emrys i Siôn ac   i Mair ganu.*
        expect.IMPF.3SG Emrys *i* Siôn and *i* Mair sing.VN

   d. *Disgwyliai   Emrys i Siôn a   Mair ganu.*
      expect.IMPF.3SG Emrys *i* Siôn and Mair sing.VN
      'Emrys expected that Siôn and Mair would sing.'

The well-formedness of (2a) doesn't come as a surprise since a coordination of *i*-clauses is clearly involved. It is much preferred to (2b), where the second clause is not preceded by *i*. (2d) doesn't raise any special difficulty: The subject phrase is comprised of a coordination of two proper names depending on a single occurrence of *i*. It is the ungrammaticality of (2c) that is significant. According to Harlow, it should be taken as a robust indication that *i*, when it functions as a complementizer, doesn't behave as prepositional *i*. Indeed, the coordination of two prepositional phrases headed by *i* systematically gives rise to a well-formed sequence (cf. 3a), just as the coordination of two nominal expressions complements to the same *i* does (cf. 3b).

(3) a. Rhoddodd   Siôn blodau   *i* Mair ac   *i* Rhian.
give.PAST.3SG Siôn flowers to Mair and to Rhian
'Siôn gave flowers to Mair and to Rhian.'

b. *Rhoddodd Siôn blodau i Mair a Rhian.*

The ungrammaticality of (2c) would also be difficult to explain in an approach where *i* would be analyzed as a dummy case marker adjoined to the subject DP, according to the schema [$_{DP}$ *i* DP]. It corresponds to the expected situation if the analysis of *i*-clauses is as in (4), where *i* has a complementizer status and the *i*+DP$_s$ sequence doesn't qualify as a constituent.[4]

(4) (V) [$_{CP}$ [$_C$ *i*] [$_α$ DP$_s$ [$_{TP}$ [$_T$ Ø] [$_{vP}$ VNP]]]]

The relative marginality of (2b) confirms that the marker *i* has a status different from that of the preposition *i* (compare 3b). This conclusion doesn't immediately follow from the analysis schematized in (4), but is fully compatible with it: (2b) doesn't show that *i* is not realized in C/Fin or that the sequence *Mair ddawnsio* is not a constituent. The behavior of *i* in (2b) is parallel to that of the French infinitival marker *de*, which Kayne (1981) analyzes as a nonfinite complementizer and which, as he notes, must be repeated in front of each infinitival conjunct:

(5) Pierre a essayé de parler fort et *(de) chanter juste.

The same conclusion holds for the subordination marker *que* in French and for the Welsh particle *y* introducing finite tensed clauses, elements that should also clearly be analyzed as complementizers.[5]

(6) *Dywedodd*   *Siôn y darllenai*   *ac*   *(y) mwynheuai Emrys y*   *llyfr.*
say.PAST.3SG Siôn y read.IMPF.3SG and   *y* like.IMPF.3SG Emrys the book
'Siôn said that Emrys would read and like the book.'

At the same time, (6) reveals that the parallelism between the declarative complementizer *y* and *i*, which can be viewed as its nonfinite counterpart, is only

---

4 Sproat (1985) was the first to classify *i* as a complementizer.
5 (6) is from Harlow (1983).

partial. The coordination of two subjects under *i* produces a grammatical result (cf. 2d), but the result of coordination is ungrammatical if *i* is repeated in front of the second conjunct (cf. 2c). In a coordination structure associating two finite clauses, each clause-initial verb must be preceded by *y* (cf. 6). The omission of *y* in front of the second verb would give rise to ungrammaticality. This difference could follow from the fact that *y* and the finite verb form an unsplittable unit in C/Fin, contrary to *i* and the following nominal subject which occupy distinct positions, C/Fin and SpecTP respectively.

In conclusion, *i* occupies an autonomous functional head, which can plausibly be identified with Fin, that is, with the lowest head of the left periphery in Rizzi's (1997) cartographic schema.

26.2 *i* as a case licenser

The way the embedded subject is case licensed must be made explicit. If *i* is lacking in exemples (1), the sentence is ungrammatical, suggesting that it plays a crucial role in the syntactic licensing of the subject.

(7) * *Dywedodd Emyr Siôn fynd i Gaerdydd.*

Conversely, the occurrence of *i* in the structures under discussion is strictly limited to the situations where the nonfinite complement clause contains an explicit subject in pre-VN position.[6] Some epistemic/declarative predicates, as well as future *irrealis* verbs, can also function as control predicates and *i* is usually absent in this case. *i* is also lacking in obligatory control constructions.[7]

(8) a. *'Dwi   'n   cofio   siarad   efo Mair.*
        be.PRES.1SG PROG remember.VN talk.VN with Mair
        'I remember talking with Mair.'

   b. *Disgwyliodd   Siôn ennill.*
        expect.PAST.3SG Siôn win.VN
        'Siôn expected to win.'

---

6 This statement is not fully accurate. It will appear in subsection 26.3 that *i* systematically occurs in front of null-subject VN-clauses, when they are not the unique or the first objects of the matrix predicate.
7 But some control verbs also lexically select a complement clause headed by *i* as a first object: *cytuno* 'consent', *cydsynio* 'consent', *ymdrechu* 'endeavour', *ymgeisio* 'endeavour'.

c. *Bwriadai   'r athro   ddarllen llyfr arall.*
   intend.IMPF.3SG the teacher read.VN book other
   'The teacher intended to read another book.'

d. *gan obeithio   clywed   oddi wrthych ...*
   with hope.VN   hear.VN   from with.2PL
   'with the hope of hearing from you ...'

e. *Penderfynodd   y cadeirydd gyfarfod am 5.*
   decide.PAST.3SG the chairman meet.VN at 5
   'The chairman decided to meet at 5.'[8]

If one reasons within the set of assumptions made available by the Principles and Parameters framework and if verbo-nominal complements without an overt subject are analyzed as full clauses, it must be guaranteed that the embedded subject position is not governed by the matrix verb. The presence of *i* would exclusively be required to insure the case licensing of overt subjects. But *i* is absent when the subject is PRO, because the occurrence of PRO is restricted to ungoverned sites. An analytical possibility consists in the claim that there exists a null counterpart to the nonfinite complementizer *i*, say $Ø_i$. $Ø_i$ is present in control structures, where it induces a barrier to the government of the grammatical subject position by the matrix verb (two maximal projections intervene between V and PRO). The relevant structure is (9). It should be compared with (10), the representation associated with *i*-clauses.[9]

(9)   V [$_{CP}$ [$_C$ $Ø_i$] [$_α$ [PRO] [$_{TP}$ T VNP]]]

(10) V [$_{CP}$ [$_C$ *i*] [$_α$ [DP$_s$] [$_{TP}$ T VNP]]]

Still using the Principle and Parameters concepts and devices, the preceding account can be sharpened by taking up a suggestion of Pesetsky (1992) concerning English *for* and provisionally assuming that the intervening functional head [$_C$ $Ø_i$] functions as a potential governor, sheltering the embedded subject from government by the matrix verb, without itself functioning as a governor. The only element that can occupy the subject position in (9) is thus PRO. To explain the obligatory occurrence of *i* in front of lexical subjects, it suffices to say that, con-

---

[8] The partial control interpretation of the complement is available with some of these predicates, in fact it is forced when the embedded verb-noun is a collective (cf. 8e).
[9] VNP stands for v-RootP, see chapter V.

trary to its null counterpart, *i* qualifies as a full-fledged governor and as a case licenser. In (10), DP$_s$ can only be a nominal expression or a pronoun whose features are spelled out on *i* (cf. 1c, 1e).

The gist of this proposal can easily be captured within the probe-goal-Agree framework. It suffices to say that prepositional complementizers are probes (cf. Kayne 2000), that *i* has the status of a complementizer when it is first merged at the Fin-level and that it is endowed with uninterpretable φ-features that allow it to probe the overt subject and enter into an Agree relation with it. Contrary to *i*, $Ø_i$ is not be endowed with the relevant features and can't function as a probe.

26.3 *i* as a nonfiniteness marker

Up to now, two syntactic patterns have been isolated, (9) and (10). The existence of a third one potentially raises a serious difficulty against the proposal made so far. Structures exist where the verbo-nominal predicate of a nonfinite domain is preceded by *i*, although no explicit subject is present. The phenomenon can be observed in object control constructions.

(11) a. *Mae   hwn wedi argyhoeddi   Siôn i siarad   efo Mair.*
       be.PRES.3SG this PERF convince.VN Siôn *i* speak.VN with Mair
       'This convinced Siôn to speak with Mair.'

   b. *Dysgwyd   ef   i ddarllen.*
      teach.PAST.IMP 3MSG   *i* read.VN
      'He was taught to read.'

   c. *Cynghoraf   chwi i ddod.*
      advise. PRES.1SG 2PL   *i* come.VN
      'I (will) advise you to come.'

   d. *Annogodd   y dynion i geisio   maddeuant.*
      urge.PAST.3SG the men   *i* seek.VN forgiveness
      'He incited the men to seek forgiveness.'

In none of these examples is the insertion of *i* imposed by the necessity to license a lexical subject. The problem they raise is twofold: It must be explained (i) why the null infinitival marker $Ø_i$ is not legitimate, and (ii) why the presence of *i* doesn't identify the site that hosts PRO as a governed position.

The examples in (11) illustrate situations where the sequence introduced by *i* is the second object of a verbal predicate. It is easy to show that the direct argument and the verbo-nominal phrase constitute distinct syntactic entities. All the matrix predicates in examples (11) assign a θ-role to the following nominal expression, which must be animate. In this respect, they differ from *disgwyl* "expect", which imposes no comparable restriction on the associated nominal expression, whose thematic status exclusively depends on the embedded verb. (11a) is an appropriate answer to the interrogative sentence (12), which results from the substitution of an interrogative expression for the VN-complement:

(12) Beth   mae   hwn yn   argyhoeddi   Siôn ohono?
     what   be.PRES.3SG   this PROG   convince.VN   Siôn of.3.MSG
     'What does this convince Siôn of?'

In (12), the second object is built as the complement of the preposition *o* 'from'. But it is *i*, not *o*, that occurs in example (11a), which suggests that a preposition-deletion process takes place in the relevant structures, preceded or followed by the insertion of the complementizer *i*. On this basis, Jones & Thomas (1977) argue that the relevant phrase should be analyzed as the complement to a deleted preposition on the left branch of the grammar, between Transfer and PF.[10]

If one adopts the "shell" analysis initially proposed by Larson (1988) and adapted by Chomsky (1995b) and Chomsky & Lasnik (1993), the second object occupies a position lower than the first one. The vP structure of (11a), resulting from a sequence of External Merge operations, before any movement takes place, can informally be schematized as follows:

(13) [vP *hwn* v [VP [DP *Siôn*] [V' [V *argyhoeddi*] [CP *i* PRO T *siarad efo Mair*]]]]

In the course of the derivation, *argyhoeddi* adjoins to the light verb v. My contention is that the obligatory occurrence of *i* in examples (11) (and in (13)) should be traced back to the fact that the intervening first object prevents the second one from accessing the matrix verb. To fully understand what is at stake, an additional notion could be relevant, namely that of "visibility": As is the case of any nominal or propositional argument, the second object in (13), which is a verbo-nominal

---

10 The occurrence of a preposition in front of the nominal complement and its absence before a propositional complement make the Welsh construction similar to the corresponding French examples in (i)-(iii). Gross (1968) analyzes the finite clause in (iii) as a domain depending on a deleted preposition.

(i)   *Ceci a convaincu Jean de la culpabilité de Marie.*
(ii) *Ceci a convaincu Jean de parler à Marie.*
(iii) *Ceci a convaincu Jean que Marie était coupable.*

propositional domain, must be "visible" in order to be accessible to θ-marking by the selecting predicate. But contrary to tensed clauses, which are systematically headed by an overt complementizer in Welsh and seem to define inherently visible contentive entities, two kinds of conditions can make a nonfinite domain visible: Either the relevant CP is the first object of the matrix verb – in which case, CP/FinP and its head C/Fin are minimally c-commanded by the verb that has raised to the higher position in the vP-shell -, or it qualifies as a vP-internal second object and its C/Fin head must be phonetically realized and morphologically manifested. The role of *i* in (13) is precisely to make the nonfinite domain "visible", exactly as the preposition *to* in (14) makes its complement visible.[11]

---

11 The presence of *de* before the infinitive in French when it heads the second object of a ditransitive predicate like *convaincre* 'convince' can be explained along similar lines. Examining a subclass of transitive verbs that can freely cooccur either with an infinitival object or with a combination nominal object+infinitival complement, Muller (2002) observes that in contemporary French, no *de* precedes the infinitive in the first case and that *de* is necessarily present in the second.

(i)   Je   souhaite gagner   la   course.
     1SG.NOM wish   win.INF   the race
     'I wish to win the race.'

(ii)   Je   te   souhaite de gagner   la   course.
     1SG.NOM 2SG.DAT wish   *de* win.INF   the race
     'I wish you to win the race.'

The two examples also differ in that the controller of the infinitival subject is the matrix subject in (i), the direct object in (ii).

The marker *de* thus seems to function as a nonfiniteness marker in some lexical environments, making an infinitival clause visible. But contrary to Welsh *i*, it never functions as a case licenser.

It should also be observed that in the two languages, cases exist where the nonfinite marker precedes the complement in constructions where its presence is not required by visibility considerations.

(iii)   Il avait imaginé   de le   tromper.
      he had imagined   *de* 3.SG.MASC   cheat
      'He had imagined cheating him.'

(iv)   Gwnaeth   Siôn gytuno   *i* orffen ei   waith.
      do.PRET.3SG   Siôn agree   *i* finish CL.3M.SG   work
      'Siôn agreed to finish his work.'

Other subject control verbs in Welsh select an *i*-initial complement, cf. fn. 7 for examples.

(14) *John returned the book to Mary.*

It remains to be explained why *i* doesn't block the occurrence of PRO in the subject position of the verbo-nominal domain. The claim that a complementizer doesn't necessarily function as a governor with respect to the grammatical subject position should be extended to this case. But before doing this, an alternative option should be eliminated. Since the subject argument is null, we don't know a priori whether *i* is realized in C/Fin, as in (15), or in T, as in (16).[12]

(15) V DP$_o$ [$_{CP}$ [$_C$ *i*] [$_\alpha$ PRO [$_{TP}$ T VNP]]]

(16) V DP$_o$ [$_{CP}$ C [$_\alpha$ PRO [$_{TP}$ [$_T$ *i*] VNP]]]

Only in (15) does *i* qualify as a complementizer. An indication that *i* is indeed realized in C/Fin at Transfer is provided by the following paradigm, in which a lexical DP has been substituted for PRO:

(17) *Perswadiodd   yr athro   y   rhieni*
    persuade.PAST.3SG the teacher the parents

  a. ? *i 'r   plant   ddarllen   y   llyfr.*
       i the   children   read.VN   the   book

  b. ** *'r   plant   i ddarllen   y   llyfr.*
       the children *i* read.VN   the   book

  c. * *i 'r   plant   i ddarllen y   llyfr.*
       i the children *i* read   the book
  'The teacher persuaded the parents that the children had read the book.'

(17a) is marginal, but not excluded (a finite *y*-clause or a *bod*-clause would be more natural in this context); (17b), in which *i* is hosted by T, is felt as strongly ungrammatical; in (17c), *i* has been inserted both in front of the subject and in front of the verbo-nominal phrase and the result is ungrammatical. We see that none of the examples in paradigm (17) provides positive evidence that *i* is ever realized in T at Transfer. In fact, T is empty at this level.

But an additional possibility must still be eliminated, namely that in the relevant structures, *i* (or the feature matrix it is a realization of) first merges with T, then derivationally moves to C/Fin: *i* could be one of the forms taken by nonfinite

---

[12] This double possibility is discussed in Rouveret (1994).

T when it moves to C/Fin.¹³ This option can readily be eliminated once the properties of Welsh C/Fin are more carefully considered. In section 6, it was proposed that [+ finite] C/Fin in Celtic keeps its uninterpretable φ-features and doesn't transmit them to T. It is plausible to assume that tense is also represented at this level, as it is in the Irish structures discussed by Cottell (1995).¹⁴ An Agree relation is established between the uninterpretable [tense] feature on C/Fin and T's interpretable [tense], valuing the former. Suppose that the nonfinite complementizer in VN-clauses displays the same properties: C/Fin keeps its uninterpretable φ-features, including case, which coexist with an uninterpretable [tense] feature. The simplest analysis consists in claiming that *i* is first merged with nonfinite C, whose features [u-tense]/[u-φ] it supports.

26.4 Interim summary

The following generalizations hold at Transfer.

(18) a. Welsh has two nonfinite complementizers at its disposal, *i* and $\emptyset_i$;
 b. *i* is selected in all the contexts where the nonfinite domain is not structurally adjacent to the matrix verbal predicate;¹⁵ its insertion makes the clause it heads visible; $\emptyset_i$ doesn't have this effect;
 c. *i* also functions as a case licenser for lexical subjects in the contexts where the clause it heads is structurally adjacent to the matrix predicate; its covert counterpart $\emptyset_i$ never functions as a case licenser;
 d. when it functions as a case licenser, *i* is endowed with φ-features; when it functions a nonfiniteness marker, φ-features are lacking.

As they stand, proposals (18a-d) do no more than restating the facts. But their exact significance should not be missed. The occurrence of *i* is not exclusively triggered by case-licensing considerations; *i*, in some contexts, also functions as a nonfiniteness marker, providing the feature [nonfinite] with an exponent and

---

13 See Pesetsky & Torrego's (2001) proposal that *that* actually corresponds to the way T is spelled out when moved to C. The complementizer *for* is also taken to originate in T. If the *i*-as-nonfinite-T hypothesis was adopted, (4) and (10) should be rewritten accordingly, with T hosting the trace of *i*.
14 See sct. 6 for discussion.
15 A VN-domain is structurally adjacent to the matrix verbal predicate if it is the higher or the unique complement of this predicate.

making the nonfinite domain it heads visible. The structures that fall under this characterization are those where the VN-clause is the second object of a verbal predicate. Taken together, (18b) and (18c) imply that the only contexts where *i* can be dispensed with are clauses without an overt subject, which are structurally adjacent to the matrix predicate, cf. examples (8).

It is desirable to make the analysis tighter. The observations that precede indicate that the Welsh particle *i* possesses what Kihm (2007) describes as the "toggle property". By definition, toggle exponents "express either one of two non-default values". This is the case of *i*, which can either mark nonfiniteness or function as a case licenser, but never fulfills the two functions at the same time. There is no evidence that it is endowed with φ-features when it is the exponent of nonfiniteness; conversely, nonfiniteness has no exponent in the structures where *i* signals the presence of uninterpretable φ-features on C. This presentation makes very precise predictions on the distribution of *i* and on the distribution of subjects. They are detailed in the next section.

26.5 The syntactic licensing of verbo-nominal clauses and of their subjects

The analysis that follows tries to capture the generalizations in (18) and the toggle property of *i* within the probe-goal-Agree approach to syntactic dependencies.

Let us first recall the conditions that the licensing of overt subjects must obey (see 14 and 21, ch. II). (19) is just a reformulation of Landau's Finiteness Rule for OC.

(19) Conditions on the licensing of overt subjects
The overt subject of a CP/FinP clause is licensed if and only if
   (i)   [tense] is present on T or on both T and C;
   (ii) [tense] is interpretable on T; it is uninterpretable on C and valued via the establishment of an Agree relation between C and T;
   (iii) φ-features are present and overtly manifested on either T or C;
   (iv) the φ-features on T or on C are uninterpretable and valued via Agree between T and DP_{subj} or between C and DP_{subj}.

The presence of interpretable [tense] on T in nonfinite domains is motivated by semantic considerations of the type developed by Stowell, Wurmbrand and Landau. [tense], which is necessarily present and interpretable on T in NC clauses, plausibly also occurs on C in some contexts, where it is uninterpretable. When it is the case, Agree establishes a relation between the two occurrences of [tense].

φ-features, contrary to [tense] features, must be morphologically realized to be active in a given domain. It was shown in section 7.3 that this restriction need not be stipulated. Taken together, the claim that an Agree relation is established between the uninterpretable and interpretable [tense] features on C and T and the hypothesis that C transmits its uninterpretable [φ]'s to T in some languages and constructions, but not in others, is consonant with Landau's idea that both T and C must be taken into account when subject licensing is at stake. Since [finite] and [tense]/[φ] constitute two disjoint sets, it can be assumed that the features involved in subject licensing are exclusively [tense] and [φ] and that [finite] plays no role at all in the process.

Let us now consider the Welsh data more closely. The property that sets apart verb-initial languages, at least Celtic V1 languages, is that C/Fin withholds the uninterpretable φ-features it is initially endowed with from T, a characteristic that was identified via the study of Welsh finite clauses, but turns out to also be relevant to nonfinite ones. The configuration underlying i-clauses is thus as in (20).

(20) DP_i T ... [$_{CP}$ [$_C$ i]   [$_\alpha$ DP_j [$_{TP}$ T ...]]]
              [u-tense]   [i-φ]   [i-tense]
              [u-φ]

Two operations must be performed for the derivation to converge: [tense] interpretation and [φ] valuing. An Agree relation is established between C/Fin's uninterpretable [tense] and T's interpretable [tense], another one between C/Fin's uninterpretable φ-features and DP_j's interpretable ones. The presence of DP_i within the CP/FinP domain allows i to value its uninterpretable φ-features. Conversely, the case feature on i allows the case licensing of DP_j. In this case, the raising of the subject out of vP is triggered by valuing considerations. It is plausible to assume that i functioning as a probe favors the configurations where it minimally c-commands the overt subject, which makes the resort to long-distance Agree unnecessary. When the uninterpretable φ-features on C/Fin are valued via Agree with a local subject and its case feature checked, all the necessary valuation relations are performed within the minimal CP/FinP phase coinciding with the embedded VN-clause.

Two additional characteristics of the licensing process must be mentioned. First, agreement φ-features are not morphologically manifested when the subject is an overt referential expression (cf. 1a, b, d); they are spelled out as an affix only when the subject argument is pronominal (cf. 1c, 1e). This asymmetric behavior of nouns and pronouns with respect to agreement relations is a general property of Welsh syntax. This situation is quite unexpected in Landau's approach. It indicates that the Agr specification in the NC clauses that he classifies as [+T, +Agr] can be abstract in some languages and constructions. Second, overt subjects are licensed only if the presence of the relevant features is signaled by the spell-out of C/Fin as i. The overtness of C/Fin seems to be a necessary condition for its [tense] and [φ] to be active.

Control structures instantiate a different situation. The representation corresponding to an exhaustive control construction is schematized in (21).

(21) DP_i T ... [$_{CP}$ [$_C$ Ø]   [$_α$ PRO$_j$ [$_{TP}$ T ...]]]
                                                            [u-tense]

(21) differs from (20) in that neither C, nor T are endowed with φ-features. Because we are dealing with an exhaustive control complement, T is not specified for an interpretable feature. Landau's rule states that if either semantic tense or morphological agreement is lacking in a clausal domain or if both are absent, an overt subject cannot be licensed and the only option is PRO. In (21), Both PRO and C/Fin are deprived of the φ-features that would allow them to enter into an Agree relation. The null counterpart of i, $Ø_i$, indicates that the features on C/Fin, if present, are inactive. PRO, when it is inserted in the derivation, is deprived of φ-features. It thus cannot cooccur with i, which signals that the φ-features on C/Fin are active and valued locally. As a consequence, PRO can only acquire φ-features derivationally and only via Agree with matrix T or with the controller DP. The Agree relation in this case associates entities that do not belong to the same CP/FinP phase. Control structures prototypically illustrate a situation where it is necessary to establish an inter-phasal relation to achieve the licensing of the embedded subject. The embedded clause is not convergent in this case. In deciding whether the embedded subject can be overt or must be PRO, the notion of phase plays a crucial role.

We know that i has a double status and that it must also be spelled out in some environments to make the verbo-nominal clause visible. Suppose that visibility obeys the following condition:

(22) Visibility Condition:
   (i) A VN-clause is visible when structurally adjacent to the matrix predicate.
   (ii) A VN-clause is not visible in the contexts where it is not structurally adjacent to the matrix predicate, unless an explicit nonfiniteness marker is inserted.

If one assumes that clauses must be visible in order to be θ-marked, (22) states that the C/Fin head of a VN-clause doesn't have to be morphologically manifested when the clause is the unique or the higher complement of the verbal predicate.

It is easy to check that these assumptions correctly derive the generalizations in (18) and the fact that the Welsh particle *i* displays the toggle property, which either marks nonfiniteness or supports C/Fin's [tense] and φ-features, but cannot do the two things at the same time.[16] The only configurations that can dispense with *i* are those where the VN-clause is the first or the only object of the matrix predicate and has a PRO subject. Obligatory control complements such as the ones in (8) fit this description. Since they are adjacent to the matrix verb, no *i* is required to make them visible or to license the subject. The second case is represented by the control structures in which the VN-clause is the second object of the selecting predicate, as is the case in examples (11) and in structure (13). The insertion of *i* is imposed by the Visibility Condition (22). No overt subject can be licensed in this case, which reflects the fact that the corresponding C/Fin is marked for [tense], but is deprived of agreement features. The last case corresponds to the situation where the VN-clause is adjacent to the matrix verb and is headed by *i* governing an overt subject: *i* manifests the [tense]/[φ]/ [case] features of C.

Since *i* either spells out [– finite] or activates [tense]/[φ], the spell-out of [– finite], when it is imposed by visibility considerations, should have no effect on the licensing of overt subjects. In fact, it is predicted that an overt subject cannot occur in the position occupied by PRO in the constructions where the presence of *i* is required to make the VN-clause visible, a situation illustrated by the constructions where a VN-clause is the second object, as in examples (11) and structure (13). This result can be derived on a principled basis. If the wrong *i* was accidentally inserted in these constructions, the derivation would crash, because the φ-endowed *i* cannot coexist with PRO (PRO being deprived of φ-features, the uninterpretable φ's on *i* couldn't be valued). It would not converge either if a full referential DP was present in the embedded subject position (instead of PRO). The overt subject would indeed be properly licensed in this case. But the selec-

---

16 In the realizational conception of morphology in which Kihm's analysis is couched, "toggle exponents express either one of two non-default values". In the case he discusses – nominal inflection in Romanian -, a single exponent expresses either the oblique non-default case when number has the default value, namely singular, or the plural non-default value of number. A strongly supported empirical observation is that default feature values such as singular are not expressed by dedicated exponents. In the case under consideration, it could be argued that the default case is represented by the Fin heading control structures with a PRO subject and adjacent to the matrix verb. In control structures not adjacent to the matrix verb and in clausal structures with an overt subject, the corresponding Fin corresponds to two non-default cases and must be overt. Welsh resorts to the same particle *i* in both cases.

tional requirement of the matrix verb, which requires a controlled complement, would not be satisfied.[17]

26.6 Nonfinite interrogatives and relatives

The account developed in the preceding section can be extended to other structures where the verbo-nominal domain is not structurally adjacent to the matrix verb and the occurrence of *i* is required. This is the case in nonfinite interrogatives/relatives.

(23) a. Wn   i   ddim beth i 'w   wneud.
       know.PRES.1SG 1SG NEG   what *i* CL3.MSG do.VN
       'I don't know what to do.'
   b. Yr   oeddynt   yn   penderfynu beth i 'w   gael   nesaf.
       PRT be.IMPF.3PL PROG decide   what *i* CL3.MSG get.VN next
       'They were deciding what to take afterwards.'
   c. Ni   ŵyr   y   meddyg ddim pa beth i'w
       NEG know.PRES.3SG the doctor   NEG   what   *i* CL.3MSG
       ddweud wrth   y   wraig glaf.
       say.VN to   the   woman ill
       'The doctor doesn't know what to say to the ill woman.'

The well-formedness of these examples confirms that the corresponding verbo-nominal structures include a CP system and also probably a T head. The only assumption necessary to account for the obligatory presence of *i* is that, when an interrogative/relative *wh*-phrase/*p*-phrase is involved, the position that hosts it is higher than the Fin category containing the nonfinite complementizer, which is the lowest head in the complementizer system. The FinP projection doesn't stand at the edge of the complement phrase in this case. Whence the obligatory insertion of *i*.[18]

---

[17] But, as mentioned in footnote 7, some predicates select a control complement headed by [– finite] *i*.

[18] The analysis of examples (i)-(iii) containing a relative-like nonfinite clause is more delicate.

(i) Nid oedd   gan y dyn   ddim   i 'w   wario.
     Neg be.IMPF.3SG with the man nothing *i* CL.3SG spend.VN
     'The man had nothing to spend.'

The obligatory presence of *i* in nonfinite clauses that are dependent on a noun (cf. 24) or on an adjective (cf. 25) can be explained along similar lines.

(24) a. *addewid Mair i ysgrifennu i Siôn*
promise Mair *i* write.VN to Siôn
'Mair's promise to write to Siôn.'

b. *ymgais Siôn i dwyllo ei ffrindiau.*
attempt Siôn *i* cheat POSS.3MSG friends
'Siôn's attempt to cheat his friends'

c. *tuedd Mair i roi gormod o halen yn y cawl*
tendency Mair *i* put.VN too-much of salt in the soup
'Mair's tendency to put too much salt in the soup'

d. *her Dafydd i Goliatt i ymladd ag ef*
challenge David to Goliath *i* fight with 3msg
'David's challenge to Goliath to fight with him'

(25) *Mae Siôn yn awyddus i weld Mair.*
be.PRES.3SG Siôn PRED eager *i* see.VN Mair
'Siôn is eager to see Mair.'

I will provisionally assume that nominal and adjectival heads behave as if they didn't lexically *select* the clause that functions as their complement. Everything works as if they had no direct lexical access to their complement and as if their complement had no direct lexical access to them. The governing nominal or

---

(ii) *A oes gennych chwi rywbeth i'w ofyn i mi?*
Q be.PRES.3SG with.2PL 2PL something *i* CL.3SG ask to 1sg
'Do you have something to ask me?'

(iii) *Mae rhywbeth i 'w weld o bob ffenestr.*
be.PRES.3SG something *i* CL.3SG see.VN from each window
'There is something to see from each window.'

i in these structures introduces a relative-like clause. Two accounts can be proposed. It could be argued that the relevant constituent is smaller in size than CP with *i* spelling out T and that the *i*-phrase functions as an unsaturated adjunct modifying the antecedent. This option is not compatible with the characterization of *i* arrived at in this chapter and must be eliminated. An alternative possibility consists in claiming that we are dealing with a full-fledged relative CP structure in which *i* occupies the C/Fin position and in which the antecedent has raised out of the CP domain, binding a variable in the object position of the verb-noun, the PRO subject being controlled by the matrix subject or its reference being left unspecified.

adjectival head doesn't suffice to make the relevant nonfinite domains visible. The null complementizer Ø$_i$ would not achieve the desired result either and [– finite] *i* must be inserted. The grammatical subject can only be PRO, since no case is made available internally.

26.7 The case of mandatory predicates

The constructions in (26) illustrate a pattern that is potentially problematic for generalizations (19) and for the account developed so far.

(26) a. *Gofynaf iddo ddod.*
ask.PRES.1SG *i*.3M.SG come.VN
'I will ask him to come.'

b. *Caniataf iddynt aros.*
allow.PRES.1SG *i*.3PL stay.VN
'I allow them to stay.'

c. *Gorchmynnodd i 'w fab ddychwelyd yn brydlon.*
order.PASTT.3SG *i* his son come.back.VN PRED punctual
'He ordered his son to come back on time.'

d. *Gorchmynnodd Mair i'r adroddiad fod yn barod*
order.PAST.3SG Mair *i* the report be.VN PRED ready
erbyn dydd Llun.
by Monday
'Mair ordered that the report be ready on Monday.'

e. *Gorchmynnwyd iddo gael ei saethu.*
order.PAST.IMP *i*.3.MSG get.VN CL.3.MSG shoot
'The order was given that he be shot.'

Some of these examples can straightforwardly be taken to illustrate a pattern analogous to that of epistemic/declarative and future *irrealis* predicates, where the subject of predication is preceded by the marker *i*. The *i*+NP combination undoubtedly belongs to the embedded verbo-nominal domain, when the nominal expression following *i* refers to an inanimate non agentive object, as in (26d), or when the embedded clause is a passive predication, as in (26e). But in other examples, *i*+NP can *also* be interpreted as an applicative complement to the matrix verb, controlling a null subject in the embedded clause. In (26c), for example, the son can fulfill the role of addressee of the order (but it need not).

This interpretation differs from the "performative" one assigned to (26d) and (26e). The structures involved also presumably differ. They could be as follows:

(27) a; V [$_{CP}$ [$_C$ *i*] [DP T VNP]]

b. V [$_{PP}$ P DP] [$_{CP}$ [$_C$ Ø] [$_{TP}$ PRO T . . .]]

Analysis (27a) is not appropriate in the constructions where a preposition distinct from *i* is involved. In (28), only (27b) can be selected.

(28) Erfyniodd   arnaf   fynd   gydaf   ef   bob cam.
     entreat.PAST.3SG on.1SG   come.VN   with.3.MSG 3M.SG   all way
     'He entreated me to come with him all the way.'

But *i* is also a possible choice for P in (27b). In the constructions where it is the case, either analysis is possible. When (27b) is involved, it is the matrix verb that is fully responsible for the selection of the preposition that introduces the applicative complement. Predicates like *gofyn* 'ask', *caniatáu* 'allow', *gorchymyn* 'order' indeed select an *i*-complement (they also take an *i*-complement in the constructions where the two internal arguments of the verb are nominal).

The coexistence of these two structures raises an interesting question: Why is it that the availability of an overt subject in the embedded verbo-nominal clause depends on the absence of an applicative complement in the matrix clause? And, conversely, why is it that the presence of an applicative complement forces the occurrence of a controlled PRO in the subject position of the verbo-nominal clause? These questions can only be answered if one gets a clear understanding of the way the DP/PRO alternation is regulated. The propositions developed in section 26.5 constitute a step into this direction. But the existence of the applicative structure also raises a potential difficulty against the assumptions made about *i*. The fact that the applicative complement systematically precedes the VN-clause, whose subject it controls, is natural. What is unexpected is that *i* doesn't (also) occur in front of the verb-noun in the relevant structures. It should if what has been said about "second objects" in the preceding sections is correct. Welsh grammars however insist that the verb-noun must be bare and cannot be preceded by *i* in the structures under consideration (see for example Anwyl 1899: 98).

An alternative option would consist in claiming that the VN-clause doesn't in fact originate as a "second object" in the relevant structures, but is first merged in the higher complement slot in the vP-shell and that the prepositional argument stands in the lower complement slot.

(29) [DP$_s$ [$_{vP}$ v [$_{VP}$ CP [$_{V'}$ V [$_{PP}$ P DP]]]]]

In order to derive the observed word order, two options should be considered. The first one is that an extraposition process takes place in (29), moving the verbo-nominal phrase to the right of the prepositional argument. But it is argued at length in chapter IX that the VN-clauses that are deprived of a nonfiniteness marker are not visible to θ-assignment when extraposed. The lack of *i* in the relevant structures constitutes a strong indication that *i* is not necessary to make the VN-clause visible to θ-assignment. The reason why this is so is that at no point in the derivation is the VN-clause a second object and that clausal extraposition is not involved in the derivation of the relevant structures. The alternative option is to assume that it is the applicative phrase that raises above the VN-clause in (29), and adjoins to the vP shell.[19]

A third possibility should be explored, which is directly inspired by Burukina's (2020) study of Russian nonfinite complementation. The dual behavior detected in Welsh VN-clauses is manifest with Russian mandative verbs such as *velet'* 'order', *razrešit'* 'allow'. They embed nonfinite clauses whose subject is either an obligatorily controlled PRO or an overt referential DP. The analysis she proposes, because it dispenses with the extraposition of verbo-nominal clause or the raising of the prepositional controller phrase postulated in the preceding paragraphs, should be preferred. The structures corresponding to the two readings of these constructions are as follows. Instead of (27a), we have (30a); instead of (27b), we have (30b).[20]

(30) a. V [$_{ApplP}$ [$_{DP}$ Ø] [$_{ApplP}$ Appl [$_{CP}$ DP T VNP]]]

b. V [$_{ApplP}$ [DP/PP] [$_{ApplP}$ Appl [$_{CP}$ PRO T VNP]]]

The Applicative head introduces and licenses a "holder" DP, which can be implicit and thought of as a caseless φP, in which case Appl licenses the embedded DP subject (cf. (30a)), or explicit, in which case case checking takes place between it and the Appl head in the specifier of the latter (cf. 30b). The advantage of this analysis is to provide an elegant and natural explanation for why constructions with a mandatory predicate make available two interpretations of the same struc-

---

19 This process would be akin to the one involved in the English construction *he gave Mary a book* or *he ordered Paul to leave*.
20 These representations are simplified versions of the ones proposed by Burukina (2020). In particular, she claims that a deontic modal head is projected in between the Appl head and the CP (FinP) projection.

ture (the complement of the predicate is an ApplP projection in both cases). The question of whether the VN-clause is extraposed or the applicative complement raised doesn't even arise. A quite satisfactory result.

The toggle property of *i* can also receive a simple and elegant representation in this approach: *i* spells out the Applicative head in all the constructions where it occurs, whether a DP/PP projection is adjoined to ApplP or not. The only reservation that can be levelled against this analysis is that it makes it difficult to capture the parallelisms between *i*-constructions and *bod*-constructions, which require an entirely different analysis, as will be shown in section 27.

26.8 Verbo-nominal heads do not raise to T

Another facet of these constructions should be dealt with. *i* never occupies the T position at Transfer, but the verb-noun doesn't either. The distribution of negative polarity adverbs like *byth* 'ever' and *bron* 'ever' shows that verb-nouns in nonfinite clauses do not raise higher than v and never reach T. In periphrastic aspectual constructions, these adverbs freely appear between the subject and the aspectual phrase:

(31) a. *'dyw   e   bron   byth yn   smygu.*[21]
       be.PRES.3SG.NEG 3M.SG scarcely ever PROG smoke.VN
       'He scarcely ever smoke.'

   b. *'does   dim byd   byth yn   digwydd.*
       be.PRES.3SG NEG anything ever PROG happen.VN
       'Nothing ever happens.'

In these examples, the verb-noun complement to the aspectual particle has no possibility to raise across it. But the situation is not different in the *i*-initial verbo-nominal structures that contain no aspectual particle.

(32) a. *Ni   fwriadai   'r athro   i 'r plentyn byth*
        NEG intend.IMPF.3SG the teacher *i* the child ever
        ddarllen llyfr o 'r math hwn.
        read.VN book of the kind this
        'The teacher didn't intend for the child to ever read a book of this kind.'

---

21 *'dyw* is a colloquial negative form of the verb *bod* 'be' in the 3rd person singular of the present tense

b. *Ni   wyddai   'r   athro i 'r plentyn erioed ddarllen*
   NEG know.IMPF.3SG the teacher i the child   ever   read.VN
   llyfr o 'r   math hwn.
   book of the kind this
   'The teacher didn't know that the child had ever read a book of this kind.'

If one takes *byth* and *erioed* to be adjoined to the vP projection (or to the AspP one if an Aspect head is projected above vP), these examples definitely show that the verb-noun *darllen* doesn't leave the vP in (32a) and (32b).[22] To explain that lexical verb-nouns do not raise to T, let us tentatively assume that neither T, nor the verb-noun are endowed with the features that would force them to enter into the head system of the language through Agree or Move relations: T bears an interpretable [tense] feature, which doesn't require checking, and inherits no uninterpretable φ-features; the verb-noun itself is not endowed with a [tense] feature, nor with interpretable φ-features. The question is taken up again in section 4 and in chapter VII, where a similar claim is made about Middle Welsh verb-nouns.

---

22 This argument relies on the behavior of a restricted class of adverbs. *bob amser* 'always' illustrates the same phenomenon.

(i) *gwyddoch   inni   bob amser wneud   ein   gorau.*
    know.PRES.2PL i.1PL always   do.VN   CL.1PL best
    'You know we always do our best.'

But in the general case, adverbs cannot intervene between the subject and the verb-noun in structures of this type.

(ii) *Disgwyliai   Siôn i Mair ennill   y   wobr   eleni.*
     expect.IMPF.3SG Siôn *i* Mair win.VN the prize   this year
     'Siôn expected Mair to win the prize this year.'

(iii) * *Disgwyliai Siôn i Mair eleni ennill y wobr.*

27 *Bod*-initial constructions

The aim of this section is to propose a theoretically founded analysis of *bod*-initial constructions that share several properties with nonfinite *i*-clauses, but are quite different from them in other respects. They will be used to test the adequacy and the generality of the principles and generalizations put forth in the preceding section.

27.1 Analysis of *bod*-clauses

Paradigm (33) indicates that the embedding of a predication structure with an aspectual, adjectival, nominal or prepositional predicate under an epistemic or declarative verb gives rise, in some tenses, to a configuration whose initial element is the verb-noun *bod*.

(33) a. Gwn   fod Ioan yn   athro.
   know.PRES.1SG *bod* Ioan PRED teacher
   'I know that Ioan is a teacher.'

    b. Ofnaf   fod y   trên   wedi mynd.
   fear.PRES.1SG *bod* the train PERF go.VN
   'I am afraid that the train has gone.'

    c. A ydych   yn   credu   fy   mod yn   dweud y   gwir?
   Q be.PRES.2PL PROG believe.VN CL.1SG *bod* PROG tell.VN the truth
   'Do you believe that I am telling the truth?'

These structures can also function as the complements to some prepositions.

(34) a. Cyn   fy   mod wedi gofyn,   yr oedd   ef wedi dweud.
   before CL.1SG *bod* PERF ask.VN PRT be.IMPF.3SG he PERF say.VN
   'Before I had time to ask the question, he had spoken.'

    b. Er   fod y   dyn yn   hen, ...
   in.spite.of *bod* the man PRED old
   'Although the man is old, ... '

    c. Rydw   i'n   mynd allan am   fod y   glaw   wedi peidio.
   be.PRES.1SG I PROG go.VN out because *bod* the rain PERF stop.VN
   'I am going out because the rain has stopped.'

27.1 Analysis of *bod*-clauses

There is no doubt that the *bod*-initial string qualifies as a constituent. In (35), it occupies the focus position of a cleft construction.

(35) *Bod tyllau yn y berth   oedd   y   drwg.*
     bod holes in the fence   be.IMPF.3SG the problem
     'The problem was that there were holes in the fence.'

It is easy to check that *bod*-initial constructions should be identified as CP/FinP domains. Harlow (1992) observes that they can be coordinated with constituents whose propositional nature cannot be questioned, finite tensed constructions and *i*-initial VN-clauses.

(36) a. *Gwn   fod Ioan yng Nghymru*
        know.PRES.1SG bod Ioan in   Wales
        ac y bydd   ef   yn   dod   yma.
        and y be.FUT.3SG 3M.SG PROG come.VN here
        'I know that Ioan is in Wales and that he will come here.'

    b. *Rydw   i   'n   credu   i Ioan ddweud yr hanes*
       be.PRES.1SG 1.SG PROG believe.VN i Ioan say.VN   the story
       ddoe   a   'i   fod ef   yn   ei   ddweud yr awr eto.
       yesterday and CL.3SG bod 3M.SG PROG CL.3M.SG say.VN now again
       'I believe that Ioan told the story yesterday and that he tells it again now.'

The representation of *bod*-initial structures at Transfer can be schematized as follows:

(37)   [$_{CP}$ [$_C$ *bod*] [DP$_s$ [$_{TP}$ [~~*bod*~~] [$_{VNP}$ ~~*bod*~~ [~~DP$_s$~~ PredP]]]]]

These clauses are CP/FinP domains containing a T head, selecting a VNP domain headed by *bod*, itself selecting a predicative projection, which is an Aspect projection in embedded periphrastic aspectual constructions (cf. 33b, 33c), but could also be a prepositional phrase or an adjectival/nominal predicate preceded by the predicative particle *yn* (cf. *yn athro* in 33a, see 63 for further examples). *Bod* first raises to T, then to C/Fin, the lowest head position in the complementizer system, just as inflected verbs do in verb-initial finite clauses. *Bod* has the same status and displays the same properties in all constructions, irrespective of the realization site of the clause it heads, in contrast to *i* which functions as a subject licenser or as a nonfiniteness marker depending on the context. The subject argument in (33a) and (33b) instantiates the EPP effect. As schematized in (37), it presumably raises from the subject position of the predicative small clause to the specifier of TP and thus occupies the same position as the subject argument in finite clauses.

A major question remains unanswered: Why is *bod* the only verb-noun that has access to the C/Fin position? This question has two facets. First, why is *bod* allowed to raise at all? Second, why does *bod* raise to C/Fin rather than to T? The fact that *bod* raises and that lexical verb-nouns do not is reminiscent of the privilege that the verb *be* enjoys in other languages and other constructions: In English and French, it is allowed to move in structures in which ordinary lexical verbal heads do not leave the vP, as Emonds's (1978) and Pollock's (1989) discoveries have established. A tentative explanation for the fact that non-auxiliary verbo-nominal heads remain in place in *i*-initial constructions has been offered in section 26.8: neither the T nor the VN head are endowed with the kind of features that would allow or force them to enter into Agree and Move relations. But *bod* raises and it must be assumed that it shares with its host C/Fin at least one feature that ordinary verbo-nominal heads don't have. This feature could be [tense], which lexically distinguishes auxiliaries from ordinary verbal heads. Second, the fact that *bod* raises to C/Fin rather than to T is a further illustration of the inertness of T in Welsh. I will assume that the feature structures of T and C/Fin in the *bod*-initial construction are exactly the same as those of finite T and C/Fin, and that, in both clause types, C/Fin doesn't transmit uninterpretable φ-features to T, but withholds them. As a consequence, C/Fin attracts the verb-noun *bod* as it attracts inflected finite forms. Finite clauses and *bod*-constructions essentially differ in that in the latter, the [tense] feature has no morphological exponent on C/Fin.

The asymmetry between auxiliaries and ordinary verbo-nominal heads is a property that Welsh *bod*-clauses share with English Acc-*ing* gerund constructions, in which only *being* and *having* raise. They differ in that the landing site of auxiliaries in English is T, not C/Fin. Again, this contrast is directly linked to the fact that in Welsh C/Fin keeps its uninterpretable (case and φ-) features for itself, whereas in English, it transmits them to T. As a consequence, gerund T has a checking potential analogous to that of finite T. The fact that the asymmetry between T and C/Fin also manifests itself when auxiliary movement is involved provides a clue that an Agree relation of some type is involved, not only in the licensing of subjects, but also in head movement.

It is interesting to reconsider the contrast between auxiliaries and main verbs in the light of Roberts's (2010) proposals concerning head movement. In the theory he develops, the head-adjunction process involved in both cliticization and verb movement reduces to an Agree process between a probing head and a defective goal. Roberts argues that the head-movement effect is observed when the probe and the goal stand in an Agree relation, such that the goal's formal features are a proper subset of those of the probe. The resulting configuration is formally undistinguishable from a structure generated by movement. When the goal is a clitic matrix and the probe the functional head v, the subset condition is fulfilled, since, in his view, pronominal clitics are matrices of interpretable φ-features deprived of a case feature. When the two elements involved are finite T and v, the same sets of features are present on both heads. As a result of Agree, the originally unvalued features of v occur valued on T. Concerning languages and structures in which verbal heads raise – this is the situation in Romance finite clauses -, Roberts suggests that the T head is endowed with an interpretable [tense] and an uninterpretable V, whereas the inverse combination, uninterpretable [tense] and interpretable [V], is found on v. As a result, v's features are a proper subset of T's and qualify v as a defective goal. In the languages and structures where raising doesn't occur, as is the case in English, for example, it can be assumed that the subset requirement is not fulfilled and the conditions for incorporation are not met. This is the case, for example, if T lacks [V], which is an inherent property of v. Auxiliaries, Roberts claims, are different from ordinary verbs in that they are deprived of [V] (the absence of [V] reflects the fact that auxiliaries do not possess any argument structure), but are endowed with uninterpretable [tense], which allows them to incorporate into T. The effect of Agree is to create a valued [tense] matrix at the T-level.

Both Matushansky (2011) and Dékány (2018) show that this proposal runs into serious problems and in particular that, contrary to Roberts's claim, a movement of some sort is necessarily involved after all in the structures he analyzes (Agree doesn't suffice). Ignoring these reservations, let us ask how the defective goal proposal fares with respect to English and Welsh nonfinite structures.

There is no doubt that gerund and VN forms lexically head defective domains and that they are themselves defective in some sense, which should qualify them as potential targets for agreement and incorporation. It was established that, when a lexical root is involved, the gerund and VN-forms don't undergo movement to T, but that the forms of *be* in English and Welsh (and of *having* in English) do. In the Welsh structures containing the verbo-nominal form *bod* and in the English constructions including the gerundive forms *being* or *having*, the T head and the auxiliary v are endowed with an interpretable [tense] and an uninterpretable [tense] respectively. The effect of Agree is to create a valued [tense] matrix at the T- or at the C/Fin-level.

The non-incorporation of ordinary VN and gerund forms is also compatible with the defective-goal approach. For incorporation to be successful, it must be possible to form a movement-like chain between the features of the goal and the features of the probe. This condition cannot be fulfilled by T and v in gerund clauses: T is specified for interpretable [tense], gerund v plausibly lacks [tense]. In other words, T and the lexical head it c-commands cannot enter into an Agree relation, because neither T nor v are endowed with the features that would make agreement possible. The same analysis can be developed to account for the non-raising of Welsh lexical VNs to C/Fin.

There is of course a major difference between the T projected in VN-clauses and the T present in gerund clauses: the latter is endowed with inherited φ-features, the former is not. This difference is directly reflected not only in the way overt subjects are licensed in the two languages, but also in the scope of the movement of the gerund/VN auxiliaries. This movement targets the head that bears φ-features, T and C/Fin respectively, although these features play no role in the valuing of [tense]. This indirectly confirms that, when φ-features are on C/Fin, an uninterpretable [tense] also is.[23]

27.2 Parallels between propositional types

Bod-clauses share an important property with *i*-clauses. When the content of the grammatical subject position is an overt (cf. 38c) or a null (cf. 38a, b) pronoun, a full matrix of φ-features is present on the C/Fin head, doubling the subject position and realized either as a pronominal inflection (incorporated into *i*) or as a proclitic (affixed to *bod*), as examples (38) show.

(38) a. *Dywedais wrtho fy mod yn byw yma.*
say.PRT.1SG to.3M.SG CL.1SG bod PROG live.VN here
'I said to him that I was living here.'
b. *A ydych yn credu fy mod yn dweud y gwir?*
Q be.PRES.2PL PROG believe.VN CL.1SG bod PROG say.VN the truth
'Do you believe that I am saying the truth?'
c. *Ni wyddem ei bod hi. 'n gyfoethog.*
NEG know.IMPF.1PL CL.3F.SG bod 3F.SG PRED rich
'We didn't know that she was rich.'

Once again, it must be emphasized that these agreement patterns are not specific to the initial elements in nonfinite VN-clauses. The absence of full number-person inflection on the probe when the goal is an overt noun phrase and its pres-

---

[23] I assume that a [tense] feature also stands on C/Fin in the languages where φ-features are transmitted to T.

ence with null or overt pronouns is a general feature of agreement phenomena in Welsh and in other Celtic languages, which has led many linguists to claim that an incorporation process, exclusively affecting pronominal matrices, is involved.[24] The agreement patterns displayed by *bod*-constructions are strictly similar to what is observed between the noun head and the genitive dependent in possessive constructions: when the genitive is pronominal, a proclitic affixed to the head noun doubles the genitive position; when it is a nominal expression, no doubling occurs.

(39) a. *llyfr Siôn*
    book Siôn
    'the book of Siôn'

  b. *ei lyfr*
    CL.3M.SG book
    'his book'

Modulo the proclisis/enclisis divide, the pattern is the same as with inflected prepositions and the complementizer *i*. In verb-initial finite clauses, the form of the initial verb varies according to whether the grammatical subject is pronominal, in which case rich agreement occurs on the verbal stem, or is a nominal expression, in which case a poor agreement marker, homophonous to the third person singular, is selected. In VN-clauses, the relation between C/Fin and the embedded subject is no exception and transparently illustrates the agreement/ overt DP complementarity. No agreement inflection occurs on the initial *bod* and *i* when the subject is nominal. Agreement patterns are no doubt the most obvious similarity between *i*-initial and *bod*-initial clauses.

The two nonfinite types also display the same behavior as finite tensed clauses with respect to binding principles. The distributional and interpretive complementarity between lexical anaphors and pronouns which characterizes the subject position of tensed clauses in many languages is also observed in the Welsh construction. The post-*bod* subject position cannot host a lexical anaphor (cf. 40b), but a pronoun occupying this position can enter a coreference relation with an argument of the matrix clause (cf. 40a, where *ei* ... *(ef)* and *Emrys* can corefer). *i*-initial clauses display a parallel behavior (cf. 41a, 41b), which thus turns out to be shared by tensed finite clauses and the nonfinite propositional types studied here (cf. Rouveret 1987, 1990, 1994, Harlow 1992).

---

[24] See the discussion of (20).

(40) a. Dywedodd   Emrys ei   fod (ef)   yn   gweithio.
        say.PAST.3SG Emrys CL.3M.SG bod 3M.SG PROG work.VN
        'Emyr said that he was working.'

   b. *Dywedodd   Emrys ei   fod ef ei hun   yn   gweithio.
        say.PAST.3SG Emrys CL.3M.SG bod himself PROG work.VN

(41) a. 'R   oeddent   hwy wedi clywed   iddynt (hwy)
        PRT   be.IMPF.3PL   3PL PERF hear.VN   i.3PL   3PL
        ennill   y   gadair.
        win.VN the chair
        'They had just learned that they had been elected at the chair.'

   b. *'R   oeddent   hwy wedi clywed   iddynt eu hunain
          PRT   be.IMPF.3PL   3PL PERF hear.VN   i.3PL   themselves
        ennill   y   gadair.
        win.VN the chair

Another property shared by *bod*-constructions and *i*-constructions is that they both fill a gap in the distribution of embedded finite clauses. A finite complement clause cannot contain an aspectual periphrasis in the present or past indicative. Only a *bod*-initial structure is legitimate in this case. The following examples illustrate this generalization.

(42) a. Dwêd   Emyr fod Ifor yn   dod   yno.
        say.PRES.3SG Emyr bod Ifor PROG come.VN there
        'Emyr says that Ifor is coming there.'

   b. *Dwêd   Emyr y mae   Ifor yn   dod   yno.
        say.PRES.3SG Emyr y be.PRES.3SG Ifor PROG come.VN there

   c. Dywedodd   Emyr fod Ifor   yn   dod   yno.
        say.PAST.3SG Emyr bod Ifor PROG come.VN there
        'Emyr said that Ifor was coming there.'

   d. *Dywedodd   Emyr yr oedd   Ifor yn   dod   yno.
        say.PAST.3SG Emyr y be.IMPF.3SG Ifor PROG come.VN there

To account for this restriction and represent the relation between the two constructions, Awbery (1976) proposes to derive the *bod*-initial structure from the finite complement clause via a rule deleting the tense and agreement features of the inflected forms of *bod* in the present and imperfect tenses in the relevant environments. This analysis, which relies on the observation that *bod* occupies the same position as the inflected verb in standard verb-initial finite clauses, amounts to syntactically assigning to the *bod*-initial construction the status of a finite clause in narrow syntax. But the complementary distribution between finite forms and verb-nouns is not limited to finite clauses and *bod*-initial clauses: It extends to *i*-initial clauses, which also function as obligatory substitutes for finite clauses in the same contexts, as shown by the following examples:

(43) a. *Dywedodd   Emyr i Ioan ddarllen   y   llyfr.*
say.PAST.3SG Emyr *i* Ioan read.VN the book
'Emyr said that Ioan read the book.'

b. * *Dywedodd   Emyr y darllenodd   Ioan y   llyfr.*
say.PAST.3SG Emyr *y* read.PAST.3SG Ioan the book

These distributions strongly suggest that the two propositional types share a fundamental property. I propose to identify this shared property as the presence in the relevant domains of a T category, which has a semantic import (it is specified for an interpretable [tense] feature), but is syntactically inactive (it doesn't inherit uninterpretable φ-features from C). In the approach developed here, T in both *i*-initial and *bod*-initial clauses, not only supplies a structural position to tense construal, it also hosts the grammatical subject in its specifier at Transfer.[25]

A last characteristic shared by VN-clauses with an overt subject is that, as is the case with finite *y*-clauses, they cannot remain in their original argument position. The characteristics of the extraposition process will be thoroughly explored in chapter IX.

There are thus strong similarities between *bod*-initial and *i*-initial clauses and between the two nonfinite types and finite tensed clauses. How should they be interpreted?

Harlow (1992) and Tallerman (1998) propose to take them as unequivocal clues that *bod*-structures and *i*-structures are finite clauses, more precisely irregular members of the finite clausal paradigm, whose syntactic properties and temporal interpretation they share. Harlow analyzes *bod* as a defective lexical realization of the category Infl, exclusively selecting a predicative domain as its complement. The consensus today (it was not in the 90s) is that the finite predicate in verb-initial languages and structures occupies a head position at the left periphery of the clause, more precisely the category C/Fin, where it coexists with

---

[25] This analysis differs from Adger's (2007), who argues that VN-clauses in Scottish Gaelic do not include a T category.

initial particles.[26] *Bod* should also be characterized as an entity having access to the CP/FinP system. As was already observed, this conclusion is unexpected from a morpho-syntactic point of view, since, as shown in 26.8, lexical verb-nouns in the contemporary language don't raise to C/Fin nor to T in the nonfinite domains that minimally contain them. In Harlow's (1992) view, the difficulty vanishes if *bod*-initial structures are analyzed as concealed finite inflected clauses. As remarked above, the specific properties of agreement in Welsh apparently lend support to this reductionist approach. Since the clitic in *bod*-structures occurs only when a pronominal subject is present, it is tempting to assign it the same status as to the rich inflection realized on the verbal head in finite tensed clauses with a pronominal subject, although it takes the form of an enclitic in the first case, that of a pronominal suffix in the second case. In this view, there exist two distinct morphological realizations for the combination *bod*+inflection, when it minimally c-commands a subject position occupied by a pronominal entity: the form *mae/maent* (in the present tense) and the form *oedd/oeddynt* (in the imperfect tense), in which inflection is the realization of both tense and agreement features; the clitic+*bod* combination, in which only agreement features are manifested (by the clitic). The use of the second one would be limited to the verb *bod* when it occurs in embedded domains in which the tense specifications can be recovered from those of the predicate of the matrix clause. Considered in this light, the analysis of *bod*-initial clauses as concealed finite tensed clauses has a real plausibility. The fact that *bod*-constructions fill a gap in the distribution of finite aspectual periphrases provides additional support in favor of this claim.

But, as examples (43) show, the complementarity effect between finite and nonfinite forms is also observed in *i*-initial clauses. In these domains, however, inflectional marks don't appear on the verb-noun, but on *i*. And there is no way to view the verb-noun as a defective lexical realization of Infl or of C or to characterize it as a defective verbal form stripped of its tense and agreement features. The parallelism is less perfect than it appears at first.

The position adopted here is different from Harlow's.[27] In my opinion, the parallelisms found between the two nonfinite complement types and between

---

26 See sct. 6, for discussion.

27 It also differs from Tallerman's (1998). Like Harlow, but for different reasons, she analyzes the Welsh VN-clauses under consideration as finite clauses, a conclusion I disagree with as far as *i*-clauses are concerned. Her conclusion is based on the fact that pronominal matrices are spelled out on the initial *i* and *bod* when the following subject is pronominal (she suggests that the relevant domains contain a case licensing Agr head, a natural hypothesis in the framework that was used at the time). Interestingly, she characterizes the Welsh constructions as full-fledged "inflected infinitive clauses", comparable to Portuguese inflected infinitive constructions, although nonfinite structures and tensed finite clauses should not be taken as robust clues that *bod*-initial and *i*-initial (or Ø$_i$-initial) clauses both qualify as finite clauses. Although the finite analysis has a real plausibility when *bod*-constructions are considered, the properties shared by nonfinite domains and finite structures provide no evidence in favor of the finiteness status of *i*-constructions. The convergences between propositional types fall into place once one combines the specific properties of agreement relations in Welsh reviewed above, Landau's insight that the features [tense] and [φ] form a bundle that is independent from [finite] and the claim that a hallmark of Welsh syntax is that the uninterpretable φ-features present on both finite and nonfinite C/Fin heads are not transmitted to T, making C/Fin the only possible spell-out site of these features when they are morphologically realized.[28] If this approach is adopted, the grammatical dimensions that are responsible for the commonalities displayed by Welsh VN-clauses are the exclusive properties of the [tense] and [φ] features of the C/Fin and T heads they contain. [finite] is not involved at all. This conclusion is the only one that matters to us, but it is not inconsistent with the claim that *bod*-initial clauses are well-behaved finite clauses, whereas *i*-initial ones are not finite.

27.3 Differences between propositional types

i-initial clauses are appropriate complements not only to epistemic/declarative predicates, as the preceding section shows, but also to predicates of the *disgwyl*-class that select a future *irrealis* propositional object. In Wurmbrand's (2014) classification, the relevant complement is literally tenseless because it is not headed by a T head, but by a Modal one, contrary to epistemic/declarative verbs (like Welsh *dweud* 'say', *credu* 'believe', *gwybod* 'know'), which include a T head in their internal structure. An alternative option, developed by Landau is that future *irrealis* complements contain a T head. The claims made here about subject licensing force on us the conclusion that a tense specification is indeed present in the relevant domains.

---

she concedes that some differences can be detected between the two structures. She doesn't really develop this insight and ignores the contribution of tense, but the parallelism she establishes opens the way to a Landau-style analysis of both structures and of the obligatory control/no control divide. The obvious differences between the two can be reduced once a more abstract perspective is adopted.

28 The latter proviso is necessary because, as mentioned above, no agreement morphology is present on the C/Fin head in VN-clauses, when the subject is an overt DP.

Whichever way it is represented, the basic semantic distinction between assertive complements and future *irrealis* complements is real and has quite remarkable syntactic reflexes, as data discussed by Jones & Thomas (1977) and Sadler (1988: 34–44) show. First, whereas an *i*-clause complement to a declarative predicate can freely be coordinated with a tensed clause, it is much less easy when the matrix predicate is *disgwyl*.

(44) ?* *Disgwyliodd   Emrys i Mair fynd   i Gaerdydd*
     expect.PAST.3SG Emrys *i* Mair go.VN to Cardiff
     ac   y byddai   Siôn yn   mynd   i   Abertawe.
     and *y* be.IMPF.3SG Siôn PROG go.VN to Swansea

(45) *Dywedodd   Emrys i Mair fynd   i Gaerdydd ac y byddai   Siôn*
     say.PAST.3SG Emrys *i* Mair go.VN to Cardiff   and *y* be.IMPF.3SG Siôn
     yn   mynd   i   Abertawe.
     PROG go.VN to Swansea
     'Emrys said that Mair had gone to Cardiff and that Siôn would be going to Swansea.'

In (45), coordination associates two semantically tensed complements instantiating two different clause types and no problem arises. The difficulty with (44) is not necessarily linked to the clause types involved. It could stem from the fact that it is odd to put the stative verb *disgwyl* in the past in sentences of this type. The same effect is observed if the complement of *disgwyliodd* reduces to the *y*-clause, but things improve if the imperfect form is used instead of the past one.

Second, Sadler notes that the two complement types display different behaviors when their content is negated. What we find in the complement of *disgwyl* is the negative periphrasis *peidio â* 'cease to' (cf. 47), which is the usual way to negate verb-nouns (cf. 46a) and whose imperative form is used to convey negative commands (cf. 46b). On the contrary, the complement of *dweud* takes the form of a finite clause introduced by the clause-initial negative particle *na/nad* (cf. 48).

(46) a. *Dywedais   wrtho   am   beidio ag aros.*
        tell.PAST.1SG to.3M.SG about NEG   stay.VN
        'He is idling and not working.'

   b. *Peidiwch ag   ofni!*
      cease.imper.2PL fear.VN
      'Do not fear!'

(47) *Disgwyliodd   Siôn i Mair   beidio â mynd   i   Gaedydd.*
     expect.PAST.1SG Siôn *i* Mair NEG   go.VN to Cardiff
     'Siôn didn't expect Mair to go to Cardiff.'

(48) *Dywedodd   Siôn nad   oedd   Mair wedi mynd   i Gaerdydd.*
     say.PAST.3SG Siôn C.NEG   be.IMPF.3SG Mair PERF go.VN   to Cardiff
     'Siôn said that Mair hadn't gone to Cardiff.'

The periphrasis *peidio â* is essentially found in modal contexts. It is never used in finite declarative clauses to negate the main predicate and cannot appear under *dweud* either: (48) is the only sentence that can convey the relevant content. This contrast confirms that the nonfinite clauses that are complements to *disgwyl* are true nonfinite domains, that are presumably projections of a Mod head in the periphery, governing a T head in the inflectional domain, whereas the complements to epistemic/declarative predicates essentially have the semantic properties of embedded FinP finite clauses including an inflected T head. Negative contexts are one of the environments where the tenseness/tenselessness of clausal complements manifests itself syntactically. The asymmetric behavior of the verbs of the *dweud* class and those of the *disgwyl* class also shows that *i*-initial clauses, which function as complements to both types, should be assigned a double status: they are future-oriented ModP complements when they are selected by *disgwyl*, past/present-oriented FinP complements, when they are associated with *dweud* or credu.

The comparison between *dweud*-constructions and *disgwyl*-constructions brings to light a further difference between *i*-initial and *bod*-initial VN-clauses, cf. Jones & Thomas (1977), Sadler (1988). The two types differ in that the *bod*-construction is selected exclusively when the predicate phrase is an aspectual projection (or an adjectival or a propositional one), while the *i*-construction is a possible choice in the absence of explicit aspectual marking. But *i*-initial clauses also allow an aspectual specification to be present. In this case, *bod* displays the same distribution as standard lexical verbs and the result is a [V *i* DP *bod* Asp VNP] sequence. The possibility to use an aspectual periphrastic structure in *i*-initial VN-clauses considerably extends the range of embedded state-denoting constructions, the verb phrases containing an eventive predicate being turned into stative ones. But the choice between the two aspectual VN-structures is not free and depends on the identity of the selecting predicate. When the matrix verb is *disgwyl*, it is almost mandatory to use an *i*-clause and to follow the standard nonfinite pattern. When the aspectual predication is embedded under *dweud* or *gwybod*, resort to a *bod*-initial clause is strongly preferred.

(49) a. Mi   ddisgwyliodd   Siôn i Mair fod   yn   palu   'r   ardd
        PART expect.PAST.3SG Siôn i Mair be.VN PROG dig.VN the garden
        pan   gyraeddai   adre.
        when   arrive.IMPF.3SG home
        'Siôn expected Mair to be digging the garden when he arrived home.'

   b. ?* Disgwyliodd   Siôn fod Mair   yn   palu   'r   ardd
         expect.PAST.3SG   Siôn bod Mair   PROG dig.VN the garden
         pan   gyraeddai   adre.
         when   arrive.IMPF.3SG home

(50) a. Dywedodd   Siôn fod Mair   yn   gweithio.
        say.PAST.3SG   Siôn bod Mair   Prog   work.VN
        'Siôn said that Mair was working.'

   b. ?* Dywedodd   Siôn i Mair fod yn   gweithio.
          say.PAST.3SG   Siôn i Mair bod Prog work.VN

Whereas *disgwyl* 'expect' cannot take a *bod*-initial structure as its complement (cf. 50), *cofio* 'remember' can, as the following example adapted from Jones & Thomas (1977) shows.

(51) Yr   wyf   yn   cofio   bod Siôn yn   chwilio
     PRT   be.PRES.1SG PROG remember   *bod* Siôn PROG look.VN
     am y goriad pan   ddaeth   Mair i fewn.
     for the key when   come.PAST.3SG   Mair inside
     'I remember that Siôn was looking for the key when Mair went in.'

The conclusion is that *i*-initial clauses essentially are [– finite, α tense] clauses, where [α tense] is [future *irrealis*] or [past/present], depending on whether the VN-clause is embedded under a verb of the *disgwyl*-class or of the *dweud*-class and that *bod*-initial clauses exclusively appear in the contexts where a [+finite, +past/present tense] clause could occur. In (51), the *bod*-initial structure receives a "past event" interpretation, in (50a), a simultaneous interpretation. The quasi-ungrammaticality of (49b) confirms that a *bod*-initial structure cannot be assigned an "unrealized event" interpretation.

An additional property shared by the two VN-clausal types is that both license overt subjects. But subject licensing appears to follow different paths in the two structures, a difference which is confirmed by the fact that *i*-initial clauses have controlled counterparts and *bod*-initial clauses do not.

Examples (2) and (8) show that the complement clauses selected by predicates of the *disgwyl*-class can either contain an overt subject or a null one, which should be identified as PRO. In the first case, C/Fin is obligatorily spelled out as *i*, in the second it remains empty. According to Borsley (1986), Welsh is a language where overt DPs and PRO do not stand in complementary distribution. But this conclusion is warranted only insofar as the presence/absence of *i* is made abstraction of. If the sequences in competition are taken to include the preceding C/Fin head, DP and PRO don't occur in the same environments (DP in a [$_{Fin}$ *i*][$_{TP}$ __ ... environment, PRO in a [$_{Fin}$ Ø][$_{TP}$ __ ... environment) and are in complementary distribution. *Bod*-initial clauses instantiate a different situation. *Bod* signals the presence of active [tense] and [φ] features on C/Fin, which license the occurrence of an overt DP subject in the SpecTP position and block the occurrence of PRO in the same position.[29]

---

[29] Recall that when the subject argument is pronominal, it takes the form of a proclitic affixed to *bod* and doubling the empty subject position. The null pronominal in the CL *bod* [e] configuration should be identified as pro, not PRO.

28 Labeling Welsh VN-clauses

Because a great effort has been made in chapter IV to make explicit the way labeling works in gerund constructions and for the sake of completeness and symmetry, it may be fruitful to indicate how Welsh VN-clauses satisfy the labeling requirement. First, it must be specified how the syntactically derived VN head is assigned a verbal status. Second, one must determine how the whole VN-clause satisfies the subcategorization requirement of the head that governs it.

Let us look at [*i* DP-VNP] constructions first.[30] The internal functional structure of the embedded clause in (52) is as in (53), where arguments and heads are represented in their first Merge position. The structure at Transfer, after various Internal Merge operations have taken place, is as in (54).

(52) *Dywedodd   Emyr [i Siôn fynd   i Gaerdydd].*
       say.PAST.3SG Emyr *i* Siôn go.VN to Cardiff
       'Emyr said that Sîon had gone to Cardiff.'

(53) [$_{CP}$ [$_{C}$ *i*] [$_{TP}$ [$_{T}$ Ø] [$_{\alpha}$ DP$_S$ [$_{vP}$ [v [$_{RootP}$ [√aff] [√X DP$_o$]]]]]]]

(54) [$_{CP}$ [$_{C}$ *i*] [$_{\beta}$ [DP$_s$] [$_{TP}$ [$_{T}$ Ø] [DP$_S$ [$_{vP}$ [$_v$ VN [$_{RootP}$ [√aff] [√X DP$_o$]]]]]]]]

A category-defining head v is merged with the projection of the complex Root [[√aff] [√X (DP$_o$)]]. The raising of the latter to v allows the derivation of a verbal VN head. The VN head itself doesn't raise higher than v. I take it for granted that no Asp head is projected above vP in the relevant structures, this head being only present in the periphrastic aspectual structures which contain an explicit aspectual marker. As already observed, lexical verb-nouns behave as if they were heads with no inflectional features: Verb-nouns are morphologically complex forms, but the verbo-nominal suffix, which doesn't trigger any agreement or movement on the part of the verb-noun that bears it, appears to be syntactically inert.[31] The analysis of this suffix as a derivational affix with a radical status is a way to rep-

---

30 I provisionally assume that what is said about *i*-clauses embedded under declarative predicates should be extended to those that are embedded under future *irrealis* predicates, such as *disgwyl*: they include a Modal head, which occupies the same position as Fin in the clausal architecture and transmits its features to the head of the inflectional domain in some languages, but not in others.
31 Verb-nouns in aspectual periphrases support this conclusion: they function as complements to the aspectual heads *yn* and *wedi*, without their dependency being manifested in any way.

https://doi.org/10.1515/9783110769289-033

resent this property.³² T is not endowed either with features that would require it to enter into a checking relation with the verb-noun.

Concerning the labeling of VN-clauses, we observe that the external argument systematically raises to the grammatical subject position, which is here taken to be a TP-adjoined position. The reason why it raises is familiar to us. The constituent minimally containing the vP and the adjoined subject cannot be labeled. The result of raising is a clausal structure that qualifies as a predication configuration, but cannot be labeled <φ, φ> either because T has not inherited φ-features from C/Fin. How is the subcategorization requirement of C/Fin, a verbal head, satisfied? I will assume that i in C/Fin must enter into a close relation with a nominal projection. DP_s in (54) is the constituent that is closest to C/Fin if one adopts Pesetsky & Torrego's (2001) definition of "closeness", discussed in chapter III and repeated here as (55).

(55) **Closeness**
Y is closer to K than X if K c-commands Y and Y c-command X.

(55) implies that in a structure like (54), where DP_s is adjoined to TP, both β and DP count as the closest constituent to C/Fin. This is the case, because the initial position occupied by DP_s is immediately dominated by β and that c-command excludes domination.³³ If i selects [D] or [N] in (53), both the DP subject and the nonfinite clause as a whole are in a position to fulfill the subcategorization requirement of i, since they are equidistant from C/Fin. A plausible claim is that the establishment of an Agree relation between Fin and DP_s suffices to assign a nominal label to the domain embedded under C/Fin. As for the i-clause as a whole, it shares its label with its head i, which should be taken to be that of C/Fin, namely [+V, –N].

The scenario leading to the licensing of overt subjects in *bod*-initial clauses is not different from the one that has just been sketched concerning i-initial clauses. But the way the clause as a whole receives a label differs. The structure assigned to the embedded VN-clause in (56) can be schematized as in (57).

---

32 But the root status is not an exclusive property of syntactically inert derivational affixes. Gerund *-ing* has also been analyzed as a root (see chapter III).
33 Note that, if closeness is characterized as in (55), the TP projection in (54) also qualifies as the closest constituent to C/Fin. But it is not the constituent that fulfills the subcategorization requirement of i.

(56) *Ofnaf   fod y trên   wedi mynd.*
     fear.PRES.1SG bod the train PERF go.VN
     'I am afraid that the train has gone.'

(57) [$_{CP}$ [$_C$ *bod*] [$_\alpha$ [DP$_S$] [$_{TP}$ [$_T$ Ø] [$_{AspP}$ Asp [$_{vP}$ [$_v$ VN][$_{RootP}$ √aff √X DP$_o$]]]]]

In (57), the item residing in C/Fin, namely *bod*, has been identified as verbal at the beginning of the derivation. C/Fin is thus endowed with the full set of verbal features, [finite], [tense], [φ], which explains why overt subjects are the only possible choice in these structures.

29 The tense of VN-clauses

The aim of this section is to further illustrate the semantic variability of VN-clauses as far as tense construal is concerned. This variability no doubt reflects the simple fact that VNs are the only nonfinite verbal forms available in the language. It will be taken here as a clue that a T head is syntactically present in the relevant domains.

Sentences (58a) and (58b) are ambiguous.

(58) a. Cofiodd   John ddod   â   'r   gwin.
        remember.PAST.3SG John come.VN with the wine
        'John remembered bringing the wine.'
        'John remembered to bring the wine.'

    b. Mae   John yn cofio   dod   â   'r   gwin.
        be.PRES.3SG John PROG remember.VN come.VN with the wine
        'John remembers bringing the wine.'
        'John remembers to bring the wine.'

In one of its interpretation, (58a) refers to a single action in the past, no doubt is raised about its accomplishment and the English translation resorts to a gerund; in the other interpretation, it refers to an act that is not accomplished yet, maybe never will be and the appropriate translation of the verbo-nominal complement into English is an infinitive clause. Similarly, in one of the readings of (58b), what is remembered is a repetitive action in the past; in the second one, the interpretation is that John is supposed to bring the wine and remembers doing so.[34] These two interpretations seem to make accessible different options for adverbial modification. In the first one, two distinct time adverbs are possible, one in the main clause, the other in the verbo-nominal clause, indicating that the event or situation denoted by the embedded predicate is distinct from the event/situation

---

[34] The contrast between *Can you remember doing that?* and *Can you remember to do that?* in English is discussed by Bolinger (1968). See sct. 15.1 for additional examples and discussion. The only nonfinite form French can resort to in this situation is the infinitive. The difference between the factive interpretation and the nonfactive one is marked by the use of an infinitival past tense form in the first case.

designated by the matrix predicate. In the second one, only one time adverb qualifying the whole sentence is possible.[35]

(59) a. *Cofiodd   John ddoe   ddod   â   'r   gwin*
       remember.PAST.3SG John yesterday come.VN with the wine
       adeg y   Nadolig.
       time the Chistmas
       'John remembered yesterday bringing the wine at Christmas time.'

   b. *Cofiodd   John ddod   â   'r   gwin ddoe.*
      remember.PAST.3SG John come.VN with the win yesterday
      'John remembered to bring the wine yesterday.'

These distributions confirm that a T head is projected in VN-clauses embedded under *cofio* 'remember', *dweud* 'say', *credu* 'believe'. The tense of the verb-noun is past (with *cofio*), past or present (with *dweud/credu*). From a semantic point of view, T can head a proposition or specify the temporal reference of a situation or an event.

We know that *i*-initial clauses are also possible under *disgwyl* 'expect', *bwriadu* 'intend', which force an *irrealis* future interpretation of their complement. In fact, this is the only verbo-nominal propositional type that these verbs can select.

(60) *Disgwyliodd   Siôn i Gwyn weithio.*
     expect.PAST.3SG Siôn *i* Gwyn work.VN
     'Siôn expected that Gwyn would work.'

(61) a. *Disgwyliai   Emrys iddo   fod   yma yn fuan.*
       expect.IMPF.3SG Emrys *i*.3M.SG be.VN here soon
       'Emrys expected that he would be here soon.'

(i) *Jean se souvient d'   avoir apporté le vin.*
    Jean remembers *de*   have brought the wine
    'Jean remembers bringing the wine.'

(ii) *Jean s'est souvenu d'apporter   le vin.*
     Jean remembered *de* bring   the wine
     'Jean remembered to bring the wine.'

35 English is more liberal since, when this interpretation is involved, it seems to allow the occurrence of one adverb modifying the matrix predicate and one adverb modifying the infinitive phrase.
(i) John remembered yesterday to bring the wine at Christmas.

b. *Disgwyliai Mair iddo fod yma gynnau.*
   expect.IMPF.3SG Mair *i*.3M.SG be.VN here a little earlier on
   'Mair expected that he had been here earlier on.'

From a semantic point of view, we are not strictly dealing with a tensed domain in this case, but with a modal one.[36]

A major difference that distinguishes Welsh verbo-nominal clauses from English infinitives is that, contrary to their English equivalents, predicates like *cred* 'believe' allow the episodic interpretation of the embedded predicate, without giving rise to the simple present effect, that is, without the perfective reading being blocked.

(62) *Cred Julia i Lea ganu yn y tŷ gynnau.*
     believe.PRES.3SG Julia *i* Lea sing.VN in the house right now
     'Julia believes that Lea sings at home right now.'

This difference could follow from the fact that, strictly speaking, verb-nouns (*bod* excepted) are not tensed forms (the verbo-nominal affix is not specified for a [tense] feature) and don't raise to T, whereas English infinitives are tensed forms, although defective ones, and, in many syntactic situations, are closely associated with a functional exponent of tense, namely *to*.

When the embedded predicative domain denotes a state, the construction resorted to is generally the *bod*-initial structure. The small clause predicate is prepositional in (63a), adjectival in (63b), nominal in (63c), verbo-nominal in (63d).[37]

(63) a. *Credaf fod bara yn y gell.*
        believe.PRES.1SG bod food in the cellar
        'I believe there to be food in the cellar.'

---

[36] As already emphasized, authors differ concerning the implication of this semantic characterization for the syntactic representation of the corresponding clauses. See sct. 27.3. and ch. II, sct. 4.3 and 5.

[37] Harlow (1992: 111) claims that the well-formedness of these examples confirms an observation made by McCloskey (1991) about Irish, according to which there exists a range of clauses "in which Infl [T in my approach] takes a non-verbal predicative category (any of NP, AP, PP) as its complement" and that it supports the idea that *bod* is a realization of Infl/T. Welsh doesn't differ from Irish in this respect. An analysis of this type is argued for by Rouveret (1990, 1994). I now believe that an account in which *bod* heads a verbal projection, selects a predicative domain, is selected by T and raises to Fin should definitely be preferred. This account aligns the syntax of *bod*-constructions on that of ordinary finite forms.

b. *Dwêd   ei   bod hi   'n   anodd.*
   say.PRES.3SG CL.3F.SG bod 3F.SG PRED difficult
   'He says it's difficult.'

c. *Gwn   fod Siôn   yn   athro.*
   know PRES.1SG bod Siôn PRED teacher
   'I know that Siôn is a teacher.'

d. *Dywedais   wrtho   fy   mod yn   byw yma.*
   say. PAST.1SG to.3M.SG CL.1SG bod PROG live there
   'I said to him that I was living there.'

In these constructions, the situation denoted by the embedded predicate and the situation denoted by the matrix clause are simultaneous. The reference of the embedded null tense coincides with that of the matrix tense. Contrary to what happens in *i*-initial constructions, the embedded tense exhibits a complete dependency on the tense of the matrix predicate that binds it.

The *bod*-construction is also available when the embedded predicate is eventive, cf. (64). In this case, it refers to an ongoing event at the reference time or to a past one, depending on whether the selected aspectual particle is progressive *yn* or perfective *wedi*.

(64) a. *Dwêd   ein   bod ni   'n   mynd.*
        say.PRES.3SG CL.1PL bod 1PL PROG go.VN
        'He said that we were leaving.'

     b. *Dywedodd   fod ei   fab   wedi colli   can   punt.*
        say.PAST.3SG bod CL.3M.SG son PERF lose.VN hundred pound
        'He said that his son had lost a hundred pounds.'

     c. *Mae   ef   yn   credu   eich   bod wedi clywed.*
        be.PRES.3SG 3M.SG PROG believe.VN CL.2PL bod PERF hear.VN
        'He believes that you heard.'

The sentences in (64) do not contradict what has been said about the interpretation of *bod* in examples (63). The temporal interpretation of *bod* is still dependent on the tense interpretation of the matrix verb. The combination of *bod* with aspectual particles allows the construal of a progressive or an anterior interpretation of the embedded event predicate. But the structure involved is the same as the one used to express properties and refers to an ongoing situation or to a resulting state.

In the minimalist approach sketched in the preceding sections, the features of Fin are not transmitted to embedded T, but remain in situ, and tense is also represented at the C/Fin-level. C/Fin thus defines a natural *locus* for the checking of the features of *bod* and for the interpretation of embedded tense. This interpretation can only be established in reference to the tense of the matrix clause and is also determined by other factors, such as the lexical identity of the matrix predicate and the eventive or stative status of the embedded predicate.

30 Conclusion

Let us recapitulate the results that have been achieved in this chapter.
(i)   Several phenomena point to *i*-initial clauses being CP/FinP or CP/ModP projections and to *bod*-initial clauses exclusively being CP/FinP ones.
(ii) A strong parallelism exists between the two verbo-nominal clausal types and between them and finite tensed clauses, concerning agreement patterns, binding properties, coordination facts and also the obligatoriness/optionality of extraposition (see chapter IX). These commonalities do not show that the two clause types should receive a uniform analysis nor that they should be characterized as finite domains. Rather, they reflect overarching characteristics of Welsh syntax, the uniform functioning of agreement relations across categories and the spell-out of agreement inflection on phase heads.
(iii) These shared properties should ultimately be traced back to one salient feature of Welsh clausal syntax, holding for both root and embedded clauses and for both finite and nonfinite domains: the generalized non-transfer of C/Fin's or C/Mod's uninterpretable φ-features to T (combined with the representation of tense at the C/Fin-level). The non-transmission property constitutes a parametric difference between Welsh and other Celtic languages on the one hand and English and Romance on the other, which explains several superficial and subtle differences between these language families, concerning the licensing of overt subjects, the distribution of agreement patterns and the raising of the auxiliary *bod* to C/Fin.
(iv) The fact that verb-nouns do not raise to T in *i*-initial constructions follows from both T and verb-nouns being deprived of the features that would allow them to establish an agreement relation.
(v)   The tense interpretation of the two nonfinite types essentially depends on the lexical identity of the matrix predicate and on the choice between the *bod*-construction that is both tensed and aspectually marked and the *i*-construction that should be viewed as a tense-deficient structure that functions as a tensed domain in some contexts and as a modal one in others. In the former, aspectual particles function as tense markers: Perfective *wedi* marks anteriority, progressive *yn* refers to a simultaneous action or state. In *i*-constructions, infinitival tense can be fixed by temporal adverbs. The origin of the semantic temporal flexibility of nonfinite clauses should precisely be traced back to verb-nouns not being themselves specified for tense or aspect and not moving to T. This explains why tense construal in these domains is essentially dependent on the lexical and syntactic environment.

VII Verbo-nominal root clauses in Middle Welsh

Verb-nouns in Middle Welsh could function as the main predicates of embedded complement clauses, but the internal syntax of these nonfinite domains was different from what it is in contemporary Welsh (cf. ch. VI). They were also found in root contexts, in coordinate structures where a series of clauses was involved. They could also stand as the main predicates in root clauses in structures that have been referred to as "historic infinitives" by Tallerman & Wallenberg (2012). At first sight, the verbo-nominal projection involved seem to display a nominal internal organization. If correct, the nominal analysis would imply that the relevant projections illustrate a kind of category-mixing, with a nominal domain having a clausal external distribution. Upon closer scrutiny, however, it turns out that this conclusion is unwarranted. Willis (2007, 2009) and Tallerman & Wallenberg (2012) forcefully argue that the observed syntactic pattern in fact follows from a specific choice made by Middle Welsh concerning the alignment of arguments, which relies on an ergative-like argument-marking strategy.[1] The present chapter fully endorses this analysis.[2] Its aim is necessarily modest : It is to tackle some of the questions that weren't fully dealt with in the previous contributions on this topic. First, it must be explained why the ergative analysis of these structures should be preferred to the nominal one. Second, since the structures under consideration are morphologically nonfinite, it should be decided whether their selecting an ergative argument-licensing strategy is in one way or another linked to their nonfiniteness. Third, it is potentially interesting to check whether the formal analyses that have been developed for the alignment of arguments in genuine ergative languages can be extended to account for the Welsh case and, since ergativity comes up in different guises in different languages, to determine which options Middle Welsh has selected.

---

[1] The notion of argument alignment refers to the way an argument α with a role θ fulfills a specific grammatical function γ or bears a specific case. For example, in the transitive active sentences of SVO languages, the Agent role usually aligns with the subject and the Theme with the direct object; the Agent is marked for the nominative case and the Theme for the accusative.

[2] It also uses data which, for the most part, have previously been discussed by the authors mentioned in the text and in Evans's (1976) Middle Welsh grammar. The origin of the examples is made explicit in the text or in footnotes.

31 Some remarkable data

Dealing with the evolution of the English gerund in *Growth and Structure of the English Language*, Jespersen (1912: 202) characterizes it as "a long development of a form at first purely substantival into one partly substantival and partly verbal in function".[3] This form no doubt was essentially nominal in Old English, but diachronically acquired verbal traits that allowed it to operate as a verb taking an object and a subject. It is tempting to claim that a similar scenario underlies the evolution of the verb-noun from Old and Middle Welsh to the present.[4] The determining factors in this evolution could have been the categorial ambiguity of VN-DP configurations, which can be analyzed as nominal construct states or as verb-object structures, and the development of periphrastic aspectual constructions, where the aspectual markers superficially look like prepositions, with the VN ending up behaving as a verb in non-aspectual environments. In chapter V, it was shown, essentially following Borsley (1993, 1997), that the nominal approach didn't provide an adequate analysis of verbo-nominal constructions in the contemporary language. Judging from the available textual evidence, the syntax of verb-nouns at the Middle Welsh stage also seems to have been different from the initial step of Jespersen's scenario: Verb-nouns at this period already displayed many of the features found in the contemporary language. They could function as verbal heads and be modified by an adverbial expression (cf. 1a) or be used as nominals and cooccur with an adjective (cf. 1b):[5]

---

[3] See Alexiadou (2013) for a recent updating of this idea.
[4] The Old Welsh period extends from the VIIIth century to the middle of the XIIth, the Middle Welsh period from the middle of the XIIth century to the end of the XVth (1150–1500). The sources for Old Welsh are relatively meagre. Examples (1)–(14) are borrowed from texts written during the Middle Welsh period, in particular the Four Branches of the Mabinogi (*Pedeir Keinc y Mabinogi*, abbreviated as PKM), composed in the course of the XIIth century or at the beginning of the XIIIth century, but possibly compiled later (the *terminus post quem* being the date of the most ancient manuscript, namely 1225, according to Lambert 1993).
[5] Examples (1) and (3)–(10) are taken from Evans (1976: 161–163). D. Willis (2007) provides example (2).

(1) a. *reit   yw   in   gerdet   yn   bryssur*
       necessity be.PRES.3SG to.1PL travel.VN with speed
       'We must travel with speed.' [PKM 71.1]

   b. *kerdet   araf gwastat*
      pace   slow even
      'a slow even pace'   [PKM 9.15]

As a matter of fact, most of the modern predicative uses listed in (1)–(8), sct. 22, were attested in Middle Welsh. The "serial construction", consisting in a series of conjoined main clauses where only the predicate of the first conjunct is specified for tense and person, the following ones taking the form of verb-nouns, was already found in Middle Welsh. As observed by D. Willis (2007), the aspectual periphrastic *yn*-construction, although less frequent than in the modern language, was developing steadily, "replacing the synthetic forms almost entirely in expressing present time reference".[6]

(2) *Ac y   mae   Matholwch yn   rodi   brenhinaeth Iwerdon y Wern...*
    and PRT be.PRES.3SG Matholwch PROG give.VN kingdom   Ireland to Gwern...
    'And Matholwch gives the kingdom of Ireland Gwern...'
    [PKM 41. 9–10]

But constructions existed in which both the syntax of verb-nouns in the verbal use and the syntax of their arguments were different from what they are in the contemporary language. When it was affirmative and referred to an event preceding the one denoted by the main clause (cf. 3), the clausal complement of a declarative or epistemic predicate took the form of a verbo-nominal clause with a VN head in first position. The same observation holds for the clausal complements of prepositions (cf. 4), adjective and nouns.

(3) *...mi   a   gigleu   dyuot   y 'r Deheu y   ryw bryuet*
       1.SG PRT hear.PAST.1S come.VN to the south the sort creatures
    ni   doeth   y 'r ynys   honn   eiroet
    NEG come.PAST.3SG to the island DEM.FSG ever
    '... I have heard that creatures the like of which have never come to this island have come to the south.' [PKM 68.16–17]

---

[6] The perfective *wedi*-construction existed in Middle Welsh, but was extremely rare, according to D. Willis (2007).

(4) *Kynn dyuot cwbyl o 'r oet*
    before come.VN end of the time
    'before the end of the time came' [PKM 20.3]

Verb-nouns could also function in isolation, in place of finite verbs, and behave as independent predicates, without being conjoined to a finite verb (cf. *dyuot* in 5). In this use, which is totally absent from the contemporary language, the verb-noun is generally interpreted as denoting past tense and perfective aspect, and can be assimilated to an "historic infinitive".[7]

(5) *Dyuot Caswallawn am eu penn, a llad y chwegwyr* [PKM 46.2]
    fall.VN Caswallawn upon them and kill.VN the six men
    'Caswallawn fell upon them and killed the six men.'

The *argument* syntax of independent or dependent verbo-nominal clauses in Middle Welsh also dramatically differed from what is found in contemporary Welsh, as the following examples illustrate.

(6) *a' e daktanu oll o Pwyll*
    and 3M.SG relate.VN all o Pwyll
    'and Pwyll related the whole of it.' [PKM 8. 13]

(7) *am lad o honaf uu hun uy mab*
    because kill.VN o myself CL.1SG son
    'because I myself killed my son.' [PKM 8.13]

(8) *Yna agori y safyn y 'r llew*
    then open.VN its mouth y the lion
    'Then the lion opened its mouth.' [PKM 31. 1296–7]

The pattern for marking arguments selected by each verbo-nominal construction primarily depends on the lexical class of the predicate.

(i) The sole argument of unaccusative VNs (*cyn dyfod y dyn* 'before the man came') and the direct argument of transitive VNs (*cyn gweled y dyn* 'before seeing the man') were projected as direct complements of the verb-noun. The first clause

---

[7] For further discussion, see Lewis (1928: 182–184), Morgan (1938), Richards (1938, 1950–1951), and more recently, Manning (1995), D. Willis (1998, 2007, 2009), and Tallerman & Wallenberg (2012).

of (5) and (6)–(8), respectively containing an unaccusative and a transitive predicate, illustrate this point.

(ii) The external argument of transitive predicates took the form of a prepositional phrase. The preposition could be *o* 'of' (cf. 6, 7) or, occasionally, *y* 'to' (cf. 8), in configurations where the subject followed the VN; the prepositional phrase *y* + subject could also precede the verbo-nominal projection in dependent clauses (cf. 9). As emphasized by D. Willis (2007), both the first and the second pattern have completely disappeared in contemporary Welsh, the third one has been generalized to all verbo-nominal dependent clauses (cf. ch. V, 2a, 2b, and ch. VI).[8]

(9) A   thebygu y 'r   brenin cadw   y   edewit   wrthaw
    and think. VN y the king   keep.VN the promise to.3M.SG
    'And he thought that the king would keep his promise to him.' [RB 278. 10–11]

(iii) As for prefixed/infixed "genitive"/"accusative" pronouns, they were obligatorily interpreted as the subject of the verb-noun when attached to an intransitive VN (*cyn fy nyfod* 'before I came', cf. 10) and as its object when affixed to a transitive VN (*cyn fy ngweled* 'before seeing me'). The pronominal subject of a transitive VN took the form of an inflected preposition (both *o* and *y* inflect) (cf. 11).

(10) a   gwedy y dyuot   y   gynted   y neuad[9]
     and after he come.VN the upper.part the hall
     'and after he came to the high hall . . .' [PKM 16.8]

(11) Canu englyn idaw   ynteu yna
     sing.VN englyn i.3M.SG 3M.SG then
     'He sang an englyn then.' [PKM 90. 9]

---

8 But Modern Irish seems to instantiate a pattern quite similar to the Welsh post-VN *y*-construction with the preposition *do*.
9 According to the traditional analysis, the *y* preceding the verb-noun *dyuot* in (10) is the normal prefixed form of the 3rd person singular of the possessive (genitive) pronoun.

32 A short excursus on unergative VNs

The behavior of intransitive predicates is not as simple as the preceding sketch could suggest. At first sight, the unique argument of intransitive predicates is built as the direct complement of these predicates, without the mediation of a preposition. This is at least what examples (4) and (5) containing a semantically unaccusative predicate suggest. But some unaccusative predicates, if they allow the unaccusative pattern in some meanings, prefer the transitive one in others. The [+/− human] status of the unique argument appears to play a role, as indicated by the following examples drawn from Manning's (1995) study of verbo-nominal syntax in a Middle Welsh text, *Y Seint Greal* (referred to as SG) When the argument is [− human], the unaccusative pattern is generally selected, when it is [+ human], there is a strong preference for the prepositional transitive pattern.[10]

(12) a. *rac dyuot   bwystuilot or   fforrest*
       lest come.VN beasts   from the forest
       'lest beasts come from the forest'   [SG 214]

   b. *dyuot   ohonat ym   castell i   y lettyu   heno*
      come.VN o.2SG   to.CL.1SG castle 1SG to lodge.VN tonight
      'You came to my castle to lodge tonight.' [SG 25]

Second, as indicated by Manning, semantically unergative verbs can enter constructions where the unique argument is projected as the direct complement of the VN and constructions where it takes the form of a prepositional phrase. According to him, the choice between the transitive pattern and the unaccusative one is determined by a constellation of interacting factors. Besides the [+/− human] status of the unique argument, the agency of the process and the aspectual properties of the predicate play a role. When the verb-noun is an atelic predicate denoting an agentive activity, the argument is generally projected as transitive subjects are (cf. 13a, 13b); when it is telic and involves an action potentially subject to control, both constructions are possible, as already illustrated by the unaccusative predicates in (12a) and (12b); the verb *bot* 'be', intrinsically non agentive, atelic states and poorly controlled processes usually select the unaccusative construction (cf. 14). Here are examples borrowed from Manning's study.

---

[10] Examples (12)–(13) are discussed by Manning (1995).

(13) a. *marchogaeth   o Galaath*
       ride.VN   o Galaath
       'Galaath rode.'   [SG 16]

   b. *A gwedy kerdet   ohonunt*
       and after walk.VN   o.3PL
       'and after they walked'   [SG 40]

(14) *a   gwedy   marw   vynggwr   i*
      and   after   die.VN 1SG husband 1SG
      'and after my husband died'   [SG 53]

In other words, if the unique argument of a monovalent predicate is projected as a prepositional phrase, one cannot conclude that it is the subject of an unergative predicate. No firm conclusion can be drawn either when the argument is projected as a direct dependent of the predicate. The latter can be unaccusative, but also unergative. Rather the oppositions illustrated by the syntax of intransitive VNs confirm D. Willis's (2007) observation that what counts as unaccusative or as unergative is not (exclusively) determined on lexical grounds. They also recall Ramchand's (1997) conclusion that the argument structure of predicates in Scottish Gaelic is lexically determined, but that their aspectual class is in large part contextually determined, and also what has been said in chapter V, section 24 about the role of the context, in particular of the Aspect head, in defining the eventive profile of predicative roots.[11] It must be acknowledged however that the semantically-based groupings achieved by the dimensions of variation identified by Manning are quite coherent. It is comforting to observe that, at the two ends of the scale, we find atelic agentive activity predicates with a [+ human] argument, which are generally considered to be unergative, and non agentive out-of-control states with a [− human] argument, which are generally considered to be unaccusative.

---

[11] There is another situation in (contemporary) Welsh in which the unaccusatives verbs denoting an action potentially subject to control behave like unergative ones: the predicates of the two classes are acceptable in the impersonal construction.

33 Against the nominal analysis

Welsh traditional grammarians were convinced that the way the subject and object of Middle Welsh verb-nouns were constructed in the independent and dependent uses illustrated above points to their internal syntax being of the nominal type. As emphasized by Melville Richards,

> the nominal character of the verb-noun in the Celtic languages is clearly seen in the relation of the verb-noun with the subject or the object. This relationship is always genitival, whether it be simple apposition or the addition of the genitive constructions with the preposition *o* and *i* in Welsh (Richards 1950–1951: 51).

In their view, the range of options available to express the VN-object and the VN-subject relations was analogous to the ones used to build the relation between a nominal head and its complements. A possessive/genitive and a prepositional phrase with *o* (or marginally *i*) could cooccur within the same nominal domain (and still can). The same situation used to hold in the verbo-nominal constructions of the type illustrated by (3)–(8), which indeed suggests that the latter were modeled on nominal constructions.

If the internal syntax of verbo-nominal expressions in Middle Welsh indeed followed a nominal pattern, which is of course the expected situation when they occur in nominal contexts, but is not in the numerous structures where they function as predicates, VNPs would combine a nominal internal make-up and a verbal/clausal external distribution, instantiating a typical case of weak category mixing. It can be shown, however, that this analysis is not the correct one and that the generalizations on which it is based are spurious.

In evaluating the nominal analysis, two cases must carefully be distinguished, verbo-nominal phrases in the periphrastic aspectual construction (cf. 9) and verbo-nominal phrases in the historic infinitive construction (cf. 10–14). In the first case, the VNP is just a phrase, dependent on an aspectual marker and coexisting with an auxiliary; in the second, it is the sole verbal predicate in an independent clause.

33.1 Aspectual periphrastic constructions

In order to reach a firm conclusion, it is absolutely necessary to decide whether the Middle Welsh equivalents of (16)–(18), ch. V, should be analyzed along the same lines as in the modern language. With respect to the latter, I have endorsed Borsley's (1993) conclusion, extended to Irish by Borsley & Kornfilt (2000) and

Carnie (2011), that they do not provide compelling evidence that predicative VNPs in contemporary Welsh combine an internal nominal make-up with an external verbal distribution. If it ever existed, the casual evidence in favor of the "nominal" mapping of argument structure has faded away, which supports the decision to consider modern VNPs as essentially verbal. The general conclusion of chapter V was that VN forms in Modern Welsh are better analyzed as transcategorial (either verbal or nominal) items, even when they appear to show some signs of mixing.

Should this conclusion be extended to the Middle Welsh situation? The only piece of data that provides robust evidence in favor of a nominal analysis of Celtic VNPs doesn't come from Middle Welsh, but from literary Irish, where the direct argument of VNs is marked for the genitive case, both in the nominal and in the verbal uses, cf. (19a), ch. V, repeated here as (15).

(15) Tá   mé ag ól   an leanna.
     be.PRES 1SG PROG drink the beer-GEN
     'I am drinking beer.'

Comparable evidence is not available in Middle Welsh, where morphological case marking is completely absent. But the logical possibility exists that verbo-nominal constructions, which are predominantly verbal in Modern Welsh, instantiated a nominal pattern in Middle Welsh. Suppose that this conjecture is correct. The internal structure of the periphrastic aspectual construction (9), repeated here as (16), would be as in (17):

(16) Ac y   mae   Matholwch yn   rodi   brenhinaeth Iwerdon y Wern
     and PRT be.PRES.3SG Matholwch PROG give.VN kingdom   Ireland to Gwern
     'And Matholwch gives the kingdom of Ireland to Gwern ... '
     [PKM 41. 9–10]

(17) C ... [bod [$_{AspP}$ DP$_{ext}$ [yn] [$_{vP}$ ~~DP$_{ext}$~~ v [$_{nP}$ n-√ [~~√~~ DP$_{int}$]]]]]

The reason why the genitive, rather than the accusative, is a plausible contender to mark the complement of the verb noun in (17) could be that nP forms a closed nominal domain, that n's complement reduces to a single argument (*brenhinaeth Iwerdon*) and that the unique structural case assigned within a nominal domain is generally the genitive case. The "other" argument (*Matholwch*), which is the external argument, necessarily originates higher. If it is first merged at the vP-level, it derivationally raises to SpecAspP (but it could as well directly be merged there), then move to the specifier of the inflectional head that hosts *bod*, which itself raises to C, the spell-out site of finite verbal forms in Middle Welsh and in the contemporary language.¹² Structure (17) thus correctly predicts that the abstract case assigned to the internal argument is genitive. A similar analysis could account for the genitive marking in (15). The v inserted immediately above nP would function as a category switch, identifying the verbo-nominal projection as a mixed projection.

One could push the traditional insight even further and claim that, at the Middle Welsh stage, the items *yn*, *wedi*, which today must clearly be viewed as functional heads, more precisely as aspectual markers, were still analyzed as prepositions subcategorized for a nominal complement.¹³ This conjecture would leave us with the following structure, incorporating no category switch.

(18) C ... [*bod* [$_{vP}$ DP$_{ext}$ v [$_{PP}$ P [$_{nP}$ n-√ [√ DP$_{int}$]]]]]
      where P is the Aspect marker.

Note however that the claim that *yn* retained a lexical prepositional meaning when used as an aspectual particle is highly implausible.

Alternatively, if the morpho-syntactic evidence concerning the parallelism between nominal and verbo-nominal syntax is considered to be inconclusive (see the discussion of (16)–(18), ch. V) and if the fact that Welsh is a system in which nouns have no morphological case at their disposal is given some significance, there is no compelling reason to assume that verbo-nominal expressions in the relevant structures have a nominal core. Paradigm (16)–(18), ch. V, can thus be analyzed along the same lines at the various stages of the history of the language. If this decision is correct, we have to look elsewhere for an explanation of the difference between Middle and contemporary Welsh.

But this account of periphrastic aspectual constructions, both in Middle Welsh and in the contemporary language, doesn't really solve the difficulty. It is not sufficient to show that the object of verb-nouns is not assigned genitive case to prove that verbo-nominal projections are verbal in nature. The case assigned to objects must still be identified. What makes the decision difficult is that the historic infinitive construction, which is the topic of the next subsection, uncontroversially shows that the accusative case cannot be the solution either in Middle Welsh, since verb-nouns, at least in this construction, are unaccusative heads. I will leave the question open for the moment, but a tentative proposal will be made in section 36.

---

12 On the V2 status of Middle Welsh, see D. Willis's (1998) foundational work.
13 Recall D. Willis's (2007) observation that the development of the periphrastic aspectual construction had just begun in Middle Welsh.

33.2 The "historic infinitive"

The aspectual construction teaches us something about the syntax of the verb-noun form within the VNP projection it heads. The case of embedded verbo-nominal clauses and of the "historic infinitive" construction is different, because a full proposition is involved, not a subpart of an aspectual construction. How should the syntax of the VN form be characterized when it is the lexical head of a full clause?

As recalled in the introduction to this section, the traditional consensus, as it is spelled out in Melville Richards's (1950–1951) article, is that paradigm (3)–(14) unambiguously shows that when the projection of the argument structure of VN heads is at stake, the language resorts to the nominal pattern. If the nominal analysis was confirmed, the apparent mismatch between the external distribution of independent verbo-nominal clausal domains and their nominal internal structure would make a large subset of VNPs in Middle Welsh mixed projections of some kind. Several considerations militate against the nominal analysis, however.

(6), (7), (8), (11) indicate that more than one argument can be syntactically expressed using this pattern. It should be noted at the outset that the situation exemplified by these examples appears to be the exact opposite of the one that is instantiated by English Acc-*ing* gerunds: In English, a gerund constituent that has the internal structure of a verb phrase or of a clause appears to have the external distribution of a nominal expression; in Middle Welsh, a verbo-nominal constituent that apparently has the internal structure of a nominal uncontroversially displays the external distribution of a verb phrase or a clause. If a category switch is present in the relevant structures, it is a verbalizer, not a nominalizer. This goes against Panagiotidis's (2015) generalization that mixed projections generally are nominalized verb-phrases, not verbalized noun-phrases.

Second, a nominal analysis of VNPs should explain why, although the argument-marking strategies in verbo-nominal clauses and in nominalizations basically resort to similar devices, they distribute differently. Here are some revealing contemporary Welsh examples.[14]

(19) a. *Mae   disgrifiad   y   tyst   yn yr adroddiad*
　　　 be.PRES.3SG description the witness in the report
　　　 'The witness's description is in the report.'

---

[14] Examples (19), which are discussed in Rouveret (1994), illustrate the contemporary Welsh usage. Unfortunately, I don't have Middle Welsh data at my disposal, illustrating the syntax of nominal expressions, in order to check whether they displayed the same regularities.

b. *Mae   disgrifiad   o 'r ddamwain   yn yr adroddiad*
   be.PRES.3SG description of the accident   in the report
   'The description of the accident is in the report.'

c. *Mae   ei   ddisgrifiad yn yr adroddiad*
   be.PRES.3SG CL.3M.SG description in the report
   'His description is in the report.'
             meaning 'the witness's description'.

In (19a), the "subject" argument of the nominalization is realized as a dependent genitive. In (19b), the "object" argument is obligatorily preceded by the preposition *o* 'of'. The pronominal article adjoined to the noun in (19c) is assigned a subject interpretation. These three properties are the exact opposite of what is observed in the verbo-nominal constructions (7), (8), (11), where the subject of transitive verbs is realized as a prepositional phrase, never as a dependent genitive, where the object is never introduced by *o*, and where the pronominal clitic attached to the transitive form is never interpreted as a subject. Examples (19) show that the alleged similarity between verbo-nominal syntax and nominal syntax is spurious and that the nominal analysis of verbo-nominal constructions cannot be correct.[15]

---

[15] The nominal analysis could be maintained if it was assumed that several structural patterns are available to build nominal constructions. But then it would be necessary to explain why verbo-nominal root constructions precisely select the "ergative" one.

34 The ergativity of verbo-nominal root and embedded clauses

D. Willis (2007: 327–330, 2009: 151–152) and Tallerman & Wallenberg (2012) observe that the syntactic mapping of arguments in Middle Welsh verbo-nominal constructions is reminiscent of what is found in ergative languages.[16] The internal argument of transitive predicates receives the same syntactic treatment as the sole argument of intransitive predicates; the external argument of transitive predicates is built differently, namely as an ergative-like oblique PP. This pattern is found in both matrix sentences and in the clausal complements to epistemic/declarative predicates and to prepositions (cf. 3, 4, 7, 8, 9). The patterns of argument-marking in Middle Welsh clausal VNPs are thus remarkably similar to those observed in the root and embedded clauses of ergative languages.[17]

Other features of Middle Welsh recall what is observed in well-behaved ergative languages. In 32., it was shown that two argument-marking strategies were available in Middle Welsh clauses headed by an unergative predicate. In some cases, the unique argument is treated as the subject of a transitive predicate and surfaces as a prepositional phrase; in others, it is treated as the argument of an unaccusative predicate. This oscillation is a recurrent feature of ergative languages. In Basque, Georgian, Hindi, some intransitive arguments display the ergative morphology,[18] while others show the expected absolutive morphology.[19] It is in fact difficult to find languages that display a uniformly ergative pattern, with the unique argument of intransitive predicates never surfacing with ergative morphology.

A remarkable feature of a subset of ergative languages is the fact that verbs seem to exhibit fewer verbal properties than verbs in nominative-accusative

---

16 In his study of the verb-noun in Old and Middle Irish, Gagnepain (1963: 17) evokes the possibility of analyzing the VN + DP_{int} + *do* DP_{ext} construction as a case of ergative alignment.

17 Several authors have observed that the patterns displayed by nominalization and more generally by the syntax of nominal expressions in nominative-accusative languages "are strikingly similar to aspects of the syntax of ergative languages" (Alexiadou 2001). This similarity is partial at best, as examples (19) show.

18 This behavior tallies well with Hale & Keyser's (1993) claim that unergative predicates should be viewed as concealed transitives. But the definition of lexical classes in ergative languages is a complex matter. On Georgian unergatives, see Nash (2022).

19 Besides the major distinction between unergative and unaccusative predicates, another split internal to the unergative class should be discussed, namely the split between the verbs that mark their argument with the ergative case and those that resort to another case, for example the dative used for non-agentive roles such as the Experiencer. On this question, see Sheehan (2017).

systems. Ch'ol and other Mayan languages, Tagalog and other Austronesian languages lack overt tense morphology. The verbal form occurring in the Welsh verbo-nominal constructions is a form, which, even in its predicative use, doesn't seem to have been fully verbal at the time.

As emphasized by Tallerman & Wallenberg (2012), verbo-nominal root clauses in Middle Welsh coexisted with well-behaved verb-second finite clauses, instantiating a nominative-accusative alignment of arguments. At no stage in the history of the language did finite clauses display an ergative alignment. A similar coexistence is observed in ergative languages, which are almost never uniformly ergative, as a long tradition of research has established. A characteristic of ergative languages is precisely that they give rise to various splits. The most remarkable ones involve viewpoint aspect and person-number. In the first case, sentences in the past tense/perfective aspect display the ergative alignment – with the internal argument bearing the absolutive case and controlling verbal agreement and the external argument marked with an oblique case -, whereas in sentences in the present tense/imperfective aspect, the subject in the unmarked case controls agreement and the object bears a marked case. In the second case, first and second person external arguments control agreement and are found in the absolute form, rather than in the ergative case that is obligatory with third person referents. Basque, Hindi, Georgian and Samoan display an aspectual split; Dyirbal and Sakha a person split. Splits are important in that they open a window on two distinct alignment patterns at work within the same language, making it possible to reach a better understanding of each. The notion of split itself should be made more precise. Person and aspect are not the only dimensions that give rise to distinct alignment patterns. The Middle Welsh data will be shown to support a conception of splits integrating additional dimensions.

Finally, an overarching property of ergative languages should be mentioned, which is a plausible candidate to the status of defining property, namely (20)

(20) **Mahajan's (1994) generalization**
Ergative case marking patterns are found in verb peripheral languages (within SOV and VSO languages). Verb medial (SVO) languages are never ergative.

(20) states that ergative alignments are incompatible with the SVO order, that is, cannot be found in structures where the verb occupies a medial position between the external and the internal argument. (20) can be criticized on several grounds. First, it takes into consideration linear order, which usually doesn't play any active

role in syntax.[20] Second, as observed by Taraldsen (2017), the incompatibility of the SVO order with ergative alignement can *a priori* result either from the impossibility to mark O for the absolutive case or to mark S for the ergative case in the relevant structures. Now, it is well known that there is more than one way to derive the SVO order. And ergative argument alignment itself can arise in several distinct ways. It is urgent to determine for which of these derivations of word order and case marking Mahajan's generalization really holds. Several proposals have been made in the literature which aim at deriving (20) on principled grounds, see Mahajan (1997), Nash (2002), Müller (2008), Lahne (2008), Roberts (2021). For the moment, it is sufficient to observe that root verbo-nominal constructions in Middle Welsh are not SVO. They thus display two defining properties of ergative alignments, the distinctive marking of transitive subjects and the non-availability of the SVO order.

One additional remark should be made at this point. The term "ergative" primarily refers to the distinctive case form marking the subject of transitive verbs in morphologically ergative languages, contrasting with the "absolutive" case used for intransitive subjects and transitive objects. One could question the validity of the reference to ergativity to account for languages which, like Middle Welsh, are deprived of overt case morphology. Fortunately, the evidence based on case morphology is not the only dimension that can be resorted to to diagnose ergativity. One could also capitalize on agreement, a highly complex phenomenon in these languages, which will be ignored here because no agreement morphology is present in the Welsh verbo-nominal constructions under consideration. But ergativity should not be confined to morphology. Independently of morphological case and agreement, the notion of ergative alignment should be conceived of in syntactic terms and extended to cover all the languages and constructions that treat intransitive subjects on a par with transitive objects to the exclusion of transitive subjects. The absolute (nominative) case assigned to the internal argument (IA) of transitive verbs and to the unique argument of intransitive verbs (call it S) can be morphologically manifested, but it also very often remains silent. The external argument (EA) of transitive predicates can be realized as a nominal bearing an ergative suffix, but it can also take the form of a standard prepositional or postpositional phrase. The Middle Welsh data presented in section 1 clearly fit the characterization of ergativity: The absolutive case is left unpronounced, the ergative case is prepositional.

---

20 However, as observed by Ion Giurgea (personal communication), one should be cautious when referring to the alleged syntactic irrelevance of linear order. Linear order, if taken to be partly independent from structural hierarchy, contrary to what the Linear Correspondance Axiom claims, could very well be correlated to other syntactic properties. This is exactly what (20) says.

A priori, these convergences can teach us something about the appropriate analysis of verbo-nominal constructions, about the nature of ergativity or about both. They indicate that ergative patterns can be found in the verbo-nominal structures of at least some nominative-accusative languages. They certainly don't show that large parts of the Middle Welsh grammatical system were ergative in nature, but they indicate that UG makes available alignment strategies that are systematically used in ergative languages and are also occasionally resorted to in nominative-accusative languages. In other words, these strategies are widespread and dominant in ergative systems, but they are not specific to them.

35 Making the ergative analysis explicit

35.1 Is a unitary analysis of ergative structures possible?

The variation found across ergative languages appears to be as considerable as the one displayed by non-ergative ones. It gives rise to incompatible, often irreconciliable proposals, to the point that one may wonder whether a unitary characterization of ergative languages is possible. Some of these proposals are discussed in Appendix, sct. 39.[21] The variable properties of ergative v, the prepositional vs. affixal status of ergative case, the presence vs. absence of inflectional morphology, the very existence of splits cast serious doubts on the possibility to isolate a macro-parameter distinguishing ergative systems from non-ergative ones. Some researchers however have tried to identify a defining property of ergativity that would transcend the considerable variation between ergative systems. Nash (2017) claims that

(21) the fact that the transitive subject in ergative languages is licensed within vP, which is also the minimal domain containing the direct object, is a defining characteristic of ergative languages.[22]

This converges with the often made observation that subjects in ergative constructions seem to stand lower at Spell-Out than subjects in nominative-accusative languages (see Appendix, sct. 39). An objection that could be leveled against (21) is that in current theorizing, external arguments in SVO nominative-accusative languages are also licensed *within* vP by a probing c-commanding T. But they have to leave the vP either to satisfy the EPP or, as assumed here, to ensure the proper labeling of the clause. What distinguishes ergative languages is that the external and internal arguments are included in the same derivational phase at Spell-Out.

---

[21] For different approaches to ergativity, see, among others, Baker & Bobaljik (2017), Bok-Bennema (1991), Bobaljik (1993a, 1993b), Laka (1993), Mahajan (1994, 1997), Dixon (1994), Nash (1995, 2002, 2017, 2022), Montaut (1997, 2004, 2006), Woolford (1997, 2006), Mahieu (2007), Müller (2008), Coon (2013, 2014, 2017), Baker & Atlamaz (2014), Manzini, Savoia & Franco (2015), Polinsky (2016), and the contributions in Johns, Massam & Ndayiragije (2006), *Lingua* 122 (2012) and Coon, Massam & Travis (2017a).
[22] (21) should be distinguished from another claim made by Nash in her 1995 dissertation, with which it only partially overlaps, namely that what holds the key to ergative alignment is an impoverished functional skeleton of the sentence.

Lahne (2008) pushes this idea further and claims that a defining property of ergative languages is that the two arguments "always end up as specifiers of the same head", with the result that there is no head in between them that the verb could fill. She explains this property by the order of application of Merge and Agree in the two classes of languages. In her view and in Müller's (2008) one, the order of application of the two operations is Merge > Agree in ergative languages, Agree > Merge in nominative-accusative languages, a double option that results from an uncertainty in the way the Earliness Principle works. In the former, the structure of the whole extended verbal projection vP, is built by Merge, before Agree takes place. This means that, at the time when Agree occurs, the external argument stands in the specifier of vP and is closer to v than the other argument. It is thus assigned the v-related "internal" case (the ergative in her approach). The other argument is probed by T, which licenses its absolutive/nominative case. In nominative-accusative languages, the Agree operation between v and the internal argument, which has the effect of licensing accusative on the latter, takes place before the external argument is projected as the specifier of vP and is licensed there. If this argument raises, and it indeed does, it is to satisfy an additional principle, namely EPP. It must be acknowledged that the Müller-Lahne account successfully represents the fact that the external argument in ergative structures is assigned the "internal case". But, in spite of its elegance and efficiency, it has two defects. First, the analysis presupposes that the content of vP's specifier is closer to v than the element in the complement of V, a costly claim that gives greater importance to the notion of m-command. Second, although it has been argued for by prominent linguists (cf. fn. 34, sct. 39, Appendix), the identification of ergative with nominative seems to me highly implausible. It should also be noted that, if one adopts the derivation by phase hypothesis, as formulated by Chomsky (2001, 2008), there is no uncertainty as to the application of the Earliness Principle: A phase must have been extensively built by Merge, before Agree relations occur. Universal Grammar should probably not allow such uncertainty situations to occur, especially concerning such overarching operations as Merge and Agree.

35.2 Deriving ergative alignment in VN-initial structures

The aim of this section is to propose an analysis of the Middle Welsh constructions showing ergative alignment. As already mentioned, one of their remarkable features is that they display a relative freedom concerning the alignment of the arguments of transitive predicates: A verb-noun in initial position can be immediately followed either by the internal argument or by the external one, a property that recalls the VSO/VOS alternation found in the transitive constructions of Austronesian and Mayan languages. Both (22), repeated from (8), and (23), repeated from (7), are well-formed.

(22) *Yna agori   y safyn   y 'r   llew.*
     then open.VN   its mouth y the lion
     "Then the lion opened its mouth."

(23) *am   lad   o honaf uu hun uy mab.*
     Because   kill.VN   o myself   my son
     "because I myself killed my son ... "

The analysis that follows is intended to account for this apparently free choice situation. It is based on the descriptive generalizations and theoretical assumptions (24)–(29), which extend to Middle Welsh some assumptions deriving from current discussions on ergativity (see Appendix, sct. 39):

(24) In the structures displaying an ergative alignment, the two arguments coexist within the same extended verbal projection at Spell-Out (Nash's generalization 21);

(25) The v head in the relevant verbo-nominal structures is unaccusative;

(26) The Voice head projected above vP is the head of the extended verbal projection, it doesn't transmit features to the lower head v and identifies the position it c-commands as a θ-position, locus of the ergative case (cf. Nash 2017, Roberts 2021);

(27) The ergative marking is of the prepositional type;

(28) Absolutive is T-related; although morphologically deficient, T is able to case license the internal argument;

(29) The verbo-nominal forms that occur in the historic infinitive constructions and the embedded complement clauses showing ergative alignment behave as morphologically uninflected forms.

Let us now make explicit the steps involved in the derivation of (22) and (23). They are listed in (30) and (31) respectively.

35.2 Deriving ergative alignment in VN-initial structures

(30) a. [$_{vP}$ DP$_{ext}$ v [V DP$_{int}$]]
 b. [$_{vP}$ DP$_{int}$ DP$_{ext}$ VN ~~DP$_{int}$~~]
 c. [$_{TP}$ T [Voice [$_{vP}$ DP$_{int}$ DP$_{ext}$ VN ~~DP$_{int}$~~]]]
 d. [$_{TP}$ T [[$_{Voice}$ VN] [$_{vP}$ DP$_{int}$ DP$_{ext}$ ~~VN~~ ...]]]

(31) a. [$_{vP}$ DP$_{ext}$ v [V DP$_{int}$]]
 b. [$_{vP}$ DP$_{ext}$ DP$_{int}$ VN ~~DP$_{int}$~~]
 c. [$_{TP}$ T [Voice [$_{vP}$ DP$_{ext}$ DP$_{int}$ VN ~~DP$_{int}$~~]]]
 d. [$_{TP}$ T [[$_{Voice}$ VN] [$_{vP}$ DP$_{ext}$ DP$_{int}$ ~~VN~~ ...]]]

The syntactic derivation of ergative VN-structures, like that of any other construction, proceeds by phase. Two phases are involved: the lower one, VoiceP, and the higher one, TP/CP. For reasons that are detailed below, I assume that a Voice head is merged above vP (the VN head is complete at the v-level and raises to Voice). As a phase head, it is endowed with uninterpretable φ and case features. But it doesn't transmit them to v, with the result that DP$_{int}$ cannot get rid of its uninterpretable case feature at the vP- level. Non-transmission can be viewed as a general property of verb-initial/Celtic languages (see the discussions in chapters II and VI) or as a feature linked to the verbo-nominal nature of the predicative head. Whatever the correct option, the resulting structure is an unaccusative construction, in which v has no feature to pass to V.

For the phasal derivation to converge, DP$_{int}$ must have raised to the edge of vP before Spell-Out takes place, becoming a specifier of vP. Two options should be considered. The word order observed in (22) is derived if the internal argument adjoins to the original vP projection, see (30b). The order in (23) is derived if the movement involved is a "tucking in" movement, as Lahne proposes, inserting the raised internal argument in between the v head and the external argument, see (31b). The Spell-Out representations corresponding to (22) and (23) are (30d) and (31d) respectively. The two arguments end up as specifiers of the same v head. In (30d), DP$_{int}$ is realized as the outer specifier of vP, in (31d) as its inner specifier.

The derivations schematized in (30) and (31) both raise a difficulty, which all the researchers working on ergative languages have met in some form or another. We would expect each argument to define a potential intervener for the relations in which the other can enter. Taking for granted that the [absolutive] feature on DP$_{int}$ can only be checked by T, which is endowed with the same case feature, and that DP$_{ext}$ is case licensed via its relation with the content of Voice, it must be explained how T can have access to DP$_{int}$ over DP$_{ext}$ in (31c). Because DP$_{ext}$ intervenes between T and DP$_{int}$, the relation should be blocked by Relativized Minimality. Similarly, if DP$_{ext}$ is case licensed by Voice in (30c), one doesn't expect this licensing to be possible across DP$_{int}$.

In the case of (22), the difficulty vanishes if a smuggling derivation à la Roberts is adopted, (see Appendix, sct. 39). No relativized Minimality effect should arise because there is no intervener between Voice and DP$_{ext}$ and because T has a direct access to DP$_{int}$. But the derivation of (23) remains problematic.[23]

Two other options can be contemplated. The first one consists in the claim that when the derivation reaches the higher phase, T has access to the two specifiers at the edge of vP, which are equidistant from it.[24] If the two vP-internal arguments in (31d) are equidistant from T, we don't expect DP$_{ext}$ to function as an intervener blocking the establishment of an agreement relation between T and DP$_{int}$. The difficulty raised by derivation (30d), resulting from the non-adjacency of DP$_{ext}$ and Voice also disappears, if Voice is assumed to be endowed with an [ergative] feature matching a feature on the prepositional head of the expression occupying the inner specifier of vP.

A more radical line of research could be based on the idea that the conditions for one of the two arguments to function as a potential intervener for the relations in which the other one enters are in fact never met. This result can be achieved if one assigns a special status to the ergative case. This can be done in one of two ways. The prepositional ergative case can be conceived of as an inherent case, that is, as a case that is licensed at the moment when the argument is inserted and θ-marked. Because the external argument bears an inherent case, the only available structural case targets the other argument, namely the internal one. Only the licensing of the internal argument requires the establishment of an Agree relation. Under this view, there is no competition between the two cases involved. An alternative possibility consists in capitalizing on the fact that the expression bearing the ergative case is projected as a prepositional phrase, not as a nominal one. This would suffice to explain why the intervening argument doesn't give rise to a minimality effect. The implications of these proposals should be carefully explored. The analysis resorting to the equidistance idea seems to me to be the more convincing, however. One doesn't expect potential intervention effects to be voided by the nature of ergative case, whatever it is.

It is time to indicate why an additional head intervenes between T and v (Voice in 30 and 31) in Welsh verbo-nominal root clauses. If the verbo-nominal form VN functioning as the predicate is not endowed with the features that would allow it to enter into an agreement relation with T, which is also deficient, and if VN moves, the head hosting the latter is necessarily distinct from T, since both the verb-noun and T are deprived of the features that would make possible the raising

---

[23] As already mentioned, Roberts assumes that remnant movement is involved.
[24] They are also equidistant from the intervening Voice head, to which the VN (v-V) head raises.

35.2 Deriving ergative alignment in VN-initial structures — 243

of v-V to T. Following previous analyses, I assume that the additional verbal head that is projected immediately above vP in verb-initial ergative constructions is Voice. This head not only provides a landing site for the raised VN head, it is also directly involved in the case licensing of the external argument at the edge of vP.

We are now in a position to understand why VN-initial sequences in languages that have verb-nouns at their disposal naturally instantiate an ergative syntax in the projection of arguments, rather than a nominative-accusative one. The ergative alignment of arguments arises as an effect of several independent factors: (i) Celtic verb-nouns, like Latin and Romance passive participles, are deprived of [accusative]; (ii) the Voice head licenses [ergative] on the prepositional head of the DP in vP's specifier; (iii) T probes the internal argument which is accessible because the two arguments are equidistant from T; (iv) VN, which doesn't have the features that would allow it to enter into the T system, raises to a head distinct from T, namely Voice, which allows the PP argument to function as the syntactically and thematically licensed external argument of the clause. In the relevant structure, v keeps its function as a category-defining head, Voice plays a crucial role in the licensing of the external argument, T is responsible for the case licensing of the direct argument.

Finally, part of the reason why the ergative alignment is compatible with the VSO order and incompatible with the SVO order, in Middle Welsh and in other languages, a regularity expressed by Mahajan's generalization (20), could be that DP_{ext} is licensed *in situ* by the c-commanding Voice head. Since no further movement is required for convergence, none takes place. Importantly, movement is not imposed by labeling considerations either. It could be assumed that, although morphologically deficient, the initial T suffices to provide the whole domain with a label. Recall that it is an active head since it case licenses the internal argument. Another possibility is that the raising of the verbo-nominal head to Voice suffices to ensure the labeling of the whole clause. Recall that the external argument keeps its first Merge position, but the verbal word doesn't.[25]

---

25 At first sight, the SOV languages showing an ergative alignment, such as Hindi and Georgian, raise a potential difficulty against this account. Nash (2002) suggests that in these systems, all arguments are allowed to move out of the verbal projection because the pre-T field is scopal (it exclusively contains A'-positions).

36 Coexistence of ergative-absolutive and nominative-accusative patterns

The verb-initial order found in contemporary Welsh finite clauses clearly displays a nominative-accusative alignment. Transitive v is endowed with [accusative] and φ-features. If v transmits no feature to V, raising the internal argument to the edge of vP is both necessary and sufficient to case license it. The direct object of finite transitive clauses is thus licensed within the first phase. The T involved in these structures also differs from ergative T: It is exclusively endowed with an interpretable [tense] feature and it is c-commanded by a C/Fin head bearing φ-features and a nominative case feature. The claim is, once again, that the head of the phase, C/Fin, withholds its uninterpretable features from T. The finite verb thus raises to C/Fin and case licenses the external argument, adjoined to TP. Since no transmission of uninterpretable features from C/Fin to T takes place, the subject first raises to SpecTP and the finite verb raises to C/Fin over the subject. The latter is thus licensed during the second phase, when the derivation reaches the appropriate level.

In ergative alignments, both the internal argument and the external argument are licensed within vP, the latter by Voice, which is the head of the lower phase, the former by T, which is external to it. The fundamental difference between the nominative-accusative and the ergative derivational paths is that in the latter, T targets the internal argument when the derivation has reached the appropriate level, the external argument being independently case licensed within the extended verbal projection.

We already know why the subject moves to a preverbal position in non-pro-drop SVO languages. The structure resulting from the movement of heads and phrases must satisfy the Labeling Requirement (cf. ch. II). In a language where T is weak, raising the subject and adjoining it to the TP projection solves the difficulty. But contrary to what could appear at first, this requirement is also at work in the VSO structures instantiating a nominative-accusative alignment: The subject first raises to SpecTP and the verb later raises to C/Fin over the subject. The configuration resulting from the first movement is labeled <φ, φ> ; the second movement ensures the labeling of the clause as an unambiguously verbal projection. But the fact that, in the vast majority of clause types, the finite verb coexists with propositional particles in C/Fin suggests that the latter play a crucial role in the labeling of the whole clause and that the verb cannot achieve this result by itself. This situation holds in contemporary Welsh. It can be extended to the so-called "abnormal sentence" in Middle Welsh, which instantiated a type of verb-second structure and included a particle.

The truth is that, during the Middle Welsh period, that is, until around 1500, VN-initial clauses displaying an ergative alignment coexisted with verb-second structures. In Willis's words, Middle Welsh instantiated "a complex and fully developed V2-system". Several changes, most notably the phonological erosion of clause-initial referential or expletive pronouns and their reanalysis as preverbal particles, triggered the loss of the V2-order in the XVIth century. Willis also notes that in the V2 period, V2 was already suspended in two types of contexts, first the contexts of "narrative continuity", particularly in conjoined clauses, second those involving the non-copular uses of the present and imperfect tenses of the verb *bot* 'be' ". In other words, literary texts made accessible three types of evidence concerning the syntax of Middle Welsh sentences: finite verb-second clauses, a restricted set of finite verb-initial clauses, both showing a nominative-accusative alignment of arguments, embedded verbo-nominal clauses and historic infinitive root clauses, displaying an ergative alignment.

I will assume that the scenario sketched for the derivation of verb-initial finite clauses can readily be extended to that of verb-second ones. A C/Fin head is obviously involved in their derivation. Since the ergative and the non-ergative alignment patterns coexisted at this stage, a situation that is strongly reminiscent of the aspectual splits described in section 34, it is interesting to ask which grammatical dimensions governed the choice between the two.

Aspectual periphrastic clauses could take the form of nonfinite *bot*-initial structures, when they occurred in the complement to an epistemic/declarative predicate or to a preposition. Tallerman & Wallenberg (2012) supply the following example.

(32) *Pan   wybu   Gei yn   diheu   y   vot   ef   yn   kyscu*
     when know.VN Cei PRED sure   3M.SG be.VN 3M.SG PROG sleep.VN
     'When Cei knew for certain that he was asleep ...'

The embedded *bot*-clause in (32) can be taken to illustrate an ergative pattern with *bot* occupying the Voice position and the grammatical subject, originally the subject of the small clause selected by *bot*, marked absolutive, and *bot* itself occupying the Voice position.[26] When the VNP complement of the aspectual particle is transitive, its object is case licensed locally and receives the genitive case, if one adopts the traditional way of thinking. But, interestingly, (32) can also be analyzed as a structure instantiating a nominative-(un)accusative pattern. Since

---

[26] In structures (32), the aspectual particle is selected by the verb *bod* and should not be taken as a defining feature of Middle Welsh clausal structure.

bot/bod is a prototypical unaccusative predicate, the nominal argument receives the structural case that the C/Fin-T pair makes available in this environment. This is the situation in the modern/contemporary language, where *bod*-initial clauses can plausibly be analyzed as concealed finite clauses (see ch. VI). We observe that, for the latter analysis to be available, a more complex structure, incorporating a C/Fin head, must be associated with the *bot/bod*-initial complement. The nominal argument raises to SpecTP and *bot/bod* is hosted by the C/Fin head projected above TP.

Willis and Tallerman & Wallenberg are right to emphasize that C/Fin was available in Middle Welsh, since finite root clauses and a subset of embedded ones instantiated a verb-second pattern. But, in my view, the Middle Welsh historic infinitive constructions were simpler structures than finite clauses and incorporated no C/Fin. One can speculate that VN-DP$_{ext}$-DP$_{int}$ sequences were analyzed as TP-VoiceP-vP structures in Middle Welsh and were lost when the C/Fin-TP-vP analysis was generalized.[27] After this change has taken place, the grammar of the language includes nominative-accusative structures in which the highest head position in the clause is occupied by a verbal element. This element is necessarily marked for tense in root clauses, but in complement clauses, it keeps its verbo-nominal status when *bod* is involved. For some reason, *bod* is the only non-finite verbal predicate that has access to C.

Another piece of data discussed by Tallerman & Wallenberg seems to me to point towards the same direction. They observe that the historic infinitive construction is incompatible with negation. A finite form must be selected.

(33) a. Ny   welei   ef   y   twrwf   rac
       NEG see.IMPF.3SG 3M.SG the commotion from
       tywyllet   y   nos
       darkness the night
       'He couldn't see the commotion, because of the darkness of the night.'

   b. ac   yn   gwybot   nat ef   bioed   y da...
      and PROG know.VN NEG 3M.SG own.IMPF.3SG the goods
      'and knowing that it was not he who owned the goods...'

In my view, this restriction doesn't show that the verb-noun and negation compete for the same position, namely C/Fin, but rather that the structure underlying the

---

[27] This analysis presupposes that T in ergative alignments has a case-feature of its own, which is not inherited from C. This property could reflect the fact that the CP analysis wasn't yet generalized to all clause types at the time.

historical infinitive construction is of a smaller size than that of full finite clauses. Neg stands in C/Fin in Welsh, the site where sentential particles and complementizers are located, and no C/Fin is projected in historical infinitive constructions. The selection of the nominative-accusative alignment is thus the only choice when the clause is negative and also when it is a present/imperfective complement clause. These observations show that other dimensions than aspect should be included among the factors blocking the resort to ergative alignment. One shouldn't conclude however that the VN-initial structures that display ergative instantiate a more elementary type of structural organization than the ones illustrating nominative alignments. It is true that the structures displaying the latter include a peripheral C/Fin head, which introduces [nominative] and [φ] features in the derivation. In this respect, these structures have a more complex organization than ergative structures. At the same time, if the analysis presented here is correct, the latter contain a Voice head, which is dispensed with in nominative-accusative structures.[28]

The historic infinitive construction in Middle Welsh also coexisted with a structure whose exact analysis, at this stage of the language, has been left as a moot point, the aspectual periphrastic construction, which, as Willis reports, was already available, see examples (8)/(22), (38), representation (23) and the discussion in subsection 33.1. It is important to take a stand on the way the object of verb-nouns is case-licensed in this construction. The claim that the case assigned is the genitive shouldn't be dismissed a priori, even if it is concluded that verb-nouns in their predicative use are essentially verbal. This claim fits well with the idea that verb-nouns are unaccusative heads. As suggested in several places in this book, genitive case, which is abstract in Welsh, can be thought of as a default case that is available when the nominal target is the unique argument in a phrasal domain (not as a case assigned by a nominal lexical or functional head). Such a case has no place in an ergative alignment system. The fact that aspectual periphrastic constructions were developing at the time when the historic infinitive construction was beginning to fade away could be not fortuitous.

As a final remark, it should be observed that what is said here about the diachronic syntax of Welsh is reminiscent of the change that has taken place in the history of Hungarian. As shown by Bacskai-Atkari & Dékány (2014), a gradual

---

[28] Concerning Voice, it could be proposed that in nominative-accusative languages, the properties of v and those of Voice are bundled in a single category, which is usually referred to under the label v. The availability of the accusative case could result from a bundling of this kind. Alternatively, it could be assumed that a Voice head, introducing the external argument, is projected above v in all propositional types, whichever alignment is involved. For an analysis along these lines, see Alexiadou (2001), Torrego (2012), Roberts (2021). Collins (2005) restricts the presence of Voice to passive constructions.

extension of finite subordination can be observed at the expense of nonfinite subordination, which crucially goes hand in hand with the development of a rich left periphery (and, they submit, with a general change from SOV to SVO). The fact that, in Hungarian too, the availability of finite root and embedded clauses is directly related to the presence of a CP system supports the analysis developed in this section. As is the case in Welsh, finite subordination was already in place when the shift began. However, neither Celtic, nor Hungarian pushed the change as far as Greek did, a language where the category of the infinitive has completely disappeared (cf. ch II, sct 7.5).

37 The interpretation of tense

The core of the structures showing ergative alignment in Middle Welsh is constituted by embedded complement clauses. It is not obvious that the cases of ergative alignment in independent clauses, in particular historic infinitive constructions, should be given the same importance. But the fact remains that the relevant structures display strictly identical properties and have disappeared from the language at around the same time. If one focuses on the independent use, one should ask how it is possible for constructions like (22) and (23) that lack morphological tense to function as independent propositional domains. A Tense head is necessarily present for semantic reasons in the independent clauses of superficially tenseless languages: It allows them to be interpreted as finite and be assigned a truth value. But it should be asked what allows T to remain silent in (22) and (23). Massam (2005: 228), in her analysis of Niuean, a predicate-initial language deprived of tense-inflection and φ-agreement, and Coon (2014), in her account of Ch'ol and Tagalog, which lack a clear noun/verb distinction and display ergativity features, propose a similar answer: The absence of grammatical tense marking in some languages and some structures stems from a morphological problem; "T is unable to attract an appropriate lexical host and must therefore be phonologically null".[29]

Can this insight be transposed to the Middle Welsh case? The claim that, at this stage of its evolution, the language didn't distinguish neatly between nouns and verbs and didn't resort to the category-defining heads v and n would make Middle Welsh dramatically different from the contemporary language, which systematically has recourse to such categories. It must be immediately rejected. A much preferable option consists in the assumption that category-defining heads are used in Middle Welsh, as they are in the contemporary varieties, but that null T, because it has different properties in Middle Welsh, allows the resort to verbo-nominal forms in structures where they cannot be used in the contemporary language. In the latter, the content of finite T must be explicit and must find lexical support. Verb-nouns are not endowed with the features that would allow

---

[29] According to Coon, the specific reason why the difficulty arises in these terms in Ch'ol and Tagalog is that "there is no means to create lexical verbs in these languages" and that "overt morphology in T requires a *lexical category* as its host". In her view, this explains why Mayan and Austronesian languages have no Tense marking of any sort. The combination of a property-denoting root and of an internal argument suffices to create a predicate phrase. Only PredPs are available, not lexical categories.

them to enter into agreement and movement relations with them and to provide the required support.

The serial construction can help us to understand how null T differs in Middle Welsh and in contemporary Welsh. This construction, already a feature of Middle Welsh, is still available in contemporary Welsh, but the independent use of verb-nouns is not anymore: (5) has no equivalent in the contemporary language.[30] This contrast can be taken to reflect a difference in the status of null T. In Middle Welsh, null T has non-anaphoric uses: It could be referential/discourse-dependent and was not forced to find a local antecedent in the sentence; in contemporary Welsh, it is either anaphoric to or dependent on the matrix tense. In the modern language, the verb-noun *bod* is allowed to head embedded clauses, where T is anaphoric or dependent, but not finite root clauses, where T cannot remain silent because it is referential. Put in different terms, the existence of ergative alignments in Middle Welsh root clauses is tied up with the possibility of using non-finite verbo-nominal forms in these clauses, itself linked to the possibility of construing null T as referential/discourse-dependent.

For the sake of completeness, it should also be explained why the interpretation of the historic infinitive is systematically past/perfective. There is a general tendency for activity verbs in languages with much impoverished verbal inflection or with no inflexion at all to be interpreted as past/perfective, in sharp contrast with stative verbs that generally receive a present time interpretation. The situation in Middle Welsh is partly different. Activity predicates, which are largely dominant in the construction under consideration, receive a past interpretation, but stative verbs also do, as *wybu* in example (27) shows.

---

30 In Rouveret (1994), a null Tense head is postulated in the coordinated clauses of serial verb constructions.

38 Conclusion

It turns out that the nominal account of verbo-nominal structures is appropriate neither for the contemporary Welsh constructions, nor for the Middle Welsh ones. One could ask why it has been the consensual analysis among Celticists for so long. There is no doubt that the account of the syntax of the modern language was modeled on that of the Middle Welsh one. And as far as Middle Welsh is concerned, it cannot be denied that there is some similarity between the internal structure of verbo-nominal expressions (in their predicative use) and that of nominal ones: In both cases, we are dealing with a closed domain headed by a deficient form deprived of person and tense features. Closer scrutiny however reveals that natural languages establish a sharp distinction between verbo-nominal and nominal expressions and treat them differently.

39 Appendix: Proposals for the analysis of ergative structures

A major concern of the studies on ergativity is of course the nature, origin and use of the ergative case. Is it structural or inherent? Is the ergative argument case licensed in its first Merge position? Which is the licenser? An assumption shared by most of the contributors to *The Oxford Handbook of Ergativity* is that ergative assignment occurs rather low in clausal structure. As Coon, Massam & Travis (2017b) observe, there are a priori two ways in which this insight can be formally represented. It can be claimed either that ergative case is an inherent case assigned by v or by a higher head, say Voice, to an NP that it θ-marks or that it is a dependent case assigned to a higher NP when there is a lower NP in the same local domain. In the Principles and Parameters-style Case Theory, what is relevant to the case marking of a noun phrase is the fact it occupies a specific position in the immediate locality of a designated functional or lexical head.[31] What matters in the dependent case theory initiated by Marantz (1991) is the fact that it coexists with another NP in a given domain.[32] In this view, the ergative case is assigned to the higher of two NPs contained in the domain, the other NP being absolutive/nominative. Whatever the correct analysis, the height of the external argument appears to be a crucial dimension in the derivation of the ergative alignment. It is safe to assume that subjects in ergative languages stand lower in the Spell-Out configuration than subjects in nominative languages.

Independently of the origin of the case assigned to the external argument, another asymmetry should be taken into consideration, the asymmetry between prepositional ergative marking and affixal ergative marking. Polinsky (2016) takes it to provide the basis for a distinction between two types of ergative languages. She establishes a relatively simple correlation between the PP/DP-dichotomy and the inherent/structural status of ergative case: This case is inherent in the languages where the ergative subject is a PP, it is structural when it is a DP.[33]

---

[31] Under this view, ergative assignment can a priori involve a head-specifier relation (both the ergative argument and v occupy their first Merge position) or a c-command relation (if the v head has been raised). Coon (2017) claims that ergative marking in Mayan languages is the reflex of an agreement relation that takes place internal to vP, between the head v and its specifier. Anyway, ergative languages show that transitive subject agreement does not always reflect agreement with finite T.

[32] For a full presentation of the two theories and for arguments in favor of the dependent case one, see Baker & Bobaljik (2017).

[33] In order to decide whether the subject is a PP or an NP marked for an inherent case, binding phenomena should be useful: A NP embedded in a PP should not be able to bind a possessive

39 Appendix: Proposals for the analysis of ergative structures — 253

Claims about the origin and nature of ergative case inevitably have consequences for the proper characterization of the "other" case, the so-called "absolutive case". Whether passive participial constructions or possessive-like structures are taken to be at the source of ergativity, transitive verbal forms, in a large subset of ergative languages, do not seem to make an accusative/objective case available. The claim that ergativity should be characterized by the inability of transitive verbs to assign structural case amounts to making ergativity a particular case of unaccusativity (see Bok-Bennema 1991, Nash 1995, Torrego 2012). Summarizing Bok-Bennema's (1991) position, Alexiadou (2001) writes that "one way to solve the case problem in an ergative language is to have an exceptional case for the subject, so that the nominative case becomes free to be assigned to the object". In this approach, absolutive is a T-related case, ergative is v-related or Voice-related in a way that remains to be made precise.[34]

The idea that ergative v, if it exists, has properties distinct from those of the Chomskyan v, is shared by most researchers, but they develop it in different directions. Relying on Chomsky's (2008) claim that accusative case assignment requires the joint work of v and V, Torrego (2012) suggests that, as far as Hindi transitive clauses are concerned, a split should be postulated between the workings of V that introduces the internal argument and the head v or Voice that introduces the external argument. In her view, this split is directly responsible for the lack of accusative case in ergative languages.

The properties of Voice also play a decisive role in Roberts's (2021) characterization of ergativity. In an attempt to explain the relative similarity between ergative structures and passive constructions, he proposes to extend Collins's (2005) smuggling analysis of the passive to the analysis of ergative structures with a transitive predicate. He shows that a smuggling derivation of these structures successfully accounts for their alignment properties. The relevant parts of the clause are schematized in (34).

---

internal to the direct object. But the results are sometimes unexpected. Mahieu (2007) studies Finnish constructions in which the subject looks like an ordinary PP, but behaves in this respect as a case-marked NP.

34 This presentation presupposes that absolutive should be identified with nominative, but leaves the status of ergative open, as well as the nature of the relation between the ergative-absolutive and nominative-accusative case systems. Several options can be contemplated. If absolutive is taken to be nominative, the ergative can be identified with the accusative, as argued by Müller (2008), or ergative and accusative can be treated differently, as in Bittner & Hale (1996). Early analyses identified ergative with nominative and absolutive with accusative, see Bobaljik (1993) and Laka (1993) among others.

(34) T [$_{\text{VoiceP}}$ [$_{\text{VP}}$ V DP$_{\text{int}}$] [$_{\text{Voice}}$ erg] [$_{\text{vP}}$ DP$_{\text{ext}}$ v [$_{\text{VP}}$ ~~V DP$_{\text{int}}$~~]]]^{35}

In (34), VP-fronting has taken place, raising the phrase V + DP$_{\text{int}}$ to the specifier of VoiceP. Voice, which "withholds its φ-features from v", licenses DP$_{\text{ext}}$ in its first Merge position. The raising of [V DP$_{\text{int}}$] places the internal argument in a position where it can be probed and licensed by T. DP$_{\text{ext}}$ is licensed as ergative by Voice, DP$_{\text{int}}$ as absolutive by T. The idea that Voice withholds its φ-features immediately explains why ergative v behaves like an unaccusative head. In clauses containing an unaccusative predicate, the unique argument is directly licensed by T.

The languages that display ergative verb-object-subject alignments also often instantiate ergative verb-subject-object orders. This is the case of many Austronesian and Mesoamerican languages. Roberts's smuggling analysis, that relies on the movement of the verb-object complex to the specifier of a higher functional head, namely Voice, successfully accounts for the existence of ergative VOS structures. In his view, ergative VSO alignments result from a derivation in which the object has been extracted out of the VP, before the latter moves. We are thus dealing with a case of remnant movement. In ergative VSO/VOS languages, the external argument is licensed within the VoiceP projection by the Voice head that c-commands it.[36]

But not all ergative constructions can be characterized as unaccusative structures. This is the case of two Polynesian languages, Niuean, studied by Massam (2000, 2001, 2005), and Tongan, analyzed by Polinsky (2016). Polinsky claims that the direct argument checks its absolutive case with a verbal head in the verbal projection. Mesoamerican languages point towards the same direction. Within the Mayan languages, Coon (1917) distinguishes two types of ergative systems depending on whether the object must move up to TP in order to receive case (Q'anjob'al) or is allowed to remain in its original low position (Ch'ol). If the second option is selected, the absolutive case is assigned either by a v head inside the vP or by the head of a higher projection in the inflectional domain, Aspect in her view.

---

[35] In (21), erg can be an ergative affix or a preposition. One of the basic ingredients of Collins's account of passive constructions is that *by* is first merged rather high in the structure, as the head of the VoiceP projection and minimally c-commands the original vP, whose specifier hosts the external argument.

[36] In fact, Roberts's (2021) primary aim is to show that the typological generalization (20) put forth by Mahajan (1994) can be derived via the combination of a smuggling analysis of ergative alignment and the Final over Final Condition (FOFC, see Sheehan, Biberauer, Roberts & Holmberg. 2017). Alternative accounts of Mahajan's generalization have been proposed, which resort neither to smuggling and remnant movement, nor to the FOFC, see Nash (2002), Müller (2008), Lahne (2008).

39 Appendix: Proposals for the analysis of ergative structures

The question of the status of ergative v arises in a specific way in the languages where the lexical N/V distinction, if it exists, is not as robust as it is in English. Many of the Polynesian and Mesoamerican languages referred to above fall under this characterization and often share two additional characteristics: They are isolating languages with no inflectional morphology; they display a verb-initial (or rather a predicate-initial) order. Since the verb/noun distinction is not as prominent as it is in English, one could ask whether the recourse to the category-defining functional head v is fully appropriate in this case. Some experts resolutely answer "no" to this question. Dealing with Niuean, an ergative predicate-initial language in which "verbs are less verbal and less distinguished from nouns than in English" and in which both verbs and T lack finiteness features, Massam (2005: 228) adopts a more conciliatory position. She argues that the crucial factor in this language is not the relation of an unspecified root to a category-defining functional head, but the impossibility to establish a relation between the latter and T. In other words, the absence of grammatical tense marking in some languages stems from a morphological problem. "Because they lack such [finiteness] features, Niuean verbs (or predicates) are not verbs at the level of morphosyntax, ... and consequently they will not enter into the head system of the language through any Agree or checking relation, but rather they will remain independent". In other words, the fact that the relevant Niuean lexical items do not bear finiteness features rules out any chance for them to raise to a higher inflectional head such as T and excludes the occurrence of inflectional morphology on the latter. These observations allow us to reach a better understanding of the possible link between the lack of inflectional morphology in some ergative systems and ergative alignment. Welsh undoubtedly is an inflectional language, but the verbal forms that occur in the historic infinitive construction and in embedded complement clauses significantly are uninflected verbo-nominal forms.

VIII The syntax of inflected infinitives in European Portuguese

40 Introduction

In European Portuguese (henceforth E.P), one finds a class of infinitival structures that display two properties that distinguish them from standard non-inflected infinitives and make them closer to finite complement clauses: (i) the verb is an *inflected* or *personal* infinitive form unspecified for tense, but bearing a person/number affix agreeing with the subject; (ii) the grammatical subject, when it is expressed, bears nominative case, as the structures in which the subject position is occupied by a personal pronoun clearly show.[1]

Let us briefly consider the forms E.P inflected infinitives can take. These forms result from the adjunction of a person-number affix to the infinitival stem ending with the morpheme -*r*. No agreement marker is added to the stem at the 1st and 3rd person singular, which makes the corresponding forms formally identical to bare infinitives. The full paradigm is as follows.

(1) singular: 1st person: *amar*   plural: 1st person: *amar-mos*
    2nd person: *amar-es*   2nd person: *amar-des*
    3rd person: *amar*   3rd person: *amar-em*

The general tendency has long been to consider the inflected infinitive form as "uma forma extremamente curiosa, estranha às linguas irmãs como a quaisquer outras fora do dominio romanico" (Said Ali [1908] 1966: 61). Research on this topic has progressed a lot in the last fifty years, showing that this early characterization is faulty on several points and cannot be maintained. Other Romance languages have inflected infinitive forms at their disposal, in particular Galician, Sardinian, Old Neapolitan (see Rohlf 1949 for details and dialectal evidence). It is also tempting to establish a link between the European Portuguese construction and the Italian structure which has been referred to since Rizzi (1982) as Aux-to-Comp, exclusively found in the complement to epistemic and declarative predicates and in which the raised auxiliary, although not inflected, appears to case license a nominative postverbal subject. Contemporary Spanish and Romanian also display uninflected infinitive structures with a nominative subject.[2]

---

[1] I will henceforth refer to inflected infinitive constructions under the label IICs and to European Portuguese as E.P.

[2] See Ambar & Jiménez-Fernández (2017) for an in-depth comparison between Portuguese and Spanish "overtly and non-overtly inflected infinitive" constructions. Rouveret (1980) and Raposo (1987) both establish a parallel between the E.P construction and the Italian one, whose distribution is more restricted.

Diachronic studies have also contributed to the definition of a new perspective on IICs. Diez (1882), in his *Grammatik der Romanischen Sprachen*, had already established a connection between the Portuguese, Italian and Spanish constructions. More recently, Romanist scholars, notably Meier (1955), have provided evidence that all Romance languages, at one stage of their history, have tried to express a referential subject next to the infinitive and that the Portuguese construction should in no way be considered as an isolated phenomenon in this respect. Adopting a demanding formal grammar perspective, Martins (2018) traces the diachrony of three types of infinitival complementation, the *faire*-infinitive, the exceptional case marking infinitive and the IIC and shows that the *faire*-infinitive construction found as complement to causative and perception verbs is the earlier pattern, that the ECM structure is a subsequent innovation and that it is precisely this structure that creates the conditions for the appearance of the IIC. The overall evolution can be characterized as "a functional enrichment of infinitival complements of causative and perception verbs". Martins's conclusion offers a highly plausible alternative to the traditional view, according to which the inflected infinitive derives from the Latin imperfect subjunctive.[3]

The discovery that IICs display a considerable distributional and syntactic variety across different dialects of Portuguese and at different stages of its evolution suggests that the properties of this construction could support a scalar view of finiteness.[4] This is the conclusion arrived at by Fiéis & Madeira (2017), who distinguish three types of inflected infinitives, which, they claim, differ in their degree of finiteness, ranging from forms that exhibit characteristics quite similar to finite ones to forms that strictly behave like uninflected infinitives. Examples (2)–(5) are arranged according to a decreasing order of finiteness, beginning with

---

[3] This Latin form was in particular found after volitional verbs, often without the mediation of the expected complementizer *ut*. (i) and (ii), containing the present and imperfect second person of the verb *curare* 'mind' respectively exemplify the dependent and independent uses of the subjunctive. The form *cures* is the subjunctive present second person singular form of *curare* 'to look after', the form *curares* is the subjunctive imperfect second person singular form.

(i) Te oro (ut) rem tuam cures.
 'I entreat you to mind your own business.'

(ii) Rem tuam curares.
 'You ought to have minded/to be minding your own business.'

For discussion, see Maurer (1968) and more recently Martins (2001, 2006) and Scida (2004). Both Maurer and Scida argue in favor of the imperfect subjunctive theory. The fact that IICs occur as complements to many types of verbal predicates in E.P, but are excluded precisely as complements to volitional verbs raises a serious difficulty against this theory.

[4] On the scalar view of finiteness, see ch. I, sct. 1.

the ones with the highest degree of finiteness and ending with the ones that are undistinguishable from uninflected infinitive structures.[5]

(2) Eu   espero   até   tu   teres
    1SG.NOM wait.1SG until 2SG.NOM have.INF.2SG
    acabado o   livro.
    finished the book
    'I'll wait until you have finished the book.'

(3) Pensam   /afirmam   ter   a polícia mentido.
    think.3PL/claim.3PL   have.INF.3SG the police lied
    'They think that the police lied.'

(4) a. Surpreendeu-me   tu   teres   saído.
       surprise.PRET.3SG-1SG.ACC 2SG.NOM have.INF.2SG left
       'It surprised me that you left.'

    b. Lamento   os deputados   terem   aprovado a   proposta.
       regret.1SG the deputies have.INF.3PL approved the proposal
       'I regret that the deputies have approved the proposal.'

(5) a. O Pedro   convenceu   os filhos   a estudarem.
       the Pedro convince.PRET.3SG the children a study.INF.3PL
       'Pedro to convinced his children study.'

    b. O Pedro preferiria   reunirem-se   mais tarde.
       the Pedro prefer.COND.3SG meet.INF.3PL-se more late
       'Pedro would prefer to meet later on.'

    c. Os professores disseram   aos   alunos   que era
       the teachers   say.PRET.3PL to.the students that was
       preciso   trabalharem.
       necessary work.INF.3PL

---

[5] (2), (4a), (6a) and (6b) are from Madeira (1994), (3), (5a) from Fiéis & Madeira (2017), (5b) and (5c) from Sheehan (2014), (4b) is adapted from Raposo (1987). Madeira (1994) provides a list of IICs that includes structures that are not considered here (complements to perception verbs, complements to causative predicates).

(6) a. * *Preferias chegares a tempo.*
prefer.PRET.2SG arrive.INF.2SG on time
'You preferred to arrive on time.'

b. * *Os deputados querem publicarem o relatório.*
the deputies want.3.PL publish.INF.3.PL the report

c. *Os deputados querem publicar o relatório.*
the deputies want.3PL publish.INF the report.
'The deputies want to publish the report.'

This paradigm confirms that the distribution of IICs and that of uninflected infinitival clauses only partially overlap. In (2), the inflected infinitive displays properties similar to those of finite verbs. Examples (5) exemplify situations where IICs define control structures. (5a) behaves in all respects like an obligatory object control structure, not licensing nominative subjects, which leads Gonçalves, Santos & Duarte (2014) to characterize an example of this type as a "pseudo-inflected infinitive". Examples (5b) and (5c), from Sheehan's (2014) study, are cases of partial control and control at a distance respectively: Inflected infinitives are legitimate in both cases. They contrast with (6a), which indicates that inflected infinitives are banned in subject obligatory control structures. The inflected form *chegares* is ungrammatical in (6a), the inflected form *publicarem* is ungrammatical in (6b). Only non-inflected infinitive clauses are allowed as complements to volitional predicates, as the contrast between (6b) and (6c) illustrates. In Raposo's (1987) view, only (3) and (4) should be viewed as "true inflected infinitives".[6]

Fiéis & Madeira's (2017) contention that IICs distribute along a scale of finiteness is an innovative claim that has many ramifications yet to be fully explored. It shows that the answer to the question of whether IICs should be conceived of as finite domains or not cannot be simple.[7] The fundamental interrogation underlying this question is whether it is possible to dissociate the φ-completeness of subject agreement and the defective status of tense in the grammatical function-

---

[6] Subject clauses (4a) and the complements to factive predicates (4b) are grouped together in the list given above. It turns out that they display strictly the same range of properties. In what follows, I will often refer to factive complements in situations where actually both object factive clauses and subject clauses are at stake.

[7] Rouveret's (1980) conclusion was that IICs should be considered as finite clauses because they exhibit both nominative case marking on the "distinguished argument", namely the subject, and person-number agreement on the verb. It is this double marking that makes the corresponding proposition finite. But paradigm (2)–(6) shows that things are much more complex.

ing of these clausal domains.[8] The scalar effect could as well be interpreted as a reflex of the interaction of several independent factors, none of them specific to Portuguese or to inflected infinitives. This is the view that this chapter intends to defend: The syntactic properties of IICs result from the interplay between the lexical requirements of the various predicate classes involved and a collection of independently motivated principles. It will appear that many central aspects of the syntax of IICs involve general notions and mechanisms that are operative elsewhere in E.P and in other languages. Concentrating on a restricted set of IICs, precisely the ones that should be considered as "true inflected infinitives", I wish to reopen a debate that was at the core of the first generative studies on E.P complementation in the 80s and 90s, namely, the syntactic contrast between factive and epistemic/declarative inflected infinitive complements. When this problem was first raised at the beginning of the 80s, most of the leading ideas and analytic devices potentially leading to a better understanding of the real nature of the inflected infinitive phenomenon had not yet been developed. The situation has changed a lot with the advent of the Minimalist Program, the development of an Agree-based approach to syntactic dependencies and the discovery of the decisive role of labeling in syntactic representations, as well as with the new perspective on the periphery of clauses opened by the cartographic approach.

Two grammatical processes will figure prominently in the explanation of the sensitivity of IICs to the lexical class of both the selecting predicate and the embedded one and of the specific form these complements take: tense construal and labeling.

First, because the notion of finiteness is elusive and difficult to handle, I will base my characterization of IICs on tense. Building on Stowell's (1982) demonstration that a restricted subset of infinitive clauses in English are tensed and on Landau's (2004, 2013) and Wurmbrand's (2001, 2014) classifications of English infinitival domains as tensed or untensed, I will show that the relevant diagnostics, when extended to IICs, unequivocally designate non factive and factive IICs as semantically tensed domains. At the same time, their tense is morphologically deficient, which suggests that they should be conceived of as defective domains. But, to the extent that they make a complete φ-matrix available, the case licensing of their subject raises no difficulty.

Second, just as non-defective ones, defective domains must be labeled, if only to satisfy the subcategorization requirements of the verbal heads that select them. It will be shown that the word order observed in each IIC type directly reflects the strategy selected to satisfy the Labeling Requirement. Epistemic/declarative

---

[8] See Sitaridou (2006) for a clear statement of this question.

predicates and factive predicates do not select the same type of complement, a difference which directly determines the choice of the (abstract) complementizer occurring in each IIC. Each complementizer type in turn imposes specific restrictions on the categorial membership of its complement. This is where Labeling Theory becomes relevant. Word-order restrictions on the two infinitival types ultimately follow from the necessity to meet the subcategorization requirements of the peripheral categories that select them. The constructions in which labeling doesn't provide the appropriate result are excluded. All in all, it will appear that some IICs are excluded because they cannot be appropriately labeled, others because the tense construal of the predicate they contain turns out to be impossible, making them uninterpretable.[9]

---

9 Subcategorizarion relations play a crucial role in the account proposed here. This account can be easily reformulated within the probe-goal-Agree framework, taking the null complementizers in IICs to function as probes, cf. sct. 26.2. In this approach, it is natural to assume that an Agree relation underlies subcategorization relations.

41 Three asymmetries

In the first generative treatment of inflected infinitive constructions in European Portuguese, Raposo (1975) observes that epistemic/declarative predicates and factive predicates can both govern clausal complements analyzable as IICs, but impose different conditions on the syntactic realization of these complements.

When the inflected form is a main verb, it generally cannot precede the subject, cf. (7b), (8b). When the matrix verb is a factive predicate, the order DP_s-V_{IInf} is grammatical, cf. (7a). It is excluded when it is an epistemic/declarative predicate, cf. (8b).

(7) a. *Lamento   os deputados   aprovarem   a   proposta.*
       regret.1SG the deputies   approve.INF.3PL the proposal
       'I regret that the deputies approve the proposal.'

   b. * *Lamento   aprovarem   os deputados a   proposta.*
       regret.1SG approve-.INF.3PL   the deputies the proposal

(8) a. * *Penso   os alunos   comprarem   o   livro.*
       think.1SG the pupils   buy.INF.3PL   the book

   b. * *Penso   comprarem   os alunos   este livro.*
       think.1SG buy.INF.3PL   the pupils   this book

When the inflected form is an auxiliary, it obligatorily precedes the subject in the complement to epistemic/declarative predicates, cf. (10b) vs. (10a), it optionally precedes it in the complement to factive predicates, cf. (9a) vs. (9b).[10]

(9) a. *Lamento   eles   terem   perdido os documentos.*
       regret.1SG 3PL.NOM   have.INF.3PL   lost   the documents
       'I regret that they have lost the documents.'

   b. *Lamento   terem   eles   perdido os documentos.*
       regret.1SG have.INF.3PL   3PL.NOM   lost   the documents
       'I regret that they have lost the documents.'

---

10 Examples (9), (10) are taken from Madeira (1994).

(10) a. *Pensam   a   policia   ter   mentido.
        think.3PL the police   have.INF.3SG lied

   b. Pensam   ter   a policia mentido.
        think.3PL have.3SG the police lied
        'They think that the police has lied.'

The factive/nonfactive divide appears to manifest itself in a particular way in examples (7)–(10): (i) the sequence V_{IInf}+subject (V a main verb) is well-formed neither as the complement to factive predicates nor as the complement to nonfactives; (ii) the unmarked order in the complement to factive predicates is subject+Aux/V_{IInf}, where the embedded inflected form can be an auxiliary or a main verb; (iii) epistemic/declarative predicates systematically impose an Aux_{IINF}+subject order on their complements. The goal of the early analyses of the IIC and of several later ones was to capture the properties of paradigm (7)–(10), which can be labeled "Raposo's paradigm", cf. Raposo (1975), Rouveret (1980), Raposo (1987), Madeira (1994).

This initial picture was modified by a major discovery made by Manuela Ambar (cf. Ambar 1994): (i) as far as nonfactive complements are concerned, the claim that the inflected infinitive forms of main verbs never occupy a position higher than that of the subject is descriptively wrong;[11] (ii) the lexical class of the embedded predicate, i.e its being eventive or stative, is the major factor determining the distribution of the verb in the relevant structures. Perlmutter (1976) had already discussed examples of the verb-first order, with V a modal or an inherently stative unaccusative predicate denoting the emergence of an event.

(11) a. Penso   poderem.   / deverem   eles
        think.1SG can.INF. 3PL/ must.INF.3PL 3PL.NOM
        resolver   o   problema.
        solve.INF the   problem
        'I think they can/must resolve the problem.'

   b. Ele   disse   existirem   muitos candidatos
        3M.SG.NOM say.PRET.3SG exist.INF.3PL many candidates
        nesta   eleição.
        in.this election
        'He said that there are many candidates in this election.'

---

11 The label "main verb" simply refers to the items that are not auxiliary heads.

c. *Ele   disse   acontecerem   coisas*
   3SG.NOM say.PRET.3SG   happen.INF.3PL things
   como essas só   nos   Balcãs.
   like   these only in.the Balkans
   'He said that things like these only happen in the Balkans.'

But Ambar shows that eventive verbs can also be found in the clause-initial position of inflected infinitive structures, provided that the embedded domain is not interpreted as reporting a single event located at the utterance time, but receives a habitual or generic reading. Although the following data are not judged plainly natural by all native speakers, they no doubt exist.

(12) a. *Penso   comprarem   eles   frequentemente livros*
        think.1SG buy.INF.3PL 3PL.NOM   frequently   books
        de física.
        on physics
        'I think that they frequently buy books on physics.'

   b. *Penso   comprarem   eles   muitos livros.*
      think.1SG buy.INF.3PL 3PL.NOM   many   books
      'I think they buy many books.'

   c. *O João afirmou   comprarem   eles*
      the João declare.PRET.3SG   buy.INF.3PL 3PL.NOM
      o   jornal   todas as   sextas-feiras.
      the   newpaper all   the   Fridays
      'João declared that they buy the newspaper every Friday.'

   d. *Ele   pensa   surgirem   rinocerontes*
      3SG.NOM think.3SG   crop.INF.3PL   rhinoceros
      na   praia   todos   os   dias.
      on.the   beach   all   the   days
      'He thinks that rhinoceros crop on the beach every day.'

It is important to decide whether the second case (involving eventive verbs) can be subsumed under the first (auxiliaries, modals and a subset of unaccusative/ stative predicates). The presence of an adverbial or of a determiner favoring a generic or habitual interpretation certainly doesn't turn a verb like *comprar* into an unaccusative predicate. But it is a fact that, once it is flanked by an expression of this type, an eventive predicate receives a generic/habitual construal, not an episodic punctual one, and semantically behaves just like a stative predicate, locating a habit or a generic property at the utterance time.[12]

In conclusion, three major asymmetries seem to play a role in the syntax of IICs and should be articulated in an adequate account:

(i) the main verb/auxiliary asymmetry, illustrated by the contrast between (8b) and (10b);
(ii) the factive/nonfactive asymmetry, illustrated by the contrast between (9a) and (10a);
(iii) the asymmetry between eventive and stative predicates, illustrated by the contrast between (7b), (8b) and (11b), (11c).

To what extent does each of these dimensions of variation contribute to an explanation of the syntactic differences between factive complements and nonfactive ones? In order to provide a principled answer to this question, I intend to examine each of these dimensions in turn, in the light of some of the assumptions put forth by current syntactic research, and evaluate their respective contributions to the syntax of IICs.

---

[12] The fact that a predicate like *surgir* 'to arise' is welcome in the initial position of the clausal complement of a declarative verb only if a frequency expression or a nominal quantifier is present in the clause shows that *surgir* illustrates the second case, not the first.

(i) ??Ele   disse   surgirem   controvérsias como essas
    3.SG.NOM say.PRET.3SG arise.INF.3PL controversies like these

(ii) Ele   disse   surgirem   frequentemente
     3SG.NOM   say.PRET.3SG   arise.INF.3PL   frequently
     controvérsias como   essas.
     Controversies   like   these

(iii) Ele   disse   surgirem   muitas   controvérsias   como essas.
      3SG.NOM say.PRET.3SG   arise.INF.3PL   many   controversies   like these

42 The non-existence of an auxiliary/main verb asymmetry

Early accounts take it for granted that when the auxiliary precedes the subject in an IIC (cf. 9b, 10b), it occupies the C position. This analysis, modeled on Rizzi's (1982) account of Italian "Aux-to-Comp" constructions, can straightforwardly be extended to the structures discussed by Ambar (1994), in which the subject follows a main verb. It is fair to acknowledge that, at a time when subjects were thought to originate in the specifier of the inflectional head Infl, the movement of the verbal head to C provided the simplest account of the existence of Aux-subject orders – in fact, it was the only available option. The vP-internal subject hypothesis, that is, the claim that external arguments originate inside the verbal projection, in the specifier of the semi-lexical head v, makes accessible a second analytic option that shouldn't be dismissed a priori, according to which the subject in auxiliary/verb-initial structures keeps its original position within vP and the verb raises to the inflectional head above vP and possibly stops there. Ambar (1994) and Madeira (1994) both suggest that a third position is accessible to auxiliaries in auxiliary+subject constructions. Ambar argues that auxiliaries do not reach C on the basis of the following example.

(13) a. *Penso   só   ontem   terem   eles   recibido*
        think.1SG only   yesterday have.INF.3PL 3PL.NOM   received
        a   noticia.
        the   news
        'I think that they received the news only yesterday.'

   b. * *Penso terem só ontem eles recibido a noticia.*

In her view, the fact that the focalized adverbial *só ontem* must precede the raised auxiliary *terem* for the derivation to converge shows that the auxiliary occupies a position *internal* to the embedded TP. If the adverbial expression is adjoined to the inflectional domain, as she assumes, it must be concluded that the auxiliary doesn't itself leave TP. To characterize the relevant target site, several technical options present themselves. Madeira (1994) proposes to resort to an intermediate category projected between T and C to account for the optionality of Aux-raising in the IICs complements to factive verbs. This site looks like a copy of the head T, projected immediately above TP, the type of category that Nash & Rouveret (1997) dub "proxy category". If Rizzi's (1997) finely structured version of the left periphery is adopted, a different conclusion can be contemplated: The adverbial in (13a) occupies the specifier of the Focus head, the auxiliary itself plausibly being realized in the lowest head of the CP system, namely Finite. The question of whether the higher heads in the periphery, namely Force and Topic are projected above Focus in (13) but remain silent, or whether they are not projected at all, will be left open at this point, although the second possibility seems to be more plausible.

Turning now to the question of the main verb/auxiliary asymmetry, no principled reason a priori prevents main verbs from targeting the sites in which auxiliaries are found. This generalization will be tested by looking at the behavior of inflected infinitives in the complement to epistemic/declarative predicates. But the infinitival structures showing a main verb in initial position are not confined to the complements to these predicates. Auxiliaries optionally raise to the edge of embedded factive domains; lexical eventive verbs can also reach the edge, provided that the relevant complements are assigned a habitual/generic construal. Some native speakers even prefer the verb-initial option.

(14) a. *Lamento   os deputados   comprarem   o   jornal*
      regret.1SG the deputies   buy.INF.3PL the newspaper
      todas as sextas-feiras.
      all   the Fridays
      'I regret that the deputies buy the newspaper every Friday.'

   b. *Lamento   comprarem   os deputados   o   jornal*
      regret.1SG buy.INF.3PL the deputies the newspaper
      todas as sextas-feiras.
      all   the Fridays

It is natural to assume that the position accessible to main verbs in clauses with a habitual interpretation, whatever it is, is the same as the one that hosts auxiliaries in auxiliary-first IICs. The claim that some positions are accessible to auxiliaries, but cannot host main verbs is directly contradicted by the facts and should be abandoned.[13]

---

13 For example, Madeira (1994) assumes that the obligatory subject-auxiliary inversion in non-factive complements results from the movement of the agreeing form to C, forced by the checking requirement of an [agr] feature in C, which is a nominal feature. In factive complements, auxiliaries, but not main verbs, are allowed to raise to an intermediate projection XP between TP and CP, whose head X is also endowed with an [agr] feature. In her view, nominal C and X are both incompatible with main verbs (making inversion generally impossible), but they can host auxiliaries, which are "pure bearers of agreement features". If indeed position X exists, it should not be restricted to auxiliaries.

In order to reach a more fine-grained and better supported account, it may be fruitful to systematically compare the behavior of auxiliaries and that of main verbs in IICs and in main clauses. The asymmetry between auxiliaries and main verbs illustrated by examples (8b) and (10b) is reminiscent of the one observed in English finite tensed clauses. The consensus today, following Emonds (1978) and Pollock (1989), is that the English auxiliaries *have* and *be*, when finite, raise higher than main verbs: The former have access to the highest inflectional heads; the latter remain trapped within vP. In French, both main verbs and auxiliaries move out of the vP and target the highest inflectional head in declarative finite clauses. Finite inflected forms in European Portuguese instantiate a behavior different from that of their English or French counterparts. They move out of the vP, but appear not to have access to the highest inflectional head. The latter conclusion is arrived at by Costa (1996) on the basis of examples like (15) and (16).

(15) a. *O Rui agarrou vivamente o braço do irmão.*
the Rui seize.PRET.3SG brusquely the arm of.the brother
'Rui brusquely seized the arm of his brother.'

b. ?* *O Rui vivamente agarrou o braço do irmão.*
the Rui brusquely seize.PRET.3SG the arm of.the brother

(16) a. ? *O João resolveu provavelmente esse problema ao mesmo tempo.*
the João solve.PRET.3SG probably this problem at.the same time

b. *O João provavelmente resolveu esse problema ao mesmo tempo.*
the João probably solve.PRET.3SG this problem at.the same time
'João probably solved this problem at the same time.'

While examples (15) confirm that finite verbs raise to the inflectional domain, since they precede manner adverbs which mark the edge of vP, examples (16) indicate that they don't reach the highest inflectional head in the clause, since they follow both the subject and sentential adverbs. Costa (1996) interprets these distributions as a clue that finite verbs stop in T, the category immediately above v, and don't reach the highest head, the one that used to be labeled Agr$_s$ in the 90s and occupied the same rank in the functional hierarchy as Finite in today's cartographic schema. He also takes the possibility of interpolating a sentential adverb in between the finite verb in T and the subject as a clue that the position SpecTP is simply not accessible to subjects in declarative affirmative clauses. If one resorts to an enriched conception of the left periphery, we end up with the following analysis: The inflected verb raises to T and follows the subject that has moved to the specifier of a higher head, plausibly Fin (or has been adjoined to the corresponding FinP prjection). The intervening adverb is itself adjoined to the TP projection.[14] The distributional contrast between *vivamente* and *provavelmente* should be traced back to the fact that *provavelmente* is a fully natural candidate for adjunction to TP, whereas *vivamente* is not.

The distribution of auxiliaries introduces an additional factor of complexity since some native speakers reject the finite declarative affirmative sentences in which an adverb is interpolated between the auxiliary and the past participle, treating the auxiliary+participle complex as an unsplittable unit. Modulo this variation, auxiliaries seem to follow the same pattern as main verbs. For the speakers who don't allow splitting, the preferred position for manner adverbs is the one following the past participle; they are not welcome in the pre-auxiliary position. Sentential adverbs on the contrary tend to precede the auxiliary and are marginally tolerated in the position following the participle. The speakers that don't object to splitting also allow the adverbs of both classes to intervene between the auxiliary and the participle.

(17) a. *O Rui   tinha   agarrado vivamente o braço*
        the Rui have.IMPF.3SG seized   brusquely the arm
        do   irmão.
        of.the   brother
        'Rui had brusquely seized the arm of his brother.'

   b. (?) *O Rui   tinha   vivamente agarrado.*
           the Rui have.IMPF.3SG brusquely seized
           o   braço do   irmão
           the arm   of.the   brother

---

14 Nash & Rouveret (1997) take Costa's examples as evidence in favor of the "proxy category" approach they develop. The higher head would be a proxy T (T₁ in a T₁ [TP0 ... T₀ ...] configuration). When an adverb like *provavelmente* intervenes between the subject and the inflected verb, cf. (16b), it occupies the specifier of the lower TP projection and the subject the specifier of the higher (proxy) TP projection. In order to make the exposition easier to follow, I will henceforth ignore the possibility that the landing site of the moved subject could be the specifier of a proxy T. The term *specifier* is used in its conventional meaning here, referring to the nominal position that is daughter-of-XP and sister- of-X' (along the lines of the standard X-bar theory).

c. ?? *O Rui   vivamente   tinha   agarrado*
   the Rui   brusquely   have.IMPF.3SG   seized
   o   braço   do   irmão.
   the   arm   of.the brother

(18) a. *O   João   provavelmente   tinha   resolvido*
   the João   probably   have.IMPF.3SG   solved
   esse problema   ao   mesmo tempo.
   this problem   at.the same   time
   'João had probably solved this problem at the same time.'

b. (*) *O João tinha provavelmente resolvido esse problema ao mesmo tempo.*

c. *O João tinha resolvido provavelmente esse problema ao mesmo tempo.*

These distributions confirm that auxiliaries and main verbs in finite declarative affirmative tensed clauses have access to the same inflectional head, namely T.

The syntax of participles raises many complex questions that cannot be adequately dealt with here. The first one concerns the nature and origin of the supposedly unsplittable units they form with auxiliaries in some languages and in some constructions. Examples (17) suggest that in declarative affirmative finite clauses, Portuguese participles do not stay confined in the VP, since they occur to the left of vP peripheral adverbs. But this doesn't show that they form a cluster with the auxiliary when they are adjacent to it, as is the case in (17a), (18a) and (18c). They could have raised to a position that stands in between the landing site of auxiliaries and the edge of vP (marked by adverbs). Conversely, there are situations where the participle is separated from the auxiliary by the subject and possibly by adverbs. This is the case in the structures that involve the raising of the auxiliary to the periphery. Root interrogative sentences are a case in point.

(19) a. *O que tinha   o João   estupidamente   entornado?*
   what have.IMPF.3SG   the João stupidly   spilled
   'What had João stupidly spilled?'

a'. ? *O que tinha   estupidamente   o João   entornado?*
   what have.IMPF.3SG   stupidly   the João   spilled

b. *Quando tinha   o João   cuidadosamente fechado as janelas?*
   when   have.IMPF.3SG the João carefully   closed the windows
   "When had João carefully closed the windows?"

b'. ? Quando tinha cuidadosamente o João fechado as janelas ?
   When have.IMPF.3SG carefully the João closed the windows

c. A quem tinha o João ontem lido o livro?
   to whom have.IMPF.3SG the João yesterday read the book
   'To whom had João read the book?'

c'. A quem tinha ontem o João lido o livro?
    to whom have.IMPF.3SG yesterday the João read the book

d. A quem tinha o João provavelmente lido o livro?
   To whom have.IMPF.3SG the João probably read the book
   'To whom had João probably read the book ?

d'. A quem tinha provavelmente o João lido o livro?
    To whom have.IMPF.3SG probably the João read the book

Costa (2004) interprets the full grammaticality of examples like (19a), (19b) and (19c) as an indication that the SpecTP position, which is not accessible to subjects when the finite verbal form stands in T, becomes available to them when it has raised to C. Interestingly, the speakers who freely allow adverbs of different classes to intervene between the auxiliary and the participle in affirmative declarative clauses reluctantly accept interrogative configurations in which an adverb immediately follows the auxiliary, disrupting the adjacency between the auxiliary and the subject, as the relative marginality of (19a') and (19b') shows. This could follow from the fact that in the relevant structures, the positions respectively occupied by the adverb, the subject and the participle cannot be clearly identified. One can dismiss the possibility that the adverb stands in SpecTP. The subject would then reside in a lower position, maybe SpecvP, although it is not interpreted as a focus, and the participle itself would not have left the vP, contrary to what is generally the case in E.P. But if the subject is realized in SpecTP and the adverb is adjoined to TP, we are left with no explanation for the fact the corresponding examples are not perfect. All adverbs don't give rise to the same contrast, however, which indicates that the adjunction possibilities are tightly dependent on the lexical class the adverb belongs to. As (19c)/(19c') and (19d)/(19d') show, the sentences containing *ontem* or *provavelmente* are grammatical, irrespective of the relative positions of the subject and the adverb: These adverbs undoubtedly are more natural candidates to adjunction to TP than *estupidamente* and *cuidadosamente*.

Costa claims that his conclusion about subjects is further supported by the syntax of two adverbs, *bem* and *sempre*, which display radically distinct distributional properties. The adverb *bem* 'well' never intervenes between an auxiliary and the participle associated with it and in fact never precedes the participle.

(20) a. A   Maria tinha   desenhado bem   algumas figuras.
         the Maria have.IMPF.3SG designed   well   some   figures
         'Maria had designed well some figures.'

   b. *A Maria tinha bem desenhado algumas figuras.

   c. *A Maria bem tinha desenhado algumas figuras.

   d. Que   tem   desenhado bem   a   Maria?
      what have.PRES.3SG designed   well the Maria
      'What has Maria designed well?'

   e. *Que tem bem desenhado a Maria?

   f. *Que tem a Maria bem desenhado?

   g. Que tem a Maria desenhado bem?

   h. O que leu o José bem?

Paradigm (20) shows two things: First, only the sentences in which *bem* follows the participle, immediately or not, are well-formed; second, it can precede the subject only when the latter follows the participle. These distributions can be made sense of if the adverb *bem* occupies a designated position at the edge of vP, if participles systematically raise out of vP, and if subjects are realized in a position internal to the inflectional domain (or remain within vP). In (20g), *a Maria* stands in the SpecTP position, as it does in (h); in (20d), it occupies a site internal to vP.

A second argument supporting the claim that SpecTP is available to subjects only in constructions involving T to C/Fin, not in those in which T doesn't raise, is provided by the syntax of the adverb *sempre*, which, when it is adjoined to the TP projection means 'after all'. Costa gives the following examples.

(21) a. O   João sempre   tinha feito   o   trabalho.
         the João after all   had done the work
         'João had done the work after all.'

   b. *Sempre   o João   tinha feito o   trabalho.
         after all the João had done the work

c. ? *Que trabalho tinha sempre o João feito?*
which work had after all the João done
'Which work had João done after all ?'

d. ? *Esses trabalhos todos, tinha sempre o João feito. Não tinha?*
these works all had after all the João done. NEG had
'All these works, João had done after all. Hadn't he ?'

In (21a), *o João* occupies the specifier of FinP, *tinha* has raised to T, *sempre* is adjoined to the TP projection. The ungrammaticality of (21b) shows that the subject can't be realized in SpecTP in this case. In (21c) and (21d), which are A'-structures, *o João* follows the adverb and the result is not fully grammatical (see the discussion of 19b and 19d).[15]

The provisional conclusion that can be drawn from these distributions is that both subject-first and auxiliary/verb-first structures should be analyzed as FinP projections and that main verbs and auxiliaries have access to the same positions in the two configurations, T in subject-first structures, Fin in auxiliary/verb-first ones.

---

15 Costa's (2004) generalization is interesting in itself. But it would be of greater significance if it could be derived on principled grounds. See Costa (2004) for suggestions. An alternative possibility should be considered. It would consist in the claim that only one licensing relation can take place within a given checking domain. The Single Licensing Condition, adapted from Nash & Rouveret (2002), achieves the desired result.

(i) **Single Licensing Condition**
A functional category can enter into a licensing relation with the feature content of only one terminal node in its checking domain.

The notion of "licensing relation" ranges over the case checking of a nominal expression via DP-raising, the labeling of a projection via untriggered DP-movement and agreement, the valuation though head movement of a functional head's feature. The overall effect of (i) is to exclude the configurations in which both the specifier and the head of a functional projection have been targeted for valuation or labeling purposes. (i) predicts that the specifier of the TP projection cannot host the subject if the verbal head has moved to T to check the latter's φ-features and that conversely, the verbal head cannot reside in T in the structures where the specifier of TP is occupied by the subject. But an adverb can be interpolted between a raised subject and a verb standing in T, because adverbs are not involved in licensing relations (cf. fn. 14). On additional effects of (i), see Nash & Rouveret (2002). (i) could also be relevant to explain why, in the cartographic schema, a focalized expression in the clausal periphery necessarily occupies a site distinct from the specifier of FinP, when the head Fin itself enters into a relation with a verbal form or a complementizer, see the end of footnote 12, section 51. Note that the notion of checking domain must be rethought if Chomsky's claim that the applications of Internal Merge systematically create set-merge symmetric exocentric structures is adopted. The resolution of this challenge will be left for further research.

Let us now look at adverbial distributions in IICs. In the factive complements that involve no auxiliary-subject inversion, the word-order patterns are roughly the same as in finite clauses.

(22) a. ??*Lamento   a   Alicia vivamente   agarrar*
         regret.1SG the   Alicia brusquely   seize.INF.3SG
         o   braço   do   pai,   quando a   mãe   chega.
         the   arm   of.the father when   the mother arrive.PRES.3SG

   b. *Lamento a Alicia agarrar vivamente*
      regret.1SG   the   Alicia seize.INF.3SG brusquely
      o braço do pai, quando a mãe chega.
      the   arm   of.the father when   the mother arrive.PRES.3SG
      'I regret that Alicia brusquely seizes the arm of his father, when her mother arrives.'

(23) a. **Lamento   obviamente   os deputados   terem*
         regret.1SG obviously   the deputies   have.INF.3PL
         aprovado   a   proposta.
         approved   the   proposal

   b. *Lamento os deputados obviamente terem aprovado a proposta.*
      'I regret that the deputies obviously have approved the proposal.'

   c. *Lamento os deputados terem obviamente aprovado a proposta.*
      'I regret that the deputies obviously have approved the proposal.'

   d. ? *Lamento os deputados terem aprovado obviamente a proposta.*

The contrast between (22a) and (22b) is reminiscent of what is observed in finite clauses (cf. 15). The quasi-ungrammatical status of (22a) shows that inflected infinitives cannot follow manner adverbs, confirming that raising to the inflectional domain obligatorily takes place in these constructions. This is also what Romance uninflected infinitives (except the French ones) do: They raise to T. Structures like (22b), where the manner adverb follows both the subject and the inflected infinitive verb, are perfect, as expected. The ungrammaticality of (23a) indicates that there is no position at the left edge of IICs that defines an appropriate site for sentential adverbs. These adverbs are perfectly natural when they intervene between the subject and the auxiliary (cf. 20b) or between the auxiliary and the participle (cf. 20c). They cannot as easily be inserted between the participle and its object (cf. 20d). In all the well-formed examples, the subject *os deputados* can be assumed to occupy the specifier of FinP and the auxiliary *terem* to stand in T. The participle *aprovado*, which is not necessarily adjacent to the auxiliary, is free to move out of the vP or not to move.

Adverbial distributions in the complements to epistemic/declarative predicates give us further clues as to the correct analysis of the corresponding structures. Let us look first at the examples in (24).

(24) a. *Penso   ter   a   Alicia agarrado*
        think.1SG have.INF.3SG the Alicia seized
        o   braço do   pai,   quando a   mãe   chegou.
        the   arm   of.the father when   the mother arrive-PRET.3SG
        'I think that Alicia seized the arm of her father when her mother arrived.'

   b. ?*Penso   ter   agarrado a Alicia o   braço do   pai,*
        think.1SG have.INF.3SG seized   the Alicia the arm   of.the father
        quando a   mãe   chegou.
        when   the mother arrive-PRET.3SG

   c. *Penso   terem   eles   resolvido esse problema dificil*
        think.1SG have.INF.3PL 3PLNOM   solved   this problem difficult
        ontem.
        yesterday
        'I think that they have solved this difficult problem yesterday.'

   d. ?*Penso   terem   resolvido eles   esse problema dificil*
        think.1SG have.INF.3PL solved   3PL.NOM this problem difficult
        ontem.
        yesterday

(24a) is more natural than (24b), (24c) is more natural than (24d), which suggests that no auxiliary+participle cluster in formed at the C/Fin level. The subject *a Alicia* occupies the specifier of TP in these examples, which confirms that this position is only accessible when the verbal head raises to C/Fin. Ana Madeira and Alexandra Fiéis inform me that assigning a contrastive focus reading to the post-participle subject would make (24d) fully acceptable. This is the interpretation that Romance languages usually assign to the post-verbal subjects that have not left the vP in finite clauses. In this example, the participle has raised out of vP and the subject *eles* remains in its vP-internal original position.

The distribution of manner adverbs is as expected.

(25) a. ?* *Penso   ter   vivamente a   Alicia agarrado o braço*
         think.1SG have.INF.3.SG brusquely the Alicia seized   the arm
         do   pai,   quando a   mãe   chegou.
         of.the father when   the mother arrive.PRET.3.SG

   b. *Penso ter a Alicia vivamente agarrado o braço do pai, quando...*

   c. *Penso   ter   a   Alicia agarrado vivamente o   braço*
      think.1.SG have.INF.3SG the Alicia seized   brusquely the arm
      do   pai,   quando...
      of.the father when
      'I think that Alicia brusquely seized the arm of her father, when...'

   d. ?* *Penso ter agarrado vivamente a Alicia o braço do pai, quando...*

   e. ?? *Penso ter agarrado a Alicia vivamente o braço do pai, quando...*

(25a) is quasi-ungrammatical, confirming that manner adverbs can't occupy a position higher than that of the subject. (25b) and (25c) illustrate a situation where both the auxiliary and the subject have raised out of vP. In (25c), the participle has also left the vP, but it doesn't form a cluster with the auxiliary, since the subject intervenes between the two. (25d) and (25e), which are less than perfect, illustrate the distribution of unsplit auxiliary+participle units. Native speakers judge (25e) better than (25d), preferring the sequence where the manner adverb follows the subject, which is a clue that the latter has raised.

Paradigm (26), which documents the distribution of sentential adverbs, points towards the same conclusions.

(26) a. * *Penso   provavelmente terem   resolvido os meninos*
         think.1SG probably   have.INF.3.SG   solved... the boys
         esse problema difícil.
         this problem difficult

   b. *Penso   terem   os meninos provavelmente resolvido*
      think.1SG have.INF.3.SG the boys   probably   solved
      esse problema difícil.
      this problem difficult

   c. *Penso terem provavelmente os meninos resolvido esse problema difícil.*

   d. *Penso terem provavelmente resolvido os meninos esse problema difícil.*

e. ? *Penso terem resolvido os meninos provavelmente esse problema difícil.*

f. ? *Penso terem resolvido provavelmente os meninos esse problema difícil.*

(26a) indicates that sentential adverbs cannot stand at the left edge of IICs. (26b), (26c) and (26d) show that raised auxiliaries occupy a position above TP. The lower acceptability of (26e) and (26f), as compared with that of (26b) and (26c), should be taken to show that the position occupied by the auxiliary in (26b) and (26c), namely Fin, is not naturally accessible to auxiliary+participle combinations. In other words, auxiliaries and participles don't cluster at the CP/FinP level, nor at the TP level (if they did, they would move to the periphery as a unit). As for the subject, it is realized in SpecTP in the structures where it immediately follows the auxiliary or the adverb *provavelmente* (cf. 26b, 26c). In the structures where it follows the participle, it occupies its original position within vP (cf. 26d).

For the sake of completeness, it is necessary to look at the positions of verbs, subjects and adverbs in the complement to non-factive predicates in the absence of an auxiliary (we know that these constructions are legitimate when they can be assigned a habitual/generic reading).

(27) a. *Penso   agarrarem   todos os meninos vivamente o   braço*
think.1SG seize.INF.3PL all   the children brusquely the arm
do   pai,   quando têm   medo.
of.the father when   have.3PL fear
'I think that all the children brusquely seize their father's arm, when they are frightened.'

b. ? *Penso   agarrarem   vivamente todos os meninos*
think.1SG seize.INF.3PL brusquely all   the children
o   braço do   pai,   quando têm   medo.
the arm   of.the father when   have.3PL fear

c. *Penso   resolverem   provavelmente os meninos   problemas*
think.1SG solve.INF.3PL probably   the children problems
difíceis quando dormem   bem.
difficult when   sleep.3PL well
'I think that the children can solve difficult problems when they sleep well.'

d. ? *Penso resolverem os meninos provavelmente problemas difíceis, quando dormem bem*

These examples confirm that in non-factive complement structures, main verbs have access to the same positions as auxiliaries. The fact that they preferentially precede manner adverbs and the subject indicates that they leave the vP. The fact that they also precede sentential adverbs shows that they raise to Fin. As for nominal or pronominal subjects, they uncontroversially stand in the specifier of TP in the well-formed examples (27a) and (27c).

The distributions in (22)–(27) support the following descriptive generalizations:

(28) In IICs, (at least) two positions are accessible to inflected auxiliaries:
(i) a position immediately above vP and manner adverbs, but below the realization site of sentential adverbs; this low position should be identified with T;
(ii) a position higher than the realization site of sentential adverbs; this high position should be identified with Fin, the lowest head in the left periphery.

(29) When raising to the periphery is involved, auxiliaries raise alone, leaving the participle stranded; unsplit auxiliary+participle sequences can be found in the inflectional domain, but the auxiliary and the participle do not necessarily form a cluster.[16]

(30) In the complement to factive predicates, inflected infinitive auxiliaries either follow or precede the subject – they are realized either in the low (T) or in the high (C/Fin) position; main verbs usually follow the subject, but can precede it when they are stative predicates or when the embedded infinitival clause can be assigned an habitual/generic reading.

(31) In the complement to epistemic/declarative predicates, inflected infinitive auxiliaries systematically precede the subject – they occupy the high position; inflected infinitive verbs follow the same distributional pattern as inflected auxiliaries, provided that they are stative predicates or eventive predicates that are assigned a habitual/generic reading.

(32) Costa's (2004) generalization also holds in inflected infinitive structures. The specifier of TP is not accessible to subjects in subject-initial structures; it is accessible to them in the structures involving T-raising to C/Fin.

---

[16] The syntax of direct questions indicates that both auxiliaries and main verbs have access to the lowest head in the left periphery, but that auxiliary+participle complexes have not.

(33) There is no evidence that the structures in which the inflected infinitive clause is not the source of an nterrogative expression and doesn't include a focalized or a topicalized phrase, the functional heads above FinP are projected, which means that the IICs considered so far qualify as FinP projections. The embedded domain in (13a), which includes a focalized phrase should be analyzed as a FocP projection. But topicalization cannot take place within an IIC, as (i) shows.

(i) * Eu lamento, esse livro, terem eles lido.

The ungrammaticality of (i) stands in sharp contrast with what is observed in embedded finite clauses, where embedded topicalization is legitimate.

These generalizations provide further support for the claim that a site that could host auxiliaries, but would be incompatible with main verbs doesn't exist in E.P IICs: Auxiliaries and main verbs potentially have access to the same range of positions in finite and inflected infinitive clause types.

43 The case licensing of IIC subjects

It is not possible to reach firm conclusions concerning verbal syntax in IICs without having formed a clear idea of the distribution of subjects. In Rizzi's (1982) analysis, the reason why uninflected auxiliaries raise above the subject in some languages and constructions is to achieve the proper case licensing of the latter. The case licensing of infinitival subjects is also at the heart of Raposo's (1987) account. According to him, the subtheories of government and case should be exported from their initial domain of application, namely NPs, to the Infl node itself. The account of IICs he proposes is closely modeled on Reuland's (1983) analysis of gerund constructions: "A tenseless Infl positively specified for Agr can assign nominative case to a lexical subject only if it is itself specified for case", that is, if the corresponding IP finds itself in the domain of a case assigner.[17] In his view, factive predicates subcategorize for a nominal maximal projection, not for a CP. An IP whose lexical head is an inflected infinitive is thus expected to be able to satisfy the subcategorization and selection requirements of the matrix predicate, since IP in this case is equivalent to NP. This analysis must be extended to subject clauses, which display the same properties, see (4a). On the contrary, the infinitival complements to epistemic and declarative predicates should be analyzed as instances of the category CP. Because of the intervening C, Agr in the embedded IP is not governed and cannot receive case. But if the Aux raises to C, the Agr element becomes accessible to government by the matrix predicate.[18] More generally, the IICs in which no inversion occurs are IPs, those displaying inversion are CPs.

---

[17] In her review of Raposo's analysis, Madeira (1994) observes that the prediction that IICs should not be allowed to occur in non-Case-positions is not confirmed by the data. Inflected infinitive structures are able to function as root exclamatives. She provides (i), (ii) is from Rouveret (1980: 97).

(i) *Poderes tu ajudar-me!*
 to.be.able.INF.2SG 2SG.NOM help.INF-1SG.ACC
 'If only you could help me!'

(ii) *Terem morrido homens de tanto valor!*
 to.have.INF.3PL died men of such value
 'And to think that men of such value have died!.'

[18] As for volitional predicates, they do not take the type of tensed complement epistemic/declarative predicates select, nor nominal complements. IIC are thus ungrammatical in this context, only bare infinitives are possible.

https://doi.org/10.1515/9783110769289-049

Should a direct link be established between the raising of the auxiliary in the complements to epistemic/declarative predicates and the licensing of nominative case on the post-auxiliary subject, as Raposo's account assumes? Is raising itself triggered by the necessity to check the features of the auxiliary or those of the host head, whether this head is the embedded C or a lower category? We know that not all IICs impose the raising of the auxiliary. In some cases, raising is optional, as factive complements show; in others, it is simply excluded, as the IICs complements to prepositional complementizers illustrate, see (2) and Madeira (1994). The fact that auxiliary raising takes place in some structures and doesn't in others suggests that it is a last resort strategy in the configurations where it occurs and, at the same time, confirms that an alternative derivational option is available in the other structures to guarantee both the checking of the auxiliary's features and the case licensing of the subject. The question is why the strategy used in one case cannot be used in the other. Raposo's treatment relies on the claim that an additional factor is involved in the phenomenon, which is independent from nominative licensing but has an effect on it, namely the complement type selected by each predicate class. A reasonable line of research would be to claim that case licensing functions along the same lines in the two complement types and to try to identify and characterize the "other factor".

The minimalist approach to syntactic dependencies makes available a novel theory of case licensing that has precisely the required property. The case licensing of the subject in Romance finite tensed clauses is taken care of by an Agree relation established at the T-level between the person, number *and case* features of the T head hosting the inflected verb and those of the subject it c-commands. The crucial implication of these independently motivated assumptions is that case checking occurs early in the derivation, when the subject still resides in the vP. If the subject raises from its original position – and it undoubtedly does in the vast majority of constructions-,[19] its movement is triggered by some other princi-

---

[19] This framework of assumptions predicts that at least a subset of the constructions in which an inflected verbal form precedes the subject can be analyzed as structures in which the verbal form is in T and the subject keeps its position inside vP. (24b) and (24d) ar plausible candidates for this analysis. The examples in which the auxiliary precedes, but the subject follows a manner adverb, also are. But the result is often rather marginal, as (25a), (25d) indicate, which confirms that subjects strongly prefer to leave the vP (at least in non-presentational clauses). In the structures in which the inflected auxiliary precedes sentential adverbs and occupies the high position, the subject can a priori be realized inside vP, as is the case in (26d), or in the specifier of the immediately higher inflectional head, namely T.

ple, plausibly some version of the EPP principle, which is totally dissociated from case checking.[20]

In section 42, I have shown that auxiliaries and main verbs potentially have access to the same range of positions in all complement types: Both can target the T head or a higher category, namely Fin, when they raise. There is no reason to assume that the features associated with these items differ in any relevant respect in the two complement types, in terms of their identity or in terms of strength or weakness.[21] I conclude that the explanatory principle accounting for the word-order differences displayed by factive complements and nonfactive complements cannot be located in the specific choices made by each construction concerning the syntactic restrictions on verb movement or the conditions governing case licensing: They are necessarily identical in the two structures.

Now that the first of the three asymmetries that have been identified at the end of section 2, that between auxiliaries and main verbs, has been removed from the list of potential sources of variation, it is time to look at the other two, the eventive/stative one and the factive/nonfactive one.

---

20 In her (1994) analysis, Madeira already argues that in Aux+subject structures, the movement of the auxiliary isn't triggered by Case licensing considerations.

21 It was argued in chapter VI that the auxiliary *bod* in Welsh differs from main verbs in that it is endowed with a [tense] feature, which explains their different syntactic behaviors. There is no evidence that a similar divide exists in E.P.

44 The eventive/stative divide

Ambar's (1994) contribution has revealed the importance of the divide between eventive and stative predicates for the internal syntax of the complements to epistemic/declarative predicates. Eventive and stative lexical classes display recurrent and remarkably uniform properties across languages and constructions. One of these is that they give rise to different tense construal of the independent and embedded finite and infinitival clauses that contain them. Contrary to stative predicates, eventive predicates trigger the "present tense effect", which, when it is observed, provides a clue that tense is semantically and also plausibly syntactically present in the corresponding domains. The aim of this section is first to briefly recall the arguments that support the claim that some infinitival domains are tensed and other are not and then to determine where E.P IICs stand in this respect.[22] The picture that emerges is that the present tense effect indeed manifests itself in most of the inflected infinitive domains containing an eventive predicate, supporting the conclusion that the internal structure of the corresponding IICs includes a T head. But it is not observed in the complements to the predicates that are generally considered to select a tenseless complement in English, such as "restructuring verbs" like *try, begin*, suggesting that the corresponding predicates in E.P do not govern an IIC.

In some languages, the use of the present with eventive predicates in finite root clauses gives rise to a specific phenomenon known as the "present tense effect", which has been the topic of a considerable literature, see among others Stowell (1995), Pancheva & von Stechow (2004), Wurmbrand (2014). In English, the present tense cannot be used to report a single event ongoing at the utterance time, or initiated at the utterance time, or completed at the utterance time. To refer to an ongoing event, the progressive construction must be used, cf. (34a). The simple present is not impossible, but can only be assigned a generic or habitual interpretation, cf. (34b). As for sentences containing an individual-level stative predicate, they are naturally assigned a present-time interpretation, cf. (34c), (34d):[23]

---

[22] For an extensive presentation of the various proposals concerning the semantics and the syntax of tense in finite and nonfinite domains, see ch. II, sct. 8.

[23] The case of stative predications based on stage-level predicates is more complex, as Ion Giurgea observes. In English, some of them must be in the progressive, as is the case in the following examples:

(i) *He is sitting on the throne.*
(ii) *He is lying on the beach.*

and in expressions like

(34) a. Lucy *reads/is reading the newspaper now.
 b. Lucy reads the TLS every week.
 c. Pat knows Pete.
 d. Homer enjoys epic poems.

The present tense effect also manifests itself in the tense construal of finite embedded domains, as well as in that of uninflected infinitive constructions, as shown by Wurmbrand's (2014) study of the tense properties of infinitives.[24] Only propositional attitude predicates like *believe* or *claim* select a complement that has a tense of its own and manifest the present tense effect. In Wurmbrand's view, this effect should be characterized as a restriction on aspect: The present tense in English is only compatible with imperfective aspect.

Portuguese stands on the same side as English as far as the imperfective restriction is concerned. Contrary to French, German and Italian, it belongs to the family of languages that don't associate a present-time interpretation to the simple present tense. (35a), (35b) and (35c) can only denote a habitual behavior:

(35) a. *A Maria fuma.*
   'Maria smokes.'

 b. *A Maria faz desporto.*
   'Maria does sport.'

 c. *O Pedro lê um livro todos os meses.*
   'Pedro reads a book every month.'

It is easy to check that E.P uninflected infinitive constructions display the same temporal properties as their English counterparts. And it is natural to extend the semantic criteria used to establish the tense status of finite and infinitive clauses to IICs, which instantiate an intermediate type between the two. IICs appear to

---

(iii) *He is being polite.*

in which the event denoted by the predicate requires an active participation of the subject. But other stage-level states do not take the progressive form:

(iv) *I like that.*
(v)   *I think that now's the time.*
(vi) *I see.*

The fact that generic and habitual predications based on eventives don't impose the progressive is a strong indication that they are equivalent to states.

24 For a full discussion, see ch. II, sct. 5.2.

transparently illustrate the imperfective restriction. The ungrammaticality of examples (36a) and (36b), repeated from (8a) and (8b), and the well-formedness of (31d) should be interpreted as clues that the imperfective restriction is operative in the complements to predicates like *pensar* 'to think', *acreditar* 'to believe', *achar* 'to think', *dizer* 'to say', *afirmar* 'declare'.

(36) a. * *Penso   os   alunos   comprarem   este livro.*
         think.1SG the pupils buy.INF.3PL this book

   b. * *Penso   comprarem   os   alunos   este livro.*
         think.1SG buy.INF.3PL the pupils this book

   c. * *O João   afirmou   eles   comprarem   o jornal*
         the João declare.PRT.3SG 3PL.NOM   buy.INF.3PL the newspaper
         todas as   sextas-feiras.
         all   the Fridays

   d. *O João   afirmou   comprarem   eles   o   jornal*
      the João declare.PRT.3SG buy.INF.3PL 3PL.NOM the newspaper
      todas as   sextas-feiras.
      all   the Fridays
      'João declared that they bought the newspaper every Friday.'

The joint ill-formedness of (36a) and (36b) confirms that eventive predicates in the present tense cannot refer to a single event located at the utterance time; (36d) shows that this tense can be used to temporally locate a habit or a generic property. These distributional patterns confirm that the infinitival complements of this type are tensed. Note that word-order variation is not at stake here, only interpretation is. The fact that the subject never precedes the embedded predicate in this complement type (cf. 36a, 36c) should be traced back to an independent constraint that must still be identified.

A major question is whether the characterization of the tense of inflected infinitives based on epistemic/declarative constructions can be extended to factive/psychological predicates like *lamentar* 'regret', *aprovar* 'approve', *criticar* 'criticize', *detestar* 'hate', *odiar* 'hate'. It was concluded in chapter II, section 8.2.3, that factive complements should indeed be analyzed as tensed domains. Let us check whether this conclusion holds for factive IICs. Paradigm (37) documents the relevant properties.

(37) a. *Lamento   os deputados   aprovarem   a proposta.*
    regret.1SG   the deputies   aprove.INF.3PL the proposal
    'I regret that the deputies approve the proposal.'

b. *Lamento   eles   perderem   os documentos.*
    regret.1SG   3PL.NOM lose.INF.3PL   the documents
    'I regret that they lost the documents.'

c. ? *Lamento eles perderem os documentos ontem.*
    'I regret that they lost the documents yesterday.'

The IICs in (37a) and (37b), which are complements in the present tense, are understood as describing punctual events. The favored interpretation in this case is a simultaneous present tense reading. But *aprovar* in (37a) can also be assigned a stative reading. In (37b), the accomplishment predicate *perder* can also be assigned an anterior/past interpretation, as the translation of (37b) indicates. (37c), in which a past-denoting adverb is adjoined to the embedded predicate is marginal, but not excluded (the construction with the auxiliary *ter* would be strongly preferred). But in the general case, native speakers don't perceive the factive complement as past. The constructions that contain a controlled subject display similar interpretative properties.

(38) a. *Eles odiavam   saberem   os resultados das   eleições.*
    they hated.IMPF.3PL know.INF.3PL the results   of.the elections
    'They hated to know the results of the elections.'

b. ? *Ele odiava   anunciar   os resultados das   eleições.*
    he hate.IMPF.3SG announce.INF.3SG the results   of.the elections

c. *Ele detestou   saber   os resultados das   eleições.*
    he detest.PRT.3SG know.INF.3SG the results   of.the elections
    'He detested to know the results of the elections.'

d. *Chocou-me   saber   os resultados das   eleições.*
    shock.PRT.3SG-1SG.ACC know.INF.1SG the results   of.the elections
    'It shocked me to know the results of the elections.'

Factive IICs can also be assigned a habitual/generic reading when the embedded predicate is eventive, provided that adverbs or determiners favoring this interpretation are present (cf. 39a). Stative predicates, like *saber* or *gostar*, also freely occur in this context (cf. 39b, 39c, 39d).

(39) a. *Lamento   eles   perderem   os documentos sistematicamente.*
       regret.1SG 3PL.NOM   lose.INF.3PL   the documents systematically
       'I regret that they systematically lose the documents.'

   b. *Eu   odiava   saberem   os resultados   das   eleições.*
       1.SG.NOM   hated.IMPF.3SG   know.INF.3PL   the results   of.the   elections
       'I hated that they knew the results of the elections.'

   c. *Lamento   eles   saberem   a noticia.*
       regret.1SG 3PL.NOM   know INF.3PL   the news
       'I regret that they know the news.'

   d. *Lamento   eles   gostarem   de comer.*
       regret.1SG 3PL.NOM   like.INF.3PL   de eat
       'I regret that they enjoy eating.'

There are two ways to interpret the suspension of the present tense effect and the neutralization of the eventive/stative divide in these environments. They could be traced back to a property of factive predicates themselves, which would somehow extend the reference time of the embedded clause, ensuring that it includes a fragment of the past, in which case the imperfective restriction wouldn't apply.[25] Another option would consist in taking into account the *realis/irrealis* status of the complement, as Pesetsky (1992) does in his discussion of English factives (cf. sct. 8.2.3). But no noticeable difference can be detected between the structures with a *realis* complement and the structures with an *irrealis* one. Compare (37a) and (37b) with (40a), in which an *irrealis* matrix with a conditional mood is involved, with (40b), where we have a *realis* matrix and an episodic complement, and (40c) with a *realis* matrix and a generic complement.

(40) a. *Ele   detestaria   perderem   este jogo.*
       3SG.NOM   detest.COND.3SG   lose.INF.3PL   this game
       'He would detest them losing this game.'

   b. *Eu   odeio   (eles)   perderem   aquele   jogo.*
       1SG.NOM   hate.1SG   3PL.NOM   lose.INF.3PL   this   game
       'I hate them losing this game.'

---

[25] The situation instantiated by these constructions would be analogous to that of the present tense clauses in languages like French and German.

c. Eu   odeio   (eles)   perderem   jogos.
   1SG.NOM hate.1SG 3PL.NOM   lose.INF.3PL   Games
   'I hate them losing games.'

The preceding discussion is somewhat inconclusive, because no robust explanation has been offered for the absence of present tense effects in these contexts and for the interpretive differences manifested by the embedded tense in the complements to factive predicates and in the complements to propositional attitude predicates. In spite of these uncertainties, I will conclude that (at least a large subset of) factive complements are tensed. More precisely, in a framework in which the different syntactic types of infinitival constructions are taken to reflect their semantic properties, factive complements should be analyzed as semantically tensed clauses headed by a C/Fin head.

The tense value of the periphrasis *ter*+past participle should also be commented on. It is well-known that in E.P and English independent finite clauses, this complex doesn't refer to a single past event and is incompatible with positional adverbs. But when embedded into an IIC, it functions as a periphrasis conveying a past tense interpretation of the event, not an imperfective/habitual interpretation, as it does in finite clauses. This is the case in examples (9a), (9b) and (10a). This interpretive difference could be linked to the fact that the value of each of the three tenses – present, simple past, present perfect (*pretérito perfeito composto*) – seems to be tightly dependent on the value of the other two.[26] Morphology makes only two tenses available in the infinitive, simple (present) and compound (non-present). The latter necessarily includes past among its values. A more straightforward way to capture the interpretation of the *ter*+participle periphrasis in IICs would consist in adopting Ambar's (1994) observation that *ter* is itself a stative predicate. As we know, the present time construal of stative predicates raises no difficulty (they inherently observe the imperfective restriction). *Ter* counts as a stative (individual-level) predicate even when its participial complement is eventive (stage-level).

In guise of a conclusion, it should be observed that the presence of a T head in IICs, which is empirically supported by their displaying the present tense effect, could also be made to follow from quite independent considerations, having to do with well-formedness conditions on phrase structure configurations. A theoretical assumption concerning agreement morphology, which is supported by various phenomena across languages, is that it is usually affixed to functional

---

[26] See Pancheva & von Stechow (2004) for a semantic analysis of English tenses along these lines.

heads, which mediate the relation between lexical heads and agreement affixes, never directly to lexical heads. If it is correct, this assumption implies that a T head necessarily mediates the relation between the infinitival inflection and the verbal stem.[27] In IICs, the relevant T head happens not to be morphologically manifested.

This analysis of the tense of IICs opens the way to a straightforward explanation of the ill-formedness of a subset of them. For example, the IICs complements to propositional attitude verbs, whose predicate is a bare eventive VP (without any auxiliary being present) are excluded because they are not interpretable. The matrix predicate imposes a simultaneity reading and thus an imperfective aspectual interpretation of the embedded domain, which is not available with eventive infinitives.

In this respect, there is no difference between (36a), which is subject-initial, and (36b), which is verb-initial. It is clear that the value of tense in each construction is determined by a semantic calculus, which proceeds along the same lines in clauses with an auxiliary and in clauses without, in verb-initial clauses and in subject-initial ones. It is indeed sensitive to the semantic class the matrix predicate belongs to, but not to the syntactic form of the domain it applies to, in particular to word order.[28]

---

27 A principle having the required effect is proposed in Rouveret (1991: 357).

(i) Agreement morphology can only be affixed to an F-head.

(i) holds whether the agreement marker is conceived of as an affix directly adjoined to the functional head or as an independent Agr head (the implication of (i) for E.P inflected infinitives is discussed in Rouveret 1991, fn. 5). In current syntactic theorizing, the effect of the well-formedness condition (i) immediately follows from the relevant F-head being endowed with uninterpretable φ-features that need to be valued.

28 In this respect, I depart from Ambar's (1994) clever feature-based analysis, couched in the 1993 version of the checking theory, in which the strength/weakness of the features associated to functional heads (here, Tense and Agr) and also to lexical categories (here, eventive and stative inflected infinitives) plays a crucial role. One of the features verbs come from the lexicon endowed with is [tense], which checks or is checked by [tense] in T and which may be strong or weak, depending on the class of the verb: eventive verbs have a strong [tense], stative ones have a weak [tense]. The derivation crashes if a strong verbal [tense] meets with a weak [tense] in T. This situation presents itself when an eventive predicate is involved in an IIC, whose head T by definition bears a weak [tense]. On the contrary, no problem arises with stative predicates, since both the feature of the verb and the feature of T are weak. Ambar specifies that "weak tense [is] correlated with the generic/habitual reading, compatible with stative predicates, and strong tense with existential quantification of the event time, compatible with eventive predicates". When coupled with eventive predicates, adverbials such as *muitas vezes* or quantifying determiners inside DP objects "have scope on the tense of the verb, universally quantify it, neutralizing the existential quantification associated with the original tense". As Mensching (2000) observes,

In conclusion, the eventive/stative divide which, at first sight, could be thought of as directly determining the syntactic shape taken by each complement type, is exclusively relevant to the semantic calculus that derives the tense/aspectual interpretation of these domains.[29] The word order variation displayed by the complements to factive predicates (cf. 10a) and to epistemic/declarative ones (cf. 9a/12a) presumably results from distinct, plausibly syntactic principles.

---

the idea that the strength of its features depends on the syntactic and lexical environment in which an item occurs is difficult to maintain in a minimalist perspective. In my view, the eventive/stative divide is exclusively relevant at the interpretive level, when the semantic calculus determining tense construal is at work. Recall that this calculus is in no way specific to E.P IICs.
29 On the form this semantic calculus could take, I refer the reader to Pancheva & von Stechow (2004).

45 The factive/nonfactive asymmetry and the categorial identity of IICs

Besides the auxiliary/main verb asymmetry, which is spurious, and the stative/eventive divide, which confirms the generalized presence of a T head in the relevant domains,[30] a last asymmetry that is potentially relevant to the problem under consideration is the lexico-semantic distinction between factive and nonfactive predicates. Before a syntactic treatment can be proposed, it is necessary to reach a better understanding of this semantic distinction.

45.1 A fundamental semantic divide

A recurrent characteristic of complementation across languages is that the complements to factive and to epistemic/declarative predicates display distinct and even opposite syntactic properties. The complements to factive verbs (i) require the presence of an overt complementizer, when they are finite, (ii) can be preceded by *the fact* or by *it*, (iii) can be introduced by a *wh*-word, (iv) can take the form of a gerund, (v) define a strong or a weak island with respect to extraction (it behaves like a complex noun phrase in the first case, as a *wh*-island in the second). Epistemic and declarative predicates share none of these properties. These diverging characteristics are interesting in themselves and should be tackled in syntactic terms. But they undoubtedly reflect a fundamental semantic split among clause-embedding predicates. Early semantic studies argue that the relevant difference is that between events and propositions, see Melvold (1991).[31] Roussou, who characterized the semantic difference between nonfactive and factive predicates along these lines in her (1992) article, prefers to deal with it today in terms of situations: Factive complements (*pu*-complements in Modern Greek) are individual propositions with a fixed truth value; nonfactive complements (*oti*-complements) are closer to indefinites, referring to a set of situations/truth-values (cf. Roussou 2018).

The crucial question for us is to identify the syntactic forms these two argumental types, factive and nonfactive ones, project on in E.P.

---

30 Exhaustive control structures should be exempted from this claim.
31 On this distinction, see chapter XI. Non-factive verbs select a proposition-type argument as their complement; factive verbs select an event-type argument. Non-factive complements, which are propositional, also are non-presuppositional; factive complements, which are presuppositional, can be compared with definite noun phrases, which are specific.

45.2 Complementizers

If one grants the claim that the complements to factive predicates and to epistemic/declarative ones both qualify as CP domains, their distinct semantic properties can only be represented on the complementizers heading them.

Several attempts have been made in the past to reduce the complementizer items to the basic categorial feature matrix [αN, βV]. Kayne (1982) attributes the nominal distribution of complement clauses to the complementizer that introduces them, arguing that its role is to turn the clause into an argument. Viewed in this perspective, nonfinite clauses don't need a complementizer because they are essentially nominal. This idea resurfaces in Manzini (2010) who also argues that complementizers in Romance languages are nominal and that the postulation of a nominal structure of some sort for sentential complementation should not be restricted to factive complementation, as in Kiparsky & Kiparsky (1970), but should be extended to most types of finite complementation. As for Emonds (1985), he takes all complementizers to be prepositional, i.e [−N, −V].

An opposite stand consists in claiming that different complementizers are resorted to to introduce different complement types. Roussou (2018) adopts Kastner's (2015) proposal that the complements of presuppositional predicates are DP projections, while the complements of non-presuppositional predicates are (bare) NPs headed by a complementizer. She proposes the following characterization:

(41) a. Presuppositional complement = [$_D$ [$_N$ Complementizer [TP]]]
b. Non-presuppositional complement = [$_N$ Complementizer [TP]]

If (36) is right, the abstract complementizers involved in the two types share their nominal character, qualifying the corresponding complements as nominal domains of a kind (as Kayne and Manzini propose), but they nevertheless differ. Presuppositional complements project an additional DP layer, containing the sentential domain, which is absent from non-presuppositional complements, which are thus equivalent to bare NPs. Recall that the categorial features [C], [D], [N] defining the categories C, D, N have a grammatical meaning and are thus in a position to establish the necessary link between the semantic properties of the relevant domains and their syntax.

As the preceding sections amply illustrate, the factive/nonfactive divide is explicitly manifested in E.P inflected infinitive complementation. The complementizers involved are non overt, but should be conceived of as endowed with distinct feature matrices. The challenge is to identify the content of these matrices.

An essential aspect of the problem under discussion falls within the competence of Grimshaw's (1991) notion of extended projection and van Riemsdijk's

(1998) proposals concerning categorial features. Grimshaw claims that the crucial property that ties together lexical projections and their associated functional heads is categorial identity: D is nominal, T is verbal. Van Riemsdijk gives to this generalization the name of Categorial Identity Thesis. (42a) states that, within a projection, the values of the categorial features must be uniform. This thesis must be completed with an additional principle, (42b), dubbed by van Riemsdijk the Unlike Feature Condition, which deals with the relation between a projection and the external categorial environment.

(42) a. **Categorial Identity Thesis**
In the unmarked case, the lexical head and the corresponding functional head have the same categorial features.

b. **Unlike Feature Condition**
* { [+F] [+F]P }, where F is N or V.

Taken together, (42a) and (42b) imply that the (positively specified) features attract one another inside a projection, via a kind of "magnetism", but repel each other externally. A nominal projection functioning as the direct complement to a verbal head has nominal and verbal features that have a reverse value of the ones of the selecting head: The verbal head is [−N, +V], the nominal projection is [+N, −V]. But what is the status of C in the categorial sequence C − T − v- V? There are two possibilities to consider: Either C is part of the extended verbal projection, in which case it is itself an ordinary functional head, sharing the features of the lexical category it c-commands, namely [−N, +V] (this is the analysis Grimshaw argues for); or C is a category of its own, maybe a (semi-)lexical head defining its own projection and endowed with a matrix of features different from the featural make-up of its TP complement.

45.3 The categorial status of inflected infinitive clauses

The intuition that their complementizer systems hold the key to the explanation of the differential syntactic behaviors of factive and nonfactive complements in E.P IICs was at the core of some of the early analyses of these constructions, see Raposo (1987), and was partly endorsed by some later accounts, see Madeira (1994).[32]

---

[32] In an early analysis building on Raposo's (1975) work, I proposed that factive verbs select a domain headed by a [−N, +V] complementizer and that nonfactive verbs select a domain headed by a [+N, −V] complementizer (cf. Rouveret 1980). A mechanism was defined, ensuring that a

45.3 The categorial status of inflected infinitive clauses

It must be acknowledged that the periphery of nonfinite clauses has been little studied and that our knowledge of nonfinite CP systems is relatively poor as compared to that of finite ones.[33] The fact that nonfinite complementizers are often non overt greatly increases the difficulty.[34]

Nouniness is a property generally associated with the complements to factive predicates. Madeira (1994) proposes that the clausal complement to factive predicates is characterized by the presence of the iota operator in SpecCP licensed by a C-head bearing the feature [+ definite] and binding an event position (in the sense of Davidson 1980 and Higginbotham 1985) in the factive complement. This analysis is "intended to represent the fact that clausal complements of factive predicates denote an individual event" (op. cit. p. 191). Concerning the complements to declarative/epistemic predicates, a natural option would consist in claiming that a different feature in C licenses a different operator in SpecCP. This feature could of course be [tense] and the operator an existential operator. But, if this was the case, it would mean that some operators in SpecCP block extraction and that others don't. This is the reason why Madeira rejects the tense analysis and proposes that the relevant feature is [+ agr] (see fn. 13).

There are alternative ways to syntactically represent the distinct semantic properties of the two complement types, the presuppositional/definite character of factive complements and the propositional/indefinite status of nonfactive ones. In what follows, I will maintain the idea that the category C/Fin is present in the internal structure of the complementizer systems of the two clausal structures, with the same specification (Fin is [−N, +V]), but that the peripheries at the edge of factive and nonfactive complements are distinct: FinP directly combines with the matrix verb in nonfactive structures and is embedded in a DP projection in factive structures. This account duplicates Kiparsky & Kiparsky's (1970) classical analysis of factivity and is undistinguishable from characterization (36)

---

verbal complementizer can only govern a [+N] expression (standing in the embedded subject position), while a nominal complementizer can only govern a [+V] expression. The gist of this analysis is that the observed word-order differences between the two complement types should be traced back to the opposite subcategorization requirements of the complementizers introducing the complements of factive predicates and that of nonfactive ones. This partial account encounters a major difficulty however. The complement of factive predicates is generally thought of as more nominal than the complement of nonfactive ones: *I regret John's death/*I believe John's death*; *I regret him having done that/*I believe him having done that*), a fact that the analysis under discussion didn't capture at all.

33 Nonfinite is here used as a generic label for morphologically untensed domains.
34 Nonfinite complementizers can also be overt, as shown by the alternation between *de* and *à* in French. Tellier (2018) successfully shows that *de* is the default nonfinite complementizer, whereas *à* tends to express modality.

(except that D is provisionally taken to be a full-fledged category). How can this analytic choice be justified?

Concerning factive complements, the question has always been to determine whether the [+ definite] feature is a specification added to the matrix of the C/Fin category or whether it is associated with an independent head, say D, that would be projected in the corresponding complement structures, as suggested by Roussou (2018) for Modern Greek. The constructions in which the clausal complement is preceded by the definite determiner *o* suggest that a D head is indeed present.[35] Here are some relevant examples.

(43) a. *Lamento   o eles   terem   partido a jarra.*
         regret.1SG o 3PL.NOM have.INF.3PL broken the vase
         'I regret it that they have broken the vase.'
    b. *Lamento   o terem   eles   partido a jarra.*
         regret.1SG o have.INF.3PL 3PL.NOM broken the vase

(44) a. * *Lamento   o as meninas terem   partido a   jarra*
            regret.1SG o the little girls have.INF.3PL broken the vase

    b. * *Lamento   o coisas como essas acontecerem   hoje.*
            regret.1SG o things like these happen.INF.3PL today

    c. *Lamento   o terem   as meninas   partido a jarra.*
         regret.1SG o have.INF.3PL the little girls broken the vase
         'I regret that the little girls have broken the vase.'

(45) *O ele   ganhar   as eleições significa uma mudança radical.*
      o 3.SG.NOM win.INF.3SG the elections means   a   change. radical
      'Their winning the elections means a radical change.'

For a reason that remains obscure, while subject personal pronouns freely intervene between *o* and the inflected infinitive (cf. 43a, 45) and can also follow it (cf. 43b), this is not possible when full noun phrases are involved: (44a) and (44b) are systematically rejected by native speakers, who generally resort to the auxiliary-first order in this case (cf. 44c). The ungrammaticality of (44a) could suggest that the sequences of two definite determiners tend to be avoided, but (44b) with an indefinite subject is also ungrammatical, although it doesn't contain such a

---

35 See Madeira's (1994) discussion. See also Brito (2013) for an in-depth study of the inflected infinitive structures preceded by *o*.

45.3 The categorial status of inflected infinitive clauses — 299

sequence. (45) indicates that subject clauses follow the same pattern as the complements to factive predicates.

But a coherent analysis of *o* + IIC sequences can only be attained if an additional piece of data is taken into account, namely the fact that, when a finite clause is the complement of a factive predicate, *que* cannot coexist with *o*, as shown by (46).

(46) * Lamento   o que eles   tenham   partido a   jarra.
      regret.1SG   o that 3PL.NOM have.SUBJ.3PL Broken the   vase

The analysis of the *o*+IIC sequences in (43) and (45) will be successful only if sequences like (46) are properly excluded. If the periphery is reduced to a single C head and its projection, as in pre-cartographic accounts, an obvious possibility is that there is a D head above CP and that *o* occupies this position. An alternative option, also considered by Madeira (1994), is to assume that *o* directly spells out a [+ def] feature on C. In this view, [+ def] C is undistinguishable from [+ def] D. If the first hypothesis is correct, the auxiliary *terem* in (49b) occupies the C position. If the second one is adopted, either the auxiliary is hosted by T (and the subject keeps its original position inside vP) or, much more plausibly, it raises to a head position X projected between TP and C, an option which is compatible with the ungrammaticality of (46). None of these options is fully satisfactory. If one reasons in the terms of a finely structured left periphery, the ungrammaticality of (46) could support a different conclusion. If the complementizer *que* is inserted into Force,[36] (46) could simply show that a ForceP projection cannot function as a complement to the definite article. The situation is different in nonfinite domains, since there is no evidence that Force is ever projected and since *o*, being nominal, cannot reside in Fin, which is an inherently verbal head. The well-formedness of (43b), (44c) would indicate that [– finite] FinP projections can function as complements to D. The structure involved, before the raising of the verbal form, the movement of the subject and the merger of *o*, would roughly be as follows:

(47) V [$_{DP}$ [$_D$ [+ def]] [$_{FinP}$ Fin [$_{TP}$ T [$_\alpha$ DP$_s$ [$_{vP}$ v [V DP$_o$ ...]]]]]]

(47) is also the structure associated with the complements to factive predicates in their "bare" form exemplified in (43a) and (43b), the only difference being that D

---

[36] This seems to be the general situation in Romance, where the complementizer precedes topicalized and focalized expressions in embedded finite clauses, cf. Rizzi (1997).

remains silent. In other words, the factive complements that are not introduced by *o* are headed by a phonologically null determiner.

(48) a. *Lamento os deputados aprovarem a proposta.* (cf. 37a)
    b. *Lamento terem eles partido a jarra.* (cf. 43b)

If *o* can optionally be used in front of the IICs complements to factive/emotive predicates, it is strictly excluded with the complements to epistemic/declarative predicates and the subjects of *true/false* constructions. I will assume that the syntactic form that functions as a vehicle for the relevant propositional object is a verbal projection, identified as such by its Fin head. The representation of a nonfactive complement in the standard case (with an auxiliary present, cf. 49), before any movement takes place, is as in (50).[37] (50) takes the Fin head to be included in the extended projection of the embedded V.

(49) *Penso terem os estudantes comprado esse livro.*

(50) V [$_{FinP}$ Fin [$_{TP}$ [$_T$ [tense]] [$_{vP}$ [$_v$ Aux] [$_α$ DP$_s$ [$_{vP}$ v [V$_{part}$ DP$_o$ . . .]]]]]]

What remains to be done is to provide an explanation for why (50) can only give rise to an auxiliary-first (or a verb-first) order, not to a subject-initial order, and why (47) allows the derivation of both auxiliary-first and subject-first orders. This is done in section 46.

Before concluding this section, more should be said about propositional nominalization, see (43)–(45). In the case under consideration, nominalization affects syntactic entities which, although they semantically denote states-of-affairs, not attitudinal objects (cf. sct. 65), are undistinguishable from full-fledged propositions. Moulton (2021 and section 65) argues that the high nominalization process that is involved here should be distinguished from low nominalization, the one that is closer to the root. It was established that the latter resorts to a category-defining/switching head n, the former to a determiner-like element associated with a D head.[38] This in itself is an interesting result, which shows that nominalization works differently at different levels of structure.

---

[37] In (50), the auxiliary is taken to originate as a v head selecting a vP projection including the subject and the verbal participle. Other options exist. The choice between them doesn't affect the argument presented here.

[38] This conclusion will be modified in section 46.1.

46 Labeling IICs

The recent development of labeling theory opens a new perspective on the perennial question of the distribution of clausal expressions and overt subjects. The claim made here is that an alternative account of the distribution of subject DPs in IICs can be proposed, which capitalizes on the fact that they participate in the labeling of the clause, not on the necessity for them to be case licensed. The clause of the Labeling Algorithm that is relevant to the discussion is reproduced in (51) (cf. ch. II, sct. 5 for discussion).

(51) **Labeling Algorithm**
If X and Y are identical in one respect and, in particular, share some feature, this feature is selected as the label of SO; in this case, the label is the pair of agreeing elements (Chomsky 2015).

A seldom asked question is how the labeling of infinitival clauses and other embedded verbal structures that display no signs of finiteness is achieved and what is the resulting label.[39] In standard infinitives, which display no inflectional morphology, the strategy that is used in the finite clauses of null subject Romance languages cannot be resorted to. But IICs satisfy all the conditions that make labeling via φ-feature sharing possible. They are identifiable as defective domains – inflected infinitive forms bear no temporal morphology -, but they display a person and number inflection that allows them first to enter into an Agree relation with the vP-internal subject and case license it, second to share φ-features with it, once the subject has raised and the infinitive has left the vP.

46.1 Labeling factive complements

Let us reconsider (47), repeated here as (52). How can this structure give rise to a well-formed (o) DP_{subj} V/Aux_{iinf} ... order?

(52) V [$_{DP}$ [$_D$ [+ def]] [$_{FinP}$ Fin [$_{TP}$ T [$_α$ DP_s [$_{vP}$ v [V DP_o ...]]]]]]
    (the initial V represents the matrix predicate)

---

[39] The same question has been raised about gerund clauses in chapter IV.

The embedded V raises to v, then to T, then (in a subset of structures) to Fin. We know that the subject, although it is case licensed in situ via agreement with the raised verb, doesn't remain in its original position and moves higher. A plausible explanation for the necessity to raise (and for the EPP effect observed in examples 38a, 40 and 33a) is that D cannot govern an (extended) verbal projection, its complement can only be nominal. But why is the internal merger of the DP subject with FinP (or with TP, if the inflected infinitive stops in T) necessary and sufficient for the derivation to converge? Recall that the label of the structure resulting from subject raising is the union of the features shared by the raised subject and the inflected verbal category, namely <φ, φ>, provided that the two φ's have non-distinct values. The labeled structure of a factive IIC, resulting from DP-raising and V-movement, is something like (53).

(53)   V [$_{DP}$ D [$_{<φ, φ>}$ [DP$_s$] [$_{FinP}$ [$_{Fin}$ V-v-T] [[~~DP$_s$~~] [$_{TP}$ ~~V-v-T~~ [~~DP$_s$~~ ~~v~~ [$_{VP}$ ~~V~~ DP$_o$]]]]]]]
       [+ def]

All the conditions making the resort to (46) possible are satisfied: The values of the φ-features of DP and V-v-T match, since by definition inflected infinitives agree; the raised subject has been previously case licensed; a given projection can only be assigned a single label and (51) turns out to be the only device available to label structures like (53).

I maintain the assumption that labeling via feature sharing necessarily interferes with the satisfaction of subcategorization requirements and the definition of extended projections (see the discussion in section 5). Derivation (53) converges because, in the resulting representation, a [+ def] D governs a domain labeled <φ, φ>, hence a projection endowed with nominal characteristics. The label <φ, φ> is the one required by the head D, if D is assumed to belong to the same extended projection as its complement. The semantic properties of presuppositional complements, which are event-tokens, are appropriately represented by the nominal characteristics associated with factive complements and their nominal periphery.

But auxiliary raising is not blocked in factive complements, cf. (54a). Verb raising isn't either, cf. (54b). Verb-initial and auxiliary-initial orders are also legitimate in the presence of *o*, as shown by examples (55).

(54) a. *Lamento   terem   os deputados   aprovado a proposta.*
          regret.1SG   have.INF.3PL   the deputies   approved the proposal
          'I regret that the deputies have approved the proposal.'

b. *Lamento   comprarem   os deputados o   jornal*
regret.1SG buy.INF.3PL the deputies the newspaper
todas   as sextas-feiras.
all   the Fridays
'I regret that the deputies buy the newspaper every Friday.'

(55) a. *O gritarem   as pessoas   surpreendeu-nos.*⁴⁰
o shout.INF.3PL the people   surprise.PRT.3SG-1PL.ACC
'The fact that people shouted surprised us.'

b. *O ter   ela   escrito   esses poemas*
o have.INF.3SG 3F.SG.NOM   written   these poems   NEG
não   me   espantou.
1SG. ACC   surprise.3SG
'The fact that she wrote these poems didn't surprise me.'

Can these distributions be reconciled with the labeling approach and the claim that D necessarily selects a nominal expression? If one assumes that the inflected verbal form is hosted by the inherently verbal head Fin, the lack of DP raising in the relevant constructions should identify FinP as a verbal projection, which, at first sight, doesn't fulfill D's subcategorization requirement. Yet, examples (54) and (55) are perfectly grammatical. Let us assume that in auxiliary-initial and verb-initial configurations dependent on a factive predicate, *o* in D or its silent counterpart functions as a category-switching head with respect to the phrase it minimally c-commands, more precisely as a nominalizer, undistinguishable from n, turning an essentially verbal constituent into a nominal "event-object". If one reasons in the terms of van Riemsdijk's magnetism approach, category-switching heads by definition escape the Categorial Identity Thesis (42a) and fall under the Unlike Feature Constraint (42b). In this case, the overt/covert D head in auxiliary/verb-initial structures should be conceived of as an autonomous category that is not included in the extended projection of V. This means that, in factive IICs, there are two ways in which the selectional requirement of the matrix verb can be satisfied: Either the subject raises and the clausal projection shares the nominal feature endowment of D; or the inflected form precedes the subject and the determiner functions as a nominalizer. In the first case, *o* or its silent counterpart is a clausal determiner; in the second, it is a category-switching head. *o* has thus a dual status. If this account is on the right track, it shows that determiners in propositional nominalization can function as nominalizing (category-switching) heads.

---

40 Examples (55) are discussed by Brito (2013).

A difficulty that cannot be ignored at this point is that all auxiliary/verb-initial examples cannot be assigned a uniform analysis. Some of them are Focus *in situ* constructions. In the finite version of Focus constructions in null subject Romance languages, the inflected verb precedes the focused postverbal subject which plausibly resides in a vP-internal position. A possibility is to say that an Internal Merge operation taking place at LF and moving the focused constituent to the left periphery of the sentence is involved in their derivation and suffices to provide the clause with the appropriate label. In examples (56a) and (56b), only the subject is in focus.[41]

(56) a. *Comeu a sopa o Paulo.*
ate the soup the Paulo

b. *Partiu o PAULO a janela.*
broke the Paulo the window

The same operation could be involved in the derivation and labeling of (57a) and (57b) and (43a), (43b) in one of their interpretations.

(57) a. *Lamento terem eles perdido os documentos.*
regret.1SG have.INF.3PL 3PL.NOM lost the documents
'I regret that they lost the documents.'

b. *Lamento terem perdido eles os documentos.*
regret.1SG have.INF.3PL lost 3PL.NOM the documents

Interestingly, the focused reading of the pronominal subject is the preferred one in (57a) and the only available one in (57b). If generalization (29) about the distribution of Aux+participle sequences is correct, the sentence imposing the Focus interpretation of the subject, namely (57b), is the one where both the auxiliary and the participle precede the subject, that is, the one where the subject remains in the vP. I won't pursue the discussion of this point.[42]

---

[41] Examples (56) are provided by Costa (2000), who argues against the Focus movement approach, because it destroys prosody and c-command relations which are instrumental for the determination of focus relations. I will ignore this objection for the moment.

[42] Nothing was said in this section about the labeling properties of control structures. The proposal that was made for the labeling of PRO-*ing* gerund clauses (cf. sct. 20) can be transposed to this case. I summarize it briefly here. Suppose that, contrary to what Landau's classification claims and as Sheehan's account suggests (cf. sct. 47), the syntactically relevant divide is between the exhaustive control constructions and all the other ones, including partial control ones.

46.2 Labeling epistemic/declarative complements

The structure associated with the complements to epistemic/declarative predicates given in (50) is repeated here as (58) (all the lexical heads and phrases are represented in their first Merge position).

(58) V [$_{FinP}$ [$_{Fin}$ [+ tense]] [$_{TP}$ T [$_{vP}$ [$_v$ Aux] [$_\alpha$ DP$_s$ v$_{part}$ [$_{vP}$ [V DP$_o$ ...]]]]]

We know that in this case, only the configurations in which the subject follows the inflected infinitive are well-formed. This is an indication that <φ, φ> is not an appropriate label for these complement clauses. Whether inflected verbal forms don't raise higher than T or reach the category Fin, it can safely be concluded that the label of the resulting structure is [+ tense] or [+ V]. The two options are schematized in (59) and (60), (60) being by far the more plausible of the two.[43]

(59) V [$_{FinP}$ [$_{Fin}$ [+ tense/+V]] [$_{TP}$ [$_T$ Aux] [$_{vP}$ [$_v$ A̶u̶x̶] [$_\alpha$ DPs [$_{vP}$ v$_{part}$ [V DP$_o$ ...]]]]]]

(60) V [$_{FinP}$ [$_{Fin}$ Aux] [$_\beta$ DP$_s$ [$_{TP}$ [$_T$ A̶u̶x̶] [$_{vP}$ [$_v$ A̶u̶x̶] [$_\alpha$ D̶P̶$_s$ [$_{vP}$ v$_{part}$ [V DP$_o$ ...]]]]]]]
 [+ tense]
 [+ V]

These representations raise no labeling difficulty. The first clause of the Labeling Algorithm (46 is the second) tells us that, in X-YP configurations, where X is a head and YP a projection, it is the head X accessible via minimal search that fixes the categorial label of the whole projection. In (60), the label of the the raised verbal form matches that of the host category, namely [tense]/[V]. We know, however, that the Tense of an IIC is not strong enough to label its own projection.

Suppose the former include a featureless PRO subject and an uninterpretable T with no [phi] features. This PRO can only be assigned an interpretation via an interphasal Agree relation with a higher functional head and via binding by an external antecedent. The embedded clause is not convergent and gets a label when the interphasal Agree relation has been established. On the contrary, partial control complements are not control structures in the strict sense. The [phi] features of T, which are uninterpretable, are valued via the incorporation into T of the feature matrix on the inflected infinitive. The Case-marked pro-like subject raises from SpecvP to the T- or Fin-level, exactly as overt DPs do, which ensures the early labeling of the clause.

43 This conclusion makes abstraction of the fact that the epistemic/declarative structures containing a raised auxiliary or an auxiliary+participle complex and a pronominal subject allow the Focus interpretation of the latter. When it is the case, the focussed subject probably resides in SpecvP, as assumed in (59).

The morphological deficiency and syntactic defectiveness of T could explain why the overt raising of the verbal form to Fin has to be resorted to in order to guarantee the verbal status of the auxiliary/verb-first complement structures and to syntactically represent the semantic properties of propositional/non-presuppositional tense-defective complements. Since Fin is verbal, the merger of the agreeing verbal form with it in (60) results in a well-formed representation. Raising the subject above the moved agreeing verbal form would wrongly produce a configuration labeled <φ, φ>.[44]

In conclusion, the overt raising of the inflected verbal form to a peripheral [tense]/[V] head in (60), above the realization site of the subject, is imposed by the necessity to guarantee the verbal status of the complement. The labeling approach has a considerable advantage over EPP-based accounts, since it can take care of derived verb-initial *and* of subject-initial structures, which both require to be labeled.

---

[44] No specific syntactic proviso has to be made to account for the grammaticality of embedded clauses with a main verb preceding the subject, when a habitual/generic reading is involved. The feature endowment of T and Fin are the same as in auxiliary structure; verbal forms are allowed to raise to a higher head, just as auxiliary forms are.

47 Inflected/uninflected infinitive clauses with a null subject

Wurmbrand's categorization is also relevant to the clausal domains selected by predicates of other lexical classes, in particular controlled IICs. Examples (61) show that future *irrealis* infinitives allow the episodic interpretation of their verbal predicates: The uninflected infinitive form of the VP is used to report a single event potentially taking place in the future, as adverbial distributions confirm.

(61) a. *Ontem,   o   João decidiu partir   amanhã.*
      yesterday the João decided leave.INF tomorrow
      'João decided yesterday to leave tomorrow.'

   b. *Ele   espera   estar   a trabalhar amanhã   às 5.*
      3SG.NOM expects   be.INF   *a* work.INF tomorrow at.the 5
      'He expects to be working tomorrow at 5.'

   c. *Os rapazes   esperam   receber   a carta*
      the children expect.3PL receive.INF the letter
      da   Maria amanhã / hoje.
      from.the   Maria tomorrow/today
      'The children expect to receive Maria's letter tomorrow/today.'

The use of the inflected form *receberem* in (56c) would cause ungrammaticality.[45] This suggests that future *irrealis* structures functioning as complements to predicates like *esperar* 'to hope', *projectar* 'to project', *decidir* 'to decide' should be analyzed as ModP projections of a modal head, as Wurmbrand proposes, not as FinP/CP projections (but I assume they include an inactive T head).

Verbs like *tentar* 'to try', *começar* 'to begin', which belong to the class of "restructuring verbs" and impose their reference time as the reference time of the embedded infinitive, cannot govern an IIC either. They don't allow any independent time modification of the embedded infinitive, cf. (62a), suggesting that they select a tenseless complement, as their English counterparts do. The subject

---

45 Some declarative verbs display the same behavior when used as control predicates.

(i) *Ontem,   o João   anunciou /afirmou / declarou   partir   amanhã.*
     yesterday the João announced / asserted / declared leave.INF Tomorrow

control verb *preferir* 'to prefer' in (5b), repeated here as (57b), also belongs to this class.

(62) a. * *Ontem,   o   Leo tentou   partir   amanhã.*
       yesterday the Leo tried   leave.INF tomorrow

   b. * *Preferirias   chegares   a tempo.*
       preferred.COND.2SG arrive.INF.2SG on time
       'You would prefer to arrive on time.'

   c. * *Preferiríamos   recebermos   um salario maior.*
       prefer.COND.1PL receive.INF.1PL a   salary higher
       'We would prefer to receive a higher salary.'

Wurmbrand (2001, 2014), Cinque (2008) argue that the exhaustive control interpretation results from restructuring and that a PRO is present only in the structures displaying partial control. They analyze the infinitive complements of *try* and *attempt* in English as vP or AspP projections, that is as CP-less, TP-less domains. If it is indeed what these complements are, examples (62) indicate that IICs cannot be too small – they must at least qualify as TP projections. Alternatively, the relevant predicates can be assumed to select a clausal uninflected complement whose subject is necessarily PRO. In this analysis, all control structures are clausal, hence contain a subject.[46] If the latter analysis is correct, which is the one proposed by Landau (2004) and the one adopted in this study, inflected infinitives are banned from exhaustive control clauses, because these clauses do not include an interpretable/dependent tense. It is now necessary to determine the nature of the null element in both structures. Landau claims that PRO is involved in all cases. The simple analysis that is adopted here consists in the claim that a PRO is present in exhaustive control local structures, but not in the other control constructions, which contain a pro-like subject. The control interpretation would be forced by the lexical environment. It is not implausible a priori to analyze the null subject in controlled IICs as a pro-like element rather than as PRO. This account, as already observed, clearly goes against Landau's typology of control structures, in which exhaustive and partial control are grouped together under the heading OC and both involve a PRO subject. More importantly, it should be contemplated only in the languages and constructions where the interpretation of the unrealized subject is mediated by an inflectional matrix in

---

[46] Landau (2013) observes that the restructuring idea is not compatible with the observation that OC is available in languages that completely ignore restructuring.

the embedded clause. This condition is fulfilled in European Portuguese and also by gerunds in English, if *-ing*, although invariable, is taken to be an agreement marker of some type. But it is not available in the English bare infinitive constructions instantiating the partial control interpretation. It is not either in the Welsh VN-structures instantiating this reading (illustrated by 8e, ch. VI), where no inflection of any sort occurs on the C/Fin head. We see that, crosslinguistically and sometimes within the same language, there are two clausal types in which the partial control interpretation may obtain, one in which the null element coexists with an overt agreement matrix, the other where it doesn't.

The following contrast discovered by Alexandra Fiéis and Ana Madeira (personal communication) is fully compatible with this account. They note that inflected infinitives are fine in sentences in which the reference of the infinitival subject is disjoint from that of the matrix one or properly includes the reference of the controller, awkward when an exhaustive control interpretation is intended. Compare (63) to (40b).

(63) ?* *Eles   odiavam   saberem   os resultados   das   eleições.*
      3.PL.NOM   hate.IMPF.3.PL   know.INF.3.PL   the results   of.the elections

It is time to ask whether the control patterns considered so far support the general perspective defined by Landau's Finiteness Rule or do not. Portuguese infinitive clauses with an overt subject qualify as NC structures: They are semantically tensed domains with verbal forms displaying morphological person/number marking; the complement clause is [+T, +Agr] (using Landau's notation) and nominative is available for the case marking of the subject. But some of the predicates under consideration can also take OC complements with a bare infinitive, which indicates that they also select [–T, – Agr] structures. As observed by Landau (2013), a specificity of European Portuguese is that the value of [Agr] in each structure is directly linked to that of [tense], an insignt that can be straightforwardly captured in the probe-goal-Agree approach. The infinitival domain is [+ tense] in NC environments, in which inflection is required, [– tense] in exhaustive control environments, in which inflection is banned. It must be concluded that the relevant predicates freely select a tensed complement or a tenseless one (or a complement with dependent tense and one with anaphoric tense).

Unfortunately, the situation appears to be much more complicated, when all the possible cases of control in European Portuguese are taken into consideration. In recent work, Sheehan (2014, 2018) has collected and analyzed the relevant data, respectively illustrating exhaustive control, partial control, non-obligatory control and long-distance control, which, it appears, obey different conditions. She provides examples (64)–(68) and classifies them as follows.[47]

exhaustive non-local subject control
(64) Prometemos   à   Maria comprarmos-lhe   um   presente.
     promise.PRT.1PL to the Maria buy.INF.1PL-3SG.DAT a   present
     'We promised Maria to buy her a present.'

partial local subject control
(65) O Pedro   preferiria   reunirem-se   mais tarde.
     the Pedro prefer.COND 3SG   meet.INF.3PL-se   more late
     'Pedro would prefer to meet later on.'

partial non-local subject control
(66) O Pedro acha   que eu   preferia
     the Pedro believe.3SG that 1SG.NOM preferred.IMPF.1SG
     reunirem-se   mais cedo.
     meet.INF.3PL-se more early.
     'Pedro believes that I preferred that they meet earlier.'

exhaustive object control
(67) Eu   obriguei   / persuadi   os meninos
     1SG.NOM force.PRT.1SG   / persuaded.PRT.1SG   the kids
     a lerem   esse livro.
     a read.INF.3PL this book
     'I forced the kids to read that book.'

partial object control
(68) Os professors persuadiram   o diretor   a reunirem-se
     the teachers persuade.PRT.3PL   the director a meet.INF.3PL-se
     mais tarde.
     more late
     'The teachers persuaded the director to meet later on.'

---

[47] Sheehan (2018) indicates that there is some variation as to the optionality of the inflected infinitive in the relevant structures. It is very rare in exhaustive non-local subject control structures (cf. 64), just an option in partial local subject control structures (cf. 65), quite usual in partial non-local subject control ones (cf. 66) and widespread in exhaustive (cf. 67) and partial (cf. 68) object control cases.

These data raise several difficulties against Landau's (2004) Agree-based approach to control. In Sheehan's view, they confirm Landau's (2000, 2004) conclusion that there are "two flavors of OC", which take different derivational paths. But she claims that distinct analyses are required to account for exhaustive local control on the one hand, partial control and the other control structures on the other. She observes that, in partial control structures such as (65), PRO differs from its controller both in person and number features, provided that the controller is "a potential subset of the reference of pro." This conclusion, which goes against Landau's contention that Agree is involved in *all* (obligatory) control relations, converges with some of the proposals advanced in sections 7.6 and 7.7 and is compatible with the PRO/pro distinction.[48]

A second difficulty, in my view, stems from the fact that the absence of inflectional agreement marking on the infinitive verbal head doesn't suffice to identify the relevant domain as an exhaustive control structure. Agreement morphology is indeed strictly banned from exhaustive local control structures; but control in the other constructions listed by Sheehan, partial control included, is to varying degrees compatible with both the presence and the absence of infinitival inflection. The partial control interpretation can thus be associated with two different syntactic structures. Both are semantically tensed, but one contains an inflected infinitive, that is a T head with overt φ-features, the other includes a standard infinitive with tense, but no φ's. In the first case, the fact that the relevant domain is both semantically tensed and inflected makes it difficult to explain why it doesn't fall into the NC category, that is, why control is possible at all (if one reasons in Landau's terms). To account for the second case, one can resort to the analyses that have been proposed for the English infinitive clauses displaying the partial control interpretation (cf. sct. 7.3 and 7.6). The two structures only differ as to the presence and the spell-out of φ-features on T. It is not clear whether they should be considered as related or unrelated: Are we dealing with two distinct and independent configurations that differ by the presence/absence of φ-features or with one and the same configuration in which the φ-features on T are optionally spelled out? Landau's approach doesn't provide an answer to this question.

Sheehan's major discovery is that exhaustive non-local subject control structures exist (cf. 64), which, contrary to exhaustive local subject control structures, allow the presence of an infinitival inflection. These constructions are relatively

---

[48] Recall that, in Landau's (2004, 2013) view, PRO directly agrees with the matrix probe in the exhaustive control case, only indirectly, via C, in the partial control one. A T head is projected in the clausal structures underlying exhaustive and partial control, but T moves to C in the second case, not in the first one, an analysis that has been reformulated within the probe-goal-Agree approach in section 7.6.

rare, but they give precious indications on the nature of the OC phenomenon. First, just as partial control structures, exhaustive control ones seem to admit two different sources. The exhaustive control interpretation *per se* is not incompatible with overt infinitival inflection ; only one of the strategies available to derive this interpretation is (the controlled PRO strategy resorted to derive the exhaustive local control reading). This situation doesn't fit in naturally with Landau's general approach. The obligatory control structures which display overt inflectional morphology also presumably have a dependent tense. If this is so, they should count as fully inflected domains and preclude OC.

The question raised by the existence of examples like (64) is why the incompatibility of overt inflection with the exhaustive control interpretation only manifests itself when the relation between the controlled clause and the antecedent is strictly local. The answer to this question is relatively straightforward. The presence of an inflected infinitive form in the T position of a locally controlled IIC would prevent the PRO in its specifier to access its matrix antecedent and the matrix T.[49] This option is itself available only when the embedded tense is anaphoric and the pronominal subject deprived of φ-features. Anaphoric tense and featureless PRO can only be found in clauses that are minimally c-commanded by the lexical predicate. Dependent tense and pro-like subjects are available elsewhere.[50]

---

[49] In this respect, the infinitival inflection in European Portuguese differs from the gerund *-ing* affix in English. The latter can occur in exhaustive local control structures, because it doesn't make explicit the values of the person and number features it bears. The Portuguese inflection bears these values on its sleeve.

[50] To capture the relevant differences, Sheehan proposes an alternative case-based analysis, founded on the idea that controlled pronominals "bear case, generally yielding an ambiguous exhaustive/partial control reading" and claims that OC can be derived via movement or via Agree, depending on whether the complement of the control predicate is non-phasal or phasal. I can't go into the details of her analysis here.

48 Conclusion

I hope to have carried out the program that had been set up at the beginning of this chapter and shown that the properties of E.P IICs just result from the combination of several interacting factors, none of them specific to IICs or to E.P. The only information that must be accessible to the child in the acquisition process is that E.P has at its disposal nonfinite verbal forms in which a person-number agreement affix is directly attached to an infinitival root. From a morpho-syntactic point of view, the clauses headed by inflected infinitives are indeed tense-deficient, but not person/number-defective. The following proposals have been introduced and justified:

(i) E.P IICs, in all their uses, should be analyzed as FinP/CP projections, which, when the matrix predicate is factive, are embedded in a DP projection.

(ii) A priori, three factors seem to play a role in the word-order differences observed between the various IICs: the presence/absence of an auxiliary in the embedded clause, the eventive/stative lexical status of the embedded predicate, the membership of the matrix predicate in the assertive/factive class. It was argued that neither the strategy used to case license the embedded subject, nor the eventive or stative nature of the embedded predicate can be held responsible for the word-order differences between factive and nonfactive complements. The case licensing of the subject, which capitalizes on the person-number features of the inflected infinitive form, occurs early in the derivation, when T is first merged, before the derivation reaches the left periphery. The constrasting behavior of eventive and stative embedded predicates is directly linked to the construal of the infinitive tense, semantically active in the two complement types. The semantic mechanisms involved are not sensitive to word order and are not expected to affect it.

(iii) Rather, the word-order asymmetries displayed by the complements to factive and nonfactive predicates should be traced back to the necessity of assigning them a label satisfying the subcategorization requirement of the matrix predicate or of the D head. Merging the subject with the FinP projection has the effect of creating a syntactic object labeled $<\varphi, \varphi>$, a label that fits the requirement of the D head of factive complements. Raising the inflected auxiliary or main verb to Fin has the effect of producing a [+ V] structure that satisfies the requirement of epistemic/declarative predicates.

(iv) All in all, some IICs are excluded because they are not interpretable (i.e. cannot be assigned a tense construal compatible with the eventive status of their predicate); others are excluded because they cannot be appropriately labeled; still others because they can neither be temporally interpreted, nor appropriately labeled.

49 Appendix: Verb classes in European Portuguese

In order to determine where exactly the dividing line between the verbs that impose auxiliary-raising in their inflected infinitive complement and those that don't should be drawn, it is necessary to resort to a more fine-grained semantic classification of verbal predicates than the one based on the factive/epistemic-declarative distinction.[51] The results basically confirm the observations made in the text, except for two predicate classes that stand in between the two major sets in the lexical hierarchy.

Auxiliary-raising is obligatory in the IICs complements to the following classes:

(i) verbs of propositional attitude: *pensar* 'think', *afirmar* 'claim'

(1) Os pais   pensam/afirmam terem   os filhos   obtido
     the parents think/claim   have.INF.3PL the children got
     aprovação no   exame.
     approval   in.the exam
     'The parents think/claim that their children passed the exam.'
     *Os pais pensam/afirmam os filhos terem obtido aprovação no exame.

(ii) factive epistemic verbs : *saber* 'know', *perceber* 'perceive'

(2) Os pais   sabem/perceberam   terem   os filhos   obtido
     the parents know/realized   have.INF.3PL the children got
     aprovação no   exame.
     approval   in.the exam
     'The parents know/realized that their children passed the exam.'
     *Os pais sabem/perceberam os filhos terem obtido aprovação no exame.

---

51 I here reproduce Ana Madeira's judgments on the examples that were submitted to her.

(iii) assertive verbs : *concordar* 'agree', *negar* 'deny'

(3) Os participantes concordam terem   sido cometidos erros
    the participants agree   have.INF.3PL been committed mistakes
    dos   dois lados.
    from.the two sides
    'The participants agree that mistakes have been committed on both sides.'
    ? Os participantes concordam erros serem cometidos dos dois lados.

(4) Os deputados   negaram ter   o Partido dos   Verdes
    the deputies   denied have.INF.3SG the Party   of.the Green
    perdido as eleições.
    lost   the elections
    'The deputies denied that the Party of the Green had lost the elections.'
    ? Os deputados negaram o Partido dos Verdes ter perdido as eleições

(iv) *irrealis* predicates : *imaginar* 'imagine'

(5) Todos os pais   imaginavam poderem   os filhos
    all   the parents imagined   be-able.INF.3PL the children
    atingir o   nível mais alto.
    reach   the level more high
    'All the parents imagined that their children could reach the higher level.'
    ? Todos os pais imaginavam os filhos poderem atingir o nível mais alto.

(6) Não podiam   imaginar estar   o   curso da
    NEG could   imagine be. INF.3SG the course of.the
    história a mudar.
    history to change.INF.SG
    'They couldn't imagine that the course of history was changing.'
    ? Não podiam imaginar o curso da história estar a mudar.

(v) predicates that select a fact as an argument : *lembrar* 'remember'.

(7) Eu lembro   ter   a actual Direção   sido eleita por maioria.
    I remember have.INF.3SG the present direction been elected to majority
    'I remember that the present direction has been elected to the majority.'
    ? Eu lembro a atual Direção ter sido eleita por maioria

Auxiliary-raising is optional with the following verbal and adjectival classes

(vi) emotive factive predicates : *surpreender* 'surprise'.

(8) Surpreendeu -me o João ter trazido o vinho.
surprised me the João have.INF.3SG brought the wine
'It surprised me that João has brought the wine.'
Surpreendeu-me ter o João trazido o vinho

(vii) *é verdade* 'is the truth', *é possível* 'is possible'

(9) É verdade/ possivel o João ter estado doente.
is truth possible the João have.INF.3SG been ill
'It is true/possible that João has been ill.'
É verdade/possivel ter o João estado doente

It can be observed that some predicates that presuppose the truth of their complement and are factive to some extent nevertheless require raising in the embedded domain, cf. (7). On the other hand, some *irrealis* predicates seem to favor the raising option, but also allow the non-raising one, as factive predicates do, compare (10) with (5)–(6); others freely allow both, cf. (11) . . . .

(10) Em nenhum momento eu imaginei isso poder ocorrer
at no moment I imagined this be.able.INF.3SG occur.INF.3SG
'At no moment did I imagine this could occur.'
? Em nenhum momento eu imaginei poser isso ocorrer.

(11) Eu espero todos os deputados terem sido eleitos
I hope all the deputies have.INF.3PL been elected
'I hope that all the deputies have been elected.'
Eu espero terem todos os deputados sido eleitos

IX Extraposition phenomena

The term *extraposition* was introduced by Rosenbaum (1967) to refer to the transformational process by which examples (b), which contain a sentential subject in clause-final position and the expletive element *it* in the grammatical subject position, were derived from examples (a), where the sentence occupies the subject position, which was taken at the time to be its original position.

(1) a. *That John left early disappointed us.*
    b. *It disappointed us that John left early.*

(2) a. *That John will come is unlikely.*
    b. *It is unlikely that John will come.*

(3) a. *For the house to be painted would irritate him.*
    b. *It would irritate him for the house to be painted.*

Extraposition, which initially designated a transformational process, came to refer to the construction this process gives rise to. Extraposition phenomena were much discussed in the wake of Rosenbaum's (1967) definition of this operation and Emonds's (1970) distinction between root and structure-preserving transformations. One of the challenges they raised was to determine whether extraposition is categorially restricted. In Rosembaum's account, embedded sentences (labeled S) are uniformly dominated by an NP node; in Emonds's (1970) view, *that*-clauses and infinitive clauses never are noun phrases. Another issue was whether extraposition, when it affects a subject clause, was to be conceived of as a rightward movement process from the subject position (Rosenbaum) or as a subject-replacement operation (Emonds). Much care was also devoted to identifying the locality conditions governing the process (the Right Roof Constraint, Subjacency . . .), if indeed movement is involved, or, if no movement occurs, to discovering the interpretive rules that build the relation between the extraposed expression and the position where it is interpreted. It was also discovered that extraposition can affect other expressions than complement clauses. Other clause types (relative, comparative or result clauses) and prepositional phrases are also found at the right edge of the propositional domains that minimally contain them.

A caveat is necessary at the outset concerning the range of structures covered by the term *extraposition*. When it was introduced at the end of the 60's, propositional arguments, when they functioned as subjects, were first merged in the grammatical subject position (now, the specifier of TP), considered to be a θ-position. It is from this site that they were supposed to move to the right edge of the clause. In contemporary syntactic theorizing, the specifier of TP is not a θ-position anymore. It is not the position where nominative case is assigned or licensed either. The valuation of nominative expressions in finite clauses takes place in SpecvP, which is also the position where external arguments are θ-marked. This means that the subject clause in (1a) doesn't occupy its first Merge position (it has been raised from inside vP). When it occurs postverbally, the clause can thus a priori occupy its first Merge position internal to vP or a right peripheral position at the edge of the clause. In (1b) and (3b), the tensed clause coexists in postverbal position with a nominal phrase and the respective orders of the two phrases cannot be modified (cf. *It disappointed that John left early all the guests present). This situation is compatible with the tensed clause having been extraposed to the left periphery or with its being the projection of the internal argument of psychological verbs. The question also arises in the case of the complement clause in (4a). In (4b), the presence of *it* is usually interpreted as a clue that extraposition has taken place.

(4) a. *Mary resents that Peter left.*
    b. *Mary resents it that Peter left.*

In what follows, the term *extraposition* will exclusively be used to refer to the situations where a clausal domain has been moved from its first Merge position to a site at the right periphery of the clause.

The phenomenon appears to raise a number of theoretical challenges that have not yet received fully satisfactory solutions. For example, languages seem to differ as to whether extraposition is optional, as is the case in the English examples above, or obligatory, as in the following Welsh example.[1]

(5) a. * Synnodd   y byddai   angen   mwy   o arian   bawb.
         surprised y be.IMPF   need   more   of money   everyone

    b.   Synnodd bawb   y byddai   angen   mwy o   arian.
         surprised everyone   y be.IMPF   need   more of money
         'It surprised everyone that more money would be needed.'

The fact that the extraposition of finite clauses is at first sight obligatorily performed in some structures, optionally in others no doubt requires an explana-

---

[1] *Synnu* raises specific difficulties that are discussed in section 51.2. The grammatical subject position in Welsh extraposition structures is not filled by an overt expletive element, which is consistent with the claim that Welsh displays some of the properties of null-subject languages.

tion and indicates that, beyond the conditions that make it possible, there are also conditions that make it obligatory. A similar observation also holds for the various nonfinite types. They appear not to display a homogeneous behavior in this respect: In English, infinitival domains extrapose, as shown by example (3), but there is a ban on the extraposition of gerund clauses; Welsh VN-clauses with a subject obligatorily move to the right edge of the clause that minimally contains them; inflected infinitive clauses in European Portuguese only optionally do so. The observed variation between languages and constructions provides additional support for the claim that the various nonfinite domains should be assigned different analyses. As a matter of fact, extraposition phenomena can be used as probes into the proper analysis of each of these domains.

50 The extraposition of embedded finite clauses

Although we are primarily interested in the distribution of nonfinite domains, it is worth looking at the way the extraposition of finite clauses has been dealt with in the literature. It appears that there is a potential conflict between the principles that are resorted to to account for obligatory extraposition and the commonly held analysis of embedded finite clauses as nominal projections.

Emonds (1970) was the first to observe that there are several ways in which sentential subjects in English do not behave like ordinary nominal subjects: Extraposition is obligatory in the context of subject-auxiliary inversion, whether or not a questioned phrase stands at the beginning of the clause, resulting in the occurrence of the expletive *it* in the grammatical subject position, cf. (6b), (6d). That finite subject clauses are not allowed to occupy this position is further confirmed by the ungrammaticality of the structures in which a clause coexists with a topicalized phrase in preverbal position, cf. (7).[2]

(6) a. * Did that John showed up please you?
 b. Did it please you that John showed up?
 c. * Who did that John left early disappoint?
 d. Who did it disappoint that John left early?

(7) * Such things, that he reads so much doesn't prove.

This restriction wasn't dealt with by Rosenbaum. In order to account for it, Emonds, in his (1970) dissertation, proposes that sentential subjects are base-generated in a VP-internal or adjunct position and then "intraposed" into the grammatical subject position by a rule of Subject Replacement, which, he assumes, has the status of a root transformation in his system. Higgins (1973) shows that none of the two claims on which Emonds's analysis is founded can be upheld: Subject Replacement is necessarily a structure-preserving transformation; the claim that *that*-clauses are never noun phrases cannot be maintained. In his (1976) book, Emonds reverts to the standard account of extraposition constructions, but claims that the sentential subjects that precede the verb at S-structure (and are inserted into the grammatical subject position at D-structure) are topicalized. His general conclusion is that "non-gerund clauses will appear only in extraposition and topicalization NP positions" (Emonds 1976: 127), a claim that is further developed by Koster (1978). For some reason, complement clauses can't

---

2 Examples (6) and (7) are given by Koster (1978) and are discussed by Davies & Dubinsky (2009).

be maintained in the grammatical subject position and must either be extraposed or topicalized. Let us provisionally assume that this generalization about sentential subjects in English is descriptively correct. It has an interesting consequence. Contrary to what the contrast between (1a) and (5a) could suggest at first, finite clauses in English and Welsh obey the same restriction: They cannot occupy or target the grammatical subject position of the sentence that minimally contains them (in Welsh, the subject position is the postverbal position). Can it be derived on principled grounds? Three lines of research have been explored, one founded on the Case Resistance Principle, another one relying on the nominal analysis of complement clauses, the last one based on thematic considerations. None of them is fully satisfactory.

50.1 The Case Resistance Principle

A first option consists in resorting to Stowell's (1981) idea that case assigning features (on [+ tense] or [– N] heads) and case marking (of the corresponding projections) are mutually exclusive. The relevant principle is formulated in (8).

(8) **Case-Resistance Principle** (Stowell 1981: 146)
Case may not be assigned to a category bearing a case assigning feature.

If one ignores the presence of a filled C in finite clauses and if the [nominative] feature on T suffices to qualify the corresponding CP as a "category bearing a case assigning feature", (8) predicts that these clauses cannot be found in the SpecTP position or in the direct object position of transitive predicates.[3] Because it contains a [nominative] feature, a finite tensed clause cannot be marked for the nominative case. (8) also correctly excludes the constructions in which a finite tensed clause is the object of a preposition, by definition a case assigner.

(9) a. * We blamed it on that Bill was too strict.
    b. * We were asking about that John went to China.
    c. * We pondered over for Bill to take a slow boat to China.

---

[3] The presence of the intervening C ceases to be problematic if one reasons in the terms of Chomsky's feature inheritance theory: [+ nominative] is part of the bundle of uninterpretable φ-features originating on C and transmitted to T.

Another piece of data that seems to be fully consistent with an explanation in the terms of (8) is the strong tendency of SOV languages to position clausal complements in postverbal position. Davies & Dubinsky (2009) attribute this observation to Dryer (1980), who cites Turkish and Persian in support of it.

In spite of its initial success, an account of extraposition based on (8) meets with serious difficulties. The first one is a side effect of the adoption of the probe-goal-Agree approach to syntactic dependencies. As repeatedly emphasized in this book, the valuation of nominative expressions takes place in SpecvP, via the establishment of an Agree relation with T. The positions from which finite clauses are supposedly excluded are not only the ones where nominative and accusative case are assigned or checked, but also all the other A-positions where clausal subjects and objects potentially occur at Transfer. This result doesn't follow from (8). Second, if (8) predicts in which situations extraposition is *obligatory*, it says nothing about the conditions that make extraposition *possible* in the first place, in other words it provides no robust characterization of the syntactic objects that are eligible for extraposition. Third, it predicts that a difference should be observed between finite and infinitive clauses: Extraposition should be obligatory with the former, optional with the latter, because infinitival T bears no case feature. The data in (3) and (1)–(2) do not reflect such a divide. A fourth difficulty is that (8) excludes the constructions in which a finite tensed clause is the object of a preposition, a correct prediction as far as English is concerned (cf. 9). But well-formed structurally analogous constructions exist in many languages, in particular in European Portuguese, where *que*-clauses can be embedded under a preposition.

(10) Convenci   o   Pedro de que a   Maria era muito competente.
     convince.PRET.1SG   the Pedro of that the Maria was much competent
     'I convinced Pedro that Maria was much competent.'

Finally, some linguists claim that the distribution of finite clauses is not as restricted as Emonds and Koster assume and as the Case Resistance Principle predicts. In particular, the evidence supporting the claim that sentential arguments cannot occur in subject positions is far from robust. Davies and Dubinsky (2009) mark (11a) and (11b) as fully grammatical.

(11) a. *To whom is that pigs can fly most surprising?*
     b. *Is that I am done with this homework really amazing?*

An account based on (8) predicts that these examples should be ungrammatical. Several linguists also observe that if some SOV languages show a strong preference for extraposing sentential object complements, others ones, such as Chocktaw and Japanese, allow clause-internal ones.

50.2 The nominal nature of propositional domains

Alternative approaches adopt an opposite stand. They take clauses to be nominal domains that require to be assigned case. They are nominal because the complementizer that heads them is itself nominal.

It must be acknowledged that no consensus has yet been reached concerning the categorial specification of complementizers. Emonds (1985), for example, assigns to all complementizers a prepositional status. But most linguists working on Romance and on other languages of the Indo-European family maintain the view that, since finite sentential complements are introduced by complementizers that derive from the pronominal system (English *that*, Romance *que/che*, Greek *oti, pu*, Russian *čto* . . .), they are expected to have the distribution of NPs. Rosenbaum's proposal that embedded clauses (S) are dominated by an NP node was intended to capture the nominal nature of complement clauses.

Beside morphological evidence, other arguments militate in favor of the nominal status of clauses. Starting from the observation that some speakers allow tensed clauses in subject positions (compare 11a/11b to 6a-6c), Davies & Dubinsky (2009) claim that generalizations are missed if *that*-clauses and infinitive phrases are never generated as noun phrases, as Emonds once assumed. There is no doubt that sentential subjects display some nominal properties: They move to the matrix subject position in raising constructions; they trigger subject agreement on the verb . . . In fact, clauses appear to display NP-like properties and to need case *precisely when they stand in subject position*.[4] In their view, this explains why *that*-clauses are banned as subjects of infinitives (cf. 12), which are caseless, but are often welcome in the subject position of finite clauses.

(12) * *It was believed that John loves Mary to be surprising.*

In order to draw the required distinctions, Davies & Dubinsky revive Rosenbaum's original analysis according to which sentential subjects are dominated by an NP

---

4 Bošković (1995) had reached a similar conclusion. He writes:
Although clauses can appear in caseless positions, they need case when they function as subjects.

node or, if one adopts today's assumptions, are embedded in a DP layer. They have the structure in (13):

(13) [$_{DP}$ Ø [$_{CP}$ that Earl can play the blues]] is quite obvious.

But if sentential subjects are indeed DPs, as Davies and Dubinsky assume, the reason why examples of the type of (11) are so exceptional and rejected by the majority of speakers remains a mystery. Their claim that English only admits DPs in subject position sheds no light on the phenomenon and seems to go in the wrong direction.

Basing his argument on semantico-logic considerations, Takahashi (2010) independently reaches the conclusion that sentential complements must consist of a DP structure headed by a covert determiner. He assumes that a clausal complement is allowed to move only if it is first merged in a position where a DP could appear. In other words, "the base-generated position of a moved complement must show properties of DPs even though the moved constituent appears to be a CP". His argument relies on the observation that reconstruction effects are observed when clausal complements are moved, which confirms that they participate in the formation of movement chains, and on the properties of the mechanism necessary for interpreting structures under the copy theory of movement. In Takahashi's view, the existence of reconstruction effects constitutes sufficient evidence to conclude that "whenever a clausal complement undergoes movement, there must exist a covert determiner on top of the CP complement".

If the nominal analysis, whichever form it takes, is on the right track and if it is generalized to all finite complement clauses, whatever their function, the status of propositional case, that is the possibility that complement clauses have to fulfill the case requirement, should be reconsidered. Complement clauses, being nominal as a function of their complementizer, are expected to be subject to the conditions that regulate the distribution of NPs. In the conception developed by Chomsky and Aoun in the early 80s, case was the grammatical dimension that made nominal expressions visible for θ-assignment. The *Visibility Condition* states that arguments must have case in order to be visible for θ-marking. Both Knyazev (2016) and Roussou (2018) argue that finite complement clauses are not exempt from this requirement.[5] To explain the restrictions on the distribution of *čto-* clauses in Russian, Knyazev proposes that these clauses project a

---

5 An alternative possibility, which would not force the generalized nominal analysis Roussou and Knyazev defend, would be to argue that finite embedded clauses are exempt from the Case requirement, because they are inherently visible domains. This proposal, however, doesn't fit in with Bošković's conclusion, reported in fn. 4.

DP-layer by virtue of the nominal properties of their complementizer. They are assigned either a structural case, or an inherent (prepositional) one. The distributional differences observed between Russian and English finite complement clauses stem from the fact that D in Russian can be left unpronounced and case remain unrealized in some positions, whereas the grammar of English includes a rule that moves *that* to D, generating structures where D is systematically filled.[6] Roussou (2018) adopts an integrated theory of case, based on Manzini & Savoia's (2010, 2011) idea that each case corresponds to a specific categorial feature: Nominative is D, accusative is N, oblique is "inclusion", often realized as a preposition. An Agree relation, which results in φ-feature sharing, is established between the case marked expression and the corresponding head. She develops an account of Greek complementation in which the *pu*-complements of factive/emotive predicates are oblique arguments, whereas *oti*-complements are direct ones. Of course, it remains to be determined whether the DP/NP analysis should be generalized to finite complement clauses in all languages and holds whatever their function. It must also be decided whether a link can be established between the obligatoriness of extraposition and the categorial identity of the complementizer involved.

In these approaches, a reevaluation of the status of the Case Resistance Principle is in order: If it has positive effects, how should they be captured? How can the nominal status of clauses, if it is confirmed, be reconciled with their falling under (some version of) the Case Resistance Principle? The following scenario can be contemplated. (8) prevents complement clauses from occupying positions in which case is assigned or positions that have access to case. The forbidden sites are the first Merge position of the clause and the positions that are included in the same A-chain. The A-chain, which by definition includes a case position, fulfills the case requirement, making the clause visible for θ-role assignment. But once extraposed or topicalized, the clause stands in a peripheral position that is the head of an A'-chain which contains the A-chain, voiding the potential violation of the Case Resistance Principle.

It remains that the failure of English complement clauses to occur as objects of prepositions and the highly marginal status of examples (11) render the nominal analysis of clauses highly suspect. The data from Spanish and European Portuguese that will be discussed in chapter XI, sections 65 and 66 indicate that the nominalization of clauses, when they function as complements to a nominal-selecting predicate, must be signaled by a specific marking.

---

[6] Unrealized case is not available in SpecTP and in the object of P.

50.3 The thematic properties of propositional arguments

Aiming at characterizing the distribution of clauses in general terms, some proposals establish a link between the argumental/predicative status of expressions and their categorial identity, with no reference to case. This is the case of principles (14) originally put forth by Kayne (1982):[7]

(14) a. A projection [+ V] cannot be an argument.
 b. A projection [+ N] cannot be a predicate.

Koopman (1984) observes that (14a) can be subsumed under the well-formedness condition (15), which amounts to the claim that verbal projections cannot bear a θ-role (only nominal ones can).

(15) Only [– V] categories can occupy θ-positions.

(15) excludes verbal projections from θ-positions, but says nothing about the other positions that cannot host these projections. To achieve the desired result, (15) should be reformulated as (16).

(16) A [+ V] CP projection cannot be realized at Transfer in a lexically related position, that is, in a nominal site internal to the extended projection of a lexical head.

(16) states that θ-positions and the specifiers of the lexically related functional heads cannot host propositional expressions as easily as nominal ones. Given (16), the fact that propositional expressions do not define appropriate contents to occupy nominal A-positions corresponds to the expected situation, at least in the languages where they qualify as [+ V] projections.[8]

---

[7] Holmberg (1986: 135–145) observes that principles (14a) and (14b) do not make available an appropriate representation of the predicative properties of adjectival and prepositional phrases and proposes to formulate a Predicate Principle, stating that a predicate must be [+ V], an Argument Principle, stating that an argument must be [– V], and to adjoin to them a Modifier Principle, stating that a modifier must have a neutral value, which he notes [% V]. (15) and (16) in the text can be thought of as an Argument Principle and as a Predicate Principle respectively.
[8] (16) says nothing about the distribution of the propositional domains that are larger than FinPs. This is the case of embedded interrogative clauses, for example, which should be analyzed as FocP.

We are thus left with two explanatory principles, which are both plausible candidates to account for the obligatory extraposition phenomenon. If propositional arguments in a language L are analyzed as FinP projections, that is as projections of an inherently [+ V] head, (16) states that they do not define appropriate contents for θ-positions and lexically related A-positions. If, on the other hand, nominal CPs exist, the combination of the nominal analysis and of the Case Resistance Principle predicts that complement clauses have to move from their first Merge position and from the case marking positions they eventually occupy to an A'-site that allows them to form an A'-chain including these positions. In other words, it seems that extraposition is forced whether propositional arguments are analyzed as [+ V] or as NP/DP projections. In the first case, they have to move because they cannot remain in a θ-position, in the second case, because they cannot occupy a case or case-related position.

These considerations also suggest that the obligatory extraposition phenomenon cannot *exclusively* be traced back to a case property or to a thematic characteristic of propositional domains. Reference to both seems to be necessary, depending on the categorial identity of the propositional domains involved. But the exact categorial status of finite tensed clauses has been left open in this rapid survey. It should be clear that what is proposed here is not a generalized nominal analysis of propositional domains. We know that a subset of them is not nominal at all and we know that the clausal domains that are plausible candidates for the nominal analysis should be analyzed as "augmented" CPs, that is, as CPs topped by a nominal functional apparatus.[9]

Our major concern is to determine whether nonfinite domains must satisfy the same restrictions as embedded finite clauses and, if the answer is positive, how this result is achieved. In the following sections, the extraposition behaviors of Welsh verbo-nominal clauses, English gerund constructions and European Portuguese inflected infinitive structures are carefully looked at, in the hope of discovering the "best theory" of extraposition and, at the same time, of confirming the analyses of the various nonfinite domains that were proposed in the preceding chapters.

---

[9] This is at least what the Spanish examples discussed by Moulton (2021) suggest, cf. sct. 65.

51 Why Welsh VN-clauses obligatorily extrapose, why Welsh VN-phrases cannot

Welsh is one of the languages where the extraposition of nonfinite VN-clauses with an overt subject is strictly obligatory. But VN-phrases with a silent subject (or without a subject) display an opposite behavior: They cannot extrapose.

51.1 Extraposition of verbo-nominal *i*- and *bod*-clauses with an overt subject

An often overlooked property of Welsh verbo-nominal complement clauses with an overt subject, which could lead to a drastic modification of the account developed in chapter VI, is that, when they function as the internal arguments of transitive predicates, they never occupy the direct object position at Transfer, but are obligatorily extraposed to the right periphery. This is the case in (17a) and (18a) (examples from Awbery 1976).

(17) a. *Dywedodd Ifor i Wyn i ni. orffen.*
  Said Ifor to Wyn *i* 1PL finish.VN
  'Ifor said to Wyn that we had finished.'

  b. * *Dywedodd Ifor i ni orffen i Wyn.*

(18) a. *Soniodd Ifor wrth Emyr fod angen mwy o arian.*
  mentioned Ifor to Emyr *bod* need more of money
  'Ifor mentioned to Emyr that more money would be needed.'

  b. * *Soniodd Ifor fod angen mwy o arian wrth Emyr.*

Neither *i*-initial clauses, nor *bod*-initial ones (nor finite tensed ones) can remain in their basic vP-internal position. They aren't allowed to occur in the grammatical subject position either, when they function as the external arguments of the verb.

(19) a. Cafodd ei   chyhoeddi   gan y   cadeirydd
       got   3M.SG   announce-VN   by the chairman
       fod angen mwy o arian.[10]
       bod need more   of money
       'It was announced by the chairman that more money would be needed.'

   b. * Cafodd fod angen mwy o   arian   ei   chyhoeddi.
          got   bod need more of money   3M.SG announce-VN
          gan y   cadeirydd
          by the   chairman

An extraposition process adjoining the clause to the right edge of the propositional domain that minimally contains it (or an interpretive process establishing a relation between the edge and the argument position where the clause is interpreted) necessarily takes place in the derivation. The correct representation of a sentence containing a selected *i*-clause is thus (20), not the one given in (4) or (10), ch. VI.[11]

(20) (V) ... [$_{FinP}$ [$_{Fin}$ *i*] [$_{TP}$ DP$_s$ [$_T$ Ø] [$_{vP}$ VNP]]]

It was shown in the preceding section that Case Theory and θ-theory conspire to force the extraposition of finite subject and object clauses. The account of VN-clauses in chapter VI has established that both *i*-initial clauses and *bod*-initial ones should be analyzed as FinP projections and that the initial Fin head is occupied by a [– N] element, which can be the preposition-like particle *i* or the verb-noun *bod*. The obligatoriness of extraposition should thus be traced back to (16). This well-formedness condition prevents the expressions analyzable as FinP projections from remaining in their original vP-internal θ-position or to occupy a nominal site belonging to the extended projection of the θ-marking head.

---

10 (19a) illustrates the periphrastic passive construction that resorts to the verb *cael* 'get' combined with a verb-noun preceded by a proclitic agreeing with the grammatical subject.

(i) Cafodd   y   bachgen ei   rybuddio gan   y   dyn.
     got   the boy   3M.SG warn-VN by   the   man
     'The boy was warned by the man.'

11 In the early analyses of extraposition structures, complement clauses in their surface position are not minimally c-commanded by the matrix predicate. The perspective changes if ones adopts the approach to the relation between linear word order and constituent structure based on Kayne's (1994) Linear Correspondance Axiom. In this approach, the extraposed clauses that stand at the right edge of the sentence necessarily occupy a position that is structurally lower than the ones hosting the phrases that precede.

Recall that extraposition is also obligatory when finite complement clauses are involved, as shown in section 1.

(21) a. *Dywedodd* Ifor *i*   *Wyn y byddai*   *angen mwy o arian.*
 said   Ifor to   Wyn *y* be.COND   need   much of money
 'Ifor said to Wyn that more money would be needed.'

 b. * *Dywedodd Ifor y byddai angen mwy o arian i Wyn.*

Finite embedded clauses are headed by the complementizer *y/yr* that is homophonous to the definite article, which should suffice to identify the corresponding projections as nominal. When extraposed (or topicalized), these clauses satisfy both the Case Resistance Principle and the Visibility Condition. The contrast between (5a) and (5b) can also be subsumed under an account of this type. But the nominal analysis cannot naturally be extended to VN-clauses, which were argued to be FinP projections. The observed parallelism between the finite and nonfinite clausal types could be taken to show that the FinP status of VN-clauses is not the dimension that forces them to extrapose. Or it could be lead to the conclusion that finite tensed clauses are FinP projections themselves. The latter claim is indirectly supported by McCloskey's (1996) discovery that clauses and adverbials/adjunct PPs in Irish interact with subordinating particles in an interesting way. The complementizer *go* is located at the right of the adverbial expression in (22); in English, *that* precedes it, as the translation shows (McCloskey's example).

(22) *Deiridís*   *an chéad Nollaig*   *eile*   *go dtiocfadh*   *sé aníos.*
 say.IMPF.3PL   the first Christmas   other   C come-COND   he up
 'They used to say that next Christmas he would come up.'

Rizzi (1997) interprets this variation as a clue that declarative complementizers may cross-linguistically occupy different heads in the periphery: In English, *that* is hosted by Force and in Irish, *go* is realized in Fin, the lowest head in the left periphery. A comparable, but not identical phenomenon can be observed in Welsh, as (23) shows.[12]

---

[12] In fact, the Irish pattern is not available in Welsh. Native speakers reject (i) and resort to (23) instead, even when there is no special emphasis on the interpolated adverb.

(i) ??*Dywedodd*   *ef yfory*   *y bydd*   *yn*   *gadael.*
 say.PAST.3SG   he tomorrow   C be.FUT   PROG   leave
 'He said that he'll be leaving tomorrow.'

(23) *Dywedodd   ef mai yfory   y   bydd   yn   gadael.*
     say.PAST.3SG he C tomorrow C   be.FUT.3SG PROG leave
     'He said that it is tomorrow that he'll be leaving.'

It can thus be safely concluded that finite embedded clauses and VN-clauses have the same size in Welsh and that both are projections of the FinP-level and fall under (16). This is the reason why the two propositional types display a parallel behavior.

But the fact that *i*-initial and *bod*-initial clauses (and finite clauses) can function as prepositional objects raises a serious difficulty against (16), since there is absolutely no indication that the relevant clauses are extraposed within the prepositional domain or out of it.

(24) a. *Yr. oedd   y   tŷ   yn   wag   wedi i bawb adael.*
        PRT was   the house   PRED empty after *i* all.   leave.VN
        'The house was empty after everyone's departure.'

   b. *Gwelais i ddamwain wrth i fi   fynd adre neithiwr.*
      saw   I accident while *i* me go.VN home last night
      'I saw an accident when I was returning home last night.'

The specificity of the construction exemplified in (23) is that it contains two complementizers, a lower one (*y*), which is the affirmative declarative complementizer in Welsh, and a higher one, whose occurrence is restricted to embedded cleft sentences. Tallerman (1996) and Rouveret (1996) suggest that these constructions should be analysed as CP-recursion structures. In Welsh, the marked property of C to select a CP complement would be signalled by the special complementizer *mai* or *taw* (depending on the dialect), which can be assumed to be specified in the lexicon for the selection of a CP domain. Roberts (2004, 2005) shows that the cartographic approach makes accessible an illuminating analysis of these structures. The lower particle/complementizer is merged in Fin, the higher occupies Force and marks the focalized/topicalized status of the embedded clause. The Welsh construction teaches us something interesting about re-complementation structures (which were also available in Medieval Romance languages). In the absence of a focalized (or topicalized) expression, the selected complementizer is systematically *y/y*, never *mai*. If *mai* is indeed a declarative force marker, it must be concluded that Force in Welsh is spelled out or projected in embedded clauses only if a focalized (or topicalized) expression is present. Some languages do not even spell out Force in this situation, as the Irish example (22) shows, which indicates that a parameter is involved. But the Welsh case raises an intriguing question: How can the spell-out or the projection of Force in embedded contexts be sensitive to the specifier of the lower projection being filled ? It could be proposed that Force must be given an autonomous expression when it is not structurally adjacent to Fin, that is, when an additional projection intervenes between the two. This could be so, because in this case, Fin and Force cannot be grouped into a single bundle.

c. *Cymerwch gwpanaid o de cyn i chi fynd.*
   Accept   cup   of tea before *i* you leave.VN
   'Accept a cup of tea before leaving.'

d. *Euthum allan am i'r glaw beidio.*
   I went out because *i* the rain stop.VN
   'I went out because the rain stopped.'

The PP as a whole seems to be systematically extraposed, a property which, as Ion Giurgea suggests, could reflect the wish to avoid central embedding. The P+CP combinations under consideration cannot occur in the environments where P+Adverb or P+ DP are welcome.[13]

51.2 A note on *synnu*

The analysis of the constructions containing the verb *synnu* "surprise" raises an interesting problem. Like the preceding examples, (25)–(27) can be taken to illustrate the extraposition phenomenon:

(25) a. *Synnodd bawb i ni orffen mor gyflym.*
        surprised everyone *i* us finish.VN so fast
        'It surprised everyone that we have finished so fast.'

   b. ** Synnodd i ni orffen bawb.*
        surprised *i* us finish.VN everyone

(26) a. *Synnodd bawb fod angen mwy o arian.*
        surprised everyone *bod* need more of money
        'It surprised evryone that more money would be needed.'

   b. ** Synnodd fod angen mwy o arian bawb.*

---

[13] The following French examples illustrate this difference:

(i) *Il était depuis lontemps malade.*
    he was since a long time ill

(ii) ** Il était depuis qu'il était rentré malade.*
     he was since he had come back ill

(27) a. *Synnodd   bawb   y byddai   angen   mwy o   arian.*
       surprised everyone y be.IMPF need   more of money
       'It surprised everyone that more money would be needed.'

   b. * *Synnodd y byddai angen mwy o arian bawb.*

We know that in these examples, *bawb* is analyzed as the direct object of *synnu* because its initial consonant has undergone lenition, as is the case with the objects of finite verbs in Welsh. What is the derivational origin of the complement clause in (25)–(27)? Many researchers take it for granted that the predicate-argument structure of a subset of psychological predicates doesn't include an external argument, but is comprised of two internal arguments. In Belletti & Rizzi's (1988) treatment, Italian *temere* "fear" selects an external argument, but *piacere a* "please", *preoccupare* "worry" do not. In both cases, the Object-of-Experience is syntactically realized as the first object, but the Experiencer in the *preoccupare* class is the second object of the verb, whereas it is the subject with verbs belonging to the *temere* class. Suppose that *surprise* and its Welsh equivalent *synnu* belong to the *preoccupare* class. If one uses a Larson's shell, the initial representation associated with *the earthquake surprised John* is the one schematized in (28).

(28) ... T [$_{vP}$ v [$_{VP}$ [$_{DP}$ the earthquake] [$_{V'}$ [$_{V}$ surprise] [$_{DP}$ John]]]]

When it is nominal, the higher argument is moved to the grammatical subject position after being licensed via the establishment of an Agree relation with T's features; the lower one is assigned an inherent case by the verb. If one reasons along these lines, the internal structure of the verb phrase in (25a) is as in (29).

(29) ... T [$_{vP}$ v [$_{VP}$ [$_{CP}$ i ni orffen] [$_{V'}$ [$_{V}$ synnu] [$_{DP}$ pawb]]]

The expression that bears the Object-of-Experience role is the VN-clause hosted by the specifier of vP; the Experiencer occupies the lowest position in the vP-shell. The fact that the VN-clause obligatorily follows the Experiencer argument at Transfer (cf. 25a/25b) shows (i) that the clause cannot keep its original VP-internal position, (ii) that it cannot occupy the canonical inflectional subject position either, and (iii) that it has been extraposed to the right edge of the clause. This account amounts to analyzing (25a) as an impersonal construction (cf. *It surprised everyone that more money would be needed*). It just happens that expletive pronouns are systematically excluded as subjects of inflected non-auxiliary verbs in Welsh. (30) is ungrammatical.

(30) * Synnodd.   hi bawb   fod   angen   mwy   o   arian.
      Surprised   it everyone   bod   need   more of   money

At this point, it is important to make sure that the ill-formedness of (25b), (26b) and (27b) results from the violation of a deep grammatical principle and is not stylistic/prosodic in nature (one could suggest that the lighter constituent cannot stand at the end of the clause). The contrast between (31a) and (31b) and between (32a) and (32b) provides the answer. The (b) sentences are not only unnatural, they are uncontroversially ungrammatical.

(31) a. Synnodd   yr   holl   ddynion   oedd
        surprised the   all   men   were
        yn yr   ystafell   i ni orffen   mor gyflym.
        in the   room   i us finish   so fast
        'It surprised all the men that were in the room that we have finished so fast.'

   b. * Synnodd i ni orffen   mor gyflym yr   holl   ddynion   oedd   yn
        surprised i us finish so   fast   the all   men   were   in
        yr   ystafell
        the   room

(32) a. Synnodd   yr   holl   ddynion   oedd yn yr ystafell
        surprised the   all   men   were in the room
        fod angen   mwy   o   arian.
        bod need   more of   money
        'It surprised all the men in the room that more money was needed.'

   b. * Synnodd   fod angen   mwy   o   arian   yr   holl   ddynion oedd
        surprised bod need   more of money   the all   men   were
        yn yr   ystafell.
        in the   room

The strength of this argument is weakened, however, by the observation that many native speakers do not analyze *synnu* as an unaccusative verb, but as a transitive one, that is as a predicate selecting an external argument, analogous to Italian *temere*. If this option is selected, we are not dealing with an impersonal construction anymore, *synnu* doesn't mean "surprise", but "be surprised" and *pawb* is not a direct object, but a subject. Subjects do not undergo mutation in Welsh and it is precisely the absence of mutation that provides a clue that the speakers under consideration adopt the subject analysis. They do not use sentence (25a), but (33).

(33) *Synnodd   pawb   i ni orffen   mor gyflym.*
     was.surprised everyone   i us finish.VN   so fast
     'It surprised everyone that we had finished so fast.'

For those speakers, no firm conclusion concerning the extraposition phenomenon can be drawn from the *synnu*-construction, because the *i*-clause could a priori either occupy its original VP-internal position, or be extraposed. The ungrammaticality of (31b) and (32b) could reflect the fact that the inversion of nominal subjects is not permitted in Welsh.

51.3 The non-extraposition of verbo-nominal phrases

A careful examination of the data reveals that, with respect to extraposition, there is a sharp contrast between VN-clauses with an overt subject and VN-phrases without a subject (or VN-clauses with a null subject) – the former obligatorily extrapose, the latter simply cannot -, which suggests that only clauses with an overt subject should be included in the scope of (16).

51.3.1 Adjectival constructions

We know that a bare verb-noun with no complements and no subject can occupy the grammatical subject position of a tensed clause. A verb-noun with complements and adjuncts, but with no overt subject is also allowed to occupy this position. Here are some examples involving adjectival predicates.

(34) a. *Mae gadael   i'r funud yn.   amhosibl.*
         is   leave.VN on time   Pred impossible
         'Leaving on time is impossible.'

     b. *Mae gwau   sanau   yn ôl   yr hen arfer   yn   anodd*
         is knit.VN stockings according to   the old custom   Pred difficult
         i   ferched.
         for   girls
         'Knitting stockings according to the old custom is difficult for girls.'

     c. *Mae ei   ddarllen yn   anodd.*
         is CL.3M.SG   read.VN   PRED   difficult
         'Reading it is difficult'.

51.3 The non-extraposition of verbo-nominal phrases

I leave it an open question whether the verbo-nominal phrase in examples (34) originates as a complement selected by the evaluative adjectives *amhosibl* and *anodd* or is first inserted as the specifier of the corresponding Adjective Phrase or Predicative Phrase. Whatever the correct analysis, the verbo-nominal phrase derivationally raises to the grammatical subject position.

On the contrary, in the adjectival constructions where a DP subject is associated with the VNP projection, the resulting [*i* DP VNP] constituent cannot occupy the SpecTP position (and be governed by the clause-initial finite verb in a VSO structure), it can only occur at the right edge of the clause.

(35) a. *Mae 'n hawdd i Ifor weld Carys.*
       is   PRED easy *i* Ifor see.VN Carys
      'It is easy for Ifor to see Carys.'

   b. * *Mae i Ifor weld Carys yn hawdd.*
       is *i* Ifor see.VN Carys PRED easy

(36) a. *Mae 'n anodd i ferched wau sanau*
      is   PRED difficult *i* young girls knit.VN stockings
     yn ôl yr hen arfer
     according to the old custom.
     'It is difficult that young girl knit stockings following the old custom.'

   b. * *Mae i ferched wau sanau yn ôl yr hen arfer*
       is   *i* young girls knit.VN stockings according to the old custom
     yn anodd.
     PRED difficult.

Again, the distributional pattern illustrated by (35) and (36) matches that of tensed complement clauses introduced by the declarative complementizer *y/yr* and that of *bod*-initial clauses, whose propositional status cannot be challenged. Tensed clauses are not tolerated in the grammatical subject position either, they must occupy an extraposed position at the right edge of the clause.[14] Similarly, subject *bod*-constructions are not legitimate in argument positions, they are in extraposed ones.

---

[14] They can also be topicalized and precede the clause-initial particle.

(37) a. Mae 'n amhosibl ei fod wedi gadael gynnau.
    is PRED impossible CL3M.SG bod PERF leave on time
    'It is impossible that he left on time.'

b. * Mae ei fod wedi gadael gynnau 'n amhosibl

The only difference with the examples discussed in section 51.1. is that we are not dealing with verbal constructions in this case, but with adjectival structures. They fall under the scope of principle (16) if the specifier of the adjectival phrase and the grammatical subject position are taken to be lexically related positions.

These distributions can be interpreted in one of two ways. Either the grammaticality of examples (34), where no subject is associated with the verb-noun, is taken to show that the constituent in SpecTP doesn't have a CP/FinP status and hence doesn't fall under principle (16). In this case, the contrast between examples (34) and (35)–(37) would indicate that verbo-nominal constituents should be identified as CP domains when coupled with a lexical subject, thus falling under (16), but as smaller truncated structures when subjectless. Or a subject position is assumed to be projected in all the relevant domains, a position that can be occupied either by an overt nominal expression or by PRO. Note that the presence of the adverbial expression *i'r funud* in (34a) and the fact that the clitic affixed to the verb-noun in (34c) can only be interpreted as the direct argument of *darllen* suggest that we are indeed dealing with a verbal VN.[15] Suppose that the clausal analysis is correct. The comparison between paradigms (34) and (35)–(37) could suggest that the extraposition process is also sensitive to whether the corresponding Fin is filled and an overt subject is present. If this conjecture is correct, the well-formedness condition (16) should be reformulated as in (38).

(38) A FinP domain with a filled Fin head and an overt subject cannot occupy a lexically related position at Transfer, that is, a site internal to the extended projection of a lexical head.[16]

(38) can be viewed as a partial reformulation of the generalization underlying Landau's Finiteness Rule for OC.

---

[15] But this property doesn't necessarily imply that a clausal domain is involved – a truncation process could have taken place.
[16] This formulation implies that a major difference exists between clauses, which are FinP projections, and nominal expressions, which are DP projections. The former are banned from the positions where the latter are legitimate.

51.3.2 Subject control structures

Recall that in subject control structures that function as complements to predicates like *cofio* and *disgwyl*, the verb-noun directly stands in construction with the matrix verb, without *i* being inserted in between, as illustrated by (39a) and (39b), repeated here from (8a) and (8b), ch. VI.

(39) a. *'Dwi 'n   cofio   siarad   efo Mair.*
        I.am PROG remember.VN talk.VN   with Mair
        'I remember talking with Mair'.

   b. *Disgwyliodd Siôn   ennill.*
        Expected   Siôn   win.VN
        'Siôn expected to win'.

If the verbo-nominal phrases in the relevant structures are taken to be subjectless vPs, selected by the matrix predicate, nothing forces them to extrapose. If these examples are analyzed as standard control structures, they don't fall under (38) either because the subject is null and the complementizer silent.

The generalizations that emerge from the preceding discussion can be summarized as follows:
(i) the presence of a lexical subject in Welsh VN-clauses systematically goes along with the occurrence of FinP and TP projections in the structure;
(ii) phrases without an overt subject should also be analyzed as FinP projections;
(iii) the possibility/necessity to extrapose is linked not only to the FinP status of the syntactic object involved, but also to C/Fin being overtly manifested and to SpecTP being filled.[17]

If assumption (iii) is on the right track, the verb-noun phrases in (34 a, b, c), which should be analyzed as clauses with a null subject, don't have to extrapose. This conclusion is fully compatible with the predictions of (16), reformulated as (38). The joint absence of an overt subject and of a complementizer explains why the relevant verb-noun phrases are allowed to remain in situ and also why they cannot extrapose.

---

[17] In examples (35a) and (36a), the constituent [*i* DP VNP] has the same behavior as in the structures where it is the direct argument of an epistemic or declarative predicate, although adjectives do not lexically select the way verbs do. This suggests that the verbo-nominal clause has probably been extraposed in this case too. The obligatory presence of *i* doesn't come as a surprise.

Although the well-formedness condition (38) is no more than a descriptive generalization for the moment, it makes clear that, when extraposition is considered, the relevant divide is not between finite and verbo-nominal clauses, but between clauses with an overt subject and a complementizer and those that lack both.

Only VN-clauses with an overt subject and an overt complementizer and VN-clauses that lack both have been discussed in support of (38). It remains to check that these two properties really go hand in hand in the relevant structures. If it turns out that they do, the reference to either complementizers or to subjects should be dispensed with. The structures studied in chapter VI (cf. paradigm 11), where the second object of a verbal predicate is a *i*-initial verbo-nominal clause with a null subject could give us a clue as to what the correct answer is. Unfortunately, it is difficult to imagine contexts where these clauses unquestionably occupy an extraposed position.

52 A principled approach to extraposition

Let us suppose that (38) is indeed correct. It is now time to provide it with a status. What is its motivation? Why does it hold at all? (38) establishes a link between the internal categorial make-up of propositional domains, the thematic and casual properties of the sites they originate in or move to, and the obligatoriness of extraposition. Whether a given structure satisfies these requirements can only be evaluated in the overt syntax or on the LF branch of the grammar. But (38) also specifies that extraposition is sensitive to the presence of an overt subject in the extraposed clause and to the overtness of Fin. The sensitivity to these dimensions could motivate the claim that extraposition should not be taken as an exclusively narrow-syntactic phenomenon and that PF considerations also play a role. The distinction between overt and covert subjects and that between filled and empty C's/Fin's can only be operative on the PF branch of the grammar. As a matter of fact, some authors argue that extraposition is a PF phenomenon, see for example McCloskey (1999).[18] Making extraposition an *exclusively* PF-phenomenon would impose non trivial adjustments in current linguistic theory. But it cannot be denied that PF considerations play a role. Part of the difficulty would disappear if (38) was taken to be operative at Transfer.

The alert reader has no doubt observed that the morphological and syntactic dimensions necessary to achieve the required distinction between the clausal domains that can and must extrapose and those that are prevented to do so are roughly the ones that are involved in Landau's "calculus of control", that is, in the partition between the clausal domains that take an overt DP as a subject (NC structures) and those that select a controlled one (OC structures). In other words, the pairing of a semantic [tense] feature and of overt morpho-syntactic [φ] features on C and/or on T also plays a prominent role in deciding whether a sentential domain must or cannot extrapose. Reinterpreted in the light of Landau's generalization, the well-formedness condition (38) amounts to the claim that the clausal structures that can and must extrapose are the FinP domains whose head is endowed with a semantic [tense] feature and an overt φ-feature matrix. We know

---

[18] Additional evidence that PF-considerations indeed play a role in extraposition phenomena is provided by the fact that extraposed finite complement clauses in English are necessarily headed by an overt complementizer.
(i)   Peter told Mary that John had failed the exam.
(ii) * Peter told Mary John had failed the exam.
(iii) It was announced from London that the pandemy had started again.
(iv) * It was announced from London the pandemy had started again.

that the relevant domains can be characterized as featurally complete syntactic objects (as far as the features on inflectional heads are concerned)[19] and give rise to convergent phases (that is, phases that contain no unvalued feature when they are completed). Both *i*-clauses and *bod*-clauses satisfy this description. In Welsh VN-clauses, Fin is spelled out as *i* or filled by *bod*. Arguments have been given in favor of the Activity Condition (40), formalizing an observation made in chapter VI.

(40) [tense] and [φ] on Fin are active only if Fin is spelled out.

On the contrary, the domains that are not allowed to extrapose are featurally defective syntactic objects, whose inflectional feature endowment doesn't make the local valuation of the relevant uninterpretable features possible and hence doesn't give rise to a convergent phase.[20] Fin is not active in the possibly tensed domains that do not include an active (overt) [φ]. PRO is then the only option in subject position. It only acquires φ-features derivationally, which means that it couldn't value uninterpretable φ-features on C/Fin, if they were present, and is forced to enter an inter-phasal relation with its antecedent and a higher functional head. The propositional domains that are not allowed to extrapose are precisely the defective ones, those whose inflectional heads have no active (overt) [φ].

In other words, the joint presence of overt φ-features and semantic tense in the clause, two properties that work in tandem when the licensing of subjects and the distinction between NC and OC clause types are at stake, should not be considered separately either in the account of extraposition. The same notion of completeness/defectiveness turns out to be relevant to the two phenomena. (38) should be reformulated as in (41).

(41) A FinP domain headed by a featurally complete Fin head (that is, a Fin positively specified for [tense] and whose overt φ-features are valued within the minimal CP/FinP phase) cannot occupy a lexically related position at Transfer and must be extraposed or topicalized.

A FinP domain headed by a featurally deficient Fin head (that is, a Fin that is negatively specified for [tense] or whose φ-features have no morphological exponent) cannot be extraposed.

---

[19] Either inflectional head can a priori be relevant. The reason why it is Fin that provides the relevant information in Welsh is that Fin doesn't transmit any uninterpretable feature to T.
[20] On the link between convergence and completeness, non-convergence and defectiveness, see the discussion in chapter II, section 7.7.

The implication of the Extraposition Principles formulated in (41) is that the different extraposition behaviors displayed by the two clause types stem from the distinct values assigned to the [tense] and φ-features on C. Another aspect of this account is that it strictly dissociates [tense] and [agreement] from [finite]. The clauses that have been dealt with in this section are not descriptively finite clauses, but nonfinite ones that can be endowed with semantic [tense] and overt [φ]'s.

One could ask why (41) or a variant of it holds at all. A defining characteristic of extraposition processes could be that only the domains that qualify as closed syntactic objects and correspond to convergent phases are *allowed* to extrapose. This is so because the checking by valuation procedure is entirely performed within the boundaries of the phase. These domains *must* extrapose because, being FinP/[− N] projections, they cannot be maintained in their first Merge A-position. The defective domains in which not all the features of Fin are active define open syntactic objects, do not correspond to convergent phases, and are dependent on material present in the external environment, for example in the immediately higher phase, for the valuation of some of their internal features. Extraposing them would break the locality that is a necessary condition on the valuation process.[21] But they are allowed to occupy different positions in the A-chain that includes their first Merge position.

The completeness/defectiveness divide can also be interpreted in different terms, namely in terms of visibility. A syntactic domain that is specified for the full range of inflectional features would be inherently visible and hence a natural candidate for extraposition. A defective domain would only be visible in the immediate vicinity of the lexical head that selects it or in a lexically related position. This would prevent it from extraposing. But an account based on visibility is less satisfying than the one proposed in this section because it doesn't explicitly represent the link between the ability to extrapose and the licensing of subjects.

---

21 In Chomsky's framework, defective domains generally do not define derivational phases, but can also qualify as phases. Raising structures and ECM complement clauses, which are TPs, are not phases. Obligatory control structures, which illustrate a type of defectiveness, are CPs and define phases. In the approach defended here, the only relevant divide is between the domains that can be characterized as convergent phases and those that cannot. Neither raising structures nor OC structures define convergent phases.

53 Why gerund clauses don't extrapose

It is possible to reach a better understanding of the nature of extraposition if one tries to identify the reason underlying the ban on the extraposition of gerund clauses. (42) documents the behavior of Acc-*ing* gerund clauses.

(42) a.   * *It surprised me John solving this difficult problem.*
       a'. *John solving this difficult problem surprised me.*
       b.   * *It is surprising Elmer looking for a place on the seashore.*
       b'. *Elmer looking for a place on the seashore is surprising.*

In this respect, Acc-*ing* constructions display a behavior that is the opposite of that of English finite tensed clauses: Contrary to the latter, they are allowed to occupy the grammatical subject position, as (43a) and (43b) show, and they are not legitimate in postverbal/extraposed position, as (43c) confirms:

(43) a.   *Is the lady bothering you any reason for you to come bothering me?*
               [from Jespersen 1933: 328]
      b.   *John reading* War and Peace *surprises me.*
      c.   * *It surprises me John reading* War and Peace.

These distributions are potentially problematic for Emonds's (1970) subject replacement account. Why are gerund phrases prevented from standing at the edge, but perfectly at ease in the grammatical subject position? If subject replacement is involved, as Emonds (1970) claims, what prevents gerund phrases from being first merged in the "extraposed" position and stay there? Higgins (1973), who raises the question, suggests that the reason why gerunds cannot extrapose (Rosenbaum) or be directly generated in extraposed position (Emonds) is that they are not clauses, but verbo-nominal domains with no complementizer. The presence/absence of an overt complementizer could be a discriminating factor here, but the case of Portuguese inflected infinitive clauses, which are "extraposable", although deprived of an overt complementizer, indicates that a more abstract perspective should be adopted (cf. sct. 54).

But if they are welcome in the grammatical subject position of active sentences, gerund clauses are not felicitous in all nominal argument positions: They must occupy a case position at some point in the derivation, that is, belong to an A-chain (by definition including a case marked position) at Transfer. This condition is not fulfilled by the gerund phrases occurring in the object position of a passive predicate.[22]

(44) * It was expected Frank reading this novel.

The result is ungrammatical although the gerund clauses complements of *expected* in (44) and objects of *surprised* in (42a) satisfy the subcategorization requirement of the governing predicate. These distributions are strictly parallel to what is observed in structures like (45a) and (45b), which also illustrate the ban on extraposition, but where subcategorization is not at stake. Finite tensed clauses are free to occur in the relevant positions (cf. 45c).[23]

(45) a. * It was tragic Paul losing the elections.
      b. * It was a joy Susan encountering that book in such out of the way shop.
      c. It was tragic that Paul lost the election.

Reuland (1983) and Pires (2006) propose that Acc-*ing* gerund phrases must themselves be case licensed. But no case is available in the object position of passive and unaccusative predicates ((42a, 44)) or in non-selected positions ((45 a, b, c)). The external environment makes a case available only when the gerund phrase is the object of a preposition or of a transitive verb or occupies the grammatical subject position of a tensed clause.[24]

Examples (42a) and (43c), which include a gerund clause that I have carefully avoided to analyze as a nominal projection, are judged ungrammatical by native speakers. But inserting a pause between the clause at the right periphery and the preceding context seems to improve things a lot, as the discussion of examples (26), ch. IV, repeated here as (46), has shown.[25]

(46) a. It surprised me # Mary leaving town.
      b. * It surprised me Mary leaving town.

---

[22] The ungrammaticality of examples (42a) and (42b), containing an unaccusative predicate could reflect the same restriction.
[23] Examples (45a) and (45c) are given by Pires (2006), (45b) is provided by Milsark (1988).
[24] They also claim that the case licensing of the whole clause is a necessary condition for its subject to be licensed. I agree that gerund clauses must be case licensed, but I reject the claim that this case licensing makes the licensing of their subject possible.
[25] This behavior is not specific to gerund clauses, it is also observed with noun phrases, which can occupy a position at the right edge only if they are separated from what precedes by a pause.

(i) *It surprised me a lot, her new hat.*

Finite tensed clauses, whose complementizer head is overt and which include verbal forms that are explicitly marked for agreement, are free to extrapose, without the insertion of an intervening pause being necessary, cf. (45c). Acc-*ing* structures, which lack an overt complementizer and do not include a person-number agreement marker, are not. This contrast could suggest that an account in terms of visibility is on the right track. Contrary to finite tensed clauses that are inherently visible, gerund clauses are not and thus cannot inherit a θ-role, when extraposed. For some reason, the pause present in (46a) seems to have the same effect on visibility as an overt complementizer.

But one should also look at gerund constructions from an alternative perspective, the one relying on Landau's approach to subject licensing. They have already been shown to raise a potential difficulty against this approach (cf. sct. 20). The ban on the extraposition of Acc-*ing* structures is also unexpected in this system because, being CP/FinP domains, having a temporal interpretation and fulfilling the description of "clause with an overt subject", they should qualify as featurally complete syntactic entities and thus as candidates for extraposition (the analysis developed in chapter IV claims that uninterpretable φ's are transmitted from C to T in these constructions). This prediction however holds only if the -*ing* affix is taken to qualify as an agreement matrix, spelling out (unspecified) person-number features. Acc-*ing* structures are also admittedly deprived of an overt complementizer. But in Landau's view, which is the one adopted here, it is sufficient that one of the inflectional heads, C/Fin or T, be endowed with the relevant features for the completeness condition to be satisfied.

The problem would vanish if gerund clauses could be shown to be φ-defective (incomplete) domains. As was shown in section 20, some considerations support this analysis. First, parallel structures with null subjects exist without any difference in the internal structure of the gerund clause being detected. Second, it seems difficult to consider the suffix -*ing* as spelling out an agreement matrix, since it doesn't vary in person and number. These negative characteristics could identify the C-T pair in these domains as featurally defective. We know that only clausal domains with a non-defective C-T pair can extrapose. As shown in section 20, this analysis is fully compatible with the existence of well-formed gerund constructions with an overt subject, provided that -*ing* is taken as an admittedly φ-deficient agreement marker, but as an agreement marker nevertheless.

The way their behavior contrasts with that of Welsh VN-clauses points towards the same conclusion. Recall that [*i* DP VNP] configurations are excluded from the grammatical subject position and are only legitimate in topic or extraposed positions, as examples (47) further illustrate.

(47) a. *Mae   'n   dda gennyf   iti   ddweud y gwir.*²⁶
       be.PRES.3SG PRED good with.1SG i.2SG tell.VN the truth
       'I'm pleased that you told the truth.'

   b. * *Mae   iti   ddweud y   gwir yn dda gennyf.*
       be.PRES.3SG i.2SG tell.VN the truth PRED good with.1SG

In the analysis proposed in chapter VI, *i*-clauses were analyzed as featurally complete syntactic objects, defining convergent CP/FinP phases.²⁷

Contrary to gerund clauses with overt subjects, gerund phrases that are not associated with an overt subject are allowed to occur in extraposed adjunct positions.

(48) a. *It's pleasant walking around the city in December.* [Milsark 1988]
   b. *Mary finds it a delight swimming for hours in mountain ponds.* [Milsark 1988]
   c. *It's no use telling me lies.*
   d. *It's no fun weighing a quintal.*

The well-formedness of examples (48) directly bears on the question of whether gerunds in these sentences are the lexical heads of clausal domains with a PRO subject or have no subject of their own. If we were dealing with ordinary nominal expressions, the well-formedness of these examples would be totally unexpected, because nominal expressions don't extrapose. In the structures under consideration, the gerund phrase could be thought of as a vP or AspP projection in adjunct position, with the vP hosting a PRO subject in its specifier. Once again, the behavior of gerund clauses and phrases is the exact opposite of that of Welsh VN-clauses: Gerund clauses with an explicit subject cannot extrapose, those without a subject can occur at the right edge of the clause, but it is not clear whether an extraposition process is involved in this case.

Let us now briefly consider the extraposition properties of Poss-*ing* constructions. They are basically identical to the properties of Acc-*ing* ones, since Poss-*ing* constructions cannot extrapose.

---

26 *gennyf* is the inflected form of the preposition *gan* 'with' at the first person singular, *iti* is the inflected form of the preposition *i* 'to' at the second person singular.
27 Their being headed by an inherently [+ V] head, namely Fin, makes the corresponding projection a content inappropriate to occupy nominal positions. It was shown in chapter VI that [*i* DP VNP] configurations define constituents.

(49) a. *It surprised me Mary's leaving town. [Williams 1975: 262]
 b. *It was expected Frank's reading this novel.
 c. *It's amusing John's walking around the city in December.
 d. *It surprised me Paul's loss.

This restriction, which is also observed with ordinary nominal expressions (cf. 49d), has a different origin from the one relevant to the parallel Acc-*ing* gerund phrases. Poss-*ing* constructions are featurally complete DP structures and (41) is irrelevant in this case. If the gerund phrases in the ungrammatical examples (49) share one characteristic, it is the lack of Case. In (49a), (49b), (49c), we are dealing with nominal projections and nominal projections cannot extrapose (cf. 49d). They can be displaced only if their landing site belongs to a case-marked A-chain.

54 Why Portuguese inflected infinitive structures sometimes extrapose, sometimes don't

An important aspect of the syntax of IICs is that they can occupy the focus position in pseudo-cleft sentences and be extraposed. In the corresponding structures, factive and nonfactive complements are not minimally c-commanded by the predicate that selects them. It is easy to check that they display the same properties in these structures as when they stand in their first Merge position.

Pseudo-cleft constructions, at the beginning of the 70s, were derived via movement and the problem at the time was to decide whether pseudo-cleft movement exclusively involved noun phrases or could also affect other projections. Finite tensed clauses are indeed allowed to occupy the focus position of a pseudo-cleft.

(50) a. *What is most likely is that Susan said she would be late.*
     b. *What John resents is that you refuse even to discuss the matter.*

This fact can be interpreted in one of two ways: Either finite clauses themselves are noun phrases (this was the favored option at the time) or projections that are not noun phrases can undergo pseudo-cleft movement.

Where do IICs stand in this respect? When the selecting verb is a factive predicate, the IIC can be focalized. Its properties are the same as when the clause is positioned in its first Merge position: The null complementizer can be preceded by *o*, subject-auxiliary inversion is optional and, in the absence of an auxiliary, verb-initial structures are marginally possible when the reference is to a habitual event or a generic situation.

(51) *O que mais me surpreende é*
     what most 1SG surprises is
  a. *os deputados terem aprovado a proposta.*
     the deputies have.INF.3PL approved the proposal
  b. *terem os deputados aprovado a proposta.*
  c. *o terem os deputados aprovado a proposta.*
  d. * *o os deputados terem aprovado a proposta.*
  e. *o todos eles terem aprovado a proposta.*
     D all them have.INF.3PL approved the proposal

(52) O que mais me surpreende é
what most 1SG surprises is
a. os deputados aprovarem a proposta.
the deputies approve INF.3PL. the proposal
b. o eles aprovarem a proposta.
c. comprarem eles o jornal todas as sextas-feiras.
d. o comprarem eles o jornal todas as sextas-feiras.

When the selecting verb is an epistemic/declarative predicate, the associated IIC can also occupy the focus position of a pseudo-cleft. All the restrictions governing the distribution of the infinitive in the uncleffted version are also operative in the pseudo-cleft one: obligatory subject-auxiliary inversion, absence of *o*, ban on subject-initial structures, ban on verb-initial structures, except in habitual or generic contexts.

(53) O que o Presidente afirmou é
what the President asserted is
a. * os deputados terem aprovado a quinta proposta.
the deputies have.INF.3PL approved the fifth proposal
b. terem os deputados aprovado a quinta proposta.
c. * o terem os deputados aprovado a quinta proposta.
d. * o os deputados terem aprovado a quinta proposta.
e. * os deputados aprovarem a quinta proposta.
f. * aprovarem os deputados a quinta proposta.

These distributions can be made sense of if it is claimed that IICs in pseudo-cleft sentences are introduced by an abstract complementizer, which is the one that occurs in the corresponding uncleffted constructions. The fact that the differences between the two complement types are preserved when the IICs stand in the focus position of a pseudo-cleft (compare (51)–(52) and (53)) indicates that the silent complementizers are part of the material occupying the focus position and confirms that they impose restrictions of their own on the TP domain they c-command. It also shows that the focus position of a pseudo-cleft is not exclusively accessible to nominal expressions, since the relevant chunks of structure must be analyzed as FinP projections when declarative/epistemic predicates are involved (cf. 53b).

With respect to extraposition, IICs follow the same pattern as Portuguese (and English) finite clauses. As already shown by pseudo-cleft constructions, they freely occupy positions which are not in the domain of a Case assigner at Transfer. (54a) from Raposo (1987) and (54b) from Madeira (1994) illustrate this point.

(54) a. *Será   difícil   eles   aprovarem   a   proposta.*
       be.FUT.3SG difficult they   approve.INF.3PL   the   proposal
       'It will be difficult for them to approve the proposal.'

   b. *É   possível eles terem   perdido o   comboio.*
      be.PRES.3SG possible they have INF.3PL missed the   train
      'It is possible that they have missed the train.'

The IICs in these examples are subject clauses in positions where no Case marking from an external lexical head can be invoked.[28] The availability of extraposition/topicalization in structures containing the verb *surpreender* 'surprise' is also as expected.

(55) a. *Muito me surpreendeu   eles aprovarem   a   proposta.*
        much me surprised   they approve.INF.3PL   the   proposal

   b. *Eles aprovarem   a   proposta muito me surpreendeu.*
      they approve.INF.3PL   the proposal much me surprised

In (55b), the IIC has raised from a vP-internal site to the grammatical subject position or to a topicalization one. The IIC in (55a) can a priori occupy the vP-internal θ-position where it was first merged, or have been extraposed to the right periphery. IICs do satisfy the conditions that make extraposition possible. The relevant structures can safely be characterized as CP/FinP domains in which the inflectional head T is fully specified and the C-T-subject relation active, two conditions that make extraposition possible. The fact that none of C's features is morphologically spelled out is irrelevant.

However, the distribution of *o* in the relevant structures shows that the situation is more complex. It was concluded in chapter VIII that inserting *o* in front of an IIC turns it into a nominalized clause. Interestingly, native speakers systematically reject the constructions in which an extraposed clause is preceded by *o*. Examples (54a) and (54b) are generally considered as slightly marginal, but the

---

[28] The contrast between European Portuguese IICs and English gerund clauses in this respect casts some doubt on the appropriateness of extending to IICs the type of account that was proposed for gerund clauses by Reuland (1983), as Raposo (1987) does. On the other hand, one cannot object to Raposo's claim that factive IICs should occupy positions for which a case is available on the ground that it conflicts with the predictions of Stowell's (1981) *Case Resistance Principle*. That the latter principle cannot by itself account for the full complexity of the data and meets with considerable difficulties has been established in section 50.1. This conclusion is confirmed by the syntax of European Portuguese IICs.

versions of the same examples with *o* inserted at the beginning of the extraposed clause (cf. 56 a, b) are judged ungrammatical. Why are these examples not well-formed? (41) cannot be invoked since nominal domains, which are not FinPs, do not fall within its scope. The reason why these examples are ungrammatical is that the lexical environment makes available no A-position that the propositional DP could occupy – *difícil* doesn't select a nominal argument – and it cannot extrapose either, because nominal expressions do not.

(56) a. * *Será   difícil   o eles aprovarem   a   proposta.*
         be.FUT.3SG difficult *o* they approve.INF.3PL the proposal

   b. * *É   possível o terem   eles perdido o   comboio.*
         be.PRES.3SG possible *o* have.INF.3PL they missed the train

In chapter VIII, it was argued that the inflected infinitive complements to factive/psychological predicates are FinP projections, embedded within a DP layer, D being optionally spelled out. The contrast between the structures with *o* and those without is less marked in this case, cf. (55a), repeated here as (57a).

(57) a. *Muito me surpreendeu eles aprovarem   a   proposta/*
         much me surprised   they approve. INF.3PL the proposal

   b. ? *Muito me surpreendeu   o eles aprovarem   a   proposta.*
         much me surprised   *o* they approve.INF.3PL the proposal

The coexistence of the (a) and (b) versions in (57) suggests that the complement clause can either extrapose or keep its original position within vP. In the first case, it necessarily is a FinP domain, since DPs cannot be found in extraposed positions. In the second case, the IIC occupies an argument position and the DP analysis is an option. Let us assume that D can host an overt determiner or remain silent.

But then, how should the constructions with an IIC in preverbal subject position be analyzed? Both the version without *o* and the one with *o* are well-formed, although the former is preferred.

(58) a. *Eles aprovarem a proposta muito me surpreendeu.* (= 55b)
   b. ? *O eles aprovarem a proposta muito me surpreendeu.*

The *o*/Ø alternation can be interpreted as above. When *o* is present, the IIC qualifies as a full DP and can only be found in the grammatical subject position. The absence of *o* can be taken as a clue that the IIC reduces either to a FinP projection, which can be topicalized, or to a DP one with a non-overt D, which is welcome in subject position.

The intriguing distributional behavior displayed by the IICs dependent on a factive/emotive predicates thus points towards their having a dual categorial analysis.

These distributions have an important consequence concerning the proper characterization of extraposition. The nominal analysis of clauses was rejected in section 50.2. But clauses can be nominalized via the adjunction of a D system. One would expect that, as long as an extraposed nominalized clause binds a Case-marked A-chain, the resulting structure is well-formed. Examples (56a), (56b) and (57b) show that this prediction is wrong. Propositional DPs behave just as standard nominal expressions in this respect, which are prevented from being extraposed from an argument position to the right periphery.

55 Conclusion

An adequate account of extraposition phenomena must provide an answer for two partly independent questions:
(i) Which syntactic objects must extrapose?
(ii) Which syntactic objects are allowed to extrapose?

(i) asks which syntactic objects have to leave the site where they have been positioned by first Merge and move to a left- or right-peripheral position and which ones are not forced to do so. (ii) asks which syntactic objects have the possibility to extrapose and which ones must be maintained in their first Merge position.

It appears that there is a divide between nonfinite clausal domains in this respect: Those that do not qualify as fully specified domains (with semantic tense and agreement inflectional morphology) cannot move to the edge; those that have a complete non defective feature endowment must be extraposed. This distinction cuts across the standard finite/nonfinite distinction. If one tries to identify the deep reason behind these patterns, it seems that two explanatory principles can be invoked. The reason why some clausal domains cannot extrapose could be that they would not be visible to θ-assignment in their landing site. Only the domains which remain visible when extraposed can move to the edge. The ones that belong to the first category are defective domains, the ones that belong to the second category are complete ones. But the reference to visibility can be dispensed with. It can be proposed that only the domains that are featurally complete and correspond to convergent phases are allowed to extrapose; defective ones, which do not define convergent phases, are not.

The preceding observations exclusively hold for CP/FinP nonfinite domains. Those that qualify as nominal domains never extrapose, because nominal phrases can only occupy a site included in an A-chain.[29]

This account of extraposition phenomena leaves several questions unanswered. For example, is it legitimate to group together extraposition and topicalization/focalization, as was done in section 54 for European Portuguese? Are movements to the right periphery (extraposition) and leftward movements related to information structure (topicalization/ focalization) allowed in the same environments? This question should be raised about each of the clause types in Landau's classification. For example, finite control constructions in Greek and Hebrew, that are characterized as [–tense, +agreement] defective domains, should

---

[29] This claim raises the question of the status of the specifier of TopP in the structures where a noun phrase is topicalized.

not be extraposable, since they do not qualify as fully specified domains. If extraposition and topicalization obey the same constraints, they shouldn't be topicalizable either. Looking at the Modern Greek data, we discover that it is indeed difficult to imagine contexts where a *na*-complement clause is extraposed, but it is easy to build sentences where such a clause is topicalized or focalized.[30]

(59) a. [*na elegsi   tin oreksi   tis*] *prospathi   i.   Maria.*
       na control.3sg   the appetite   her try.3sg   the Maria
       'Maria tries to control her appetite.'

   b. [*na pari   tin ipothrofia*]   *elpizi   o Yannis.*
      na get.3sg   the scholarship   hope.3sg the Yannis
      'Yannis hopes to get the scholarship.'

   c. [*na kolimbao*]   *ksero.*
      na swim.1sg   know.1sg
      'I know how to swim.'

   d. [*na diavasi*]   *parakalese   i Maria   ton Yannni.*
      na read.3sg   ask.pret.3sg   the Maria   the Yanni
      'Yannis asked Maria to read.'

These distributions can be interpreted in one of two ways: They either show that the two syntactic processes should not be grouped together and don't fall under the same principles, or that *na*-complement clauses in Modern Greek do not systematically behave as defective domains. I will leave this important question open, although the first option seems to me to be the correct one. It is safe to claim that the Topic and Focus positions don't share the characteristics of extraposed ones.

---

[30] I am most grateful to Anna Roussou for help with the Greek data.

X **The Latin *ab urbe condita* construction**

This chapter deals with the *dominant participle construction* in Latin. This grammatical label refers to "noun phrases that are comprised of a noun and a participle in which the participle is not understood as a modifier of the nominal head, but as a predicate".[1] Camille Denizot, to whom we owe this characterization (cf. Denizot 2017: 37), observes that the expression "dominant participle" is not fully satisfying. It conveys "the idea that semantically (and maybe syntactically), the participle is dominant, although, being in a noun phrase, it should be a simple modifier of the nominal head" (Denizot 2017: 38, fn. 3). But at the same time, since it leaves open the possibility that what is at stake is a purely interpretive phenomenon, possibly deprived of any syntactic basis, this characterization leads one to think that dominant participle constructions (henceforth DPCs) could essentially have the same structure as the participial constructions in which the participle is construed as a modifier of the noun.

Latin scholars agree that expressions like (1a) and (1b) constitute prototypical examples of the DPC.

(1) a. *ab   urbe   condita*
       since city   founded   'since the foundation of the city'

    b. *Sicilia amissa*
       Sicily lost   'the loss of Sicily'

It is easy to check that they fully satisfy the characterization proposed by Denizot: They are nominal expressions in which a predication relation is established between the participial phrase and the noun phrase. A perennial source of puzzlement for the Latin scholars interested in the DPC seems to have been the difficulty to reconcile their predicative/propositional interpretation, a semantic characteristic in their opinion, with the clearly nominal status of the constituent [NP PartP] formed by the noun phrase and the participial phrase. This is the reason why some researchers propose to identify the complex noun phrase formed by the DPC, not as a nominal expression, but as a clause, cf. Longrée (1995), Storme (2010). The position argued for in this study is quite different. I will follow Bolkenstein's (1981, 1989a, 1989b) proposal that what is involved is not a proposition, but an embedded predication, which happens to have an external nominal distribution. It is thus necessary to ask what type of syntactic object the DPC is, which allows the integration of a predicative structure into a typically nominal expression. It will appear that only a syntactic approach that takes into account

---

[1] The label "dominant participle" was introduced by A. G. de Man (1965) in his Latin method.

the structural constraints on predication and that wonders about the nature of participles, as well as about the cooccurrence within the same domain of verbal and nominal properties, is in a position to provide an explanation for the categorially mixed behavior of participles in the DPC. It must also be discovered why the distribution of the predicative structures [NP PartP] appears to be much more constrained in contemporary French, where they are at best marginally acceptable or even absolutely excluded in nominal argument positions, as illustrated by examples (2a) and (2b) (but see fn. 40).

(2) a. * *La   révolte   réprimée   n'   a   pas   mis   fin*
        the   revolt   repressed   NEG   has   NEG   put   end
        aux   troubles.
        to-the   troubles

   b. * *Depuis   la   digue   reconstruite,   les   touristes*
        since   the   dyke   rebuilt   the   tourists
        affluent   au   Mont Saint-Michel.
        come in flocks   to-the   Mont Saint-Michel

As a matter of fact, Latin grammars for schools emphasize a specific property of DPCs, the possibility and sometimes the quasi-necessity to translate the NP+PartP combination by the abstract noun derived from the same root as the participle, followed by a dependent genitive corresponding to the subject of predication. *Sicilia amissa* translates as 'the loss of Sicily', *ab urbe condita* as 'since the foundation of the city'. I will refer to this phenomenon as the "*Sicilia amissa* effect" and try to discover what makes it possible and take a stand on its nature.

These questions are not only of interest for Latin syntax, they also have implications for syntactic theory as a whole. Solving them is a necessary step for anyone who tries to provide the DPC with a status in general linguistics. The working hypothesis adopted in this study is that the Latin construction cannot be reduced to an artificial or learned stylistic innovation, but corresponds to a deep syntactic phenomenon, which Latin syntax made possible and the syntax of contemporary French excludes.

56 Domain of study

If one adopts the characterization proposed above, the use of the participle in the DPC should be distinguished not only from its use as an attributive modifier, in which its status is analogous to that of a determinative adjective (cf. 3, 4), but also from its use as an adjunct (cf. 5, 6, 7).[2,3]

(3) seruus   currens
    slave.NOM   run.PART.PRES.NOM
    'the slave that never stops running' (a recurrent type in New Comedy)

(4) aqua   denique   feruenti   a   Rubrio
    Water.ABL   finally   boil.PART.PRES.ABL   by   Rubrius.ABL
    ipso   Philodamus   perfunditur.
    himself.ABL   Philodamus.NOM   souse.PRES.PASS.3SG
    'finally, Philodamus is soused with boiling water by Rubrius himself.'
    Cic, Verr 2. 1. 67.

(5) Dionysium,   qui   cultros   metuens   tonsorios
    Denys.ACC   who.NOM   razors.ACC   fear.PART.PRES.NOM   shaving.ACC
    candente   carbone   sibi   adurebat   capillum, ...
    glowing.ABL   coal.ABL   himself.DAT   burn.IMPF.3SG   hair.ACC
    'Denys, who, being afraid of the barber's razor, used to have his beard singed off with a glowing coal ... '
    Cic, Off 2. 25.

(6) pugnam,   qua   T. Manlius   Gallum,   cum quo
    fight.ACC   which.ABL   T. Manlius.NOM   Gaul.ACC   with who.ABL
    prouocatus   manus   conseruit,   in conspectu
    provoke.PART.NOM   hands.ACC   join.PFT.3SG in.view.ABL

---

2 The Latin corpus on which this study is based is constituted by the material collected by Heick (1936), by the examples discussed in various advanced Latin grammars and syntaxes – Riemann (1908), Gildersleeve & Lodge (1895), Ernout & Thomas (1951), Blatt (1952), Woodcock (1959), Touratier (1994) – in Bolkestein's (1980, 1981, 1989a, 1989b) and Longrée's (1995) papers, in Laughton's (1964), Pinkster's (1990) and Joffre's (1995) books.
3 Present and future participles are glossed PART.PRES and PART.FUT respectively. Passive past participles, which are overwhelmingly more frequent, are simply glossed PART, with no mention of their passive and past value. The glosses associated with common nouns simply mention the morphological case they bear and make no reference to their gender or number.

	duorum	exercitum	caesum	torque	spoliauit...
	two.GEN	armies.GEN	kill.PART.ACC	collar.ABL	strip.of.PFT.3SG

'the fight in which T. Manlius, challenged by a Gaul, came to blows with him, in the sight of both armies, killed him and despoiled him of his collar.'
Liv 6. 42. 5.

(7)   ...*C. Flaminio*   *tribuno*   *plebis*...   *restitit*
        C. Flaminius.DAT   tribune.DAT   people.GEN...   oppose.PFT.3SG
agrum   *Picentem*   *et*   *Gallicum*   *uiritim*
land.ACC   Picene.ACC   and   Gallic.ACC   to each man separately
contra   *senatus*   *auctoritatem*   *diuidenti*;...
against   senate.GEN   authority.ACC   distribute.PART.PRES.DAT

'he opposed the people's tribune C. Flaminius who was endeavoring to parcel out the Picene and Gallic public domains, against the will of the Senate...'
Cic, Sen 11.

Latin grammars in the German scholarly tradition assign a particular function to the participles in examples (5)–(7), namely "praedicatiuum".[4] The participial phrase is in apposition to the nominative noun phrase in (5), to the accusative one in (6), to the dative one in (7). But from a semantic point of view, it is often possible to interpret it as a secondary predicate, grafted on the main predication, rather than as an adjunct to the nominal expression with which it grammatically agrees (this is the case in (5) and (6) for example). This indeed suggests that the participle can be merged at different levels of structure. If it is accusative, it can be analyzed as syntactically adjoined to one of the verbal projections. If it is nominative, it can be analyzed as adjoined to the highest projection of the verbal complex or to an even higher one. The only restriction is that the participial predicate should not occupy a position structurally higher than the one of the term it relates to. It should be noted that in all these constructions, present participle forms seem to freely alternate with past participle forms.

    Now that we have said what the dominant participle is not, it is time to say what it is. Difficulties appear, however, when one tries to make precise the con-

---

[4] It is sometimes difficult to distinguish the *praedicatiuum* use from the modifier use. The decision is easy when the participial phrase is clearly external to the noun phrase with which it agrees in gender, number and case or when the noun is a proper name. Proper names generally cannot be modified by attributive modifiers that would restrict their reference, nor by restrictive relatives (here, I abstract away from some obvious exceptions, such as constructions like *Plinius Maior* or *the Cynthia that he knew doesn't exist anymore*).

tours of this grammatical concept. If *ab urbe condita* and *Sicilia amissa* should clearly be included in the DPC class, it is not the case for some of the constructions that are sometimes analyzed as belonging to it. Pinkster (1990) for example, without further discussion, includes the complements to perception predicates (*uidere, audire, sentire*) and to representation predicates (*facere, fingere, inducere*) in the DPC category.

(8) *saepe illam audiui furtiua voce*
often her.ACC heard.PFT.1SG hushed.ABL voice.ABL
loquentem / solam cum ancillis haec
talk.PART.PRES.ACC alone.ACC with servants.ABL these.ACC
sua flagitia,
her.ACC escapades.ACC
'I've often heard her talking in hushed whispers alone with her maid-servants, about her escapades.'
Catul 67, 41–42.

(9) *prodiga non sensit pereuntem*
wasteful.NOM NEG realize.PRES.3SG going.away.PART.PRES.ACC
feminam censum.
woman.ACC money.ACC
'the prodigal woman doesn't realize that the money is running away.'
Juv 6, 362.

We are clearly dealing here with constituents that combine a noun phrase subject and a participle functioning as a predicate, semantically denoting a propositional entity or rather, in Higginbotham's (1983) characterization, the "indefinite description of an individual event". But from a syntactic point of view, these domains cannot be categorized as nominal phrases. They are bare clauses that, contrary to infinitival clauses which are also legitimate with the same verbs, are alien to temporal deixis and reduce to the predicative relation.[5] Note that they can occur in structures in which they are coordinated with an infinitival clause, a constituent that no one would dream of analyzing as a noun phrase.

---

[5] The main predicate in (9) forces the propositional reading of its complement. *censum* cannot be interpreted as the direct object of *sentit*.

(10) … *Polyphemum   Homerus   cum ariete   etiam*
          Polyphemus.ACC Homer.NOM with ram.ABL even
      conloquentem   facit   eiusque   laudare   Fortunas …
      discussing.PART.PRES.ACC make.3SG he.GEN.and praise.INF lot.ACC
      'Homer even makes Polyphemus discuss with a ram and praise his lot.'
      Cic, Tusc 5. 39. 115.

A similar observation holds for the absolute ablative construction. According to Pinkster (1990) and Longrée (1995), the absolute ablative constitutes a particular case of DPC, even though obvious differences distinguish the two constructions.[6] The NP+PartP combination again constitutes a propositional domain that is reduced to the predicative relation, but this domain is not selected by a verbal predicate and in no way can be analyzed as nominal.

(11) *salute   nostra   atque   urbe   capta   per*
      safety.ABL our.ABL   and   city.ABL take.PART.ABL   by
      dolum, /   domum   reduco   integrum
      stratagem.ACC home.ACC   bring.back.PRES-1SG integer.ACC
      omnem   exercitum.
      all.ACC   army.ACC
      'without risking my life, the city being taken by a stratagem, I bring back home all our army safe.'
      Plaut, Bacch 1070–1071.

These two constructions share at least one characteristic. They don't allow an action nominal to be substituted for the participle and the argument to be realized as a dependent genitive. In other words, they cannot be identified with nominal expressions and don't manifest the "*Sicilia amissa* effect", in contrast with the DPC. These domains should thus be sharply distinguished from predications embedded in a noun phrase.

---

6 In *The Philosophy of Grammar*, Jespersen claims that none of the grammarians that have studied the particular "nexus" that the *ab urbe condita* construction represents – he refers to Madvig and Brugmann – "thinks of classing the phenomenon with the rest of the constructions which [he] mentions in the same chapter (absolute ablative, etc.)" (cf. Jespersen 1924: 124–125). These grammarians were probably fully aware that different constructions were involved. As Daniel Petit observes, the fact that these participial constructions have survived in languages in which the DPC was lost, Slavic for example, is an additional clue that they are independent from one another.

It is indeed possible to follow Pinkster and Longrée and assume that the existence of a predication relation between a NP and a participle suffices to qualify the corresponding domain as a DPC. This would amount to adopting a broad definition of this notion. Alternatively, one can stick to a narrow definition and restrict the notion to the structures in which the predicative relation is included within the boundaries of a noun phrase. This is Denizot's stand in the characterization reproduced at the beginning of this article. This is also Bolkenstein's position, who analyzes the DPC as the nominalization of an embedded predication (cf. Bolkestein 1989a, 1989b). The *ab urbe condita* construction clearly satisfies this characterization: (i) a predication relation is established between the noun *urbe* and the participle *condita*; the NP+PartP combination, built as the complement to the preposition *ab* whose categorial selection it satisfies, is itself analyzable as a noun phrase, (iii) the predicative relation is morphologically manifested by the feature sharing relation observable between the two constituents involved in the predication relation: The participle bears the same case, gender and number specifications as the noun phrase. In this study, I adopt the narrow definition of the DPC.[7]

---

[7] As emphasized by Riemann (1908) and Woodcock (1959), the DPC in Latin didn't enjoy the same extension at all periods of the history of the language. Relatively rare in early and preclassic Latin, where it occurred in prepositional expressions like *ante solem orientem* 'before the rising of the sun' (Pl. Bach. 424), it was fully developed only in classical times and became relatively frequent in Caesar's and Cicero's prose. It was later much appreciated by poets and mannered historians such as Tacitus. Its use was clearly connected to the narrative form, more precisely to the historical or mythical narratives.

But there is no doubt that the DPC appeared early in the history of the language, as shown by the construction (*quid*) *opus est*, which governs a DPC. It was very frequent in early and preclassical Latin and much rarer afterwards, providing a clue as to the antiquity of the construction. Laughton (1964) provides the following examples.

(i) celeriter mi hoc homine conuento est opus.
 fast 1SG.DAT this.ABL man.ABL meet.PART.ABL is need
 'I really must meet with the man right now.'
 Plaut, Curc 302.

(ii) quid istis nunc memoratis opust, quae commeminere?
 why these.ABL now remind.PART.ABL need-is, which remember.PRF.3PL
 'What need is there to remind them of these things now, which they remember so well?'
 Plaut, Mil 914.

(iii) Quid opust me aduocato, qui utri
 what need.is 1sg.ABL advocate.ABL who.NOM one.or.the.other.DAT
 aduocatus nescio?
 advocate.NOM NEG.know.1sg
 'What's the use of my being an assistant, when I don't know which of the two to side with?'
 Plaut, Amphitryon 1038.

57 Basic syntactic and semantic properties of the DPC

The list of the sites accessible to DPCs is easy to establish: They are the nominal positions hosting the arguments selected by a verbal, adjectival or prepositional predicate and the dependent genitive position in a nominal expression.[8]

DPC complement to a preposition

(12) *post* transactam fabulam ...
 after complete.PART.ACC play.ACC
 'after the performance of the play'
 Plaut, *Cas* 84.

DPC in genitive position

(13) *et pudor* non lati auxilii.
 and shame.NOM NEG bring.PART.GEN help.GEN
 'and the shame of not having sent help to them'
 Liv 21. 16. 2

DPC complement to an adjective

(14) uenturae*que* hiemis *memores*,
 come.PART.FUT.GEN-and winter.GEN remembering.NOM
 aestate /laboremand experiuntur.
 summer.ABL work.ACC experiment.PRES.3PL
 'and thinking of the coming winter, they dedicate themselves to work during the summer.'
 Verg, *Geor* 4. 156.

---

8 For many more examples, further references and additional discussion, see Rouveret (2018b). Only a small part of the corpus that was used in the previous study is mentioned in this reduced version. The constituent forming the DPC is written in Roman characters in the Latin text in italics.

https://doi.org/10.1515/9783110769289-065

DPC in subject position

(15) *atque ea   res   saepe temptata*
     and   this.NOM   thing.NOM often attempt.PART.NOM
     etsi   impetus   eius   consiliaque   tardabat, ...
     even.if   progress.ACC he.GEN   plans.ACC-et   delay.IMPF.3SG
     'and although these repeated attempts delayed his progress and his plans ...'
     Caes, B.C 1. 26. 2.

(16) *angebant   ingentis   spiritus   uirum   Sicilia*
     vex.IMPF.3PL   immense-GEN   pride.GEN   man.ACC   Sicily.NOM
     Sardiniaque   amissae.
     Sardinia.NOM-and   loose.PART.NOM.PL
     'what vexed this man of immense pride was the loss of Sicily and Sardinia.'
     Liv 21.1. 5.

(17) *fugiens   denique Pompeius   mirabiliter homines   mouet.*
     flee.PART.PRES.NOM finally Pompey.NOM   amazingly   people.ACC move.3SG
     'the flight of Pompey is having an amazingly strong effect on people.'
     Cic, Att 7. 11. 4.

(18) *illustrium   domum   aduersa ...   solacio*
     illustrious.GEN   houses.GEN   misfortunes.ACC   consolation.ABL
     adfecit   D. Silanus   Iuniae   familiae
     provided.with   D. Silanus.NOM   Iunia.DAT   family.DAT
     reditus.
     given.back.PART.NOM
     'the misfortunes of illustrious houses were softened by D. Silanus's restitution to the Junian family.'
     Tac, Ann 3. 24. 1.

DPC in direct or indirect object position

(19) *Carthaginienses   quoque   Capuae   amissae*
     Carthaginians.NOM   also   Capua.DAT   loose.PART.DAT
     Tarentum   captum   aequabant.
     Tarentum.ACC   take.PART.ACC   compare.IMPF.3PL
     'the Carthaginians likewise put on the same level the loss of Capua and the capture of Tarentum.'
     Liv 26. 37. 7.

This sample contains a huge proportion of DPCs involving a passive past participle, even though active present intransitive participles (cf. 17) and future intransitive ones (cf. 14) are not absent.[9] The overwhelming dominance of the passive past participle probably in part reflects the relative poverty of the Latin participial system, which includes no active past participle and no passive present participle.

Linguists working on Latin observe that it is not an easy matter to distinguish the DPC from the other participial structures, where the participle is an adjunct or an attributive modifier. Some of the examples given above are ambiguous between two interpretations. Longrée (1995) notes that in (18), *reditus* can be interpreted as the predicate of a DPC or as an adjunct. In the first case, the appropriate translation is 'the restitution of D. Silanus to the Junia family', in the second case, it is 'D. Silanus, once released and returned to the Junia family, ...'. A similar observation holds for (15). *ea res saepe temptata* allows a reading corresponding to the DPC ('these repeated attempts ...'), but can also endorse an alternative interpretation in which the participle functions as an adjunct ('this manoeuvre/operation, because it had been often attempted before, ...'). Among the criteria that Bolkestein (1980) proposes to identify DPCs, two seem to be really efficient: (i) impossibility to omit the participle, which is necessary to the semantic well-formedness of the sentence and is a confirmation of its dominant status;[10]

---

[9] According to Woodcock (1959: 76), the use of the DPC became more frequent in Cicero's time. The authors who provide most examples are Livy and Tacitus. Cicero is the first to use the present participle in this kind of construction, Livy inaugurates the use of the future participle.

[10] The subject itself can be omitted in constructions that look like passive impersonal structures. In this case, the participle bears a mark of neuter. The following example from Livy is provided by Woodcock (1959).

(i) diu   non perlitatum   tenuerat   dictatorem.
    for.a.long.time NEG obtained.PART.ACC favorable omens detain.PLPFT.3SG dictator.ACC
    'The failure for a long time to obtain favorable omens had detained the dictator.'
    Liv 8.5.

The DPC can also reduce to a participle when the missing subject is recoverable from the discourse context.

(ii) *perdita*   perdidit   me
     loose.PART.NOM lose.PFT.3SG 1sg.ACC
     'The loss [of the casket] ruined me.'
     Plaut, Cist 686.

The construction *opus est* + past participle illustrated by example (iii) quoted by Riemann (1908: 480) is usually analyzed as involving a subject-less DPC:

(ii) possible replacement of the DPC by a *quod*-clause.[11] I will leave the question of the efficiency and reliability of these tests open, only noting that criteria (i)–(ii), if they list recurrent characteristics of these constructions, propose no analysis of them and shed no light on their functioning.

Riemann's (1908) observation that the DPC can replace a *quod*-clause or commute with it emphasizes the fact that embedded predication can rely on several syntactic structures. Bolkestein (1989a) lists all the alternative structures that can be found in the relevant positions:

(i) inflected clauses introduced by a complementizer, such as *quod* or *ut*;
(ii) infinitival clauses, either subjectless or with an accusative subject;
(iii) noun phrases containing a gerundive ("adjectival" form of the gerund);
(iv) noun phrases headed by a noun referring to an event or a state of affairs usually related to a verbal root.

Like DPCs, these syntactic objects can also occur in the argument positions associated with verbal predicates. But they rarely are in free variation in a given site. According to Bolkestein, this is due to the selectional requirements of the host position and to the fact that the objects under consideration differ as to their varying degrees of clauseness or nouniness. A *quod*-clause can only reside in the subject or direct object position of a proposition. Neither these clauses nor infinitives constitute appropriate objects to prepositional heads, which usually select complements that occupy a high rank in the scale of nominality. Conversely, epistemic and declarative verbs only allow tensed or infinitival constructions to func-

---

(ii) facto,   non consulto   in tali   periculo
    act.PART.ABL   NEG deliberated.PART.ABL   in such.ABL   danger.ABL
    opus   esse.
    need.NOM   be-INF
    'it was necessary to act, not to make plans in such a danger.'
    litt. one needs to be in the situation of having acted, not deliberated.
    Sall, Cat 43.3.

11 Bolkestein (1980) mentions an additional test. The constructions in which the "subject" of the participle is a personal, interrogative or relative pronoun cannot be analyzed as modifier structures, since pronouns cannot be modified. What is involved in the following example given by Haug & Nikitina (2016) is the dominant participle use:

(i) ... eas   leges   quas   ipse   nobis
    these.ACC   laws.ACC   which.ACC   himself.NOM   1PL.DAT
    tulit,   quibus   latis   gloriabatur ...
    pass.PFT.3SG   which.ABL   carried.PART.ABL   glorify-IMPF-PASS-3SG
    'the laws which, in your presence, he passed, in the passing of which he gloried ... '
    Cic, Phil 1.10.

tion as their direct argument, they cannot govern an NP whose head would be an action nominal incompatible with the semantic type that these predicates select. Their selectional requirement cannot be fulfilled by a DPC either, which, according to Bolkestein (1981, 1989b), presupposes that the process denoted by the participial predicate has been completed by the argument realized as the subject of predication or is about to be completed.[12] To refer to this property, which in her view is a crucial dimension in the functioning of the DPC, Bolkestein uses the term "factivity". Indeed, the divide between factive/non-factive predicates has been shown to have complex ramifications in almost all the constuctions studied in this book. A salient characteristic that distinguishes factive predicates from epistemic/declarative ones is their ability to govern nominal complements (*I regret Paul's disappearance* /**I believe/know Paul's disappearance*). If Latin DPCs are analyzed as complex nominal domains, it doesn't come as a surprise that factive predications conceptualizing states of affairs can take the form of a DPC when they are governed by a verb, a noun or a preposition. The predications that are dependent on a psychological predicate, when they denote an objective event, can also be syntactically realized as a DPC (the predication occupies the subject position in 16). On the other hand, this syntactic structure cannot be used to express the propositional content corresponding to the complements to epistemic and declarative verbs. What these conclusions teach us is that the lexical and syntactic environments in large part determine the choice between the different forms of embedded predication and directly contribute to constraining the distribution of DPCs.

But the studies that have just been mentioned say very little about the syntactic nature of the DPC, that is, about its internal structure and the details of its categorial architecture. In (20), I reproduce the formulation of the problem that its existence raises, which was given in the introduction.

(20) What type of syntactic object is the DPC, which allows the integration of a predicative structure into a typically nominal expression?

The aim of section 4 is precisely to provide a theoretically founded answer to this question. The analysis will be based on the following assumptions and proposals:

---

[12] This observation may appear to be relatively obvious, when the DPC is constructed with a passive past participle. It corresponds to the expected situation if one assigns to the Latin passive past participle the two values that are traditionally associated with the *perfectum* theme: The perfect can be semantically characterized either as a present of the *perfectum* or as an *accomplished past*. But this constraint is far from trivial when a present participle (cf. (17) is involved and it cannot easily be reconciled with the DPCs containing a future participle (cf. 14).

(21) It is necessary to establish a strict distinction between predicative relations and propositional contents. Both obey precise (and different) syntactic constraints.

(22) DPCs should be analyzed neither as syntactic, nor as semantic propositions.

(23) DPCs are categorially identifiable as complex nominal domains.

Proposing a satisfactory answer to (20) also requires that we reach a better understanding of the nature of participles, that of passive past participles in particular that are omnipresent in Latin DPCs. This reflection is carried out in section 3, taking French and English data as a basis.

58 The analysis of passive past participles: A few landmarks

It seems that passive past participle forms in English and French can receive three types of interpretation, which could rely on distinct syntactic structures. The first type usually corresponds to what is usually referred to as the "verbal passive participle"; I will use the label "eventive passive participle" instead. (24a), whose cognitive content coincides with that of (24b), and (24c) illustrate the relevant interpretation.

(24) a. *La porte de la ville avait été prestement ouverte par le bourgmestre.*
   The gate of the city had been readily opened by the burgomaster.

   b. *Le bourgmestre avait prestement ouvert la porte de la ville.*
   The burgomaster had readily opened the gate of the city.

   c. *La porte avait été délibérément ouverte.*
   The gate had been intentionally opened.

Contrary to the first type, which refers to an activity presupposing the presence of an agent, the second type refers to a state that has already been reached, explicitly presented as resulting from an anterior event. This resultative perfect interpretation is present in (25a) and (25b), which both contain a "resultative passive participle".

(25) a. *La porte est restée ouverte pendant la pause de l'après-midi.*
   The door remained opened during the afternoon break.

   b. *A mon arrivée, la porte était déjà complètement démontée.*
   On my arrival the door was already completely dismantled.

The reading of (25a) is that the door remained in the state resulting from its opening. It is easy to check that the resultative use is incompatible with the presence of a *par/by*-complement.

(26) * *La porte était restée ouverte par le bourmestre.*
   * The door had remained opened by the burgomeister.

In the third type, the participle, which also refers to a state, can be fully assimilated to an adjective. This is the case in (27).

(27) *Dans le dessin de Matisse, la porte est ouverte, les fenêtres sont fermées.*
   In Matisse's drawing, the door is opened, the windows are shut.

I will refer to this case as the stative participle (or adjective) construction.[13]

The Anglo-Saxon grammatical tradition, taken up by generative grammar, contrasts "verbal passives and "adjectival passives". Wasow's (1977) great merit is to have shown that the two types are distinguished from each other in English by several syntactic characteristics. Adjectival participles exhibit properties, adjectival properties precisely, which verbal passives do not: They can be prefixed with the privative affix *un-*; they can function as attributive modifiers and occupy the prenominal position; they can function as complements to the verbs *seem, remain, . . .* , which select adjectives, not verbs.

(28) a. *The island was uninhabited.*
   b. *the uninhabited island*
   c. *The island remained uninhabited.*

The conclusions that Wasow has drawn from these distributions are well known. Passive verbal constructions are transformationally derived in the syntactic component, via a displacement rule moving the NP from the object position to the subject position. Adjectival passives, on the contrary, result from a word-building process taking place in the lexicon, no NP-movement is involved in the derivation of the sentences that contain them. Emonds (2006) also remains loyal to the two-term distinction, ignoring the resultative/stative divide, and assumes that a movement from the object position to the subject position of V is involved in the derivation of both adjectival resultative passives and eventive passives. If this movement takes place in the two types, one can consider that it is directly correlated to the passive participial suffix, present in both. Kratzer's (1994, 2000) and Embick's (2004) analyses differ from Wasow's and Emonds's on two points. First, they establish that a two-term opposition is not fine-grained enough and that three types should be distinguished, but they differ concerning the nature of the relevant distinctions. Second, they share the idea that the derivation of the

---

[13] Embick (2004), from whom this three-term classification is borrowed, observes that in English, the resultative passive participle and the stative participle are sometimes morphologically distinguished. It is precisely the case with the root √open. (i) only allows the resultative interpretation; this interpretation is excluded in (ii), which contains the stative form, incompatible with a manner adverb.

(i) *The door remained carefully opened.*
(ii) **The door remained carefully open.*

resultative type, like that of the eventive type, takes place in the syntax and that the differences between the two should not be traced back to their being formed in distinct components, but result from differences in the functional skeleton of the participial phrase and in the properties of the functional items involved.

Several diagnostic properties can be invoked in order to distinguish statives from the two other participial types. Kratzer (1994, 2000) observes that, contrary to statives, resultatives and eventives allow modification by manner adverbs and adverbs of other classes. This observation, already illustrated by the contrast between (i) and (ii), fn. 13, confers an additional plausibility to the claim that the ambiguity of the past participle form reflects structural and categorial differences between the various interpretations. Independent modification by manner adverbs seems to be directly related to the presence of the v category in the structure, the verbalizing head at the edge of the lexical projection RootP conveying semantic properties such as eventive interpretation and agentivity. This category would be present in eventive and resultative participial constructions, but not in stative constructions. On the other hand, one can follow Embick (2004) in assuming that the head Aspect (Asp) is the site in which participial morphology is inserted – whose exponent in English and in French varies according to the morphological class the verb belongs to. This head is thus present in the internal structure of all participial constructions. If these two assumptions are combined, we end up with the claim that a structure like (29) underlies resultative and eventive passive participles, whereas stative participles are assigned a structure like (30).

(29) Eventive/resultative passive participle
 $[_{AspP} [_{Asp} ASP] [_{vP} v RootP]]$

(30) Stative participle
 $[_{AspP} [_{Asp} ASP] [RootP]]$

But there exists an essential difference between the resultative passive participle and the eventive passive participle: As already mentioned, the agentive interpretation is available in the latter, not in the former. A way to represent this difference, according to Embick (2004), consists in the assumption that the Asp head, which selects the vP projection, doesn't select the same type of v in the two constructions. The v selected by resultative Aspect contains an operator of the BECOME type, whose specification reduces to the [+ event] feature. The role of Aspect amounts to creating a state from the event denoted by the vP. Contrary to the preceding one, the v selected by eventive Aspect also includes the [+ agent] specification. In this view, the representations associated with eventive and resultative participles should be rewritten as (31) and (32) respectively.

(31) Eventive passive participle
 [$_{\text{AspP}}$ [ASP-event] [$_{\text{vP}}$ v   RootP]]
                           [+ agent]
                           [+ event]]

(32) Resultative passive participle
 [$_{\text{AspP}}$ [ASP-result] [$_{\text{vP}}$ [$_{\text{v}}$ BECOME]   RootP]]
                                [+ event]

This analysis, which essentially derives from Embick's (2004) one, is couched within a syntactic approach to the derivation of morphologically complex objects, in which words are created in the syntax by the same building mechanisms as those that build phrases and clauses (cf. Halle & Marantz 1993, Marantz 1997, 1999, 2001, 2007). Concerning inflectional dimensions, like number, and substantive categories, like tense, aspect and person, they can be assumed to be inserted into structures under the form of overt affixes or, as DM proposes, as feature matrices that take a phonological shape only late in the derivation, after being combined with lexical roots and lexical categories. If the presentation that precedes is correct, the different participial types are first distinguished by the presence or absence of a verbalizing category in the relevant structures. When v is absent, the Asp head that hosts the participial morpheme is directly combined with the projection of the root. This is the situation illustrated by statives. When v is present, Asp attaches to the vP projection. A second difference follows from the feature specification of v, which can include the [+ agent] feature (in the case of eventive passive participles) or not include it (in the case of resultative passive participles).

An aspect of the preceding analysis that could be improved concerns the distinct representations associated with eventive and resultative participles. In Embick's approach, they are very close. The functional categories involved are the same, only the feature contents and the specifications associated to these features differ. And these differences affect two distinct heads, Aspect and the v that it selects. It seems that Asp-result can only select a v containing the operator BECOME, not specified for [+ agent], and that Asp-event can only select a v specified [+ agent]. The choice of a value for Aspect immediately determines the properties of the selected v head. A redundancy exists, which no doubt should be eliminated, by stating for example that the choice of an event or non-event Aspect suffices to distinguish the two structures.

Representations (30), (31), (32) amount to analyzing past participles as exclusively verbal categories, projections of the Aspect head. But this analysis remains incomplete on two fundamental points. First, participles by definition are non-finite verbal forms that express a property directly linked to the participation of an entity in the process denoted by the verbal root they are derived from. It must be asked what the syntactic origin of the relevant nominal expression is, how it is related to the participle itself, in particular whether it is syntactically built as an argument of the participle. This initial question brings about a second one. In Romance languages, passive past participles agree in gender and number (but not in person) with the participial argument functioning as their subjects. A tight connection exists between the ability to pluralize and other nominal properties, such as the sensitivity to gender and case inflection. Participles thus cannot be given a purely verbal characterization: They function as mixed categories, combining verbal and nominal (or adjectival) properties, which manifest themselves at different levels of structure. How should the nominal (or adjectival) dimensions of the three participial types be represented?

The first question concerns the derivational origin of the "subject" of the participle. It is necessary to establish a sharp distinction between the eventive/resultative participles and the stative ones, whose representation doesn't include a vP projection. Now v is the only head able to θ-license an external argument (subject) and to casually mark an internal argument (object). The "subject" of a stative participle is thus first merged into a position external to the participial projection – similarly, the subject of adjectival phrases originates in a position external to the adjectival projection, cf. Baker (2003). On the contrary, resultative and eventive participial phrases include a v head, able to θ-license a direct argument. This argument receives the θ-role that the verbal root assigns to the direct object in active constructions. To represent this property, let us assume that the relevant expression is first merged as the direct argument of the root, occupying the complement position, is θ-marked there, and is then externalized, becoming the subject of the participle.[14] This derivation, shared by eventives and resultatives, relies on the hypothesis that the v present in the corresponding structures is a defective v, more precisely an unaccusative v, which can neither θ-license an external argument in its specifier, nor casually mark an internal argument. In (33) and (34), the participial argument DP/NP is represented in its first Merge position, that is, in the direct object position.

(33) Eventive passive participle
 $[_{AspP} [ASP\text{-}event] [_{vP} \quad v \quad\quad [_{RootP} Root\ DP/NP\ ]]]$
 $\quad\quad\quad\quad\quad\quad\quad\quad\quad [+ agent]$

---

14 For a discussion of passive participles in English and of the process of externalization in the relevant structures, see Levin & Rappaport (1986) and Emonds (2006). As already mentioned, Emonds defends the idea that resultative participle configurations are adjectival projections, in which a movement process externalizing the participial argument occurs.

(34) Resultative passive participle
[$_{AspP}$ [ASP-result] [$_{vP}$ [$_v$ BECOME] [$_{RootP}$ Root DP/NP]]]

In the case of the eventive participles, present in (24a) and (24c), the selection of a designated passive auxiliary goes along with the transformation of a transitive v into an unaccusative v, which forces the externalization of the participial internal argument. The [+ agent] feature indicates that if the passive participial morphology deprives the subject position (that is, the specifier of vP) of its status as a θ-position, turning it into a site available to movement, it leaves open the possibility for the Agent argument to remain implicit or to take the form of an oblique complement. The participial argument DP/NP, if it transits via the specifier of vP, is not casually marked in this position: The v head, being unaccusative, assigns no case. This means that the moved argument is entirely dependent on the functional material above and potentially outside the AspP projection for licensing its case. The derivation of resultative participle structures proceeds along parallel lines, also involving an externalization process.

Concerning the second point, the representation of the nominal properties of the eventive and resultative participles, two lines of research can be followed, depending on whether a category-changing head n is projected above the AspP projection, converting it into a nominal domain, or no nominalizer is included in the relevant structures.

Let us examine the first option. One can follow the standard analysis that takes a Number (Num) head to be present in nominal constructions. This head can itself appear in a structure only if it takes a nominal projection as its complement. It thus cannot be directly applied to representations (33), (34), (30): A nominalizing element is necessary to mediate the relation between the verbal projection and the Num head.[15] This category-changing element is noted n in (35) and (36).

(35) Eventive passive participle
[$_{NumP}$ Num [$_{nP}$ n [$_{AspP}$ [ASP-event] [$_{vP}$ v   [$_{RootP}$ Root DP/NP]]]]]
                                     [+ agent]

---

15 Recall that the contribution of an element of this type is to assign the label "'noun" to a bare root or to a category previously characterized as verbal. But, in the case of participles, the switching element could as well be an adjectivalizing head a, since, in many contexts, they display an adjectival syntax. Embick (2000) adopts the view that participles are some types of "deverbal adjectives", that is, are "in some sense 'derived' as opposed to 'primitive' ". Note that this status doesn't necessarily imply that participial structures involve an adjectivalizing projection AP above the verbal projection.

(36) Resultative passive participle
[$_{NumP}$ Num [$_{nP}$ n [$_{AspP}$ [ASP-result] [$_{vP}$ [$_v$ BECOME] [$_{RootP}$ Root DP/NP]]]]]

A salient feature of these representations is that they presuppose that the cooccurrence of an aspect specification and of a number specification is possible within nominal domains. On the contrary, the analysis of nominalizations in the same languages reveals the existence of a strict complementary distribution between these two dimensions. The nominalizations that allow pluralization (cf. 37a/b) include no eventive dimension; those that receive an eventive interpretation do not allow pluralization (cf. 38a/b).

(37) a. *La description de l'accident (?* par le témoin) est consignée dans le rapport.*
The description of the accident by the witness is recorded in the report.

b. *Les descriptions de l'accident sont consignées dans le rapport.*
The descriptions of the accident are recorded in the report.

(38) a. *La description de l'accident par le témoin a duré une heure.*
The description of the accident by the witness lasted an hour.

b. * *Les descriptions de l'accident par le(s) témoin(s) ont duré plusieurs heures.*
* The descriptions of the accident by the witness(es) lasted several hours.

The complementarity hypothesis is confirmed by the study of the infinitive and the supine in Romanian cf. Alexiadou, Iordachioaia, Soare (2010).[16] The data indicate that the representation of the infinitive in Romanian includes a Number head, but no Aspect head, whereas the representation of the supine includes an Aspect head, but no Number head. French and Romance participles seem to instantiate an opposite situation: They both display a mark of aspect and a mark of number. In (35) and (36), the AspP projection is embedded in the nominal structure introduced by the nominalizing head, which nominalizes the structural level AspP.

In fact, it is possible to make representations (35) and (36) simpler. If resorting to a nominalizing head n turns out to be necessary, the category that seems to require the projection of n, namely Num, can itself be dispensed with. The reason supporting this move is that the number specification could as well take the form

---

16 The authors finally abandon it, because some Bulgarian data don't behave as expected. An early version of the complementarity hypothesis is discussed in Rouveret (1994).

of a feature associated with n, not that of a feature on an autonomous head. The representation associated with eventive and resultative passive participles would then be as follows.

(39) Eventive passive participle
[nP n   [AspP [ASP-event] [vP v   [RootP Root DP/NP]]]]
[+ number]   [+ agent]

(40) [nP n   [AspP [ASP-result] [vP BECOME [RootP Root DP/NP]]]]
[+ number]

In representations (39) and (40), neither Asp, nor n are case markers. As a consequence, DP/NP has to move to a higher position, from where it has access to an external case marker.

The second option that has been alluded to above consists in dispensing with the projection of a category switch n or a above AspP and relying on the various Agree relations involved in the valuing of the uninterpretable features of the functional heads dominating the root and on the movement processes occurring in the derivation, which have an effect on the labeling of the resulting structure. There are indeed situations where it seems possible to entirely dispense with a switch, for example when the participial phrase has a clearly verbal use. This is the case in (41a), whose representation at Transfer can be schematized as (41b).

(41) a. La porte a été fermée

b. [[DP] [TP être [AspP ~~DP~~ [Asp' être [vP ~~DP~~ [v' ~~être~~
[vP Root-vPart [RootP ~~Root DP~~]]]]]]]]

The DP that occupies the SpecTP position at Transfer originates as the internal argument of the Root and successively raises to the intermediate specifiers until it can get rid of its case feature. This is what happens when it reaches the Spec-AspP position, where it enters into an Agree relation with the φ-features of the inflected form of *être* in T. The reason why it transits via the intermediate position SpecvP is that the φ-features of the Asp head are valued in this site. The final movement of DP into SpecTP has the effect of labeling the whole structure as <φ, φ>. This scenario corresponds to the standard derivation of passive constructions. An important question is to determine at which point the participial form and DP share features. A possibility is that the unaccusative past participial v, which is deprived of a case feature, is endowed with φ-features. A precondition for the raising of DP to SpecvP could be that it shares features with v.

If one now turns to Latin DPCs, it could be that they resort to a switch, whereas other participial constructions don't. Depending on whether they use a switch or not, they should be characterized as strongly mixed projections or as weakly mixed ones. These two options will be discussed in section 5. Before a decision can be made, it must be shown that DPCs are indeed mixed projections.

59 DPCs as mixed projections

Although the diagnostic properties intended to support the distinction between verbal passives and adjectival passives in English (cf. 28) identified by Wasow seem to be to a large extent transferable to Latin, one doesn't know for the moment whether the participial typology established on the basis of Romance and English data is operative in this language. The examination of the periphrases containing *esse* indicates that Latin didn't ignore the aspectual divide between eventive participles and resultative participles. It is on this basis that Riemann's (1908: 217–218) observations on the ambiguity/non-ambiguity of past participle constructions should be interpreted. He briefly discusses the following made up examples:[17]

(42) a. *templum* clausum est.
temple.NOM close.PART.NOM be.PRES.3SG
'at a particular moment in the past, the temple was closed.' or
'right now, the temple is closed.'
(i.e. a closure took place, now it is done)

b. *templum* clausum fuit.
temple.NOM close.PART.NOM be.PFT-3SG
'in the past, the temple remained closed.'
(during an unspecified period, but it is not anymore).

c. *templum* clausum fuerat.
temple.NOM close.PART.NOM be.PLPFT-3SG
'the temple had remained closed'
(during an unspecified period, but it is not anymore).

Whereas (42a) is ambiguous and can receive an aoristic value or refer to a state of affairs resulting from an anterior event and contemporary with the speech act, only the resultative interpretation is available in (42b) and (42c) and only the latter is possible in Livy's example (43).

---

17 (42a) contains the periphrasis combining a passive past participle with a form of *be* in the present tense that usually functions as a passive perfect. In (42b) and (42c) the passive past participle is associated with a perfect or a pluperfect form of *be*.

(43) bis   deinde   post Numae   regnum   [Ianus]
     twice   afterwards after Numa.GEN reign.ACC [Ianus]
     clausus   fuit...
     close.PART.NOM   be.PFT.3SG
     'twice, since Numa's reign, has the temple of Ianus been closed afterwards.'
     Liv 1.19.3.

This interpretation is also available in the following examples, which respectively contain an auxiliary form in the present tense and a perfect auxiliary form, confirming that the two forms are compatible with the resultative interpretation:[18]

(44) Gallia   est   omnis   diuisa   in partes
     Gaul.NOM   be.PRES.3SG   whole.NOM   divide.PART.NOM   in parts.ACC
     tres.
     three.ACC
     'All Gaul is divided into three parts.'
     Caes, B.G 1.1.1.

(45) omnia   fere,   quae   sunt   conclusa
     all.the.things.NOM   almost   which.NOM   are   comprise.PART.NOM
     nunc   artibus,   dispersa   et   dissipata
     now   arts.ABL   disperse.PART.NOM   and   scattered.PART.NOM
     quondam   fuerunt
     formerly   be.PRF.3PL

---

18 When a contrast is established between the two forms in a complex statement, the perfect periphrasis with *est* clearly receives an aoristic value, whereas the construction with *fuit* is interpreted as a resultative predicative structure (*latae sunt* functions as the perfect passive form of *fero* 'bear' and means 'have been proposed').

(i) ... legum   multitudine,   cum earum   quae
         lois.GEN   multitude.ABL   those.GEN   which.NOM
     latae   sunt, tum uero   quae
     proposed.PART.NOM   be.PRES.3PL (those)   which.NOM
     promulgatae   fuerunt...
     promulgate.PART.NOM   be.PFT.3PL
     'this multitude of laws, some that were passed, others that have been promulgated...'
     Cic, Sest 25.55.

(i) confirms that the opposition between eventive participles and resultative participles was active in Latin.

'almost all the things which are now comprised in the different arts were formerly unconnected and in a state of dispersion.'
Cic, De Orat 1. 187.

The major difference between the predicative periphrastic constructions with *esse* (and those that serve as a basis for Embick's participial typology) and Latin DPCs is that the latter are embedded predications that do not contain *esse* or another auxiliary. Although auxiliary choices cannot be appealed to, the necessity to identify the participial type involved in these constructions imposes itself in a sharp and acute way. In fact, it is easy to show that the participles occurring in the DPCs satisfy all the syntactic criteria that are associated with *eventive* passives.

Several authors mention the reduction of the valency of the participle in the DPC. This generalization is directly contradicted by the facts. In Classical Latin and in the following periods, one encounters DPCs that include an explicit agent complement, DPCs in which the argument selection of the participle is fully realized, and also DPCs containing adverbs and non selected adjuncts.[19]

(i) DPCs with explicit agent complements

(46) *ad me   litteras   misisti,   unas   de*
to 1SG.ACC letters.ACC send.PFT.2SG some.ACC about
legatis   a me   prohibitis   proficisci,
ambassadors.ABL by 1SG.ABL prevent.PART.ABL leave.INF
alteras de   Appianorum   aedificatione impedita,
others   about   Appiani.GEN   building.ABL block.PART.ABL
legi   perinuitus;
read.PFT.1SG   displeased-NOM.
'the letters that you sent me, one about my forbidding legates to leave, the other about stopping the building operations at Appia, were a very unpleasant reading for me.'
Cic, Ad Fam 3. 9. 1.

---

19 The status of past participle *-to-* forms and of present participle *-nt-* forms seems to have evolved in the history of the language, always tending towards a tighter integration into the verbal system. According to Meillet (1928), the *-to-* formation, which was originally adjectival, was only secondarily incorporated into the verbal system and the *perfectum* paradigm. In his study on the present participle, Marouzeau (1910) establishes that, in Plautus's works, one cannot find a single example of a participle used as a verb and taking a nominal direct object (but participles can take a clausal object). Only in the prose works of the Republican period does the present participle begin to manifest fully verbal properties. In Sallust, the participle is "more often used with a complement than intransitively" and "not exclusively in the nominative case" (Marouzeau 1910: 16).

(47) his   enim   honoribus   habitis   Ser. Sulpicio
     these.ABL indeed honors.ABL   returned.PART.ABL   Ser. Sulpicius.DAT
     repudiatae   reiectaeque   legationis
     turn.down.PART.GEN   rejected.PART.GEN-and   deputation.GEN
     ab Antonio   manebit   testificatio   sempiterna.
     by Antonius.ABL   remain.FUT.3SG testimony.NOM eternal.NOM
     'indeed, these honors returned to Ser. Sulpicius will remain an eternal testimony of the refusal and the rejection of the deputation by Antony.'
     Cic, Phil 9. 15.

(ii) DPCs with selected arguments

(48) ... non   abscisum   in duas   partis   exercitum,   cum
         NEG   split.PART.ACC   in two.ACC   parts.ACC   army.ACC   when
     altera   alteri   auxilium   ferre   non   posset,
     one.NOM   the.other.DAT   help.ACC   bring.INF   NEG   could
     causae   fuisse   cogitabant.
     cause.DAT   be.PFT.INF   understand.IMPF.3PL
     'they didn't understand that the scission of the army into two groups, which couldn't help each other, was the cause [of our defeat].'
     Caes, B.C 3. 72. 2.[20]

(iii) DPCs with adjuncts

(49) *post*   mare   Actiacum   Romano   cruore   ...
     after   sea.ACC   of.Actium.ACC   Roman.ABL   blood.ABL
     infectum   *post*   fractas   in Sicilia   classes ...
     spoil.PART.ACC   after   smashed.PART.ACC   in Sicily.ABL   fleets.ACC
     'It was after having spoiled the sea of Actium with Roman blood, ... after the fleets were smashed in Sicily ... '
     Sen, Clem 1.11.1.

It should be remembered that, according to Embick, the property that distinguishes English eventive participles from resultative participles is that the former make the explicit representation of the external argument possible (it generally takes the form of an agentive complement), while the latter don't. One concludes that in (46) and (47), the participle involved is an eventive participle. In the exam-

---

[20] But the participle in this example can also be assigned a resultative interpretation, since the state of division is considered as the cause of the defeat.

ples where no agent is explicitly present, the resultative interpretation is sometimes available, but it cannot be asserted that it is the only possible one.

On the other hand, it is well known that verbal passives essentially reproduce the argument structures that are found in active verbal constructions and, at the same time, that passive verb phrases include a gap corresponding to the moved object complement/direct argument. Eventive participles in the DPC are no exception to this claim, as examples (46)–(49) indicate. This characteristic lends further support to the claim that participles occurring in DPCs have a verbal/eventive status.

The possibility to associate some adverbial types with the participle also indicates that the participle involved is not a resultative nor a stative one. As observed by Bolkestein (1989b), not all adverbs can coexist with resultative participles. Excluded are evaluative adverbs like *recte* "rightly", modal expressions like *uerum* "certainly", "but yet", which are only legitimate in the domains that contain a clause, not a predication. Similar restrictions don't hold in the DPCs, which can contain evaluative adverbs (cf. 50), time adverbs (cf. 51) and manner (cf. 52) adverbs.

(50) *itaque   senatus   ob   ea   feliciter*
       and thus senate.NOM because of these.ACC successfully
       acta   dis   immortalibus   supplicia
       conduct.PART.ACC gods.DAT immortal.DAT thanksgivings.ACC
       decernere.
       vote.INF.
       'and thus, for the success of these well-planned operations, the Senate decreed a thanksgivings to the immortal gods.'
       Sall, Jug 55. 2.

(51) *... incusatae   paulo ante   sterilitatis   oblitus.*
            accuse.PART.GEN a little before sterility.GEN forgetful.NOM
       'forgetting that a little before he had accused her of sterility.'
       Tac, An 14. 63. 1.

(52) *ornant   igitur   in primis   orationem   uerba*
       embellish.PRES-3PL therefore above all.ABL discourse.ACC words.NOM
       relata   contrarie.
       relate.PART.NOM in a contrary way
       'words antithetically used are a great ornament to discourse.'
       Cic, De Orat 2. 263.

Up to now, the DPCs that include a present active participle (cf. 17) have not been taken into consideration. They contradict none of the assumptions that have been put forth in the analysis of past participle constructions. The essential difference that pulls apart present and past participles is that in the former case, the v head can be transitive/unergative, the argument subject of predication originating in the specifier of v, not in the complement position of the root.[21] But in both cases, the derivation of the DPC involves the movement of an argument that is not casually marked, in fact the displacement of the unique argument fulfilling this condition. The externalization of this argument out of the verb phrase creates an empty place within the latter, qualifying it as a predicative domain.

The preceding discussion leaves open the question of the representation of resultative participles. The eventive interpretation of Latin past participles is usually dominant, but some lexical choices or the context may favor the resultative interpretation, with the participial construction referring to an achieved result or to a reached state rather than to an accomplished process or a completed action.[22] The latter interpretation is only available in the absence of an explicit or implicit agent and evaluative adverbs. This way to look at things leaves open the possibility that in Latin, the resultative interpretation of the past participle has no specific syntactic representation, at least no representation distinct from the one of the eventive interpretation. It must be kept in mind that the two readings resort to the same participial affix and involve a movement of the object nominal expression into the subject position.[23] It is thus not implausible to claim that they occur in essentially the same syntactic structure. Technically, the [+ agent] feature is not present on v in the constructions receiving a resultative interpretation. But it is not present either in the eventive constructions containing an unaccusative present participle, cf. *ineunte* in (i), fn. 21. Therefore, the lack of this feature is not a sufficient condition for the resultative interpretation of a participial construc-

---

21 (17) is a structure in which the v of the DPC is unergative, (i) a structure in which it is unaccusative.

(i) qui   homo   cum animo inde   ab   ineunte
     which.NOM   man.NOM   with disposition.ABL   from   begin.PART.PRES.ABL
     aetate   *depugnat*   suo ...
     age.ABL   struggles   his-ABL
     'the man who struggles against his inclination from his earliest age.'
     Pl, Trin 305.

22 In particular, with the verbs whose participle can denote the states that Kratzer (2000) calls the "target states", the two interpretations seem to be equally available, cf. *The windows were all recently opened* and paradigm (42).

23 As observed by Ion Giurgea, unaccusative predicates often resort to distinct participial forms for the resultative and the eventive meanings: past participles are resultative (*casus* 'fallen', past participle of *cado* 'I fall', *uentus*, 'arrived', Past participle of *uenio* 'I come'), present participles are eventive (*cadens* 'falling', *ueniens* 'coming').

tion to be available. The aspectual value turns out to be the crucial dimension in the divide between the two interpretations.[24]

The specificity of the analysis schematized in (33) and (34) is to state that the participial argument in the DPC, which is the subject of predication, originates within the participial vP itself.[25] It appropriately represents the restriction of past participle DPCs to transitive roots, the fact that a specific aspectual interpretation is attached to them, the fact that they convey no deictic temporal interpretation.

The category-changing analysis of participial phrases schematized in (39) and (40), in which the verb phrase is topped by a nominalizing head that is attached rather high in the structure, captures the coexistence of verbal properties and nominal properties, resulting from the cooccurrence of number and aspect specifications. It adequately represents the fact that the past participle in the DPC manifests a range of clearly verbal properties and, at the same time, is included in a phrase that has the external distribution of a nominal expression. The high position of the nominalizer explains why the nominal characteristics manifest themselves at the periphery of the domain. In other words, (39)/(40) characterize DPCs as strongly mixed projections, resulting from a nominalization/deverbalization process.

But an alternative analysis is possible, which would dispense with the projection of a switch above AspP. Chomsky's (2013a, 2015) notion of Labeling and the Labeling Algorithm that goes with it make available an alternative way to turn a predicative domain into an expression with nominal distributional properties. The raising of the participial argument and its adjunction to Aspect in (39) and (40) should suffice to create an exocentric symmetric structure in which the two maximal projections NP and PartP (i.e. AspP) are sisters and share φ-features, if one makes the assumption that AspP, which corresponds to the participial phrase in this analysis, and the Asp head to which the agreeing participle raises are endowed with φ-features (the participial argument obviously is). The label of the whole structure would be <φ, φ>. (53) is the representation corresponding to an eventive participle phrase. The representation of a resultative one would be basically the same.

---

[24] But the aspectual value is different in the two cases, cf. fn 23.
[25] This account is reminiscent of the raising analysis of restrictive relative constructions proposed by Vergnaud (1985), in which the relative antecedent originates within the relative itself and derivationally raises to the specifier position of CP, that is, at the edge of the CP phase. Proleptic structures in Ancient Greek should also probably be analyzed along these lines. In these constructions, the term undergoing prolepsis is also realized at the edge of a CP phase.

(53) [<φ, φ> [NP]φ [AspP [Root-v-Aspevent] [vP ~~NP Root-v~~ [RootP ~~Root NP~~]]]φ]

This analysis assigns a <φ, φ> label to the participial predication structure, making it an appropriate content for nominal positions, without the projection of a category-changing head being necessary.[26] Under this view, the DPC instantiates a case of weak category mixing, as the Acc-*ing* construction does, not a case of strong category mixing, as the category-changing approach presupposes.

Several observations seem to me to militate against this option. First, whether the conditions governing the application of labeling via feature sharing are met in (53) is far from clear. In particular, we don't know whether Aspect is a φ-endowed category. Second, as observed in section 54, other types of participial predication structures exist in Latin, which display word sequences that are identical to the DPC ones, but seem to have quite different properties, which suggest that these structures and the DPC should be assigned distinct analyses. This is the case of the small clause complements to perception and representation verbs, such as (54), and of the absolute ablative construction, illustrated in (55).

(54) *Homerus* Laertam ... colentem
Homer.NOM Laerta.ACC ... cultivate.PART.PRES-ACC ...
agrum *facit.*
field.ACC ... represent.PRES.3SG.
'Homer represents Laerta cultivating his field.'
Cic, *Sen* 54.

(55) ... *regnari* tamen omnes uolebant libertatis
have.kings.INF however all.NOM want.IMPF.3PL freedom.GEN
dulcedine nondum experta.
sweetness.ABL not.yet experience.PART.ABL
'they all inclined to be ruled by a king, because they had not yet tasted the sweetness of freedom.'
Liv 1. 17. 3.

There is absolutely no way to consider them as nominal projections. Small clauses are projections of their predicate, whatever its category, or of a Relator category mediating the relation between the predicate and its subject (cf. den Dikken 2006). It seems reasonable to analyze ablative absolute constructions as seman-

---

26 It is assumed that the labels derived via φ-feature sharing count for the checking of subcategorization requirements and predication relations. See the discussion in chapter II, section 2.

tically tensed CP domains and to assign them the same <φ, φ> label as to finite (root) clauses. DPCs differ from them in not incorporating a T head and in displaying a strictly nominal distribution. These observations, in particular the clearly nominal non propositional status of the DPC, seem to me to support a category-changing account of these structures.

The following section tries to settle the issue by closely looking at the functioning of agreement and case in DPCs.

60 Agreement and case in DPCs

In DPCs, the participle and its subject agree with each other in φ-features, but also in case.[27] The shared morphological case is directly sensitive to the syntactic and categorial environment in which the construction occurs. It is ablative in the expression *ab urbe condita*, where the DPC complements the preposition *a/ab*; it is nominative in the expression *Sicilia amissa*, where the DPC is the subject of a finite verb. In other words, (i) the case of the participial argument and the case borne by the participle covary; (ii) the whole construction and its subject are both case-dependent on the categorial identity and lexical status of the external governing head. This feature of the DPC is a sure indication that its outer boundary, whatever its label, is not opaque and doesn't create a barrier blocking the establishment of syntactic relations with its internal content, at least with its subject. This situation sharply contrasts with what is observed in the English gerund Acc-*ing* construction or with Latin infinitives where the subject is systematically marked for the accusative case, whatever the context.[28] How is the case licensing of the argument subject achieved in DPCs? There are two questions to consider:

(i) How is the case relation between the DPC and the external head established?
(ii) How is case and φ-feature sharing between the participle and its subject achieved?

60.1 The problem

DPCs raise extremely interesting questions concerning the functioning of both case marking and agreement. In example (16) reproduced here as (56), the nominal argument *Sicilia Sardiniaque* controls the value of the gender and number features borne by the participle *amissae*, suggesting that some internal local agreement process is involved. At the same time, the case shared by the nominal argument

---

[27] Participles agree, whether they function as attributive participles, as predicates in a DPC or fulfill a praedicatium function. Elements of the agreeing mechanism described below can no doubt be extended to the other constructions involving a participle.

[28] In Latin infinitives, the accusative shows up on the embedded subject in contexts where no transitive verbal head in the matrix clause governs the infinitive.

(i) Certum est Petrum uenisse.
    certain be.PRES.3SG Petrus.ACC come.INF.PRF
    'It is certain that Petrus came.'

and the participle is exclusively dependent on the identity of the case-assigning head external to the DPC that minimally c-commands it.

(56) angebant   ingentis   spiritus   uirum   Sicilia
     vex.IMPF.3PL immense.GEN   pride.GEN   man.ACC   Sicily.NOM
     Sardiniaque   amissae.
     Sardinia.NOM-and   lose.PART.NOM
     'What vexed this man of immense pride was the loss of Sicily and Sardinia.'
     Liv 21.1. 5

The reason why the nominal expression *Sicilia Sardiniaque* and the participle *amissae* in (54) are marked for the nominative case is that the DPC occupies the grammatical subject position of a tensed clause, which makes nominative case available. But, as shown at length in the preceding sections, other cases than the nominative can be shared.

Haug & Nikitina (2016) argue that the Latin facts impose to adopt a theory of case and agreement different from the standard minimalist approach. I will briefly repeat the observations and ideas that motivate their claim. They observe that there are two dimensions along which theories of agreement may differ.

(i) Agreement can be conceived of as asymmetric (as is the case in minimalist approaches, which distinguish a probe and a goal) or as symmetric. Agreement is asymmetric if the controller and the target are clearly distinguished, that is, if the active features exclusively originate on the controller and are inherited by the target; it is symmetric if "target features have the same status as controller features", if they are independent from one another and if any of the two terms involved can trigger agreement on the other.

(ii) Agreement involves "feature sharing" when the agreement features are initially present on both the controller and the target (they are expressed on both positions); on the contrary, there is no feature sharing if agreement features are present only where they are interpreted.

According to Haug & Nikitina (2016), there are phenomena that require an agreement mechanism that is both symmetric and feature sharing. The DPC is precisely one of them. They characterize DPCs as domains headed by a verbal participle ultimately projecting a noun phrase and propose the following structure.

(57) $[_{NPc}\,[NP_e\,V_{head}\ldots]]$
           where the index c means 'constituent' and the index e refers to 'entity'.

The problem raised by (57) against the asymmetric theories of agreement dispensing with feature sharing is that they provide a mechanism for passing features from heads to their maximal projections – almost all agreement theories do -, "so all the information at V is in principle available at the position of NP$_c$" (p. 884) and a mechanism for passing information from the agreeing head V to its subject NPe, but "no mechanism for passing information in the other direction, from the controller to the target, that is, in the situation under consideration, from the subject NP to its agreeing head V. This is the "wrong direction" for information passing via agreement, since in theories without feature sharing (whether asymmetric or symmetric), the information is collected in the locus of the controller (NP$_e$) only, not that of the target (V) (p. 884–885). Yet this transmission is a necessary move for the structure as a whole to trigger agreement with the verb when it stands in subject position (it can be claimed that the φ-features involved in agreement reside either on the participial subject or on the DPC itself, but not on both). If, on the other hand, feature sharing is an option, it makes it possible to pass the agreement features up the structure and make them available to subsequent agreement relations. The authors conclude that the DPC requires a symmetric and feature-sharing theory of agreement.

I can't do full justice to Haug & Nikitina's (2016) careful account here. They are cautious not to overgeneralize and don't claim to have shown that agreement is always symmetric and always relies on feature sharing. They couch their analysis in a LFG framework and inevitably make assumptions that are contradictory with the minimalist approach adopted here. For example, they take for granted that the complex nominal expression corresponding to the DPC is the projection of the participle itself. NP$_c$ in (57) is the projection of the V head, a claim that surely should be avoided in a minimally constrained framework, at least under this form. The way "controller" and "target" are defined largely differs from the notions of "probe" and "goal" in the Agree theory of syntactic dependencies. The nominal argument is the controller of agreement in their account, but a goal in the minimalist approach. From the definitions they give, it is not clear whether the Chomskyan agreement should be characterized as being of the feature-sharing type or not, since features are present on the probe and the goal from the start (or as a result of inheritance), but are valued in the course of the derivation.

Can the agreement and case properties of DPCs be accounted for using a derivational asymmetric theory of agreement? The answer seems to be positive.

60.2 Formalizing agreement and case assignment in DPCs

Two possible lines of research should be explored. The first one consists in claiming that two steps are involved in the derivation of agreement and case relations in (58b).[29] Suppose that the head that makes it possible to achieve internal agreement is nothing other than n.

(58) a. *Sicilia amissa Hamilcarem angebat.*

b. T [$_{nP}$ n [NP [$_{AspP}$ [$_{Asp}$ PART] [$_{vP}$ ...]]]]
where T is the external "governing" head

The φ-features (that is, the number and gender features) of the head n functioning as a probe target both the features borne by the nominal argument and those associated with participial inflection and assigns them the same value. The case feature on *Sicilia* is also copied onto *amissa*. But this case is not valued at the nP-level because no head internal to nP makes a case feature available. Neither n, nor the participle whose φ-matrix is defective (it has no [person] feature) do. The case value shared by the two elements can only be fixed at the post-nP level, when the computation reaches the T-level.[30] At this level, T tries to establish an Agree relation with the case features on *Sicilia* and on *amissa*. The Agree relation is successful this time. Its effect is that the two unvalued case features internal to the DPC take the value of the case borne by the governing head T, namely nominative.[31] The case valuations of the two elements can be thought of as being simultaneous. But a proviso must be introduced if one assumes that they are successive. In order to ensure that *amissa* remains an appropriate goal for T after T has established a relation with *Sicilia*, a survival principle must be defined, to the effect that the features on T, although marked for deletion, aren't erased until the next higher phase head (matrix C in the case under consideration) has been

---

29 The nominal argument is noted NP in (58b), because nominal expressions can be argued to be NPs, not DPs, in Latin, see section 6.

30 One can also think of the case features on *Sicilia* and *amissa* as variable features, marked as being bound to get the same value, but a value that is known only at the post-nP level. Alternatively, one can propose that the shared case is "any case" and that all the structures where its value doesn't match that of the governing head are filtered out.

31 The alert reader has no doubt noticed that the analysis that has just been developed is a transposition of the one Chomsky (2001) proposes for the Icelandic sentences of the type of (i), where *caught* and *several fish* independently agree with T in gender, number and (nominative) Case.

(i) T seem [there to have been several fish caught]

inserted.³² A potential difficulty raised by (58b) is that the intervening n head should block the relation between T and each element of the pair NP+Asp. This difficulty vanishes if the participle form raises to n and the nominal argument raises to its specifier.³³

This category-changing analysis shares with Haug & Nikitina's one the claim that there is a kind of NP-cycle in which the relation between the participle and its subject is dealt with, before the relation between the external head and the DPC as a whole is considered. It is not fully satisfying however because it doesn't take into consideration a generally overlooked feature of the DPC: The participle seems to indifferently follow or precede the participial argument, without the position of the two elements with respect to each other being governed by emphasis considerations. The participle follows in (56)/(58), it precedes in the following, often commented Tacitus's example.

(59) ...*cum*   occisus   dictator   Caesar   aliis
       when   kill.PART.NOM   dictator.NOM   Caesar.NOM   some.DAT
     pessimum   *aliis*   *pulcherrimum*   *facinus*
      the.most.horrible.NOM   others.DAT   the.most.beautiful.NOM   deed.NOM
     uideretur.
      seem.SUBJ.IMPF.3SG
     'when the murder of the dictator Caesar appeared to some the most horrible, to others the most glorious of deeds ... '
     Tac, Ann 1.8.6.

This state of affairs shouldn't be taken as evidence that Latin word order is free, which it surely is not, but reflects a constitutive feature of DPCs. A simple option would be to claim that the participial argument has the possibility to raise to the edge either in the overt syntax or at LF (in which case the relevant Agree relations would be established in the covert syntax). An unfortunate consequence of this scenario would be that a morphological property, the overt case marking of the argument and of the participle, would be dependent on a process taking place at LF, which is quite unusual. A second option would be to claim T has access to the participial argument whatever its position within the DPC, because, when it precedes, the participle doesn't function as an intervener and because no phase

---

32 On the Survival Principle, see Pesetsky & Torrego (2001).
33 This category-changing analysis shares with Haug & Nikitina's one the claim that there is a kind of NP-cycle in which the relation between the participle and its subject is dealt with, before the relation between the external head and the DPC as a whole is considered.

boundary blocks the establishment of a relation between T and NP/Asp. There are two ways to derive this result. One can rely on Chomsky's (2001) conception of the derivation by phase in which an Agree relation can involve a probe and a goal separated by a phase boundary as long as the next higher phase head (C in the case under consideration) has not been inserted. Under this view, T has access to the participial argument whatever its position within the DPC, because, when it precedes the participle doesn't function as an intervener and because nP doesn't function as a barrier as long as C has not been inserted. A simpler option would be to assume that only DPs, not nPs, define phases. As shown in the next section, nominal expressions should be analyzed as NPs in Latin, not DPs. To explain that the participle doesn't function as an intervener when it precedes the argument, the two valuation relations can be taken to be simultaneous.

Similar scenarios can be proposed for the structures in which the external licensing head is a v head, rather than T, and the NPC and its subject are marked for the accusative case. But other situations arise that are potentially problematic for this analysis. If one looks at the morphological cases which can be shared, it appears that, besides the nominative and the accusative, the genitive and the dative case also can, as well as oblique and inherent cases, for example the ablative case that marks the complement of a subset of prepositions. The difficulty the analysis is faced with is that a governing head is not systematically present in the immediate locality of the relevant DPCs (the evidence supporting a head licensing genitive Case is not as strong as the one in favor of the categories T and v) and that, when such a head is present, it is not necessarily endowed with φ-features (this is the case of prepositions, although there is no doubt that inflected prepositions in Welsh bear such features). I cannot think of any satisfactory solution to propose to solve the difficulty, which, anyway, far exceeds the DPC question and requires a sharpening of the way morphological case is assigned.

Nothing was said up to now about the second line of research, the one that dispenses with a nominalizer and relies on a structure like (60) (repeated from 53), resulting from the raising of the argument and from labeling via φ-feature sharing.

(60) T [$_{<φ, φ>}$ [NP]$_φ$ [$_{AspP}$ [Root-v-Asp$_{event}$] [$_{vP}$ ~~NP Root-v~~ [$_{RootP}$ ~~Root NP~~]]]$_φ$]

The major difference with structure (59b) is that no phase boundary intervenes between the probe T and the goals NP and Asp. The φ- and case features of the two syntactic objects *amissa* and *Sicilia* independently agree with the φ- and case features of T at the T'-level. I leave it to the reader to check that this analysis is not in a better position than the n-analysis to account for the difficulties that have just been discussed: the free word order of participles and their argument, the functioning of morphological case. Since there is no indication that the labeling account should be preferred, I will adopt the category-switching account, which, it seems to me, has a greater plausibility, because it draws a sharp distinction between the constructions that are in no way nominal, like (54) and (55), and the DPC, which uncontroversially is.

Summarizing, a minimalist theory in which agreement is asymmetric (and in which the agreeing elements do not necessarily directly agree with each other, but indepedently share features with the same probe) is in a position to account for the salient properties of the DPC, contrary to what Haug & Nikitina claim.[34] This is indeed a satisfactory result.

60.3 A particular case

One also finds structures in which agreement involves the neuter gender. Storme (2010) provides the following example from Quintus Curtius.

(61) plerique   amicorum   Alexandri   non tam   criminum,
     most.NOM   friends.GEN   Alexander.GEN   NEG so much   crimes.GEN
     quae   palam   obiciebantur,   atrocitatem   quam
     who.NOM   overtly   be.in.the.front.IMPF.3PL   horror.ACC   than
     memoriam   occisi   per illos   Parmenionis,   quod
     memory.ACC   kill.PART.GEN by them.ACC   Parmenion.GEN   which.ACC
     tacitum   prodesse   reis   apud
     kept.silent.about.ACC   be.useful.INF   defendants.DAT in.front.of
     regem   poterat,   intuebantur.
     king.ACC   can.IMPF.3SG consider.IMPF.3PL

'Most Alexander's friends had an eye not so much to the atrocity of the crimes that were openly laid as to the memory of the murder of Parmenion, which could secretly help the defendants with the king.'
Curt, Hist 10.1.6.

As observed by Storme, the antecedent of *quod* can only be the phrase *occisi per illos Parmenionis*. The neuter form of the pronoun is used without the nominal

---

[34] To be fair, a feature-sharing approach like the one developed by Frampton, Gutman, Legate & Yang (2000), in which a mechanism of unification ensures that whatever happens to the feature set of *amissa* affects the features of *Sicilia* and conversely, would be a serious alternative to the one that has just been proposed and would come very close to Haug & Nikitina's treatment. The authors in fact refer to Frampton, Gutman, Legate & Yang's work.

argument being neuter, which suggests that agreement is here established with the nominalized predicative content. Examples of this type do not necessarily require an analysis different from the one that was developed in 60.2. There is every reason to believe that the predicative domain as a whole and the nominal argument are marked for the same Case, namely genitive. The observed mismatch exclusively concerns gender and number features;[35] the DPC as a whole has a φ-feature specification different from that of *occisi* and *Parmenionis*, the DPC being neuter singular, the nominal argument and the participle being masculine singular. It looks as if the φ-features borne by the DPC take a default value, whereas the φ-features associated with the nominal argument and the participle are the interpretable features of the nominal argument. The situation illustrated by (51) can only arise if the nominal argument and the DPC as a whole count as equidistant from the governing head (*memoriam* in Quintus Curtius's example). Otherwise, the node dominating the DPC would function as an intervener for the relation between the external head and the subject argument. This condition is fulfilled if the participial argument occupies the edge of the DPC and if one adopts Pesetsky & Torrego's (2001) definition of "closeness".[36]

(62) **Closeness**
Y is closer to K than X if K c-commands Y and Y c-command X.

Recall that the idea behind this definition is that the metrics of closeness involves c-command rather than node counting, which implies that in a structure like (63), where NP occupies the edge of the DPC, both NP and α count as the closest constituent to X.

---

[35] Concerning (61), and the way it differs from the standard case, Ion Giurgea observes that the contrast is not real because the 3rd person singular form appearing in (61) is also the default form that would be used if agreement was established with the predicative content, as is the case in (51). On the contrary, (i), which contains a plural verb, is a case where agreement *is not* established with the predicative domain as a whole.

(i) (*dixit*) se missum... qui Catilinae
he said himself.ACC send.PART.ACC who.NOM Catilina.DAT
nuntiaret ne eum Lentulus et Cethegus...
tell.SUBJ.IMPF.3SG that.NEG he.ACC Lentulus.NOM and Cethegus.NOM
deprehensi terrerent
arrest.PART.NOM frighten.SUBJ.IMPF.3PL
'He said he had been sent to inform Catilina that the arrest of Lentulus and Cethegus ought not to alarm him.'
Sall, Cat 48. 4

[36] See also ch. VI, sct. 28.

(63) X [α NP [. . .]]

This is the case, because the edge position is immediately dominated by αP and that c-command excludes domination. A standard assumption is that it is usually the closest constituent to some head that satisfies the subcategorization requirement of this head.[37] If X selects [N] in (63), both the NP subject and the αP DPC are in a position to fulfill the subcategorization requirement of X. A similar situation holds for Case licensing. Both the participial argument and the DPC itself can enter into an Agree relation with X, with the result that the Case borne by the argument and the Case borne by the DPC are the same Case and match the value of the Case feature made available by X.

---

[37] The subcategorization requirement of a head X can also be thought of as an uninterpretable feature on X, that has to be valued and eliminated via the establishment of an Agree-relation with the subcategorized element.

61 The origin of linguistic variation

It is now time to ask why French allows with great difficulty or even excludes the dominant use of the participle exemplified in (2a) and (2b), repeated here in (64a) and (64b).

(64) a. * *La révolte réprimée n' a pas mis fin aux troubles.*
       the revolt repressed NEG has NEG put end to-the troubles

   b. * *Depuis la digue reconstruite, les touristes*
       since the dyke rebuilt the tourists
       affluent au Mont Saint-Michel.
       come in flocks to-the Mont Saint-Michel

French, which has a definite article at its disposal, includes the functional head D (Determiner) in its categorial inventory and this category functions as the head of nominal expressions, therefore analyzable as DP projections. The representation associated with *la révolte réprimée* or *la digue reconstruite* in French is thus (65), not (39) or (58b) (the participial argument is represented in its first Merge position):

(65) Passive participle
   [DP D [nP n [AspP [Asp-event] [vP v [RootP Root ~~DP~~]]]]

The presence of D radically affects the way the participial argument is marked for Case. If a DP level is present in the structure, the expression as a whole is casually licensed by the local environment, but the participial argument is not. If it indeed raises to the specifier position of AspP, labeling the resulting structure α as <φ, φ>, it doesn't stand at the edge of the DP phase, that is, the specifier of D, the only position that is accessible to an external case marker in (65). A natural hypothesis is that, in the grammatical systems that are endowed with a DP, the D head blocks the casual licensing of the subject noun phrase in DPCs, which are thus excluded. The well-formedness of (66) follows from the fact that, in the corresponding representation, the noun phrase contains no nominal expression requiring to be casually marked, besides the one that is headed by the lexical noun.[38]

---

[38] This analysis implies that in languages that have an article at their disposal, the well-formed [DP + PartP] sequences are not structured as in (65). In the modifier use, the participle is adjoined to a DP projection. In other uses, like the *praedicatiuum*, it is adjoined to a higher projection.

(66) La répression   n'   a   pas mis fin aux   troubles.
      the repression NEG has NEG put end to-the troubles
      'The repression didn't put an end to the troubles.'

On the contrary, in the languages that have no explicit determiner and, in particular no definite article, nominal expressions should not be analyzed as DP projections. The DP level being absent, it is the nP projection that requires to be case marked. The representation associated to passive participles is thus (39)/(58b). But both the participial phrase as a whole and the participial argument require to be casually marked. The participial argument fulfills this condition if it moves to the periphery of the nP domain at some stage in the derivation.[39] Latin is a language of this type.

However, the Ancient Greek data collected by Denizot (2017) and those of other languages indicate that this hypothesis should be sharpened. Ancient Greek (i) has a definite article at its disposal, and (ii) allows DPCs. A possible way to solve the difficulty consists in making the following two assumptions: First, the existence of a definite article in a language L provides an unequivocal clue in favor of the presence of the D head in the categorial inventory of L; second, the crucial dimension in the DPC phenomenon is not the absence of the definite article in L, but the possibility of building nominal expressions without a determiner. In the languages where indefinite nominal expressions do not resort to an article, noun phrases are analyzed either as DP projections (in the structures with a definite article) or as nP projections (in article-less structures). This is precisely what Ancient Greek noun phrases are when no article is present: nP projections. This assumption also accounts for the well-formedness of DPCs in Old French (*lèse majesté* . . .), in Italian (*dopo letta questa risposta, Gerusalemme liberata,* . . .), in English (*Paradise lost,* . . .).[40]

---

39 See the discussion in sect. 60.2.

40 Contrary to what examples (64) seem to indicate and contrary to the predictions of our analysis, one occasionally encounters examples of DPCs in modern and contemporary French. And yet, the time when nominal expressions could be built without a determiner has long been gone.

(i) Sois beni,   juste Ciel! de   mon sort adouci. Molière, *L'Etourdi* 1386
     be blessed   God,   for my fate softened.

Lerch's (1912) lists provide a host of examples taken from Maupassant's works.

(ii) C' était   son rêve   accompli.
     it was   his dream   come true

From the point of view of general linguistics, asking why French doesn't allow DPCs as liberally as Latin does and is often forced to resort to nominalization is as important as explaining why Latin has this construction and instantiates the *Sicilia amissa* effect. With respect to Latin, the well-formedness of DPCs goes along with a defining property of the language – the fact that nominal expressions should not be analyzed as DP projections. Contemporary French, on the contrary, can only resort to nominalization in the same contexts, because the internal structure of nominal expressions includes a D category, which blocks case assignment to the participial argument by an external marker. The predicative relation thus cannot be represented, in a natural way, by a sequence nominal expression+participial phrase. Only an eventive/resultative nominalization can provide the syntactic support that this interpretation requires.

(iii) *Il s'était souvenu de la promesse faite.*
 he had remembered of the promise made

(iii) *torturé par la peur du crime découvert*
 tortured by the fear of-the crime discovered

I will assume that most of these examples should be taken as conscious and learned imitations of Latin syntax.

62 Conclusion

We are now in a position to answer the questions that were raised at the beginning of this study.[41]
(i) Latin DPCs should be analyzed as nP (non-DP) nominal projections.[42] They are strongly mixed categories.
(ii) The raising of the participial argument to the external specifier and the concomitant raising of the participle to Asp or to n explain why NP+PartP combinations define predication structures.
(iii) The participial argument and the participle are both accessible to case licensing by a minimally c-commanding external head, because no phasal boundary intervenes between these elements and the external head.
(iv) The participial argument and the participle share φ-features because they both independently agree with the nominalizer n.

Two factors seem to play a decisive role in the well-formedness of the DPC in Latin. On the one hand, participial syntax takes advantage of the fact that the language allows the coexistence of verbal (aspect) and nominal (number, gender) properties within the same domains. On the other hand, the possibility to build nominal expressions without an article in some languages makes available an analysis of participle constructions as non-DP nominal projections, in which the

---

41 Both the DPC and structures with a nominal predicate were grammatical in Latin, as the parallelism between *post te cognitum* 'after knowing you' and *post te consulem* 'after you have been a consul' shows. The property shared by the two constructions is of course that they embed a predication structure, only the nature of the predicate changes, nominal vs. participial. Both are excluded in contemporary French and in contemporary English. Jaume Mateu (personal communication) rightly observes that it would be a mistake to develop dissociate accounts of the joint grammaticality or ungrammaticality of the two constructions. The feasability of extending the analysis developed in this section to other predication structures must be carefully evaluated. Just as marginal cases of DPCs can be found in modern and contemporary French (see fn. 40), it is possible to encounter cases where a nominal predication structure is built as the complement to a preposition. But only *avec* in contemporary French seems to allow this type of construction:

(i) Avec Fouché remercié par l' empereur, une situation nouvelle s'installe.
    With Fouché dismissed by the emperor a situation new arises

(ii) Avec Fouché ministre de l'intérieur, ceci ne serait jamais arrivé
     with Fouché Home Secretary this NEG be.COND.PRES ever happened

42 This account presupposes that Latin demonstratives and possessives are not instances of D and are not syntactic heads determining a DP projection.

nominal argument is accessible to an external case marker. In this respect, the Latin phenomenon indicates that, contrary to what is standardly assumed, an abstract D category is not necessarily included in the representation of nominal expressions in the languages and constructions that do not display a definite article.

This study only tackles one type of participial embedded predicative constructions. Other types exist, which usually display word sequences that are identical to DPCs. Besides the absolute ablative construction and the small clauses complementing predicates of perception and representation, which have been briefly discussed at the end of section 57, one should mention the gerundive dominant construction, which is formally parallel to the DPC, although its distribution is more constrained and its aspectual interpretation quite different, since it is construed as an eventuality, as a virtual and prospective process. The latter difference is manifest in (67):

(67) *per totum hiemis quies. inter* labores *aut*
during all.ACC winter.GEN rest.NOM between works.ACC either
iam exhaustos *aut* mox exhauriendos...
already accomplish.PART.ACC or soon accomplish.GER.ACC...
'the winter's rest between works that had already been accomplished and those that soon would be ... '
Liv 21. 21. 8.

The dominant gerundive construction should be analyzed along the same lines as the DPC, that is as a non-DP nominal projection including a vP domain. This is not the case of the other two, which in no way are nominal.

Other participial structures, those where the participle has the status of an attributive modifier and those where it is merged as an adjunct must also rely on different functional architectures and have different derivational histories. Participial adjuncts can be thought of as included in a small clause structure with a PRO subject. No null or overt subject is associated with participials functioning as restrictive modifiers. If a category-switching head is present in their structure, it can only be an adjectivalizer a.

If these speculations are on the right track, it must be concluded that embedded prediction structures can come under different labels and, probably, in different sizes.

Abbreviations of classical sources

Caes.	Caesar	
	B.C	De bello ciuili
	B.G.	De bello Gallico
Catul.	Catullus	
Cic.	Cicero	
	Att	Ad Atticum
	De orat	De oratore
	Off	De officiis
	Fam	Ad familiares
	Phil	Orationes Philippicae
	Sen	De senectute
	Sest	Pro Sestio
	Tusc	Tusculanae disputationes
	Verr	In Verrem
Curt.	Quintus Curtius	
	Hist	Historiae Alexandri Magni
Juv.	Juvenal	
Liv.	Livy	
Pl.	Plautus	
	Amph	Amphitruo
	Bacch	Bacchides
	Cas	Casina
	Cis	Cistellaria
	Curc	Curculio
	Mil	Miles gloriosus
	Most	Mostellaria
	Poen	Poenulus
	Trin	Trinummus
Sall	Sallust	
	Cat	De coniuratione Catilinae
	Jug	De bello Jugurthino
Tac	Tacitus	
	Ann	Annales
Verg	Virgil	
	Georg	Georgica

XI Facts and events, attitudinal objects and states of affairs

It is well known that one of the salient features of Chomsky's grammatical models since the 60s has been the complete dismissal of external semantics and the development of a systematic critique of the traditional notion of reference as a relation to the external world. This position is maintained and even accentuated in the Minimalist Program (cf. Chomsky 2000b, 2013b). But in the search for a characterization of nonfiniteness encompassing all its aspects, one cannot avoid adopting a semantic perspective, at least provisionally, and inquiring about the relation of form to meaning.

The reference to propositions, facts, events and states undoubtedly is a pervasive feature of human language and thought. The identification of the syntactic forms and lexical resources that natural languages use to represent these abstract semantic entities is directly relevant to the questions dealt with in this book. It must be determined which ontological categories are involved in the syntactic functioning of nonfinite complementation and are accepted by the speakers when they use these structures. It should also be asked whether the ontological categories that natural languages commit themselves to are those that have been isolated by semantic and philosophical research. The answer that can be provided for the second question, which stands at the interface between semantics, the philosophy of language and the philosophy of mind, much depends on the ontology that is adopted. Several ones have been proposed, some of them parsimonious, others more prolific, see Vendler (1967), Menzel (1975), Portner (1991a, 1991b, 1994), Asher (1993), Zucchi (1993) and more recently Moltmann (2013). Deciding which one should be preferred far exceeds the limits of this work. I will thus focus on the first question. The aim of this chapter is a strictly linguistic one, namely to make explicit the way the various NFDs studied in this book are distributed into the major ontological classes isolated by previous research.

Let us take for granted that propositional and nominal complements act as expressions functioning as arguments in the logico-semantic relations expressed by selecting verbs. The problem can be tackled from two different but complementary angles: (i) one can classify verbal predicates in function of the semantic type of the objects they select. (ii) one can characterize syntactic structures in function of the type of predicates they function as arguments of and of the type of semantic object they represent. I will basically follow the second line of research. The question of interest to the linguist is whether and to what extent the various syntactic nonfinite structures that natural languages have at their disposal are semantically specialized.

A familiar divide that is largely reflected in the syntax of clausal/nominal embedding is that between assertion/belief and factivity. These notions were shown to provide the semantic underpinning for a wide range of complementation patterns.[1] Some languages appear to resort to distinct syntactic forms in order to refer to assertions/beliefs and to refer to facts, others use the same forms. Other semantic dimensions, which are partly independent from the preceding distinction, turn out to be relevant to the semantic characterization of nonfinite domains: the presuppositional/non-presuppositional divide, the *realis/irrealis* divide. Again, it is plausible to think that these distinctions involve categories of different ontological classes. The question that arises is how some languages can choose to represent them by resorting to distinct syntactic structures, while others do not express them at all.

The results of this survey turn out to be relatively modest. A correspondence no doubt exists between syntactic forms and categories of meaning and major tendencies can indeed be identified. But the relation is almost never strictly one-to-one. Moreover, if differentiation patterns are easily detected within a single language, this is not the case when different languages are compared. This makes it difficult to draw general conclusions.

---

[1] But the dividing line between the two classes is often blurred, see the appendix to ch. VIII.

63 Do gerund clauses name facts?

If one follows Vendler's (1967) early characterization, a divide should be established between the reference to events and the reference to facts. In (1), the nominal object refers to an event; in (2), which differs in meaning from (1) and is also a semantic proposition, the *that*-clause denotes a fact; in (3), which is synonymous with (2), the expression *the fact that*..., which has the shape of a complex noun phrase, no doubt refers to a fact.

(1) *Mary remembers John's arrival.*

(2) *Mary remembers that John arrived.*

(3) *Mary remembers the fact that John arrived*

The difference between the two sets is roughly as follows: Events (and processes and actions) are objects that are located, take place and hold at a certain time and lack truth conditions; on the contrary, facts (and results) are not located, do not take place or begin or last in any sense and have a truth-value.[2] Vendler contrasts predicates like *surprised everyone* that take a fact as an argument and time-specifying predicates like *occurred yesterday, took a long time, lasted two hours* that select event-denoting arguments. In English, derived nominals fit into both frames, *for-to*-clauses and *that*-clauses only fit into the former.

(4) a. *John's disappearance*   *surprised all of us.*
     b. *For Mary to mow the lawn*
     c. *That John disappeared*

(5) a. *The eruption of the volcano*   *occurred yesterday.*
     b. # *For the volcano to erupt* ...
     c. # *That the volcano erupted*

From (4) and (5), it can be concluded that *for-to*-clauses and *that*-clauses, which do not fit into the frame __ *occurred yesterday*, are not appropriate vehicles for eventualities, but denote facts or propositions.

---

[2] See also Asher (1993: 16): "propositions do not have spatio-temporal location or causal efficacy".

Vendler extends the discussion to the characterization of gerund constructions, which turn out to be very picky about the kind of predicates they combine with. Contrary to nominal gerunds that may function as arguments to eventuality predicates like *took a long time, is slow* . . ., Poss-*ing* and Acc-*ing* structures cannot, which could suggest that they are not appropriate vehicles for events and exclusively denote propositions of a certain type.³

(6) a. The breaking of the window   occurred yesterday.
     b. # John accidentally shooting his wife   occurred last night.
     c. # Fred shooting Bill   took place behind the bar.

(7) a. Mary's mowing of the lawn   surprised all of us.
     b. Her having mowed the lawn
     c. Mary's mowing the lawn
     d. Mary mowing the lawn

In later years, some of the ontologies derived from Vendler took the notion coupled with that of *event* to be that of *proposition*, not that of *fact*. At first sight, *facts* and *propositions* seem to be notions quite remote from each other. And nowhere in his article does Vendler use the term "proposition". But the characterization of *fact* that he provides (it has been reproduced above) is highly reminiscent of the one that is usually given for the notion of *proposition*.⁴ In his view, facts seem to be just true propositions. As Benjamin Spector oberves, there is no conflict between the possibility to embed the direct argument of a predicate like *remember* in a *the fact that* . . . structure, this argument being propositional in nature. In examples (2) and (3), *remember* is factive and since everything that Mary remembers is true, the *that*-clause complement to *remember* should admit a *the fact that* . . . con-

---

3 Vendler (1967: 126) discusses the following paradigm:

(i)   John's playing of poker is sloppy.
(ii)   *John's playing poker is sloppy.
(iii)   ? John's playing of poker is unlikely.
(iv)   John's playing poker is unlikely.

The expression *is sloppy* defines a context hosting events, processes, actions. Nominal gerunds fit naturally in this context, verbal gerunds do not, cf. (i) vs. (ii). The expression *is unlikely* defines a context where semantic propositions are welcome. Poss-*ing* gerunds roughly fit in this environment, nominal gerunds do not.

4 See also Asher (1993: 16): "propositions do not have spatio-temporal location or caisal efficacy".

struction as a paraphrase and it should be possible to say *What Mary remembers is true/an indisputable fact*, which is indeed the case.[5]

But it is easy to discover cases where only the notion of fact or that of proposition is appropriate, which suggests that they cannot be taken to be equivalent.

Asher's 1993 and Zucchi's 1993 studies confirm that the contexts where verbal gerund constructions occur are contexts where the selecting verb imposes the propositional reading of its complement. They are welcome with predicates like *remember, imagine, be aware of*. The verb *deny* can also take a gerund as its complement, which can only be interpreted as a proposition, not as an event or as a fact, since it doesn't refer to a real occurrence.

(8) a. *I imagined John('s) eating the apple quickly.*
    b. *Naima remembers Trane('s) playing My favorite things that night.*
    c. *John is informed about Chomsky('s) lecturing to a packed auditorium at the university.*

(9) *He denied seeing her at the opera.*

But it is well-known that a large number of propositional attitude verbs, which take *that*-clauses or *(for)-to*-clauses or complex NPs as objects, exclude verbal gerunds. *Believe* is one of them.

(10) a. *? Sam believed Fred hitting of Bob.*
     b. ** Sam believed Fred's hitting of Bob.*
     c. ** Sam believed Fred hitting Bob.*
     d. *Sam believed Fred to have hit Bob.*
     e. *Sam believed that Fred had hit Bob.*
     f. *Sam believed the claim that Fred had hit Bob.*

From the contrast between (8), and (10b), (10c), Asher concludes that gerunds denote facts. Indeed, gerund phrases easily combine with predicates that define prototypical contexts for facts, not only factive/emotive verbs (cf. examples 7), but also causative verbs (cf. 11), whose complements are proposition-like intensional entities.

---

[5] Note that an event-denoting expression cannot be embedded in a *the fact that . . .* or *he fact of . . .* structure.

(i) **Mary remembers the fact of John's arrival.*

(11) *John hitting Mary made her mad.*

For his part, Zucchi (1993: 207) discusses an interpretive phenomenon that shows that gerunds do not systematically name facts, but also establish that their bare denotation is not a proposition either. If Poss-*ing* constructions systematically denoted facts, (12a) should be contradictory, as (12b) is.

(12) a. *We prevented his succumbing to the temptation by hiding all the cookies from him.*
      b. *We prevented the fact that John succumbed to the temptation by hiding all the cookies from him.*

The existence of a non-contradictory reading of (12a), he claims, shows that "Poss-*ing* NPs like *the soprano's performing the song* need not denote facts" and suggests that the semantic distinction between (13a)/(13b) and (8c), repeated here as (13c)

(13) a. * *John knows the soprano's performing the song.*
      b. * *The soprano's performing the song is false.*[6]
      c. *John is informed of the soprano's performing the song.*

> is not the distinction between propositions and facts, but, more generally, the distinction between propositions, things that can be true or false and can be objects of belief, and states of affairs, things of which one may be aware, ..., but which ... cannot properly be said to have the property of truth or falsehood, or be objects of belief. [Zucchi 1993: 207]

To account for the ill-formedness of (10b), (10c), he proposes that what a gerund expression basically denotes is not a proposition, but a smaller entity, a "state-of-affairs", out of which the grammar provides a way of creating syntactic units denoting propositions.

Two additional observations should be integrated into the discussion. The first one is that, in quite specific contexts, gerund clauses can express events, not facts. This is at least what a test put forth by Menzel (1975) suggests. To better identify the type of ontological category gerund constructions refer to, Menzel resorts to constructions in which an abstract noun predicated of a complement clause in subject position "names" the semantic category to which the clause belongs. The two nouns *fact* and *event* can be found in gerund environments, as already observed by Vendler (1967).

---

6 Similarly, corresponding to (12a) and (12b), we don't have (i).

(i) *John's winning the race is true.

(14) a. *John winning the race is an indisputable fact.*
 b. *John's winning the race was a notable event.*

These data seem to indicate that gerund clauses with an overt subject can freely express facts or events.

Second, it was concluded in ch. IV that the two gerund types, Acc-*ing* and Poss-*ing*, differ as to their categorial identity - the former are CP projections, the latter DP domains. They are possible in almost the same range of contexts and neither can function as complement to the prototypical verbs of propositional attitude (*believe* ...) and verbs of saying (*assert* ...). As a consequence, the joint ungrammaticality of (10b) and (10c) and the joint grammaticality of (7c) and (7d) should not be traced back to their categorial identity. It remains that each type is semantically specialized. Poss-*ing*, which is uncontroversially nominal and definite, is also generally presuppositional (in that the semantic content conveyed by the gerund constituent constitutes specific/presupposed information with respect to the main clause). Acc-*ing*, which is clausal, is not presuppositional. The following examples show this clearly.

(15) a. *It's unlikely that Mary regretted John's coming to visit her.*
 [presuppositional]

 b. *It's unlikely that Mary regretted John coming to visit her.*
 [presuppositional]

(16) a. *It's unlikely that Mary discussed John's coming to visit her.*
 [presuppositional]

 b. *It's unlikely that Mary discussed John coming to visit her.*
 [non-presuppositional]

When embedded under a factive verb, as is the case in (15a) and (15b), a gerund clause usually designates a fact and the construction has a presuppositional interpretation. Poss-*ing* constructions are particularly suited for this role, since they are inherently definite and pick out already familiar events. Acc-*ing* constructions are also possible choices in this context. But they can also be interpreted as indefinite expressions and function as the argument of a restricted set of proposition-selecting predicates. Factive predicates are special precisely in that they define contexts in which the definite/indefinite asymmetry is suspended, so that the two types of verbal gerund phrases are possible choices. Nominal gerunds, just like action and derived nominals, are also welcome as complements to factive predicates, when they are specific, hence presuppositional in some sense.

In conclusion, neither the distinction between facts and events, nor that between propositions and events that prominently figure in the ontologies derived from Vendler are in a position to account for the full complexity of the data. An alternative dichotomy will be substituted for the Vendlerian ones in section 65. For the moment, Welsh verbo-nominal clauses will be looked at, relying on the standard distinction between propositions and events.

64 Verbo-nominal clauses

The semantic properties of Welsh *i*-clauses differ from the ones displayed by English gerund clauses. If one looks at the Welsh equivalents of examples (12), an asymmetry arises: (17a) is semantically well-formed, but (17b) is not.[7]

(17) a. *Ffaith ddiamheuol yw i John ennill y ras.*
Fact   indisputable is *i* John win the race
'That John won the race is an indisputable fact.'

b. #*Digwyddiad pwysig   oedd i John ennill y   ras.*
Event   important was *i* John win   the race

This contrast indicates that, contrary to gerund constructions, *i*-initial clauses are appropriate vehicles for propositions or facts, but can't denote events or states-of-affairs. The fact that they are not possible subjects for verbs of occurrence points towards the same conclusion.[8]

(18) a. #*Digwyddodd am hanner dydd i John wneud hyn.*
happened   on half   day   *i* John do   this

b. #*Digwyddodd y   llynedd   i'r   llosgfynydd echdorri.*
occurred   the last year *i* the volcano   erupt

c. #*Fe   barhaodd am amser hir i'r   llosgfynydd echdorri.*
PRT lasted   for time   long *i* the volcano   erupt

d. #?*Digwyddodd   ddwywaith i John ennill y   ras.*
occurred   twice   *i* John win   the race

Another property that sharply distinguishes VN-clauses from gerund constructions is that they are allowed to function as complements to epistemic/declarative verbs, which are prototypical examples of proposition-selecting predicates.

---

[7] The same contrast is found with *bod*-clauses. (i) is well-formed, (ii) is not.

(i) *Ffaith ddiamheuol yw   bod John wedi ennill y   ras.*
Fact   indisputable is   *bod* John PERF win   the race.

(ii) #*Digwyddiad pwysig   oedd bod John wedi ennill y   ras.*
Event   important was *bod* John PERF win   the race.

[8] Examples (18) are ill-formed, although the *i*-clause has been extraposed at the right edge, cf. ch. IX.

(19) a. *Dywedodd   Susan i Fred fwrw   Bob.*
said   Susan i Fred hit   Bob
'Susan said that Fred had hit Bob.'

b. *Credai   Sam i Fred fwrw   Bob.*
believed   Sam i Fred hit   Bob
'Sam believed that Fred had hit Bob.'

c. *Gwadodd   iddo   'i   gweld   yn yr   Opera.*
Denied   i.3M.SG   3F.SG   see   at the opera
'He denied seeing her at the Opera.'

The relatively marginal status of example (20) could be traced back to the fact that it doesn't strictly speaking refer to a proposition, but to the end of a process reinterpreted as an event.[9] The parallel example (21) containing a derived nominal is perfect.

(20) ?*Digwyddiad   mwyaf   pwysig   y   mileniwm cyntaf*
event   most   important   the   millenium first
oedd   i'r   ymerodraeth   Rufeining   gwympo.
was   i the   empire   Roman   fall
'The fall of the Roman empire was the most important event of the first millenium.'

(21) *Cwymp   yr   ymerodraeth   Rufeining   oedd*
fall   the   empire   Roman   was
digwyddiad   mwyaf   pwysig   y   mileniwm cyntaf.
event   most   important   the   millenium first
'The fall of the Roman empire was the most important event of the first millenium.'

But *i*-clauses are not possible choices in all the lexical environments where propositions are welcome. (22) is ungrammatical.[10]

---

9 In his discussion of the corresponding English example, which is well-formed, Menzel (1975) suggests that nominals like *fall* and gerund clauses derived from achievement verbs make an event interpretation available: The hearer interprets the completive aspect of the underlying verbs as referring to the end of the real world process.
10 The gerund equivalent of (22) in English is marginal, cf. fn. 3.

(22) * *Mae 'n   annhebygol   i Siôn chwarae pocer.*
       is   PRED   unlikely   *i* Siôn play   poker
       'Siôn playing poker is unlikely.'

VN-clauses do not fit naturally in causative environments either. The "fact" interpretation is available only if one uses a structure in which *y ffaith* 'the fact' precedes the VN-clause, which indicates that in the absence of the reifying name, the VN-clause simply cannot be assigned this interpretation.[11]

(23) *Fe. wnaeth y   ffaith i Siôn fwrw Mair ei   gwylltio.*
       PRT made   the   fact. *i* Siôn strike Mair 3F.SG be angry
       'Siôn's hitting Mary made her mad.'

It thus appears that verbo-nominal *i*-initial clauses semantically refer to propositions, rather than to facts or events. As has been shown in ch. VI, they can be selected by verbs belonging to a disparate set of verbal predicates belonging to distinct lexical classes – *dweud* 'say', *credo* 'believe', *synnu* 'surprise', *disgwyl* 'expect' -, a low selectivity that makes them close to *that*-clauses. *i*-constructions freely function as complements to both factive and nonfactive predicates and convey a presuppositional or a propositional reading. The same tests as the ones that have just been used would reveal that *bod*-initial clauses are also syntactic vehicles appropriate to express semantic propositions, but less easily refer to states-of-affairs.

Close examination reveals another interesting semantic difference between *i*-initial clauses and *bod*-initial clauses.[12] The two structures freely alternate when embedded under an epistemic/declarative predicate. But *i*-initial clauses are the only option with future *irrealis* verbs like *disgwyl* 'expect'. It can be concluded that the *realis/irrealis* distinction is what fixes the dividing line between the two constructions: *Bod*-clauses can only be assigned a realis propositional interpretation, whereas *i*-clauses can also convey an *irrealis* one, much like *for-to*-clauses in English. This short discussion confirms that, beyond the opposition between propositions and events, an additional semantic dimension must be taken into account when one deals with propositional nonfinite structures, the *realis/irre-*

---

11 The same observation can be made about *bod*-initial clauses.

(i) *Fe wnaeth y   ffaith bod Siôn wedi bwrw Mair   ei   gwylltio.*
      PRT made the fact *bod* Siôn PERF strike Mair 3F.SG be angry
      'John's hitting Mary made her mad.'

12 As already revealed by the interpretation of embedded domains including an aspectual specification. See ch. VI, sct. 27.3.

alis divide. This indicates that the notions of proposition, fact and event that are part of the semantic ontologies derived from Vendler (1967) are not in a position to account for the full complexity of the data and need sharpening.

65 On attitudinal objects

Starting from the observation that the familiar dichotomy between propositions and events is too crude to properly distinguish among the expressions of natural language that can be used as the arguments of intensional predicates and those that cannot, Moltmann defines a novel notion, that of "attitudinal object" (see in particular, Moltmann 2013). Attitudinal objects are "truth-bearing, mind-dependent objects." In a sentence like (24), what Bill never heard before is not a proposition, but rather a statement of John's:

(24) John said something Bill has never heard before.

Moltmann (2013: 142) comments:

> What *something* ranges over in [(24)] is not propositions, but the kind of things nominalizations such as *John's claim* stand for – that is attitudinal objects, concrete objects that include the attitudinal mode expressed by the verb.

Attitudinal objects are entities in between propositions and events. Their concreteness sets them apart from propositions. Their ability to bear truth conditions distinguishes them from mental events and states, which cannot be true or false. One further difference between them is that the time of occurrence is essential to mental events, it is accidental to attitudinal objects, whose status is that of "products of attitudes" rather than "objects of attitudes". Although they preferentially take the form of a nominalization such as *John's belief that Mary is smart*, attitudinal objects can come in many different guises. The contents of the complement clauses that occupy the object position of propositional attitude verbs like *believe* or *say* no doubt qualify as attitudinal objects. But not all predicate complement constructions are amenable to an analysis along these lines. Moltmann observes that there is no attitude involved in a __ *is possible* sentence that would make it possible to introduce an attitudinal object. And there are many intermediate cases between the *believe* __ construction and the __ *is possible* one, among which the complements to epistemic factives such as *know*, *realize*, and *see*, to verbs such as *agree* and *deny*, to the fact-selecting verb *remember*, to the *irrealis* predicates *imagine* and *expect*, to emotive factives such as *be surprised*. Among these, some predicates only remotely qualify as selecting a complement clause corresponding to an attitudinal object, others don't fit at all in the characterization that has just been given. If we revert to a strictly linguistic perspective, we observe that a major split displayed by natural languages is the one between the assertive clauses complements to verbs of the *believe/say*-class and the factive ones complements to verbs of the *regret/surprise*-class. This distinction in part cuts across the various kinds of attitudinal objects discovered by philosophical research.

In his study of the divide between *el que*-constructions and *lo de que*-constructions in Spanish, Moulton (2021) convincingly argues that, besides that of "attitudinal object", an additional notion is necessary to account for the full complexity of the data, which he identifies with that of "state-of-affairs", derived from Zucchi (1993).[13] The difference between the two Spanish constructions is illustrated by examples (25) and (26).

(25) Ana lamenta el que hayas   tenido que tomar
     Ana regrets   el que had.SUBJ.2 had   que take.INF
     essa difícil   decisión sola.
     that difficult decision alone
     'Ana regrets that you have had to make that decision on your own.'

(26) No   me creo   lo de que María compró una casa nueva.
     NEG me I.believe lo de que María bought a   house new
     'I don't believe that María bought a new house.'

El que cannot be substituted for *lo de que* in (26); replacing *el que* by *lo de que* in (25) would produce an ungrammatical result. There is no doubt that the two structures, the first one which naturally functions as an argument to factive predicates, the second one that complements propositional attitude verbs, are "propositional in the broad sense", but that they correspond to different propositional types. Following Moltmann, Moulton claims that the objects that combine with predicates like *believe*, *say*, *know*, *be true* should be identified as particular cases of "attitudinal objects". This is precisely what *lo de que*-clauses denote. *El que*-constructions, on the other hand, cannot serve as arguments of predicates of truth and falsity and propositional attitude verbs. Moulton resorts to the notion of "state-of-affairs" to characterize the semantics of these clauses, which naturally provide the propositional content of the complement of emotives/factives, but are not necessarily presupposed and do not necessarily denote facts or describe possible situations or events (this is the reason why he revives the notion of state-of-affairs). His major conclusion is that, for the complement to a predicate selecting an attitudinal object to refer, the presence of a content-bearing entity is necessary, much as

---

[13] Zucchi develops this notion to deal with action nominals and gerundives and gives it a different extension from Moulton, cf. sct. 63.

in nominalizations like *John's belief that Mary is smart*. Adding a D to CP doesn't suffice to insure the reference of the propositional objects of assertive predicates. He argues that in *lo de que*-constructions, a reifying term is present between *lo* and *de que*. Factive predicates do not impose a similar requirement.

66 Inflected infinitive constructions

Inflected infinitive constructions in Portuguese manifest a factive/assertive contrast similar to the one that is found in Spanish finite *el que/lo de que*-clauses. But the form it takes is quite different. There is no Portuguese equivalent to *el que* and *lo de que* constructions: *o* never cooccurs with *que* (cf. ch. VIII). The sensitivity to lexical classes manifests itself in IICs via word order differences and the presence/absence of *o*, as examples (27) and (28), (29) and (30) show.

(27) *Lamento. muito (o) ela   ter   sido obrigada*
     regret.1SG much (o) 3F.SG.NOM have.INF.3SG been forced
     a explicar   tudo isto.
     a explain.INF all   this

(28) *Não acredito   (*o) terem   eles   comprado uma casa*
     Neg believe.1SG o   have.INF.3.PL 3.PL.NOM bought   a   house
     nova.
     new

(29) *Lamento. muito (o) estarem   a trabalhar os   enfermeiras*
     regret.1SG much o   be.INF.3PL   *a* work.INF the   nurses
     dia e   noite nos   hospitais.
     day and night in.the hospitals

(30) *(*o) eles   terem   comprado uma casa   nova é verdade.*
     O   3.PL.NOM have.INF.3.PL bought   a   house new is truth

From (27) and (29), it can safely be concluded that subject-initial infinitives in European Portuguese are appropriate vehicles for expressing states-of-affairs. The optionality of *o* in front of the embedded CP could suggest that its insertion is not necessary to produce an authentic propositional nominalization. But it is plausible to assume that a D head is also projected in the absence of *o* and that this extra category provides the propositional complement with a nominal status. (28) and (30) show that the Spanish strategy is not the only one that can be used to satisfy the selection of the predicates that take an attitudinal object as an argument. Portuguese doesn't resort to a D-(N)-CP complex to fulfill the selectional requirement of these verbs. The nonfinite structures that are used to describe attitudinal objects with propositional content are auxiliary/verb-first inflected infinitive clauses, which, as argued in ch. VIII, are not nominal projections, but verbal ones, that is, propositions (in the syntactic sense).[14]

---

[14] It is true that the clausal complement to emotive/factive predicates where subject-auxiliary inversion has taken place is, in the absence of *o*, superficially undistinguishable from the complements to epistemic/declarative predicates. But, if the analysis developed in section 54 is correct, distinct structures underlie these superficially similar sequences.

67 Taking stock

We are now in a position to answer the question we started with. A salient feature of nonfinite syntactic structures is that not all NFDs are equally appropriate to function as complements to predicates of various lexical classes. Among the various nonfinite structures that have been taken into consideration, some appear to be specialized in the expression of a particular ontological category, others seem to be freely used as vehicles for both attitudinal objects and states-of-affairs. The variation observed within every language and across languages appears to fall within narrow limits and the interpretive properties of the various constructions appear to be relatively homogeneous across languages.

A convenient way to start the discussion is to check whether the domains that have been identified as nominal form a homogeneous class in this respect. The dominant participle construction in Latin, the English Poss-*ing* construction, the nominalized Portuguese inflected infinitive (preceded or not by *o*) fall under this characterization.

The Latin DPC, which should be analyzed as a noun-like projection, is ideally suited to refer to state-of-affairs and is a natural vehicle for the factive /presuppositional interpretation. It usually functions as a complement to factive predicates, as a complement or a subject to psychological predicates, as a complement to prepositions, but cannot be resorted to when the selecting predicate is a verb of propositional attitude or a declarative verb, semantically selecting an attitudinal object as its direct argument.

In European Portuguese, subject-initial structures are selected when the matrix predicate is emotive/factive and selects an argument referring to a content that can be characterized as a state-of-affairs. On the contrary, it is the auxiliary-initial construction that is used to refer to propositional contents, when the matrix verb is a declarative verb or a verb of propositional attitude selecting an attitudinal object. Word order is not the only difference between the two structures: From a semantic point of view, DP projections are generally presuppositional, FinP ones propositionnal.

English Poss-*ing* constructions, which also are uncontroversially nominal, convey a definite presuppositional interpretation, which can be absent from Acc-*ing* constructions.

The nominal nonfinite types share at least one property: Whichever form they take, they cannot convey the propositional interpretation associated with attitudinal objects and cannot function as complements to the prototypical verbs of propositional attitude (*believe* . . .) and verbs of saying (*assert* . . .). The structures specialized in the description of state-of-affairs across languages are quite generally nominal. But there are exceptions. Welsh *i*-initial and *bod*-initial constructions treat the assertive and factive predications in the same way and the VN-clauses that are used to express the contents that correspond to state-of-affairs are FinP projections, not nominal ones. This indicates that if uncontroversially nonfinite verbal/clausal structures usually convey the propositional content that corresponds to attitudinal objects, they can also, in some languages and constructions, express a specific/presupposed information with respect to the main clause, that is, a state-of-affairs.

This observation can be pushed further. When two alternative nonfinite structures are available in a language L, it is often the case that one is neutral with respect to the factive/assertive (or *realis/irrealis* or presuppositional/non-presuppositional) divide, whereas the other is specialized in one of these interpretations. For example, both Poss-*ing* and Acc-*ing* constructions in English are appropriate choices to express states-of-affairs, but only Acc-*ing* structures can (*albeit* marginally) function as vehicles for the propositional interpretation associated with attitudinal objects, as the case of *deny* shows. Similarly, both subject-initial and auxiliary-initial clauses in European Portuguese can express the semantic content associated with the complement of factive predicates, but only auxiliary-initial clauses can convey the propositional reading. This indicates that verbal projections can be used as vehicles for both the propositional and state-of-affairs interpretations, but that nominal ones cannot generally be coerced into functioning as vehicles for the propositional interpretation.[15]

---

15 The constructions in which a clause is embedded under *the fact that* are not nominal in this sense.

XII **Conclusion: The many faces of defectiveness**

The initial goal of this inquiry was to contribute to a better understanding of the nature of nonfiniteness by focusing the investigation on the core properties of some nonfinite predicative domains that have received less attention in the linguistic literature than standard infinitives and by looking at them from a unified perspective addressing their morphological, syntactic and semantic aspects. The picture that emerges is admittedly quite different from the one with which the inquiry began. The distinction between finite and nonfinite domains appears to be blurred in several constructions and finiteness turns out to be a rather fuzzy concept, whose grammatical efficacy should be called into question. This situation could simply reflect the fact that standard infinitival structures, which are usually considered to be the prototypical nonfinite domains, have been left out and that those that have been taken into consideration are bivalent or mixed projections (English gerunds) or potentially concealed finite clauses (Welsh VN-clauses) or enriched infinitival/impoverished finite domains (Portuguese inflected infinitives) or overtly nominal participial structures (Latin dominant participle constructions). One could decide that the constructions that have been selected are not representative because they are not well-behaved nonfinite structures, but that would only beg the question. In fact, it turns out that the reference to finiteness can almost entirely be dispensed with once careful attention is paid to its basic ingredients, namely tense and person-number, and to the semantic, syntactic and morphological properties of the corresponding features, an insight that lies at the heart of Landau's seminal work on the theory of control but also underlies Chomsky's probe-goal-Agree approach to syntactic dependencies.

It remains that several principles and theoretical constructs must be recruited to deconstruct the traditional finite/nonfinite divide, while accounting for the full complexity of the phenomena. The picture we end up with is inevitably a rather fragmented one.

Let me summarize the results that I hope to have achieved.

68 Semantics

Some provisional conclusions can tentatively be drawn concerning the correspondence between syntactic forms and categories of meaning. Not all nonfinite syntactic structures are equally appropriate to function as complements to the predicates of various lexical classes. Taking attitudinal objects and state-of-affairs to be the two major ontological classes that are relevant to the semantic characterization of complementation in natural languages, it can be said that the structures specialized in the description of state-of-affairs are generally nominal, the ones that convey propositional contents corresponding to attitudinal objects are systematically verbal/clausal. Nominal nonfinite types (English Poss-*ing*, nominalized European Portuguese IICs, preceded or not by *o*, Latin DPCs) cannot function as complements to the prototypical verbs of propositional attitude and cannot convey the propositional interpretation associated with attitudinal objects. The natural vehicles for attitudinal objects uncontroversially are verbal/clausal nonfinite projections (auxiliary-initial inflected infinitive structures in European Portuguese, *bod*-initial and *i*-initial VN-clauses in Welsh).

But the correspondence between syntactic forms and categories of meaning in no way functions on a one-to-one basis. Welsh resorts to the same VN-clause types to express factive predications and epistemic/declarative ones. Contrary to Poss-*ing* constructions, which are overtly nominal and are restricted to the expression of states-of-affairs, Acc-*ing* constructions, which are also possible choices to express states-of-affairs, indisputably have a verbal internal structure: They are here analyzed as CP/FinP projections with a <φ, φ> label. In other words, one should not conclude that the syntactic objects that complement factive/psychological predicates systematically qualify as NP/DP projections. In contrast, the claim that NP/DP projections cannot be vehicles for attitudinal objects seems to be correct.[1]

The tense construal of the nonfinite domains studied here gives rise to several interpretive options, which in large part match up with the classes isolated by Landau (2013) and Wurmbrand (2014). The interpretation of embedded tense is primarily determined by the lexical class of the matrix predicate and by the eventive or stative nature of the embedded one. Tense dependency (in the broad sense) is a recurrent feature of embedded nonfinite domains and reflects their morphological tense deficiency. It looks as if, faced with the absence of

---

[1] Recall that <φ, φ> Acc-*ing* projections can function as vehicles for the propositional interpretation associated with some attitudinal objects, such as the complements of *remember, imagine, deny*, but not the complement of *believe*.

finite tense, which would ensure the temporal anchoring of the clause, the computational system capitalizes both on the lexical properties of the selecting verb and on those of the embedded predicate. At first sight, the claim that Latin DPCs incorporate no T doesn't fit easily with what is said here about other nonfinite structures. But the difficulty vanishes if one assumes that the relevant constructions just name an event and don't participate in the temporal succession set up by matrix tense.

69 Morphosyntax

An optimal way to summarize the morphosyntactic results achieved in this book is to first reconsider the characterizations that were associated with the various affixes attached to the *nonfinite forms* examined here, then to make explicit their contribution to the *clausal structures* in which these forms enter.

The gerund suffix *-ing* is aspectually neutral and bears a [tense] feature and φ-features with unspecified values. This feature endowment explains why gerund forms freely coexist with anaphoric T (in exhaustive control structures) and with dependent T (elsewhere). Because φ-features are present on dependent T, overt subjects are case-licensed in the corresponding clauses. Because the value of these features is not specified, gerund forms can also coexist with PRO. This also explains why (auxiliary) gerund heads systematically raise to T: They are allowed and required to raise because they bear features that can value, or be valued by, those of T.

The verbo-nominal affix in Welsh has no properties. It is specified neither for aspect nor for voice nor for tense. When these dimensions are present in a verbo-nominal domain, they are necessarily borne by independent words (or represented by null categories). The non-movement of Welsh verb-nouns is a reflex of their being deprived of [tense] and φ-features. It is because of this property that these forms are neither required nor allowed to raise.

The affix attached to infinitival stems in European Portuguese is exactly what it appears to be, namely a mark of person and number. Inflected forms also bear a silent [tense] feature. As a result, they systematically raise to T and, in some structures, to C/Fin. Infinitival inflection cannot be found in exhaustive local control structures because its presence would prevent the establishment of an Agree relation between PRO and a functional head or an antecedent in the matrix clause. But it is welcome in all the other control constructions, exhaustive non-local control constructions included, which indicates that the presence/absence of agreement is a purely syntactic affair, with no effect on interpretation (the exhaustive control interpretation is marginally available in the presence of agreement).

Participles in Latin DPCs uncontroversially behave as full-fledged verbal (rather than adjectival) forms, endowed with an argument structure, voice and aspect. The lexical root, the participial v that immediately dominates it and the Aspect head projected above v are the sources of these verbal properties. The participial suffixes *-nt-* and *-t-* can be viewed as being the exponents of these properties. Latin participles jointly manifest nominal properties, since they agree in gender, number and case with their subject. These inflectional dimensions reflect the presence of an additional head, n, above vP. The successive merger of these heads gives rise to the participial word.

If Latin participles are left aside, the various nonfinite affixes under consideration distinguish themselves from one another by a crucial property. Some are restricted to occur in the constructions that have a dependent/interpretable tense, but are banished from the structures lacking tense (that is, where [tense] is anaphoric/unvalued). This is the case of Portuguese IICs. My claim was that, if a person-number agreement affix was present in local exhaustive control constructions, PRO couldn't Agree with an antecedent in the matrix clause. Other affixes are compatible with both exhaustive control and the other cases of control, as well as with overt referential subjects. The verbo-nominal affix in Welsh illustrates this case. This situation is not unexpected if this affix has no properties. But if it has no properties, overt subjects, when present, must be case-licensed otherwise (by the term in C/Fin in the Welsh case). The gerund affix -*ing* occurs in all construction types. This has been taken as a clue that -*ing* doesn't function as a full-fledged agreement marker, but as a substitute for agreement. The claim that -*ing* is endowed with unspecified φ-features in all situations has no unwanted consequences for exhaustive control constructions, since, in the absence of interpretable [tense], these features don't suffice to make the gerund clause featurally complete (in Landau's terms), and don't block the establishment of an Agree (control) relation between embedded PRO and its functional or nominal antecedent in the matrix (in Chomskyan terms).

70 Syntax

70.1 Classification of NFDs

As anticipated in section 68, the constructions that have been referred to here as nonfinite domains distribute from a syntactic point of view into two major classes: They are either nominal or verbal/clausal. Latin dominant participle constructions, which are nP projections, English Poss-*ing* gerund phrases, which are DPs, and European Portuguese subject-initial inflected infinitive structures functioning as complements or subjects to factive or emotive predicates, which should be analyzed as CP/FinP projections embedded in a DP, belong to the nominal class. Welsh verbo-nominal clauses and European Portuguese auxiliary-initial inflected infinitive complements to epistemic/declarative predicates belong to the verbal/clausal class.

Chomsky (2000a) argues that T's defectiveness plays a crucial role in the way infinitival subjects are licensed. In his view, "T functions in the case-agreement system only if it is selected by C, in which case it is also complete" and "T enters into feature-checking only in the C-T configuration . . . " (cf. Chomsky 2004: 13), two assumptions that are directly relevant to the study of nonfinite clauses. The data considered here provide strong additional support for the claim that the two heads T and C/Fin also work in tandem in the other nonfinite verbal/clausal constructions. T is necessarily projected in the structures headed by Fin. Both T and Fin are present in the internal structure of Portuguese inflected infinitives; both are absent in the Latin DPC. But, as Chomsky's quotation implies, the projection of C/Fin doesn't systematically go hand in hand with the projection of T. T is projected in Poss-*ing* constructions, but C/Fin is not. When C/Fin is not projected above T or when it doesn't transmit uninterpretable features to T (see 1a), T is an inactive, defective head, whose feature endowment reduces to interpretable [tense].

The fact is that, within the class of verbal/clausal projections, a further divide must be established between the structures where the C/Fin head transmits its uninterpretable φ-features to a lower T – this is the case in Acc-*ing* constructions – and those where it doesn't – this is the case in Welsh verbo-nominal constructions. It was shown that this parametric choice, which affects both finite and nonfinite clauses in Welsh, has far-reaching consequences for the valuation of the uninterpretable features present on functional heads, for the syntax of verbo-nominal heads and for the case licensing of their subjects.

Concerning the presence or absence of a TP projection in nonfinite domains, the position adopted in this study is that, with the exception of the Latin DPC, which relies on a purely TP-less participial structure, all the NFDs examined here, including strongly mixed extended projections such as Poss-*ing*, contain a T head, whose presence is attested by tense construal phenomena, such as the present tense effect or temporal mismatches between embedded and matrix tenses.

These observations lead to a better understanding of the situations where T is syntactically active and where it is defective or absent.

(1) T is syntactically active when it is not φ-defective, that is, when it inherits uninterpretable φ-features from C/Fin. When it is active, its interpretable [tense] feature generally values an uninterpretable [tense] feature on C/Fin.

(2) T is inactive when it is φ-defective. It is φ-defective when it inherits no uninterpretable features from C/Fin,
    (a) because C/Fin withholds them (Welsh VN-clauses); or
    (b) because C/Fin is not projected: in this case, T is minimally c-commanded by either the selecting matrix predicate (English ECM and raising structures) or by a nominalizer (Poss-*ing* construction).

(3) T is anaphoric/unvalued when it is the head of an exhaustive control configuration.

(4) T is absent in Latin DPCs and in nominal gerunds.

70.2 The licensing of overt subjects

In Landau's (2004, 2013) system, the overtness of inflectional φ-features on either T or C is a crucial dimension in the licensing of overt subjects in verbal/clausal structures. It was shown that this insight can elegantly be transposed into Chomsky's probe-goal-Agree approach to syntactic dependencies, which relies on the asymmetry between uninterpretable features that need to be valued and interpretable ones that already are and on the valuation of the former by the latter.

The way subjects are licensed is directly determined by the parametric options that are selected by each language and each construction, which include the properties of the nonfinite affixes that they use (cf. sct. 67). Licensing can be internal to the nonfinite domain or depend on the presence of an external governor. Among the structures that have been examined, the DPC is the only one that selects a T-less, C-less, D-less nominal structure and for which external licensing is the only option. The structures where licensing is internal should be distinguished according to the level at which it takes place. If transmission of uninterpretable features from C/Fin occurs, the Case licensing of the subject is achieved at the T'-level.

This means that case licensing cannot be held responsible for the fact that the subject generally occupies a higher position at Spell-Out. This property should rather be traced back to the necessity to properly label the corresponding structure. An untriggered movement of the vP-internal subject (that is, a movement that is not triggered by checking considerations, but is motivated by the labeling requirement) takes place in Portuguese IICs and in Acc-*ing* gerund constructions.

A recurrent theme of this study is that nonfinite subjects can also be licensed in the absence of an active category T in the clause. Welsh VN-clauses illustrate this situation: C/Fin, which has kept its uninterpretable φ-features, takes the responsibility of the licensing of the subject, which can thus only be performed at the CP/FinP-level. There are still alternative ways to license the subject in the absence of an active T, see (2). Irish VN-clauses seem to resort to a strategy in which T plays no role at all and the particle *a* is responsible for licensing one or two arguments. In this case, licensing occurs at the vP/AspP-level.

It should be added that T's case feature doesn't necessarily target the external argument. This situation arises in Middle Welsh root and embedded transitive VN-clauses, which resort to an ergative alignment strategy consisting in building the external argument as a prepositional phrase, thus making T's structural case (the absolute case) available to license the "other" argument.

In conclusion, natural languages resort to different strategies to achieve subject licensing. The one that is used in each construction is tightly dependent on the choices it makes concerning the battery of functional heads it incorporates, the properties of the nonfinite affix it uses and the possible transmission of uninterpretable features from C/Fin to T.

70.3 The movement of verbo-nominal heads

These parametric choices also have an impact on the distribution of verbo-nominal heads. If transmission has made T active, it is natural to assume that T is an appropriate host for these heads, as the distribution of auxiliaries in Acc-*ing* gerund constructions suggests. It should not when T has no φ-features, a case illustrated by Welsh VN-clauses. The affix on the nonfinite head necessarily displays properties that match those of the head that hosts it: It has the strength of a finite inflection in Acc-*ing* constructions, it is inert in Welsh verbo-nominal structures.[2]

---

[2] But Poss-*ing* constructions show that things are more complex. They are clearly nominal and project no C under the nominalizer n; yet, auxiliaries raise in these structures, exactly as in Acc-

In more general terms, if one takes the notions of probe and goal to also be relevant to head movement (not just to phrase movement), it can be assumed that the feature endowments of the defective heads that function as the goals in the relevant Agree relations necessarily match those of the higher probes (or are a subset of them, see Roberts 2010). A representation resulting from head movement is well-formed only if the lexical entity that functions as a goal is equipped with features that can participate in the valuing of uninterpretable features on the functional probe and, conversely, doesn't bear features that the probe cannot license. This condition plays a crucial role in nonfinite structures.

70.4 Labeling

A distinction is established in this book between strong and weak categorial mixing. A seldom asked question is how to deal with weak categorial mixing: How is it that some verbo-nominal domains, most notably Acc-*ing* constructions, which unquestionably display a verbal internal syntax, and should not be considered as resulting from a nominalization (deverbalization) process, have access to positions which are reserved for nominal expressions? It was argued that the <φ, φ> labeling resulting from untriggered DP raising provides the solution and, at the same time, that resort to this strategy is severely constrained. In fact, the domains where it can be used are those that are reputed to display EPP effects.

Much care has been taken here to specify the internal structure and the categorial and featural make-up of defective domains. The determination of their label plays a crucial role in their characterization, since labels directly contribute to the fulfillment of the subcategorization requirements of the matrix predicates selecting the corresponding domains. Subcategorization was argued to be directly responsible for the observed word-order differences internal to factive and nonfactive complements in Portuguese IICs. Similar considerations can be made about the ability of DPCs in Latin to complement factive/emotive, but not epistemic/declarative predicates.

---

ing structures. A possible way out is to claim that what underlies the raising of auxiliaries in the corresponding T'-domains is their being specified for tense, which main verbs are not.

70.5 Size

The question of the size of nonfinite domains has not been seriously discussed in this work. This situation in part results from the fact that size doesn't seem to be a determining factor distinguishing the various types of nonfinite predicative domains acting as arguments. But it becomes relevant when the nonfinite domains functioning as modifiers are taken into consideration. Williams (2013) was right to observe that the size of the latter is generally reduced as compared with that of the former. Note that full clauses can also function as modifiers. This is of course the case of relative clauses across languages. This is also the case of the Welsh verbo-nominal *i*-phrases mentioned in fn. 18, ch. VI, which, because they contain the particle *i*, are necessarily CP/FinP domains and should be viewed as concealed relative clauses.

71 On defectiveness

It has been observed in the first chapter that there is more than one way in which clausal domains can be nonfinite. This situation could simply reflect the fact that there is more than one way in which nonfinite domains can be defective. The claim made in this book is that the key notion that makes it possible to unlock the systematicity of nonfinite domains is indeed that of defectiveness. But the scope of this notion must be made more precise.

At a descriptive, pre-theoretical level, it appears under several different guises in the various constructions studied here. It makes sense to say that IICs in European Portuguese are tense-defective, but not φ-defective, that the non-auxiliary verbo-nominal forms in Welsh are morphologically deficient categories, which are specified neither for agreement, nor for voice, nor for tense. One can also choose to describe the target of the control process, PRO, as a deficient element, which makes the clauses that contain it defective domains.

Linguists, for their part, agree that the tense and φ-features whose absence in their matrix makes the corresponding T or C/Fin heads morphologically deficient and syntactically defective play a major role in the functioning of grammar. But they implement this general idea in different ways. In *Minimalist Inquiries*, Chomsky refers to defectiveness, conceived of as the syntactic reflex of morphological deficiency, in his characterization of infinitival T, thus accounting for the fact that a further movement of overt subjects is necessary when T is not equipped with the φ-features that would allow it to value their case feature. In Chomsky's view, defectiveness is T's φ-defectiveness (cf. (1)). Landau's (2004, 2013) contribution can be viewed as laying the foundations of an alternative conception of defectiveness, in which semantic tense and overt inflectional morphology work in tandem to determine the feature completeness of a domain or its defectiveness. His basic claim is that T's defectiveness should not exclusively be conceived of as defectiveness in φ features, but should also be made sensitive to the status of the [tense] feature. A rule governing subject licensing, incorporating Landau's insight into the probe-goal-Agree framework, has first been formulated in (23), chapter II, section 7.7, then further discussed in chapters IV, VI and VIII. Both the feature completeness of clauses (their being fully specified for [tense] and [φ]) and their defining convergent phases (in which the [φ] and [tense] features that need to be are valued within the minimal CP phase) turn out to be relevant.

Since the [tense] feature can come in several guises, it must be asked which value of [tense] makes T defective, which one contributes to its completeness. Landau's distinction between (referentially) *dependent* tense and *anaphoric* tense was adopted in this book. Various phenomena show that the tense in embedded finite clauses often depends on the matrix tense for its interpretation. A large subset of nonfinite domains also includes a *dependent* tense. Exhaustive control constructions, provided that they also incorporate a T head, include an *anaphoric* tense. In the previous chapters, it was proposed that the feature specification corresponding to anaphoric tense is unvalued [tense], the one corresponding to dependent tense is interpretable [tense]. The clauses that incorporate a dependent [tense] feature (and a full matrix of φ-features) are complete, the ones that display the anaphoric unvalued type are defective.

If the preceding observations are on the right track, the boundary between finite and nonfinite clauses should be displaced and replaced by the completeness/defectiveness divide. A subset of clausal domains, traditionally classified as nonfinite, are not defective in the relevant sense. This happens when they have both an overt subject and a fully specified (overt or non-overt) C/T system. This is the case in Welsh VN-clauses with an overt subject, where the C-DP$_{subject}$ relation is active, and in European Portuguese inflected infinitive clauses, where both the C-T and the C-DP relations are active.

Feature completeness is also what allows propositional domains to be extraposed. Defective domains absolutely resist extraposition and must remain in their first Merge position or occupy a site in the A-chain that includes it. The blocking of extraposition, when it is observed, should be taken as an indication that the corresponding structure is a CP/FinP projection with a defective C/Fin or T head. It can also be a DP projection, since DP projections, if they freely move within A-chains, do not extrapose. The clausal objects that are "extraposable" are those that, being inflectionally complete domains, give rise to convergent phases. By definition, such objects do not depend on the external environment for their licensing, only on internal grammatical information. On the contrary, the clauses that resist extraposition are those that do not correspond to convergent phases, because they are defective, and depend on the local environment and their belonging to an A-chain for their licensing. The projections that are analyzable as clausal DPs fall under this generalization.[3]

In the approach defended here, the completeness/defectiveness divide is tightly linked to another notion, that of visibility. Featurally complete clauses are autonomous domains that are inherently visible for θ-assignment; featurally defective ones, which are heavily dependent on the content of the matrix clause for their licensing and interpretation, must satisfy strict conditions to be visible.

---

[3] See what has been said about the extraposition of Portuguese *o*-clauses at the end of section 54.

Let us conclude with a general observation on the dependencies involved in complementation and the way they work. When complement clauses are at stake, the Language Faculty must generate representations in which a predication structure combining a (potentially defective) predicate and a (potentially defective) argument functioning as its subject enters into a dependency with a governing verb. How do natural languages take up this major challenge? Finite clauses and related constructions are generally constructed as closed domains whose internal structure is not accessible from the outside and in which feature valuation exclusively resorts to internal resources. This presentation presupposes that dependent tense dependencies don't make the corresponding domains defective. At the other hand of the spectrum, exhaustive control structures are built as open clauses in which tense is anaphoric and the null subject necessarily agrees with an external functional head and an external antecedent. Defectiveness in this case implies a strong dependency on the external environment. A range of intermediate cases exists, in which the nonfinite domain contains an internally or externally licensed overt subject. The dependency of a nonfinite clause is generally marked by the defectiveness of some of its components, that is, by the presence on functional heads of uninterpretable features that can only be valued by external elements.

But all in all, the licensing strategies used to accommodate nonfinite clauses do not substantially differ from the ones resorted to to account for finite clauses. The formal mechanisms that have proved to be efficient in finite clauses – probe-goal-Agree, valuation, inheritance, labeling, free untriggered Internal Merge – can readily be used to deal with the nonfinite ones. The grammar of nonfiniteness doesn't require the definition of specific devices or of specialized tools.

References

Abney, Steven. 1987. *The English Noun Phrase in its Sentential Aspect*. Doctoral dissertation, Cambridge, MA: MIT.
Ackema, Peter & Ad Neeleman. 2004. *Beyond Morphology: Interface Conditions on Word Formation*. Oxford: Oxford University Press.
Adger, David. 2007. Three domains of finiteness: a Minimalist perspective. In Irina Nikolaeva (ed.), *Finiteness: Theoretical and Empirical Foundations*, 23–58. Oxford: Oxford University Press.
Alexiadou, Artemis. 2001. *Functional Structure in Nominals: Nominalization and Ergativity*. Amsterdam: John Benjamins.
Alexiadou, Artemis. 2010a. Nominalizations: A probe into the architecture of grammar. Part I: The nominalization puzzle. *Language and Linguistics Compass* 4/7: 496–511.
Alexiadou, Artemis. 2010b. Nominalizations: A probe into the architecture of grammar. Part II: The aspectual properties of nominalizations and the lexicon vs. syntax debate. *Language and Linguistics Compass* 4/7: 512–523.
Alexiadou, Artemis. 2013. Nominal vs. verbal *-ing* constructions and the development of the English progressive. *English Linguistics Research* 2. 2.: 126–140.
Alexiadou, Artemis. 2021. D vs. n nominalizations within and across languages. In Artemis Alexiadou & Hagit Borer (eds), *Nominalization: 50 years on from Chomsky's Remarks*, 87–109. Oxford: Oxford University Press.
Alexiadou, Artemis, Gianina Iordăchioaia & Elena Soare. 2010. Number/aspect interactions in the syntax of nominalizations: a Distributed Morphology approach. *Journal of Linguistics* 46: 537–574.
Alexiadou, Artemis, Gianina Iordăchioaia & Florian Schäfer. 2011. Scaling the variation in Romance and Germanic nominalizations. In Petronella Sleeman & Harry Peridon (eds.), *The noun phrase in Romance and Germanic*, 25–40. Amsterdam, John Benjamins.
Alexiadou, Artemis & Hagit Borer (eds.). 2021a. *Nominalization: 50 years on from Chomsky's Remarks*. Oxford: Oxford University Press.
Alexiadou, Artemis & Hagit Borer. 2021b. Introduction. In Artemis Alexiadou & Hagit Borer (eds.), *Nominalization: 50 years on from Chomsky's Remarks*, 1–23. Oxford: Oxford University Press.
Ambar, Maria Manuela. 1994. Aux-to-Comp and lexical restrictions on verb movement. In Guglielmo Cinque, Jan Koster, Jean-Yves Pollock, Luigi Rizzi & Raffaella Zanuttini (eds.), *Paths towards Universal Grammar, Studies in Honor of Richard Kayne*, 1–23. Washington, D.C: Georgetown University Press.
Ambar, Maria Manuela & Ángel Luis Jiménez Fernández. 2017. Overtly/non-overtly inflected infinitives in Romance. In Martin Everaert & Henk van Riemsdijk (eds.), *The Blackwell Companion to Syntax*, 2nd edn. Oxford & New York: Wiley-Blackwell.
Anwyl, Edward. 1899. *A Welsh Grammar for Schools, part I.: Accidence*. London: Swan Sonnenschein & Co.
Aoun, Youssef. 1981. Parts of speech. A case of redistribution. In Adriana Belletti, Luciana Brandi & Luigi Rizzi (eds.), *Theory of Markedness in Generative Grammar, Proceedings of the 1979 GLOW Conference*, 3–23. Pisa: Scuola Normale Superiore di Pisa.
Arad, Maya. 2003. Locality constraints on the interpretation of roots: the case of Hebrew denominal verbs. *Natural Language & Linguistic Theory* 21: 737–778.

Asher, Nicholas. 1993. *Reference to Abstract Objects in Discourse*. Dordrecht: Kluwer.
Authier, J. Marc & Lisa A. Reed. 2009. French *Tough*-movement revisited. *Probus* 21: 1–21.
Awbery, G. 1976. *The Syntax of Welsh: A Transformational View of the Passive*. Cambridge: Cambridge University Press.
Baker, Mark. 1985. The mirror principle and morphosyntactic explanation. *Linguistic Inquiry* 16: 373–415.
Baker, Mark. 1988. *Incorporation*. Chicago, University of Chicago Press.
Baker, Mark. 2003. *Lexical Categories*. Cambridge, Cambridge University Press.
Baker, Mark. undated. On gerunds and the theory of categories. Unpublished manuscript, Rutgers University.
Baker, Mark & Ümit Atlamaz. 2014. On the relationship of case to agreement in split ergative Kurmanji. Unpublished manuscript, Rutgers University.
Baker, Mark & Jonathan Bobaljik. 2017. On inherent and dependent theories of ergative case. In Jessica Coon, Diane Massam & Lisa deMena Travis, eds., *The Oxford Handbook of Ergativity*, 111–134. Oxford: Oxford University Press.
Belletti, Adriana & Luigi Rizzi. 1988. Psych-verbs and theta-theory. *Natural Language and Linguistic Theory* 6: 291–352.
Bianchi, Valentina. 2003. On Finiteness as logophoric anchoring. In Jacqueline Guéron and Liliane Tasmovski (eds.), *Temps et point de vue/Tense and Point of View*, 213–246. Université Paris X-Nanterre.
Bisang, Walter. 2007. Categories that make finiteness: discreteness from a functional perspective and some of its repercussions. In Irina Nikolaeva (ed.), *Finiteness: Theoretical and Empirical Foundations*, 115–137. Oxford: Oxford University Press.
Bittner, Maria & Ken Hale. 1996. The structural determination of Case and Agreement. *Linguistic Inquiry* 27 : 1–68.
Blatt, Franz. 1952. *Précis de syntaxe latine*. Les langues du monde. Lyon: IAC.
Blevins, James. 2005. Remarks on gerunds. In C. Orhan Orgun & Peter Sells (eds.), *Morpology and the Web of Grammar, Essays in memory of Steven G. Lapointe*, 19–40. Stanford: CSLI Publications.
Bobaljik, Jonathan. 1993a. On ergativity and ergative unergatives. In Colin Phillips (ed.), *Papers on Case and Agreement II, MIT Working Papers in Linguistics* 19, 45–88. Cambridge, MA: MIT.
Bobaljik, Jonathan. 1993b. Nominally absolutive is not absolutely nominative, In *Proceedings of the 11th WCCFL*, 44–60. Stanford, CA: CSLI.
Bobaljik, Jonathan. 1994. What does adjacency do? In Heidi Harley & Colin Phillips (eds.), *The morphology-syntax connection, MIT Working Papers in Linguistics* 22, 1–32. Cambridge, MA: MIT.
Bobaljik, Jonathan & Andrew Carnie. 1996. A minimalist approach to some problems of Irish word order. In Robert Borsley & Ian Roberts (eds.), *The Syntax of the Celtic Languages: A Comparative Perspective*, 223–240. Cambridge: Cambridge University Press.
Bok-Bennema, Reineke. 1991. *Case and Agreement in Inuit*. Berlin: Foris Publications.
Bolinger, Dwight. 1968. Entailment and the meaning of structures. *Glossa* 2, 119–127.
Bolinger, Dwight. 1978. A semantic view of syntax: Some verbs that govern infinitives. In Mohammad Jazayeri, Edgar Polomé & Wiemer Winter, *Linguistic and Literary Studies in Honor of Archibald A. Hill*, volume II, 9–18. The Hague: Mouton.
Bolkestein, A. Machtelt. 1980. The *ab urbe condita* construction in Latin: a strange type of raising. In Saskia Daalder & Marinel Geeritsen (eds.), *Linguistics in the Netherlands* 1980, 80–92. Dordrecht: Foris.

Bolkestein, A. Machtelt. 1981. Factivity as a condition for an optional expression rule in Latin: the *ab urbe condita* construction and its underlying representation. In A. Machtelt Bolkestein & alii (eds.), *Predication and Expression in Functional Grammar*, 205–233. London: Academic Press.

Bolkestein, A. Machtelt. 1989a. Parameters in the expression of embedded predication in Latin. In Gualtiero Calboli (ed.), *Subordination and other Topics in Latin*, 3–36. Amsterdam: John Benjamins.

Bolkestein, A. Machtelt. 1989b. Latin sentential complements from a functional grammar perspective. In Marius Lavency & Dominique Longrée (eds.), *Actes du Vè Colloque de Linguistique Latine. Cahiers de l'Institut de Linguistique de Louvain*, 41–52.

Bondaruk, Anna. 2006. The licensing of subjects and objects in Irish non-finite clauses. *Lingua* 116: 1840–1859.

Borer, Hagit. 2005. *Structuring Sense*, vol II: *Taking Form*. Oxford: Oxford University Press.

Borer, Hagit. 2014. The category of roots. In Artemis Alexiadou, Hagit Borer & Florian Schäfer (eds.), *The Roots of Syntax, the Syntax of Roots.*, 112–148. Oxford: Oxford University Press.

Borsley, Robert. 1986. Prepositional Complementizers in Welsh. *Journal of Linguistics* 22: 67–84.

Borsley, Robert. 1993. On so-called 'verb nouns' in Welsh. *Journal of Celtic Linguistics* 2: 35–64.

Borsley, Robert. 1997. On a nominal analysis of Welsh verb-nouns. In Anders Ahlqvist & Vera Čapková (eds.), *Dán Do Oide, Essays in Memory of Conn. R. Ó Cleirigh*, 39–47. Dublin: Institiúid Teangeolaíochta Éireann.

Borsley, Robert & Jaklin Kornfilt. 2000. Mixed extended projections. In Robert Borsley (ed.), *The Nature and Function of Syntactic Categories*, Syntax and Semantics vol. 32, 101–131. New York: Academic Press.

Borsley, Robert, Maggie Tallerman & David Willis. 2007. *The Syntax of Welsh*. Cambridge: Cambridge University Press.

Bošković, Željko 1995. Case properties of clauses and the Greed principle. *Studia Linguistica* 49: 32–53.

Bošković, Željko. 1996. Selection and the categorial status of infinitival complements. *Natural Language and Linguistic Theory* 14: 269–304.

Bošković, Željko. 1997. *The Syntax of Nonfinite Complementation: An Economy Approach*. Cambridge, MA: MIT Press.

Bresnan, Joan. 1970. On complementizers: Towards a syntactic theory of complement types. *Foundations of Language* 6: 297–321.

Bresnan, Joan. 1972. *Theory of Complementation in English Syntax*. Doctoral dissertation, Cambridge, MA: MIT.

Bresnan, J. 1997. Mixed categories as head sharing constructions. In Miriam Butt & Tracy Holloway King (eds.), *Proceedings of the LFG 97 Conference*, Stanford: CSLI Publications.

Brito, Ana Maria. 2013. Tensed and non-tensed nominalization of the infinitive in Portuguese. *Journal of Portuguese Linguistics* 12: 7–40.

Burukina, Irina. 2019. *Raising and Control in non-finite clausal complementation*. Doctoral dissertation, Budapest: Eötvos Lorand University.

Burukina, Irina. 2020. Mandative verbs and deontic modals in Russian. Between obligatory control and overt embedded subjects. *Glossa* art 54: 1–37.

Burzio, Luigi. 1986. *Italian Syntax. A government-binding approach*. Dordrecht: Reidel.

Carlson, Gregory. 1977. *Reference to Kinds in English*. Doctoral dissertation, Amherst: University of Massachusetts.

Carnie, A. 2011. Mixed categories in Irish. *Lingua* 121: 1207–1224.
Chomsky, Noam. 1965. *Aspects of the Theory of Syntax*. Cambridge, MA: MIT Press.
Chomsky, Noam. 1970. Remarks on nominalization. In Roderick Jacobs & Peter Rosenbaum (eds.), *Readings in English Transformational Grammar*, 184–221. Waltham, MA: Ginn.
Chomsky, Noam. 1981. *Lectures on Government and Binding*. Dordrecht: Foris.
Chomsky, Noam. 1995a. *The Minimalist Program*. Cambridge, MA: MIT Press.
Chomsky, 1995b. Categories and transformations, in *The Minimalist Program*, 219–394. Cambridge, MA: MIT Press.
Chomsky, N. 2000a. Minimalist inquiries: The framework. In Robert Martin, David Michaels & Juan Uriagereka (eds.), *Step by Step*, 89–155. Cambridge, MA: MIT Press.
Chomsky, Noam. 2000b. *New Horizons in the Study of Language and Mind*. Cambridge: Cambridge University Press.
Chomsky, Noam. 2001. Derivation by phase. In Michael Kenstowicz (ed.), *Ken Hale: A Life in Language*, 1–52. Cambrige, MA: MIT Press.
Chomsky, Noam. 2004. Beyond explanatory adequacy. In Adriana Belletti (ed.), *Structures and Beyond*, vol. 3 of *The Cartography of Syntactic Structures*, 104–131. New York: Oxford University Press.
Chomsky, Noam. 2008. On phases. In Robert Freidin, Carlos Otero & Maria Luisa Zubizarreta (eds.), *Foundational Issues in Linguistic Theory*, 133–166. Cambridge, MA: MIT Press.
Chomsky, Noam. 2013a. Problems of projection. *Lingua* 130: 33–49.
Chomsky, Noam. 2013b. Notes on denotation and denoting. In Ivano Caponigro & Carlo Cecchetto (eds.), *From Grammar to Meaning: The Spontaneous Logicality of Language. Festschrift for Gennaro Chierchia*. Cambridge: Cambridge University Press.
Chomsky, Noam. 2015. Problems of projection. Extensions. In Elisa di Domenico, Cornelia Hamann & Simona Matteini (eds.), *Structures, Strategies and Beyond*, 1–16. Amsterdam: John Benjamins.
Chomsky, Noam. 2020. Puzzles about phases. In Ludovico Franco & Paolo Lorusso, *Linguistic Variation: Structure and Interpretation*, 163–168. Berlin: De Gruyter Mouton.
Chomsky, Noam & Howard Lasnik. 1977. Filters and control. *Linguistic Inquiry* 8: 425–504.
Chomsky, Noam, & Howard Lasnik. 1993. The Theory of Principles and Parameters. In Joachim Jacobs, Arnim von Stechow, Wolfgang Sternefeld & Theo Vennemann (eds), *Syntax: an International Handbook of Contemporary Research*. Berlin: Walter de Gruyter. Reproduced in Noam Chomsky. 1995. *The Minimalist Program*, 13–127. Cambridge, MA: MIT Press.
Chung, Sandra & James McCloskey. 1987. Government, barriers and small clauses in Modern Irish. *Linguistic Inquiry* 18: 173–237.
Cinque, Guglielmo. (2006). *Restructuring and functional heads*. Oxford: Oxford University Press.
Collins, Christopher. 2005. A Smuggling approach to the passive in English. *Syntax* 8: 81–120.
Coon, Jessica. 2013. *Aspects of Split Ergativity*. Oxford: Oxford University Press.
Coon, Jessica. 2014. Predication, tenselessness, and what it takes to be a verb. In Hsin-Lun Huang, Ethan Poole, Amanda Rysling (eds.), *Proceedings of the 43rd Annual Meeting of the NELS*, 77–90. University of Massachusetts at Amherst, GLSA.
Coon, Jessica. 2017. Little-v agreement and templatic morphology in Ch'ol. *Syntax* 20: 101–137.
Coon, Jessica, Diane Massam & Lisa deMena Travis (eds.). 2017a. *The Oxford Handbook of Ergativity*. Oxford: Oxford University Press.

Coon, Jessica, Diane Massam & Lisa deMena Travis. 2017b. Introduction. In Jessica Coon, Diane Massam & Lisa deMena Travis (eds.). *The Oxford Handbook of Ergativity*, 1–21. Oxford: Oxford University Press.

Cornilescu, Alexandra. 2003. *Complementation in English. A minimalist approach*. Bucarest: Editura Universității din București.

Costa, João. 1996. Adverb positioning and V-movement in English: Some more evidence. *Studia Linguistica* 50: 22–34.

Costa, João. 2000. Focus in situ: Evidence from Portuguese. *Probus* 12: 187–228.

Costa, João. 2004. *Subject Positions and Interfaces. The Case of European Portuguese*. Berlin: de Gruyter Mouton.

Cottell, Siobhan. 1995. The representation of tense in Modern Irish. *GenGenP* 3: 105–24.

Cowper, Elizabeth. 2016. Finiteness and pseudofiniteness. In Kristin Melum Eide (ed), *Finiteness Matters: On Finiteness-Related Phenomena in Natural Languages*, 47–78. Amsterdam: John Benjamins.

Davidson, Donald. 1980. *Essays on Actions and Events*. Oxford: Clarendon Press.

Davies, William & Stanley Dubinsky. 2004. *The Grammar of Raising and Control: A Course in Syntactic Argumentation*. Malden, MA: Blackwell

Davies, William & Stanley Dubinsky. 2009. On the existence (and distribution) of sentential subjects. In Donna B. Gerdts, John C. Moore, & Maria Polinksy (eds.), *Hypothesis A/ hypothesis B: Linguistic explorations in honor of David M. Perlmutter*, 111–128. Cambridge, MA: MIT

Déchaine, Rose-Marie. 1993. *Predicates across Categories. Towards a Category-Neutral Syntax*. Doctoral dissertation. Amherst: University of Massachusetts.

Dékány, Éva. 2018. Approaches to head movement: A critical assessment. *Glossa* 3. 65: 1–43.

den Dikken, Marcel. 2006. *Relators and Linkers*. Cambridge, MA: MIT Press.

de Man, A. G. 1965. *Accipe ut reddas. Ars grammatica*. Groningen: Wolters.

Denizot, Camille. 2017. Les constructions dites à participe dominant en grec ancien: motivations sémantiques et pragmatiques. In Claire Le Feuvre, Daniel Petit & Georges-Jean Pinault, *Verbal Adjectives and Participles in the Indo-European Languages*, 29–49. Bremen: Hempen Verlag.

Diez, Friedrich. 1882 [1836–1842]. *Grammatik der Romanischen Sprachen*, vol. 3, 5th edn. Bonn: Eduard Weber's Buchhandlung.

Dixon, Robert. M. W. 1994. *Ergativity*. Cambridge: Cambridge University Press.

Dryer, Matthew. 1980. The positional tendencies of sentential noun phrases in universal grammar. *Canadian Journal of Linguistics* 25: 123–195.

Embick, David. 2000. Features, syntax, and categories in the Latin perfect. *Linguistic Inquiry* 31: 185–230.

Embick, David. 2004. On the structure of resultative participles in English. *Linguistic Inquiry* 35: 355–392.

Embick, David & Rolf Noyer. 2001. Movement operations after syntax. *Linguistic Inquiry* 32: 555–595.

Embick, David & Rolf Noyer. 2007. Distributed morphology and the syntax-morphology interface. In Gillian Ramchand & Charles Reiss, *The Oxford Handbook of Linguistic Interfaces*, 289–324. Oxford: Oxford University Press.

Embick, David & Morris Halle. 2008. *Distributed Morphology. Aspects of the Latin Conjugation*. Unpublished manuscript, University of Pennsylvania and MIT.

Emonds, Joseph. 1970. *Root and Structure-Preserving Transformations*. Doctoral dissertation, Cambridge, MA: MIT.

Emonds, Joseph. 1976. *A Transformational Approach to English Syntax. Root, Structure-Preserving, and Local Transformations*. New York: Academic Press.
Emonds, Joseph. 1978. The verbal complex V'-V in French. *Linguistic Inquiry* 9: 151–175.
Emonds, Joseph. 1985. *A Unified Theory of Syntactic Categories*. Dordrecht: Foris.
Emonds, Joseph. 2006. Adjectival passives: the construction in the iron mask. In Martin Everaert & Henk van Riemsdijk (eds), *The Blackwell Companion to Syntax*, volume I, 16–60. Malden: Blackwell.
Emonds, J. 2007. *Discovering Syntax*. Berlin: De Gruyter Mouton.
Enç, Mürvet. 1987. Anchoring conditions for Tense. *Linguistic Inquiry* 18: 633–657.
Enç, Mürvet. 1990. On the absence of the present tense morpheme in English. Unpublished article, University of Wisconsin, Madison.
Ernout, Alfred & François Thomas. 1951. *Syntaxe latine*. Paris: Klincksieck.
Evans, D. Simon. 1976. *A Grammar of Middle Welsh*, 3rd printing. Dublin: The Dublin Institute for Advanced Studies.
Fiéis, Alexandra & Ana Maria Madeira. 2017. The Portuguese infinitive across varieties. In Pilar Barbosa, Maria da Conceição de Paiva & Celeste Rodrigues (eds), *Studies on Variation in Portuguese*, 280–299. Amsterdam: John Benjamins.
Fife, James. 1990. *The Semantics of the Welsh Verb, A Cognitive Approach*. Cardiff: University of Wales Press.
Frampton, John, Sam Gutmann, Julie Legate & Charles Yang. 2000. Remarks on *Derivation by Phase*: feature valuation, agreement and intervention. Unpublished manuscript, Northeastern Univesity, Boston.
Fu, Jingqi, Thomas Roeper & Hagit Borer. 2001. The VP within process nominals: Evidence from adverbs and the VP anaphor Do-So. *Natural Language & Linguistic Theory* 19: 549–582.
Gagnepain, J. 1963. *La syntaxe du nom verbal dans les langues celtiques. I. Irlandais*. Paris: Klincksieck.
Gallego, Ángel. 2017. Remark on the EPP in Labeling Theory. Evidence from Romance. *Syntax* 20: 384–399.
Gao, Mingkai. 1963. The problem of word class in Chinese grammatical study. *Collected Linguistic Papers of Gao Mingkai*. Beijing: The Commercial Press.
George, Leland & Jaklin Kornfilt. 1981. Finiteness and boundedness in Turkish. In Frank Heny (ed.), *Binding and Filtering*, 105–127. London: Croom Helm.
Gildersleeve, Basil Lanneau & Gonzalez Lodge. 1895. *Latin Grammar*, 3rd edition. London: MacMillan.
Givón, Talmy. 1990. *Syntax: A Functional-Typological Introduction*, vol. 2. Amsterdam: John Benjamins.
Gonçalves, Ana, Ana Lucia Santos & Inês Duarte. 2014. (Pseudo-)inflected infinitives and control as *Agree*. In Karine Lahousse & Stefania Marzo (eds), *Selected Papers from Going Romance 2012*, 161–180. Amsterdam: John Benjamins.
Grimshaw, Jane. 1990. *Argument Structure*. Cambridge, MA: MIT Press.
Grohmann, Kleanthes. 2003. *Prolific Domains: On the Anti-locality of Movement Dependencies*. Amsterdam: John Benjamins.
Gross, Maurice. 1968. *Grammaire transformationnelle du français: le verbe*. Paris: Larousse.
Guilfoyle, Eithne. 1990. *Functional Categories and Phrase Structure Parameters*. Doctoral dissertation, Montreal: McGill University.

Guilfoyle, E., 1997. The verbal noun in Irish nonfinite clauses. In Anders Ahlqvist & Vera Čapková (eds), *Dán Do Oide. Essays in Memory of Conn. R. Ó Cleirigh*, 187–200. Dublin: Institiúid Teangeolaíochta Éireann.
Hale, Kenneth & Samuel Keyser. 1993. On argument structure and the lexical expression of syntactic relations. In Kenneth Hale and Samuel Jay Keyser, *The View from Building 20*, 53–109. Cambridge, MA: MIT Press.
Halle, Morris & Alec Marantz. 1993. Distributed morphology and the pieces of inflection. In Kenneth Hale and Samuel Jay Keyser (eds.), *The View from Building 20*, 111–176. Cambridge, MA: MIT Press.
Harley, Heidi & Rolf Noyer, 1998. Mixed Nominalizations. Short Verb Movement and Object Shift in English. In Pius N. Tamanji & Kiyomi Kusumoto (eds.), *Proceedings of NELS 28*, 143–157. University of Massachusetts at Amherst, GLSA.
Harley, Heidi, & Rolf Noyer. 1999. Distributed Morphology. *GLOT* 4.4. 3–36.
Harlow, Stephen. 1983. Celtic relatives. *York Working Papers in Linguistics* 10: 77–121.
Harlow, Stephen. 1992. Finiteness in Welsh sentence structure. In Hans-Georg Obenauer & Anne Zribi-Hertz (eds.), *Structure de la phrase et théorie du liage*, 93–119. Saint-Denis: Presses Universitaires de Vincennes.
Haug, Dag Trygve Truslew & Tatiana Nikitina. 2016. Feature sharing in agreement. *Natural Language & Linguistic Theory* 34: 865–910.
Heick, Otto. 1936. *The Ab Urbe Condita Construction in Latin*. Lincoln, Nebraska: University of Nebraska.
Heyvaert, Liesbet, Charlotte Maekelberghe & Anouk Buyle. 2019. Nominal and verbal gerunds in present-day English: aspectual features and nominal status. *Language Sciences* 73: 32–49.
Higginbotham, James. 1983. The logic of perceptual reports. *Journal of Philosophy* 80: 100–127.
Higginbotham, James. 1985. On semantics. *Linguistic Inquiry* 16: 547–593.
Higgins, Francis Rogers. 1973. On J. Emonds's analysis of extraposition. In John Kimball (ed.), *Syntax and Semantics* vol. 2, 149–195. New York: Seminar Press.
Hoekstra, Teun. 2004. *Arguments and Structure. Studies on the Architecture of the Sentence.* In Rint Sybesma, Sjef Barbiers, Marcel den Dikken, Jenny Doetjes, Gertjan Postma, Guido Vanden Wyngaerd (eds.). Berlin: De Gruyter Mouton.
Holmberg, Anders. 1986. *Word Order and Syntactic Features in the Scandinavian Languages and in English*. Department of General Linguistics, University of Stockholm.
Horn, George. 1975. On the non-sentential nature of the Poss-*ing* construction. *Linguistic Analysis* 1: 333–387.
Hornstein, Norbert. 1999. Movement and Control. *Linguistic Inquiry* 30: 69–96.
Hornstein, Norbert. 2003. On control. In Randall Hendrick (ed), *Minimalist Syntax*, 6–81. Oxford: Blackwell.
Hu, Jianhua, Pan Haihua, and Xu Liejong. 2001. Is there a finite vs. non-finite distinction in Chinese? *Linguistics* 39: 1117–1148.
Iatridou, Sabine. 1993. On nominative case assignment and a few related things. *MIT Working Papers in Linguistics* 19: 175–196.
Jackendoff, Ray. 1977. *X' syntax: a study of phrase structure*. Cambridge, MA: MIT Press.
Jakobson, Roman. 1957. Shifters, verbal categories and the Russian verb. Russian Language Project, Department of Slavic Languages and Literatures, Harvard University.

Jakobson, Roman. 1959. Boas' view of grammatical meaning. In W. Goldschmidt (ed.). *The Anthropology of Franz Boas*, *American Anthropologist* 61. 5. part 2, October 1959, memoir n° 89 of the American Anthropological Association.

Jespersen, O. 1912. *Growth and Structure of the English Language*, 2nd edition. Leipzig: Teubner.

Jespersen, Otto. 1924. *The Philosophy of Grammar*. London: George Allen and Unwin.

Jespersen, Otto. 1933. *Essentials of English Grammar*. London: George Allen & Unwin.

Jespersen, Otto. 1940. *A Modern English Grammar on Historical Principles*, Part V, *Syntax* vol. 4. London, George Allen & Unwin.

Joffre, Marie-Dominique. 1995. *Le verbe latin: voix et diathèse*. Louvain: Peeters.

Johns, Alana, Diane Massam & Juvenal Ndayiragije (eds.). 2006. *Ergativity. Emerging Issues*. Dordrecht: Springer.

Johnson, Kyle. 1988. Clausal gerunds, the ECP and government. *Linguistic Inquiry* 19: 583–609.

Jones, Morris & Alan Thomas. 1977. *The Welsh Language. Studies in its Syntax and Semantics*. Cardiff: University of Wales Press.

Kajita, Masaru. 1968. *A Generative-Transformational Study of Semi-Auxiliaries in Present-Day American English*. Tokyo: Sanseido.

Kaneko, Makoto. 2002. *Syntaxe et sémantique du jugement thétique: étude contrastive de la construction ga du japonais et de la construction pseudo-relative du français*. Doctoral dissertation, Paris: Université Paris-8.

Kastner, Itamar. 2015. Factivity mirrors interpretation: The selectional requirements of presuppositional verbs. *Lingua* 164: 156–188.

Kayne, Richard. 1969. *The Transformational Cycle in French Syntax*. Doctoral dissertation, Cambridge, MA: MIT.

Kayne, Richard. 1975. *French Syntax*. Cambridge, MA: MIT Press.

Kayne, Richard. 1981. On certain differences between French and English. *Linguistic Inquiry* 12: 349–371.

Kayne, Richard. 1982. Predicates and arguments, verbs and nouns. *GLOW Newsletter* 8: 24.

Kayne, Richard. 1991. Romance clitics, verb movement and PRO. *Linguistic Inquiry* 22: 647–686.

Kayne, Richard. 1993. Toward a modular theory of auxiliary selection. *Studia Linguistica* 47: 3–31.

Kayne, Richard. 1994. *The Antisymmetry of Syntax*. Cambridge, MA: MIT Press.

Kayne, Richard. 2000. *Parameters and Universals*. New York: Oxford University Press.

Kayne, Richard. 2010. *Comparisons and Contrasts*. New York: Oxford University Press.

Kihm, Alain. 2007. Romanian nominal inflection: a realizational approach. *Revue Roumaine de Linguistique* 52: 255–302.

Kiparsky, Paul & Carol Kiparsky. 1970. Fact. In Manfred Bierwisch & Karl Erich Heidolph (eds), *Progress in Linguistics*, 143–173. The Hague: Mouton.

Knyazev, Mikhail. 2016. *Licensing Clausal Complements. The case of Russian čto-clauses*. Doctoral dissertation, Utrecht: University of Utrecht.

Koopman, Hilda. 1984. *The Syntax of Verbs: from verb movement rules in the Kru languages to universal grammar*. Dordrecht: Foris.

Kornfilt, Jaklin. 2007. Verbal and nominalized finite clauses in Turkish. In Irina Nikolaeva (ed.), *Finiteness: Theoretical and Empirical Foundations*, 305–332. Oxford: Oxford University Press.

Koster, Jan. 1978. Why subject sentences don't exist. In Samuel Jay Keyser (ed.), *Recent Transformational Studies in European Languages*, 53–64. Cambridge, MA: MIT Press.
Kratzer, Angelika. 1994. The event argument and the semantics of voice. Unpublished paper. University of Massachusets at Amherst.
Kratzer, Angelika. 1996. Severing the external argument from its verb. In Johan Rooryck & Laurie Zaring (eds.), *Phrase Structure and the Lexicon*, 109–137. Dordrecht, Kluwer.
Kratzer, Angelika. 2000. Building statives. In Lisa Conathan, Jeff Good, Darya Kavitskaya, Alyssa Wulf & Alan Yu (ed), *Proceedings of the 26th Annual Meeting of the Berkeley Linguistics Society*, 385–399. Berkeley, California: Berkeley Linguistics Society.
Kratzer, Angelika. 2004. Telicity and the semantics of objective case. In Jacqueline Guéron & Jacqueline Lecarme (eds.), *The Syntax of Time*, 389–423. Cambridge, MA: MIT Press.
Kuryłowicz, Jerzy. 1964. *The Inflectional Categories of Indo-European*. Heidelberg: Karl Winter.
Lahne, Antje. 2008. Excluding SVO in ergative languages: a new view on Mahajan's generalisation. *Linguistische Arbeits Berichte* 87, 65–80. Leipzig: Universität Leipzig.
Laka, Itziar. 1993. Unergative that assign ergative, unaccusatives that assign accusative. In Jonathan Bobaljik & Colin Phillips (eds.), *Papers on Case and Agreement* I. MIT Working Papers in Linguistics 18, 149–172. Cambridge, MA: MIT Press
Lambert, Pierre-Yves. 1993. *Les quatre branches du Mabinogi et autres contes gallois du Moyen Âge*. Paris: Gallimard.
Landau, Idan. 2000. *Elements of Control: Structure and Meaning in Infinitival Constructions*. Dordercht: Kluwer.
Landau, Idan. 2004. The scale of finiteness and the calculus of control. *Natural Language & Linguistic Theory* 22: 811–877.
Landau, Idan. 2013. *Control in Generative Grammar*. Cambridge: Cambridge University Press.
Landau, Idan. 2015. *A Two-Tiered Theory of Control*. Cambridge, MA: MIT Press.
Larson, Richard. 1988. On the double object construction. *Linguistic Inquiry* 19: 335–391.
Laughton, Eric. 1964. *The Participle in Cicero*. Oxford: Oxford University Press.
Lee, Thomas Hun-tak. 2018. The use of child language in linguistic argumentation: some methodological considerations. Paper delivered at the Ohio State University, october 22, 2018.
Lees, Robert B. 1960. *The Grammar of English Nominalizations*. The Hague: Mouton.
Lerch, Eugen. 1912. *Prädikative Participia für Verbalsubstantiva im Französischen*. Halle: Max Niemeyer.
Levin, Beth & Malka Rappaport. 1986. The formation of adjectival passives. *Linguistic Inquiry* 17: 623–661.
Lewis, H. 1928. Y berfenw [The verb noun]. *The Bulletin of the Board of Celtic Studies* 4: 179–189.
Lin, Tzong-Hong Jonah. 2011. Finiteness of clauses and raising of arguments in Mandarin Chinese. *Syntax* 14: 48–73.
Lin, Tzong-Hong Jonah. 2015. Tense in Mandarin Chinese sentences. *Syntax* 18: 320–342.
Lois, Ximena & Valentina Vapnarsky. 2006. Root indeterminacy and polyvalence in Yukatekan Mayan languages. In Ximena Lois & Valentina Vapnarsky (eds.), *Lexical Classes and Root Classes in Amerindian Languages*, 69–115. Bern: Peter Lang.
Longrée, Dominique. 1995. Du fonctionnement de la construction *ab urbe condita* chez Tacite. In Dominique Longrée (ed.), *DE VSV. Études de syntaxe latine offertes en hommage à Marius Lavency*, 175–188. Louvain-La-Neuve: Peeters.

Lowenstamm, Jean. 2014. Derivational affixes as roots. Phasal Spellout meets English stress Shift. In Artemis Alexiadou, Hagit Borer & Florian Schäfer (eds.), *The Syntax of Roots and the Roots of Syntax*, 230–258. Oxford: Oxford University Press.

Madeira, Ana Maria. 1994. On the Portuguese inflected infinitive. *UCL Working Papers in Linguistics* 6: 179–203.

Mahajan, Anoop. 1994. The ergativity parameter: *have-be* alternation, word order and split ergativity. In Mercè González (ed.), *Proceedings of NELS 24*, 317–331. University of Massachusetts at Amherst, GLSA.

Mahajan, Anoop. 1997. Universal Grammar and the typology of ergative languages. In Artemis Alexiadou & T. Alan Hall (eds.), *Studies on Universal Grammar and Typological Variation*, 35–57. Amsterdam: John Benjamins.

Mahieu, Marc-Antoine. 2007. *Cas structuraux et dépendances syntaxiques des expressions nominales en finnois*. Doctoral thesis, Paris: Université Paris-Diderot.

Malouf, R. 2000. Verbal gerunds as mixed categories. In Robert Borsley (ed.), *The Nature and Function of Syntactic Categories*, 133–166. New York: Academic Press.

Manning, H. Paul. 1995. Fluid intransitivity in Middle Welsh: Gradience, typology and unaccusativity. *Lingua* 97: 171–194.

Manzini, Maria Rita. 2010. The structure and interpretation of (Romance) complementizers. In Phoevos Panagiotidis (ed.), *The Complementizer Phase*, 167–199. Oxford: Oxford University Press.

Manzini, Maria Rita & Leonardo Savoia. 2010. Case as denotation: variation in Romance. *Studi Italiani di Linguistica Teorica e Applicata* 39: 409–438.

Manzini, Maria Rita & Leonardo Savoia. 2011. Reducing 'case' to denotational primitives: nominal inflections in Albanian. *Linguistic Variation* 11: 76–120.

Manzini, Maria Rita, Leonardo Savoia & Ludovico Franco. 2015. Ergative case, Aspect and Person splits: two case studies. *Acta Linguistica Hungarica* 62: 297–351.

Manzini, Maria Rita & Anna Roussou. 2019. Morphological and syntactic (non-)finiteness. A comparison between English and Balkan languages. *Quaderni di Linguistica e Studi Orientali / Working Papers in Linguistics and Oriental Studies* 5 : 195–229.

Marantz, Alec. 1978. Embedded sentences are not Noun Phrases. In Mark Stein (ed), *Proceedings of NELS 8*, 112–122. University of Massachusetts at Amherst.

Marantz, Alec. 1991. Case and licensing. In Germain Westphal, Benjamin Ao, and Hee-Rahk Chae (eds.), *Proceedings of the 8th Eastern States Conference on Linguistics (ESCOL 1)*, 58–68. Ithaca: CLC Publications.

Marantz, Alec. 1997. No escape from syntax: Don't try morphological analysis in the privacy of your own lexicon. *University of Pennsylvania Working Papers in Linguistics* 4, 201–225.

Marantz, Alec. 1999. Creating verbs above and below little v. Unpublished manuscript. MIT, Cambridge, MA.

Marantz, A. 2001. Words. Handout for the *WCCFL* 20.

Marantz, A. 2007. Phases and words. In Sook-Hee Choe (ed.), *Phases in the theory of grammar*, 191–222. Seoul: Dong-In Publishing Co.

Marouzeau, Jules. 1910. *L'emploi du participe présent latin*. Paris: Honoré Champion.

Martins, Ana Maria. 2001. On the origin of the Portuguese inflected infinitive. In Laurel J. Brinton (ed.), *Historical Linguistics 1999: Selected papers from the 14th International Conference on Historical Linguistics*, 207–222. Amsterdam: John Benjamins.

Martins, Ana Maria. 2006. Aspects of infinitival constructions in the history of Portuguese. In Randall Gess & Deborah Arteaga (eds.), *Historical Romance linguistics: retrospective and perspectives*, 327–355. Amsterdam: John Benjamins.

Martins, Ana Maria. 2018. Infinitival complements of causative/perception verbs in a diachronic perspective. In Anabela Gonçalves & Ana Lúcia Santos (eds.), *Complement Clauses in Portuguese: Syntax and Acquisition*, 101–128. Amsterdam: John Benjamins.

Massam, Diane. 2000. VSO and VOS: Aspects of Niuean word order. In Andrew Carnie & Eithne Guilfoyle (eds), *The Syntax of Verb Initial Languages*, 97–116. New York: Oxford University Press.

Massam, Diane. 2001. On predication and the status of subjects in Niuean. In William Davies & Stanley Dubinsky (eds), *Objects and Other Subjects*, 225–246. Dordrecht: Kluwer.

Massam, Diane. 2005. Lexical categories, lack of inflection, and predicate fronting in Niuean. In Andrew Carnie, Heidi Harley, & Sheila Dooley (eds.), *Verb first: On the syntax of verb initial languages*, 227–242. Amsterdam: John Benjamins.

Matushansky, Ora. 2011. Review of Ian Roberts, *Agreement and head movement. Journal of Linguistics* 47: 538–545.

Maurer, Theodoro Henrique. 1968. *O infinito flexionado português*. São Paulo: Companhia Editora Nacional.

McCloskey, James. 1980. Is there raising in Modern Irish? *Eriu* 31: 59–99.

McCloskey, James. 1983. A VP in a VSO language? In Gerald Gazdar, Ewan Klein & Geoffrey Pullum (eds.), *Order, Concord, and Constituency*, 9–55. Dordrecht: Foris

McCloskey, James. 1984. Raising, subcategorization and selection in Modern Irish. *Natural Language & Linguistic Theory* 1: 441–85.

McCloskey, James. 1991. Clause structure, ellipsis, and proper government in Irish. *Lingua* 85: 259–302.

McCloskey, James. 1996. On the scope of verb movement in Irish. *Natural Language & Linguistic Theory* 14: 46–104.

McCloskey, James. 1999. On the right edge in Irish. *Syntax* 2: 189–208.

Meier, Harri. 1955. Infinitivo flexional português e infinitivo personal español. *Boletin de Filologia de la Universidad de Chile* 8: 267–91.

Meillet, Antoine. 1928. *Esquisse d'une histoire de la langue latine*. Paris: Hachette. 6th edition 1952. Paris: Klincksieck.

Melvold, Janis. 1991. Factivity and definiteness. In Hamida Demirdache & Lisa Cheng (eds.), *More papers on Wh-movement. MIT Working Papers in Linguistics* 15.

Mensching, Guido. 2000. *Infinitive Constructions with Specified Subjects*. New York: Oxford University Press.

Menzel, Peter. 1975. *Semantics and Syntax of Complementation*. The Hague: Mouton.

Miller, D. Gary. 2002. *Nonfinite Structures in Theory and Change*. Oxford: Oxford University Press.

Milsark, Gary. 1988. Singl-ing. *Linguistic Inquiry* 19: 611–634.

Moltmann, Friederike. 2013. *Abstract Objects and the Semantics of Natural Language*. Oxford: Oxford University Press.

Montaut, Annie. 1997. L'ergativité en indo-aryen. *Faits de langues* 10: 57–64.

Montaut, Annie. 2004. Oblique main arguments in Hindi as localizing predications. In Peri Bhaskararao & Karumuri Venkata Subbarao (eds.), *Non nominative Subjects*, 33–56. Amsterdam: John Benjamins.

Montaut, Annie. 2006. The evolution of the tense-aspect system in Hindi/Urdu: The status of the ergative alignment. In Miriam Butt & Tracy Holloway King (eds.), *Proceedings of the LFG06 Conference.* Stanford, CA: CSLI Publications.

Morgan, Thomas John. 1938. Braslun o gystrawen y berfenw [Outline of the syntax of the verb-noun]. *Bulletin of the Board of Celtic Studies* 9: 195–215.

Morris-Jones, John. 1913. *A Welsh Grammar Historical and Comparative.* Oxford: Clarendon Press.

Morris-Jones, John. 1931. *Welsh Syntax, an Unfinished Draft.* Cardiff: University of Wales Press Board.

Moulton, Keir. 2004. External arguments and gerunds. *Toronto Working Papers in Linguistics* 22: 121–136.

Moulton, Keir. 2021. Remarks on propositional nominalization. Artemis Alexiadou & Hagit Borer (eds.), *Nominalization: 50 years on from Chomsky's* Remarks, 255–276. Oxford: Oxford University Press.

Muller, Claude. 2002. *Les bases de la syntaxe.* Bordeaux: Presses Universitaires de Bordeaux.

Müller, Gereon. 2008. Ergativity, accusativity, and the order of Merge and Agree. In Kleanthes Grohmann (ed.), *Explorations of Phase Theory : Features and Arguments*, 269–308. Berlin: de Gruyter Mouton.

Nash, Lea. 1995. *Portée argumentale et marquage casuel dans les langues ergatives: le cas du géorgien.* Doctoral dissertation, Paris: Université Paris-8.

Nash, Lea. 2002. The absence of SVO order and the role of Inflection in ergative languages: a case study of Georgian. Unpublished manuscript, Université Paris-8.

Nash, Lea. 2017. The structural source of split ergativity and ergative case in Georgian. In Jessica Coon, Diane Massam & Lisa deMena Travis (eds.), *The Oxford Handbook of Ergativity*, 175–203. Oxford: Oxford University Press.

Nash, Lea. 2022. Nonunitary structure of unergative verbs in Georgian. *Natural Languages & Linguistic Theory*, online November 2021.

Nash, Lea & Alain Rouveret. 1997. Proxy categories in phrase structure theory. In Kiyomi Kusumoto (ed), *Proceedings of NELS 27*, 287–304. University of Massachusetts at Amherst, GLSA. Also in A. Rouveret. 2018. *Aspects of Grammatical Architecture*, 52–71. New York and London: Routledge.

Nash, Lea & Alain Rouveret. 2002. Cliticization as unselective Attract. *Catalan Journal of Linguistics* 1: 157–199. Also in Alain Rouveret. 2018. *Aspects of Grammatical Architecture*, 150–190. New York and London: Routledge.

Nikitina, Tatiana. 2008. *The Mixing of Syntactic Properties and Language Change.* Doctoral dissertation, Stanford: Stanford University.

Nikolaeva, Irina (ed.). 2007a. *Finiteness: Theoretical and Empirical Foundations,* Oxford: Oxford University Press.

Nikolaeva, Irina. 2007b. Introduction. In Irina Nikolaeva (ed.), *Finiteness: Theoretical and Empirical Foundations,* 1–19. Oxford: Oxford University Press.

Nikolaeva, Irina. 2010. Typology of finiteness, *Language and Linguistics Compass* 3/1: 1–14.

Ó Siadhail, Micheál. 1989. *Modern Irish: Grammatical Structure and Dialectal Variation.* Cambridge, Cambridge University Press.

Ouali, Hamid. 2008. On C-to-T feature transfer: the nature of Agreement and Anti-Agreement in Berber. In Roberta D'Alessandro, Susann Fischer & Gunnar Hrafn Hrafnbjargarson (eds.), *Agreement Restrictions*, 159–180. Berlin: De Gruyter Mouton.

Panagiotidis, Phoevos. 2015. *Categorial Features.* Cambridge: Cambridge University Press.

Panagiotidis, Phoevos & Kleanthes Grohmann. 2011. Mixed projections, categorial switches and prolific domains. *Linguistic Analysis* 35: 141–161.

Pancheva, Roumyana & Arnim von Stechow. 2004. On the present perfect puzzle. In Keir Moulton & Matthew Wolf (eds.), *Proceedings of NELS 34*, 469–483. University of Massachusetts at Amherst, GLSA.

Partee, Barbara (1973). Some structural analogies between tenses and pronouns in English. Journal of Philosophy 70 : 601–609.

Perlmutter, David. 1976. Evidence for subject downgrading in Portuguese. In Jürgen Schmidt-Radefeldt (ed.), *Readings in Portuguese Linguistics*, 93–138. Amsterdam: North Holland.

Pesetsky, David. 1989. Language-particular processes and the Earliness Principle. Unpublished manuscript. MIT.

Pesetsky, David. 1992. Zero syntax II: An essay on infinitives. Unpublished manuscript. MIT.

Pesetsky, David & Esther Torrego. 2001. T-to-C movement: causes and consequences. In Michael Kenstowicz (ed.), *Ken Hale: A Life in Language*, 355–426. Cambridge, MA: MIT Press.

Pesetsky, David & Esther Torrego. 2004. Tense, Case and the nature of syntactic categories. In Jacqueline Guéron & Jacqueline Lecarme (eds.), *The Syntax of Time*, 495–537. Cambridge, MA: MIT Press.

Peyraube, Alain. 2014. Has Chinese changed from a synthetic language into an analytic language? In He Zhihua & Feng Shengli (eds.), *Adaptation and Innovation. Research on Chinese Language and Script.*, 39–66. Hong Kong: Commercial Press.

Pinkster, Harm. 1990. *Latin Syntax and Semantics*. New York and London: Routledge.

Pires, Acrisio. 2006. *The Minimalist Syntax of Defective Domains. Gerunds and Infinitives*. Amsterdam: John Benjamins.

Platzack, Christer, & Inger Rosengren. 1998. On the subject of imperatives: A minimalist account of the imperative clause. *The Journal of Comparative Germanic Linguistics* 1: 177–224.

Polinsky, Maria. 2016. *Deconstructing Ergativity. Two Types of Ergative Languages and their Features*. Oxford, Oxford University Press.

Pollock, Jean-Yves. 1989. Verb movement, Universal Grammar and the structure of IP. *Linguistic Inquiry* 20: 365–424.

Portner, Paul. 1991a. Interpreting gerunds in complement positions. In Dawn Bates (ed.), *Proceedings of WCCFL X*, 375–385. Stanford Linguistics Association.

Portner, Paul. 1991b. Gerunds and types of events. In Steven Moore & Adam Zachary Wyner (eds), *Proceedings of SALT I, Cornell University Working Papers in Linguistics* 10, 189–208.

Portner, Paul. 1994. A uniform semantics for aspectual -*ing*. In Mercè González (ed.), *Proceedings of NELS 24*, 507–517. University of Massachusetts at Amherst, GLSA.

Postal, Paul. 1974. *On Raising*. Cambridge, MA: MIT Press.

Ramchand, Gillian. 1993. Verbal nouns and event structure in Scottish Gaelic. In Utpal Lahiri & Adam Wyner (eds.), *SALT III*, 162–181. Ithaca, N.Y.: Cornell University.

Ramchand, Gillian. 1997. *Aspect and Predication: The Semantics of Argument Structure*. Oxford: Oxford University Press.

Ramchand, Gillian & Peter Svenonius. 2014. Deriving the functional hierarchy. *Language Sciences* 46: 152–174.

Raposo, Eduardo. 1975. Uma restrição derivacional global sobre o infinitivo em português. Monograph of the *Boletim de Filologia* 24.

Raposo, Eduardo. 1987. Case Theory and Infl-to-Comp: The Inflected Infinitive in European Portuguese. *Linguistic Inquiry* 18: 85–109.

Reuland, Eric. 1983. Governing -*ing*. *Linguistic Inquiry* 14: 101–136
Reuland, Eric. 2011. What's nominal in nominalizations? *Lingua* 121: 1283–1296.
Richards, Melville. 1938. *Cystrawen y frawddeg Gymraeg* [Syntax of the Welsh sentence]. Caerdydd: Gwasg Prifysgol Cymru.
Richards, Melville. 1950–1951. Syntactical Notes II: The subject of the verb noun in Welsh. *Etudes Celtiques* 5: 51–81 and 293–313.
Richards, Norvin. 2001. *Movement in Language: Interactions and Architectures*. New York: Oxford University Press.
Riemann, Othon. 1908 [1886]. *Syntaxe latine*. 5th edn revised by Paul Lejay. Paris: Klincksieck.
Riemsdijk, Henk van. 1978. *A Case Study in Syntactic Markedness: The Binding Nature of Prepositional Phrases*. Lisse: The Peter de Ridder Press.
Riemsdijk, Henk van. 1983. The case of German adjectives. In Franck Heny & Barry Richards (eds), *Linguistic Categories: Auxiliaries and Related Puzzles*, 223–252. Dordrecht: Reidel.
Riemsdijk, Henk van. 1998. Categorial feature magnetism: The endocentricity and distribution of projections. *Journal of Comparative Germanic Linguistics* 2: 1–48.
Rizzi, Luigi. 1982. Lexical subjects in infinitives: government, case and binding. In *Issues in Italian Syntax*, 77–116. Dordrecht: Foris.
Rizzi, Luigi. 1997. The fine structure of the left periphery. In Liliane Haegeman (ed), *Elements of Grammar*, 281–337. Dordrecht: Kluwer.
Roberts, Ian. 2004. The C-system in Brythonic Celtic languages, V2 and the EPP. In Luigi Rizzi, (ed.), *The Structure of CP and IP. The Cartography of Syntactic Structures*, 297–328. New York: Oxford University Press.
Roberts, Ian. 2005. *Principles and Parameters in a VSO Language: A case study in Welsh*. New York: Oxford University Press.
Roberts, Ian. 2010. *Agreement and head movement: Clitics, incorporation, and defective goals*. Cambridge, MA: MIT Press.
Roberts, Ian. 2021. Smuggling, ergativity, and the final-over-final condition. In Adriana Belletti & Christopher Collins (eds.), *Smuggling in Syntax*, 318–352. Oxford: Oxford University Press.
Rochette, Anne. 1988. *Semantic and syntactic aspects of Romance sentential complementation*. Doctoral dissertation, Cambridge, MA: MIT.
Rohlfs, Gerhard. 1949. *Historische Grammatik der italienischen Sprache und ihrer Mundarten*, vol. 2: *Formenlehre und Syntax*. Bern: Francke.
Rooryck, Johan. 1992. On the distinction between raising and control. In Konrad Koerner & Paul Hirschbühler (eds.), *Romance Languages and Modern Linguistic Theory, papers from the 20th linguistic symposium on Romance languages (LSRL XX)*, Ottawa, 10–14 avril 1990, 225–250. Amsterdam: John Benjamins.
Rosenbaum, Peter. 1967. *The Grammar of English Predicate Complement Constructions*. Cambridge, MA: MIT Press.
Ross, John. 1972. The category squish: endstation hauptwort. *Chicago Linguistic Society* 8: 316–28.
Ross, John. 1973. Nouniness. In Osamu Fujimura (ed), *Three Dimensions of Linguistic Theory*, 137–258. Tokyo, TEC Company.
Roussou, Anna. 1992. Factive complements and *wh*-movement in modern Greek. In Hans van de Koot (ed.), *UCL Working Papers in Linguistics* 4, 123–147.
Roussou, Anna. 2009. In the mood for control. *Lingua* 119: 1811–1836.

Roussou, Anna. 2018. Complement clauses: case and argumenthood. In L. Franco & P. Lorusso (eds), *Linguistic Variation: Structure and Interpretation. Studies in Honor of M. Rita Manzini*, 609–631. Berlin: De Gruyter Mouton.

Rouveret, Alain. 1980. Sur la notion de proposition finie: gouvernement et inversion. *Langages* 60: 75–107.

Rouveret, A. 1987. *Syntaxe des dépendances lexicales, identité et identification dans la théorie syntaxique*. Thèse d'Etat, Paris: Université Paris7-Denis Diderot.

Rouveret, Alain. 1990. X-bar theory, minimality and barrierhood in Welsh. In Randall Hendrick (ed), *The Syntax of the Modern Celtic Languages*, 27–79. New York: Academic Press.

Rouveret, Alain. 1991. Functional categories and agreement. *The Linguistic Review* 8: 353–387. Also in Rouveret 2018a, 23–51.

Rouveret, Alain. 1994. *Syntaxe du gallois. Principes généraux et typologie*. Paris: CNRS Éditions.

Rouveret, Alain. 1996. *Bod* in the present tense and in other tenses. In Robert Borsley & Ian Roberts (eds), *The Syntax of the Celtic Languages*, 125–170. Cambridge: Cambridge University Press. Also in Rouveret 2018a, 72–115.

Rouveret, Alain. 2015. *Arguments minimalistes. Une présentation du Programme Minimaliste de Noam Chomsky*. Lyon: ENS Editions.

Rouveret, Alain. 2017. VSO Word Order in the Celtic Languages, In Martin Everaert & Henk van Riemsdijk (eds), *The Wiley Blackwell Companion to Syntax*, 2nd edition. Oxford and New York: Wiley & Blackwell.

Rouveret, Alain. 2018a. *Aspects of Grammatical Architecture*. London and New York: Routledge.

Rouveret, Alain. 2018b. Sur la construction latine *Ab Vrbe Condita*. *Bulletin de la Société Linguistique de Paris* 113: 267–287.

Rouveret, Alain. 2020. Le nom verbal gallois, problèmes de dérivation et de représentation. In Danh-Thàn Do-Hurinville, Huy-Linh Dao, & Annie Rialland (eds), *De la transcatégorialité dans les langues. Description, modélisation, typologie*, 227–260. Paris: Éditions de la Société Linguistique de Paris.

Rouveret, Alain & Jean-Roger Vergnaud. 1980. Specifying reference to the subject. French causatives and conditions on representations. *Linguistic Inquiry* 11: 97–202.

Rowland, Thomas. 1876. *A Grammar of the Welsh Language*. 4th edition. Wrexham: Hughes & son.

Sabbagh, J. 2009. The category of predicates and predicate phrases in Tagalog. Commentary on Kaufman's article. *Theoretical Linguistics* 35: 153–165.

Sadler, Louisa. 1987. *Welsh Syntax: A Government-Binding Approach*. London: Croom Helm.

Said Ali, Manoel. 1966 [1908]. *Dificuldades da língua portuguêsa*, 6th ed. 1966. Rio de Janeiro: Livraria Acadêmica.

Schütze, Carson. 1997. *INFL in Child and Adult Language: Agreement, Case and Licensing*. Doctoral dissertation, Cambridge, MA: MIT.

Scida, Emily. 2004. *The Inflected Infinitive in Romance Languages*. New York and London: Routledge.

Sheehan, Michelle. 2014. Portuguese, Russian and the Theory of Control. In Hsin-Lun Huang, Ethan Poole & Amanda Rysling (eds), *Proceedings of NELS* 43, vol. 2, 115–126. University of Massachusetts at Amherst, GLSA.

Sheehan, Michelle. 2017. Parametrizing ergativity. An inherent case approach. In Jessica Coon, Diane Massam & Lisa deMena Travis, *The Oxford Handbook of Ergativity*, 59–84. Oxford: Oxford University Press.

Sheehan, Michelle. 2018. Control of inflected infinitives in European Portuguese. In Ana Lúcia Santos & Anabela Gonçalves (eds), *Complement Clauses in Portuguese: Syntax and Acquisition*, 29–58. Amsterdam: John Benjamins.

Sheehan, Michelle, Theresa Biberauer, Ian Roberts & Anders Holmberg. 2017. *The Final-Over-Final Condition: A Syntactic Universal*. Cambridge, MA: MIT Press.

Sitaridou, Ioanna. 2006. The (dis)sociation of Tense, φ-features, EPP and nominative Case. In João Costa & Maria Cristina Figueiredo Silva (eds), *Studies on Agreement*, 243–260. Amsterdam: John Benjamins.

Smith, Carlota. 1997. *The Parameter of Aspect*. Dordrecht: Kluwer.

Sproat, Richard. 1985. Welsh Syntax and VSO Structure. *Natural Language & Linguistic Theory* 3: 173–216.

Spyropoulos, Vassilios. 2007. Finiteness and control in Greek. In Williams Davies & Stanley Dubinsky (eds), *New Horizons in the Analysis of Control and Raising*, 159–183. Dordrecht: Springer.

Storme, Benjamin. 2010. *Sicilia amissa*: Syntagme nominal ou proposition subordonnée? *Revue de Philologie* 84: 119–136.

Stowell, Timothy. 1981. *Origins of Phrase Structure*. Doctoral dissertation, Cambridge, MA: MIT.

Stowell, Timothy. 1982. The tense of infinitives. *Linguistic Inquiry* 13: 561–570.

Stowell, Timothy. 1995. What is the meaning of the present and past tenses? In Pier Marco Bertinetto, Valentina Bianchi, Mario Squartini (eds), *Temporal Reference: Aspect and Actionality* vol. 1: *Semantic and Syntactic Perspectives*, 381–396. Torino: Rosenberg & Sellier.

Takahashi, Shoichi. 2010. The hidden side of clausal complements. *Natural Language & Linguistic Theory* 28: 343–380.

Tallerman, Maggie. 1996. Fronting constructions in Welsh. In Robert Borsley & Ian Roberts (eds), *The Syntax of the Celtic Languages*, 97–124. Cambridge: Cambridge University Press.

Tallerman, Maggie. 1998. The uniform Case-licensing of subjects in Welsh. *The Linguistic Review* 15: 69–133.

Tallerman, Maggie & Joel Wallenberg. 2012. The Middle Welsh historic infinitive. Paper presented at the Colloquium *New Perspectives on Celtic Syntax*, University of California, Berkeley, September 7–8, 2012.

Tang, C. C. Jane. 1990. Finite and nonfinite clauses in Chinese. *Language and Linguistics* 1: 191–214.

Taraldsen, Tarald. 2017. Remarks on the relation between case-alignment and constituent order. In Jessica Coon, Diane Massam & Lisa deMena Travis (eds), *The Oxford Handbook of Ergativity*, 332–354. Oxford: Oxford University.

Tellier, Christine. 2018. Modality and complementizer choice in French infinitives. Laura Kalin, Ileana Paul & Jozina Vander Klok (eds), *Heading in the Right Direction: Linguistic Treats for Lisa Travis*. McGill Working Papers in Linguistics 25:1 (Special issue), 414–425.

Terzi, Arhonto. 1997. PRO and null case in finite clauses. *The Linguistic Review* 14: 335–360.

Thompson, Sandra Annear. 1973. On subjectless gerunds in English. *Foundations of Language* 9: 374–383.

Thorne, D. 1993. *A Comprehensive Welsh Grammar*. Oxford: Blackwell.

Torrego, Esther. 2012. The unaccusative case pattern of Hindi and auxiliary *be*. *Lingua* 122: 215–224.

Touratier, Christian. 1994. *Syntaxe latine*. Louvain-la-Neuve: Peeters.

Trask, Robert Lawrence. 1993. *A Dictionary of Grammatical Terms in Linguistics*. New York and London: Routledge.
Vendler, Zeno. 1967. Facts and events. In *Linguistics and Philosophy*, 122–146. Ithaca: Cornell University Press.
Vergnaud, Jean-Roger. 1977. Letter to Noam Chomsky and Howard Lasnik on "Filters and Control," April 17, 1977. Reproduced in Robert Freidin, Carlos Otero & Maria Luisa Zubizarreta (eds). *Foundational Issues in Linguistic Theory: Essays in Honor of Jean-Roger Vergnaud*. Cambridge, MA: MIT Press.
Vergnaud, Jean-Roger. 1985. *Dépendances et niveaux de représentation en syntaxe*. Amsterdam: Benjamins.
Vinokurova, N. 2005. *Lexical Categories and Argument Structure: A Study with Reference to Sakha*. Doctoral dissertation, Utrecht: Utrecht University.
Wasow, Thomas. 1977. Transformations and the Lexicon. In Peter Culicover, Thomas Wasow & Adrian Akmajian (eds), *Formal Syntax*, 327–360. New York: Academic Press.
Wasow, Thomas & Thomas Roeper. 1972. On the subject of gerunds. *Foundations of Language* 8: 44–61.
Williams, Edwin. 1974. *Rule Ordering in Syntax*. Doctoral dissertation, Cambridge, MA: MIT.
Williams, Edwin. 1975. Small clauses in English. In John Kimball (ed), *Syntax and Semantics* vol. 4, 249–273. New York: Academic Press.
Williams, Edwin. 1980. Predication. *Linguistic Inquiry* 11: 203–238.
Williams, Edwin. 1982. The NP Cycle. *Linguistic Inquiry* 13: 277–295.
Williams, Edwin. 1996. Three models of the morphology-syntax interface. Paper presented at the Seventh International Congress of Morphology, Vienna, February 16–18, 1996.
Williams, Edwin. 2013. The size of small clauses. Handout of a lecture delivered at Université Paris7–Denis Diderot, Paris, January 2013.
Williams, Stephen. 1980. *A Welsh Grammar*. Cardiff: University of Wales Press (translation of the 1959 Welsh version).
Willis, David. 1998. *Syntactic Change in Welsh: A Study of the Loss of Verb-Second*. Oxford: Oxford University Press.
Willis, David. 2007. Historical Syntax. In Robert Borsley, Maggie Tallerman & David Willis (eds.), *The Syntax of Welsh*, 286–337. Cambridge, Cambridge University Press.
Willis, David. 2009. Old and Middle Welsh. In Martin Ball & Nicole Müller (eds.), *The Celtic languages*, 117–60. New York and London: Routledge.
Willis, Penny. 1988. Is the Welsh verbal noun a verb or a noun? *Word* 39: 201–224.
Woodcock, Eric. C. 1959. *A New Latin Syntax*, London, Methuen and Co.
Woolford, Ellen. 1997. Four-way case systems: ergative, nominative, objective and accusative. *Natural Language & Linguistic Theory* 15: 181–227.
Woolford, Ellen. 2006. Lexical case, inherent case, and argument structure. *Linguistic Inquiry* 37: 111–130.
Wurmbrand, Susi. 2001. *Infinitives: Restructuring and Clause Structure*. Berlin: De Gruyter Mouton.
Wurmbrand, Susi. 2014. Tense and aspect in English infinitives. *Linguistic Inquiry* 45: 403–447.
Yoon, James Hye Suk. 1996. Nominal gerund phrases in English as phrasal zero derivations. *Linguistics* 34: 329–356.
Zucchi, Alessandro. 1993. *The Language of Propositions and Events*. Dordrecht: Kluwer.

Index

affixes as roots 94, 159
Anchoring Principle 6
attitudinal object 300, 421–423, 424, 426, 427, 433
Austronesian languages 79, 249, 252, 254

Basque 234, 235

cartographic approach 8–9, 16, 25, 32, 34, 36, 178, 263, 271, 276, 334
case
- absolutive 40, 234–236, 239–241, 244–248, 252–254, , 439
- common 159–162
- default 123, 162–163, 169, 188, 247
- direct 91, 159
- ergative 234, 235, 236, 238, 239, 240, 242, 243, 247
- genitive 4, 21, 74, 81, 88, 129, 152, 154, 155, 157, 159, 160, 162–163, 166, 169, 201, 226, 229, 230–231, 233, 245; 247, 362, 366, 368, 397

Case Resistance Principle 324–326, 328, 330, 333, 353
Categorial Identity Thesis 296, 303
category
- bivalent 82–83, 85, 169, 431
- hybrid 83–85
- mixed xvii, 19, 48, 69, 79, 81–86, 89, 91, 93, 95, 103, 128, 132, 141, 145, 158, 160, 162, 165–166, 231–232, 362, 378, 382–391, 404, 431, 438
category mixing
- strong 82, 128, 141, 162, 164, 165, 382, 390, 404, 438, 440
- weak 82, 103, 141, 164–165, 229, 382, 390, 440

Chinese 3, 7, 30, 79
Ch'ol 235, 249, 254
Clause
- featurally complete 52–54, 138–139, 344, 348–350, 356, 436, 443
- featurally defective 344, 348, 443

Closeness 211, 399

construction
- absolute ablative 366, 390, 405
- Aux-to-Comp 259, 269
- focus in situ 304
- gerundive xvi, 405
- *na*-complement 46, 357
- *opus est* 367, 370–371
- periphrastic aspectual 149, 168, 194, 197, 210, 223, 229–231
- small clause v, xv, 16, 42, 112, 118, 133, 137, 149, 198, 215, 245, 390, 405

control
- exhaustive 7, 41, 43–44, 48, 51–54, 64, 116, 138–139, 187, 294, 304, 308–312, 435–436, 438, 443–444
- non-obligatory 7, 309
- obligatory 5, 7, 16, 25, 41, 43–48, 52, 64, 115, 137, 178, 188, 205, 262, 311, 345
- partial 7, 42–44, 48, 51–53, 139, 179–180, 262, 304–305, 308–309, 311–312

convergence 52, 54, 115, 243, 344

defectiveness v, 11–14, 15, 20, 52–53, 131, 306, 344–345, 437, 442–444
Distributed Morphology approach 72–78, 87–90, 103
Dyirbal 235

EPP see Extended Projection Principle
ergative-absolutive alignment xvii, 40, 164, 221, 234–243, 244–248
Extended Projection Principle 14, 22, 29, 30, 39, 125, 127, 238, 239, 285, 302, 306, 440
Exo-Skeletal framework 90

Finiteness rule for OC 5, 41, 43, 48, 51, 55, 137, 185, 340
Finnish 7, 161, 253
Final over Final Condition (FOFC) 254

Georgian 234, 235, 243
Greek
- ancient xv, 5, 389, 402
- modern 41, 45–49, 248, 294, 298, 356, 357

head
- category-defining 28, 73–75, 77–78, 80, 83, 87–89, 91–96, 127, 131, 133, 164, 169, 210, 243, 249, 255, 300
- category-switching 80, 83, 91–96, 100, 103, 111, 127–132, 145, 159, 162, 164–166, 303, 398, 405

Hindi 234, 235, 243, 253
Hungarian 4, 247, 248, 326, 328

inheritance xvii, 10, 17, 25, 32–38, 138, 324, 394, 444
Irish 21–22, 36–38, 45, 49, 145, 155, 156, 158, 159–163, 166, 184, 215, 226, 229, 230, 333, 334, 439
- Munster 160, 161, 162
- Old 234
- Ulster 160, 161

Japanese 3, 7, 326

Kronoby dialect 72

Labeling algorithm xvii, 25, 27–29, 125–129, 138, 301, 305, 389
Latin 69, 243, 260, 361–406
Linear Correspondance Axiom 236, 332
Logophoric Centre 6, 7

Mahajan's generalization 235, 236, 243, 254
Mayan languages 79, 235, 240, 249, 252, 254
Mesoamerican languages 254, 255
Mirror Principle 72

Niuean 249, 254, 255
nominative-accusative alignment 40, 163, 235–239, 244–248
non-convergence 52–54
nouniness 297, 371
- squish 18, 19

Old English 223

participles
- adjectival 72, 76, 375
- eventive 379, 383–387
- passive 243, 376–378, 381, 402
- *praedicatiuum* 364, 401
- resultative 374–381, 383–384, 386–388
- stative 375–378

particle
- aspectual 158, 168, 194, 216, 218
- propositional 244

Persian 325
phase 32–33, 43, 50–54, 76, 93–96, 119, 126, 131, 162, 186–188, 238–239, 241–244, 344–345, 349, 356, 389, 395–397, 401, 442–443

Polynesian languages 254
predicates
- achievement 108, 110
- accomplishment 108, 110
- activity 108, 110
- assertive 206, 313, 315, 418, 421–424
- epistemic/declarative 175, 178, 207, 234, 245, 265–266, 270, 278, 281, 283–284, 294, 300, 305, 313, 352, 419, 425, 437, 440
- eventive 56–65, 74, 151, 207, 216–217, 266–270, 281, 285–293
- factive 262, 264–266, 281, 283, 290–291, 293–300, 303, 313
- future *irrealis* 55, 57–61, 64, 105, 173, 178, 191, 205–210, 307, 419
- mandatory 191–194
- stative 12, 59, 107–108, 167, 281, 286–293

present tense effect 57, 58, 59, 62, 63, 286, 287, 290, 291, 438
probe-goal-Agree approach 10–11, 14, 25, 32, 49–52, 55, 71, 77, 96, 103, 138, 180, 185, 264, 309, 311, 431, 438, 442
prolific domain 93

Q'anjob'al 254
quantifier scope 118–119
quod-clause 371

Reference-Predication constraint 83
Russian 3, 7, 45, 193, 326, 327, 328

Sakha 235
Samoan 235
Single Licensing Condition 276

state of affairs 12, 19, 82, 105, 111, 173, 371, 383, 396, 422, 426–427, 433
Survival Principle 395–396

Tagalog 79, 235, 249
tense
– anaphoric 47, 49, 51–54, 136, 138, 142, 250, 309, 312, 436, 442, 443–444
– dependent 42, 47, 49, 52–53, 136, 138, 250, 308–309, 312, 435–436, 442–444
θ-marking 182, 327, 332

toggle property (of *i*) 185, 188, 194
Tongan 254
transcategorial item 79–80, 82–83, 86, 88–89, 103, 158, 169, 230
Turkish 4, 325

Unlike Feature Condition 296

verb-nouns
– nominal analysis of 155–158, 160, 229–233
Visibility Condition 187–188, 327, 333

www.ingramcontent.com/pod-product-compliance
Lightning Source LLC
Chambersburg PA
CBHW031748220426
43662CB00007B/324